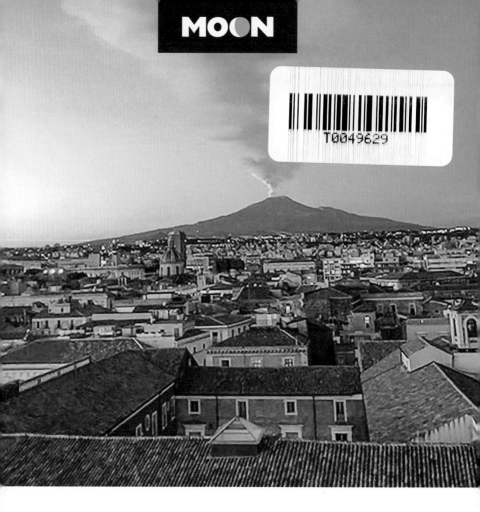

MO●N

T0049629

Sicily

LINDA SARRIS

SICILY

Area Marina
Protetta Isola
di Ustica

Riserva Naturale
Orientata
dello Zingaro

AEROPORTO
DI PALERMO
FALCONE E
BORSELLINO

Mondello

LA TONNARA
DI SCOPELLO

Palermo

A29

CASTELLO ARABO
NORMANNO

Trapani

SS187

SS113

Riserva Pizzo Cane,
Pizzo Trigna e
Grotta Mazzamuto

A19

Riserva Naturale
Marina Isole Egadi

A29dir

Riserva Monte
San Calogero

Aegadian
Islands

Camporeale

PALERMO

SS624

A29

Marsala

TRAPANI

SS189

SS115

SS118

SELINUNTE
ARCHAEOLOGICAL
PARK

SS115

AGRIGENTO

SS640

Agrigento

SCALA DEI TURCHI

Punta
Grande

VALLE DEI TEMPLI

Pantelleria

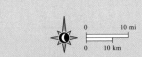

0   10 mi

0   10 km

Stromboli
Island

VIBO
VALENTIA

Filicudi
Island

Alicudi
Island   Pollara   Salina
Island   Panarea
Island

Alicudi Porto

REGGIO
CALABRIA

Lipari
Island

Aeolian
Islands

Parco Nazionale
dell'Aspromonte

Vulcano
Island

CAPO
MILAZZO
★

Milazzo

SS113dir

Messina

A2

Cefalù   A20

Castelbuono   Canneto

Riserva Fiumedinisi
e Monte Scuderi

Reggio
di Calabria

MESSINA   SS106

Parco Naturale
Regionale
delle Madonie   SS117   Randazzo   Castiglione
di Sicilia

Polizzi   SS120   Parco
Generosa   SS284   dell'Etna
A19   Linguaglossa   Taormina

Milo
A18

Petralia   A19   Mount Etna
Sottana   Nicolosi   Viagrande

Caltanissetta   CATANIA

Catania   Aci Trezza

VILLA ROMANA
DEL CASALE ★

SS626   CATANIA
FONTANAROSSA
SS117bis   AIRPORT

SS626dir

CALTANISSETTA   SS194
MUSEO REGIONALE
★ DELLA CERAMICA
SS417

SS514   SS114

PIANOGRILLO FARM
ORGANIC WINERY
SS115   SYRACUSA

AZIENDA AGRICOLA   Syracuse
ARIANNA OCCHIPINTI

Ragusa   Noto

RAGUSA   Riserva Naturale
Orientata Cavagrande
SP25   del Cassibile

Modica

Marzamemi

© MOON.COM

Contents

Trapani

WELCOME TO
Sicily

Whether you're visiting the enchanting island of Sicily for the first time, or returning to savor it again, the fact that you're really here might just hit you during the break between the late afternoon and dinnertime, when Sicilians enjoy "la passeggiata." Locals, often hooked arm-in-arm with friends or family, take part in this evening stroll each day, chitchatting about the latest news and gossip. Kids play in the street and older people relax on park benches, in front of bars playing cards, or drinking an aperitivo before sitting down to a delicious meal.

Most visitors start their journey in Palermo or Catania, then wander from there. The southeast features Baroque towns and fishing villages and beautiful ceramics, and is dotted with Greek and Roman landmarks. In western Sicily, the drive from fortified wine capital Marsala to seaside Trapani is lined with sea salt flats, often speckled with migrating flamingos. Heading north, charming and romantic towns like Cefalù and Taormina are quintessentially Sicilian destinations, perfect for first-time visitors. Take day trips from Catania to Mount Etna volcano for hiking or wine tastings, or head south to sun-drenched Ortigia, the historic center of the ancient city of Syracuse. And, of course, gorgeous, shabby, raucous Palermo merits at least a few days on its own.

No matter where you go, the history of Sicily is laid out right in front of your eyes, in the architecture as well as the food. It's a top destination for food and wine lovers from around the world; there's nothing like that first taste of freshly made sheep's milk ricotta or a glass of mineral-rich wine nourished by Mount Etna's fertile volcanic soils. A trip to Sicily is an invitation to slow down and indulge all the senses.

Soak it all in. Life in Sicily moves slower, and that is what makes it so special.

beach at Scala dei Turchi

8 TOP
EXPERIENCES

1 Lounging on **Sicily's best beaches,** from chic beach clubs dotted with colorful umbrellas to secluded rocky coves (page 28).

2 **Climbing Mount Etna,** Sicily's beating heart and the most active volcano in all of Europe, where you can grab a glass of volcanic wine after your hike (page 225).

3 Seeking out Spanish-influenced Baroque architecture in the UNESCO World Heritage Site of **Noto** (page 273).

4 Snacking on crispy, salty, sinfully good **street food in Palermo** (page 58).

5 Following in the footsteps of the ancient Greeks at the eight majestic temples of the **Valle dei Templi** (page 132).

6 Island-hopping in the **Aeolian Islands** (page 25).

7 Tasting **Sicilian wine,** from the fortified wines of Marsala to malvasia wines from the Aeolian Islands (pages 124 and 162).

8 Strolling and shopping on the island of **Ortigia,** the sun-drenched historic center of Syracuse (page 257).

Planning Your Trip

WHERE TO GO

Palermo

Start your trip to Sicily in the fascinating capital city of Palermo, where its history is marked by waves of conquerors, from the Greeks to the Romans, Arabs, Normans, French, and Spanish. Each one has left its mark and influenced the architecture, culture, landscape, customs, and culinary traditions of the island. Palermo is a hub of Sicilian art, culture, and gastronomy. The **centro storico** is filled with art museums, folksy puppet performances, noble palaces, flourishing **outdoor markets,** and some of Italy's best **street food.**

Western Sicily

Spectacular **beaches** surround Palermo and also stretch down Sicily's western coast. The seaside town of **Cefalù** is one of Sicily's postcard sights, and towns like Castellammare del Golfo, Scopello, and San Vito lo Capo dot the drive from Palermo to the western coast of Sicily. The low-key **Aegadian Islands** sit in the Mediterranean off the coast of the seaside towns of **Trapani** and **Marsala.** The latter is famous for its seafood and fortified wine. To the south, the ruins of the **Valle dei Templi** rival anything found in Greece.

The Aeolian Islands

Just off Sicily's northeast coast, head off the grid to the Aeolian Islands. The largest is **Lipari,** which can serve as a base for exploring the other six islands. Some of the best swimming, wine, fresh seafood, and nightlife in Sicily can be found on the Aeolian Islands, and **Salina** in particular is the place to splurge on a luxury resort. See

the Baroque town of Modica in southeastern Sicily

the volcano on **Stromboli** explode at night, taste wines grown on the island, and lounge on beaches only accessible by boat. **Milazzo** is the main departure point for ferries to the islands, but is beautiful in its own right—slow down to enjoy one of the region's famous granitas before making your island escape.

Catania, Mount Etna, and Northeastern Sicily

Under the shadow of Mother Etna, **Catania**'s proximity to Sicily's largest airport, Catania Fontanarossa, makes it a no-brainer stop on any trip to Sicily. This intricate black-rock city was rebuilt with lava stones after two devastating volcanic eruptions and earthquakes, but the vivacious **Pescheria di Catania** fish market shows the town to be very much alive. Within an easy drive, you can climb the slopes of **Mount Etna,** sip volcanic wines, and live large in glamorous, historic **Taormina.**

Syracuse and Southeastern Sicily

Get a glimpse into Sicily's Greek history in **Syracuse,** originally founded by the Corinthians in 734 BCE. Its **Parco Archeologico della Neapolis** is home to an impressive Greek theater and a Roman amphitheater, and the island of **Ortigia** jutting just off the city's coast is the perfect combination of historic architecture, the sea, and delicious food. Then, venture out to the towns of **Modica, Noto,** and **Ragusa,** living pieces of art with their beautiful Baroque townscapes. Along the southeastern coast, you will find lovely beaches with fewer crowds.

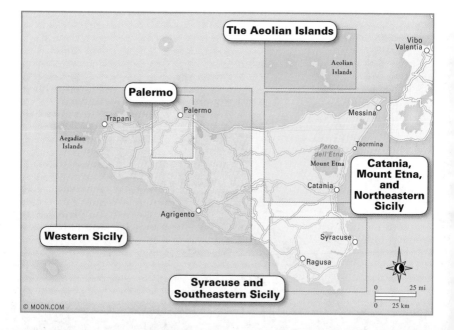

WHEN TO GO

Sicily's subtropical Mediterranean climate, with mild winters and hot, dry summers, makes it an ideal destination all year round, with the exception of a few weeks in August when the island becomes crowded with tourists on their summer holidays. However, the islands off the coast of Sicily—Aegadian, Aeolian, and Pantellaria—are seasonal, with most businesses only open April/May to September. Throughout Sicily and the islands, July and August are generally the busiest, most crowded months; the transitional months of April, May, and September offer the best balance.

BEFORE YOU GO

In general, give yourself a little wiggle room in your planning. Life moves slowly in Italy, even more so in Sicily. It will take longer than you expect to travel from place to place. There are surprises around every corner, so it's best to leave a little free time to allow for changes.

Passports and Visas
U.S., UK, Canadian, Australian, and **New Zealand** travelers do not need a visa to enter Italy, but in 2024, the ETIAS registration system (https://travel-europe.europa.eu/etias_en) is set to go into effect, and visitors from visa-exempt countries will need to apply for authorization to enter Italy (and other European Union countries). Passports should be valid for six months after your departure date from the EU.

EU citizens have no visa or registration requirements to enter Italy. For travelers from **South Africa,** a Schengen Visa (€80 for adults) is required to enter Italy.

For more information, visit Italy's **Ministry of Foreign Affairs website** (http://vistoperitalia.esteri.it).

What to Pack
Sicily is very casual, with mild winters and hot summers. Beaches figure prominently in a trip to the island, so be sure to bring swimsuits and sun protection. Water shoes can help navigate rocky Sicilian beaches. If you're planning to hike, such as up Mount Etna, well-fitting hiking footwear is essential.

For travelers from outside the EU, pack a couple plug adapters—EU outlets take plugs with two round pins—to charge your devices.

To reduce waste, bring a refillable water bottle, reusable shopping bag, and your own toiletries.

Transportation
Although there are train and bus systems in place, a car—whether self-driven or with a driver—is the recommended way to travel around Sicily.

Air
Sicily's main airports are in **Palermo** (Aeroporto di Palermo Falcone e Borsellino, also known as Punta Raisi) and **Catania** (Aeroporto di Catania Fontanarossa). There are no direct flights from North America to either airport, but both are well connected to airports across Europe and Italy. Though it is possible to travel to Sicily by train, bus, and rental car from mainland Italy, travelers with limited time should consider the quick, frequent, and cheap domestic flights.

It is not necessary to fly between destinations in Sicily. The one exception is the island of Pantelleria, which is located far enough off the coast of Sicily that flying is the best option.

Train
Train service connects major cities in Sicily, though it is generally a slower, less reliable way to travel compared to the rest of Italy. Mount Etna is also accessible by the **Ferrovia Circumetnea** train.

Ferry

You will need to take a ferry to reach the archipelagoes off Sicily, such as the Aegadian and Aeolian Islands. It also is possible to reach Palermo from Naples on mainland Italy via an overnight ferry (11 hours).

Bus

Regional bus service is available between cities and, in some cases, may be the only option for those who aren't driving. For some trips, such as between Palermo and Trapani, the bus may be faster than the train.

Car

Driving is often the best way to get around in Sicily. Outside of large cities like Palermo or Catania, it is easy to drive in Sicily, since the terrain is generally flat. That said, give yourself extra time on road trips, as many small, regional roads will not be smoothly paved.

Car rental agencies are available at most airports and in larger cities, and off-season prices for rental cars are extremely affordable. In addition, hotels will often provide shuttle services from the airport; check with your accommodations for recommendations on how to best reach them.

If driving yourself, bring an international GPS of your own. Renting them through the agency will be expensive. In off-the-grid locations, cell service might be limited, so don't depend solely

If You Have...

- **Three Days:** Head to Palermo and make day trips to Cefalù and Segesta.

- **One Week:** With seven days, visit Palermo and explore the western coast down to the spectacular Valle dei Templi.

- **Two Weeks:** You can see most of Sicily in two weeks, starting in Palermo and seeing the western coast, then crossing the island to Catania, Taormina, and Mount Etna. You can visit one of the archipelagoes off the Sicily coast as well, either breaking up the western coast portion with a night or two on the Aegadian Islands or ending your trip with a getaway to the Aeolian Islands.

on your cell phone for directions, though the Google Maps app has a great option to download regional maps offline.

Public Transportation

Within cities, public transportation can simplify your trip. In Palermo, Catania, and their immediate vicinity, buses comprise the public transportation network, and Catania also has one Metro line. Messina has a tram system.

The Aeolian island of Lipari also has bus service.

BEST OF
Sicily

Any one region of Sicily can take at least five days to explore properly, but it's possible to see the highlights in a little more than a week. You'll need to rent a car to make the most of your time.

Day 1-2: Palermo

After landing in **Palermo,** the island's buzzing, vibrant capital, get the lay of the land at **Quattro Canti,** or the "Four Corners," a beautiful Baroque landmark at the main crossroads of Palermo's old town. Nearby, stroll through **Piazza Pretoria** and the red-domed **Church of San Cataldo,** before walking south to **Mercato di Ballarò** for a deep dive into Palermo's famous street food. Spend the afternoon in the fascinating **Palazzo dei Normanni** before finding a nearby wine bar for an aperitivo and enjoying dinner at a tucked-away trattoria.

Begin your second day in Sicily with breakfast at the oldest coffee roaster in Palermo, **Casa Stagnitta,** then stop in **Santa Maria dell'Ammiraglio** church to see its Byzantine mosaics. In the afternoon, choose a museum, like the **Galleria d'Arte Moderna Palermo,** to explore, or peruse the treasures of **Mercato delle Pulci** to find a unique souvenir. In the early evening, join in the typically Sicilian passeggiata along the waterfront **Foro Italico,** heading to **Mercato Vucciria** just as its alleyways start to bustle with young people drinking, dancing, and snacking on Palermitan street food delicacies.

Day 3: West from Palermo

Rent a car and make the 20-minute drive from Palermo's city center to the stunning **Cattedrale di Monreale,** a can't-miss UNESCO World Heritage Site, built in the 12th century, when Sicily was under Norman rule. Continue driving west into the Monreale DOC winemaking region, where you can schedule tastings at wineries like **Alessandro di Camporeale** or **Tenuta Sallier de La Tour.** Spend the evening in seaside **Castellammare del Golfo.**

Mercato di Ballarò

on all the history that this part of Sicily has seen. Make your way to **Agrigento,** a 20-minute drive from the beach, for dinner and a much-needed night's sleep.

Day 5: Valle dei Templi

The next day, make a beeline for the dramatic ruins of the ancient Greek city of Akragas, known as **Valle dei Templi.** Among the remains of seven impressive temples spread out over 3,000 acres (1,200 ha), the **Temple of Concordia** is the best preserved. Be sure to stop by the **Giardino della Kolymbetra,** built to supply the city of Akragas with water, still a fertile garden to this day. In the afternoon, drive two hours across the island to reach **Catania,** on Sicily's eastern coast.

Day 4: Southwestern Coast

In the morning, drive inland from Castellammare del Golfo to the **Temple of Segesta,** and spend a few hours at the picturesque ruins. Afterward, keep heading south along the coast for about two hours to the dramatic, terraced limestone beach of **Scala dei Turchi,** a great place to meditate

Day 6: Catania

For your day in Catania, wake up your senses at the **Pescheria di Catania** seafood market, not far from the town's **Piazza del Duomo** and impressive **Cattedrale di Sant'Agata.** Admire the basalt architecture of this city built in Mount Etna's shadow, strolling past ancient Roman sites

Valle dei Templi

Villa Bellini in Catania

including a theater and thermal baths, to **Villa Bellini,** surrounded by many excellent cafés and bars, to get a pastry or aperitivo.

Day 7: Taormina

The cliffside city of Taormina, featured in the popular TV series *The White Lotus,* makes a luxurious day trip from Catania. Wander along and off **Corso Umberto** in the historic center, popping into its shops, boutiques, and cafés; take a cable car to **Isola Bella;** and don't miss **Teatro Antico di Taormina,** the ancient Greek theater carved into Monte Tauro. Head back to Catania for the evening.

Day 8: Mount Etna

Take an excursion to **Mount Etna** today, an hour's drive north of Catania. Depending on your tastes, you can hike to the **volcanic crater** from the Etna Sud visitor center, or sample some volcanic vino at one of the many **wineries** on the volcano's slopes. Consider booking a **wine tour**

if you go the latter route. Return to Catania for your final night in.

Day 9: Journey Home

For most, heading home will mean a flight through Naples or Rome, but the adventurous may want to travel to mainland Italy by the train that gets loaded onto a ferry.

Mount Etna

Sicily's Ancient Sites

Its strategic location between North Africa and mainland Europe, fertile land, and other resources meant that Sicily saw waves of settlement and conquest. Once a colony in the Greek empire, Sicily is today home to many spectacular Greek archaeological sites. Later, Romans overtook the island, building over Greek structures and constructing others. Today, visitors with an interest in archaeology and antiquity will be spoiled for choices among Sicily's many ancient treasures.

GREEK

Temple of Diana

Combine a visit to this ancient temple with a hike along Cefalù's La Rocca cliffs (page 84).

Temple of Segesta

This well-preserved temple with its intact Doric columns and location atop Monte Barbaro sets a breathtaking scene inland from the Gulf of Castellammare (page 97).

Selinunte Archaeological Park

This extensive site in southwestern Sicily was once one of the most powerful cities in the ancient Greek colonies in Italy (page 129).

Valle dei Templi

If you only go to one archaeological site in Sicily, make it Valle dei Templi, in southwestern Sicily, where eight ancient temples are spread across 3,000 acres (1,214 ha) against a backdrop of almond and olive trees (page 132).

Teatro Antico di Taormina

You can still see performances at Taormina's ancient Greek theater in the summer months. Even when not in use, the site is worth visiting to see its size and cliffside location (page 216).

Parco Archeologico della Neapolis

Syracuse's archaeological park showcases both Greek and Roman ruins, as well as the quarry that provided the materials to build these ancient structures (page 251).

Island of Ortigia

The sites in Ortigia, the oldest part of Syracuse, include the Tempio di Apollo, which might actually have been dedicated to Apollo's sister Artemis, and the mythic Fonte Aretusa (page 257).

PHOENICIAN

Mozia

Seafaring Phoenicians established a colony, called Motya, on this tiny island just off the coast of Marsala. The ruins here include burial grounds and temples (page 124).

ROMAN

Catania's Theaters and Baths

The Roman sites in Catania include two theaters, one of which was once the largest in Sicily, and a complex of thermal baths (page 201).

Villa Romana del Casale

This Roman villa in central Sicily, about halfway between Agrigento and Catania, is famous for its many intricate mosaics (page 286).

Island-Hopping Escapes

Although Sicily is itself an island, it also boasts two splendid island groups that are perfect for summer holidays. Whether you want to kick back on a pebbly beach next to deep blue waters, take a boat tour to coves and caves, pamper yourself at a luxe resort, or watch a beautiful sunset, you can make your escape to the Aeolian or Aegadian Islands—or both!

Aeolian Islands

The seven Aeolian Islands sit off the north coast of Sicily, with most visitors arriving from Milazzo on mainland Sicily, although access from Palermo or Messina is also possible. This short itinerary focuses on the highlights on four islands and traveling by ferry, though those with more time or who charter a boat may be able to get to more islands. Soak in the relaxed vibe of the Isole Eolie, as they're called in Italian. If you're wine tasting at Tenuta di Castellaro, be sure to make reservations ahead of time.

Day 1-2: Lipari

From Milazzo, board a hydrofoil in the afternoon to head to Lipari, a 45-minute ride. Check into **Hotel Mea Lipari** for three nights. Get into the island spirit by relaxing next to the pool for a few hours. **Il Giardino di Lipari** is a great spot for dinner after your lazy afternoon.

The next day, seek out some beach time at one of the stretches of white sand that Lipari is

a pebbly beach on the Aeolian island of Lipari

known for. Beautiful **Spiagge Bianche** is backed by white stone cliffs and has a beach club with beach loungers to rent. In the afternoon, head out for a wine tasting at **Tenuta di Castellaro,** using its shuttle service from Lipari's port. The views from this winery, perched high above sea level, are incredible. Make it an early night to rest up for tomorrow's day trip.

Day 3: Vulcano

Take the earliest ferry you can bear over to Vulcano (10 minutes), bringing hiking shoes, a bathing suit, and other beach supplies. Once at Vulcano's port, follow signs to the **Gran Cratere della Fossa,** the island's volcanic crater. The hike up to the top of the crater and back is 3.5 miles (5.6 km) and takes about 2.5 hours. Be sure to wear sun protection and carry water, as the route is not shaded.

Afterward, head down to **Spiaggia delle Acque Calde,** where you can pick up sandwiches and salads at the beach bar and relax on the black sand. If you lose track of time and find yourself needing dinner, get the famous pane cunzatu open-face sandwich from **Malvasia Pane Cunzatu.** Enjoy it out on the terrace with a glass of malvasia wine before catching the ferry back to Lipari.

Day 4-5: Salina

You'll be switching islands today. Hop on a hydrofoil to Salina (20 minutes). Splurge on one of Salina's luxury resorts, such as **Hotel L'Ariana** in Rinella. You won't need to move around much once you're here—just spend the rest of the day taking in the amenities. If you want a swim, you can take a dip in the sea right from the hotel via a private staircase to the water, then lie out on the terrace.

The next day, take a boat tour around the island. Make sure to go to **Pollara** to see the area made famous by the movie *Il Postino*. If you can, stick around to watch the **sunset,** which is spectacular from this part of the island. In the distance, you'll see Filicudi island, your destination for tomorrow.

Day 6: Filicudi

Head down to the port of Rinella for the 25-minute ferry to Filicudi. For something a little different, walk to the **prehistoric village,** about 15 minutes away from the Filicudi ferry terminal. Afterward, rent a boat to explore the **Grotta del Bue Marino,** the largest cave in the Aeolian Islands. Head back to Salina for a last afternoon lounging on the **beach of Rinella.** If you're not spending another night in Salina, head back to Milazzo in the early evening.

Aegadian Islands

The Aegadian Islands are located off Sicily's west coast and can be accessed via Trapani or Marsala. This trio of low-key islands—Favignana, Marettimo, and Levanzo—is still relatively off the radar of international tourists. The waters surrounding them are part of Italy's largest marine reserve, and many spots are accessed only on foot or by boat, making for an outdoorsy getaway. If you want to visit the Garden of the Impossible on Favignana and Grotta del Genovese on Levanzo, be sure to make reservations ahead of time. Also reserve a boat tour with Marettimo Giro dell'Isola con Pippo in advance.

harbor of Levanzo, the smallest Aegadian island

Day 1-2: Favignana

From the port of Trapani, take a 30-minute morning ferry ride on Liberty Lines to the nearby island of Favignana. Rent a bicycle to cruise around the flat terrain of the town center or take the one-hour steep hike up to **Santa Caterina Castle** for a bird's-eye view of the island's magnificent coves and crystal waters from 1,030 feet (314 m) up, spotting Levanzo and Marettimo in the distance. Get dinner at **Formica,** which serves seafood with locally sourced ingredients.

The next day, head up to **Scogliera di Cala Rossa** on the north coast. If you walk, it will take one hour from Favignana town. This picturesque, rocky beach is one of the most beautiful in the Aegadian Islands—and possibly all of Italy. If you have a reservation, take a tour of the **Garden of the Impossible** in the afternoon. If you need more beach time, **Spiaggia Praia** is right in town, near various bars and restaurants.

Day 3: Levanzo

From Favignana, take a day trip to Levanzo. Visit the **Grotta del Genovese** to see Paleolithic and Neolithic paintings and engravings. Afterward, stop by **Panetteria La Chicca** to stock up on lunch and snacks, then head to one of the pebbly beaches on the island. **Cala Fredda** and **Cala Minnola** are two near the harbor. Catch an afternoon or evening ferry back to Favignana.

Day 4: Marettimo

Catch the first boat to Marettimo in order to arrive in time for a morning tour with **Marettimo Giro dell'Isola con Pippo,** which will take you around the island to swimming spots and grottos. Afterward, if you want to do some snorkeling, head to **Spiaggetta dello Scalo Vecchio,** near the main port. Head back to Favignana for a nap, then toast your last night in the Aegadian Islands at **Camparia Lounge,** located in an old fishing boat repair building.

Sicily's Best Beaches

Located in coves, in nature reserves, and on offshore islands, the beaches of Sicily range from sparkling white sand to dark and volcanic to rugged and rocky. Beauty and clear waters abound. Here are a few of the best spots to enjoy sunshine and a swim.

PALERMO

- **Spiaggia di Mondello:** The golden sands of this beach just 20 minutes from the city center of Palermo are popular among travelers and locals alike (page 71).

WESTERN SICILY

- **Spiaggia di Cefalù:** This gorgeous public beach is a good spot for families with children due to the warm, calm waters (page 85).

- **Scala dei Turchi:** The dramatic scenery of white terraced cliffs makes for a unique beach experience, where you can lie on the cool white stone (page 130).

THE AEOLIAN ISLANDS

- **Spiagge Bianche:** One of the most beautiful beaches on Lipari boasts warm turquoise waters (page 154).

- **Spiaggia delle Sabbie Nere:** This beach on Vulcano stands out for its soft, black volcanic sand and shallow waters (page 174).

NORTHEASTERN SICILY

- **Spiaggia Libera di Isola Bella:** Though you'll have a lot of competition for a spot to lie down, this pebbly beach has a picturesque setting facing Isola Bella, the tiny island that has become an icon of Taormina (page 217).

- **Spiaggia di Giardini Naxos:** Also near Taormina, the beaches of Giardini Naxos have a lively nightlife scene (page 217).

SOUTHEASTERN SICILY

- **Spiaggia Calamosche:** Wildlife is a big attraction at this beach in the Vendicari Nature Reserve. See flamingos in spring and fall and sea turtles in May (page 272).

- **Spiaggia di Sampieri:** Surrounded by sand dunes and a pine forest, Sampieri is one of the most scenic landscapes along the coast of Ragusa (page 299).

Tasting Sicily

Sicily is rich with delicious gastronomic experiences. Each dish tells a story of the history of the island, with ingredients brought to Europe by way of Sicily from the Greeks, Arabs, Normans, and Spaniards. And all across Sicily, locals make the most of their pristine coasts and landscape with fresh seafood and produce featuring in their cuisine.

Seafood

Seafood is ubiquitous in Sicily, with fresh, locally caught fish and shellfish found on most menus. The coastal cuisine features sardines, swordfish, red Mediterranean tuna, and anchovies.

Markets

A highlight of a visit to Sicily is Catania's **Pescheria di Catania,** or A' Piscaria in Sicilian, (page 201). The **Mercato di Siracusa** in Ortigia is also a good place to see what locals eat and features seafood not found elsewhere on the island (page 265).

Fish Couscous

In Trapani and surrounding areas in western Sicily, fish couscous is a local specialty. A rich broth is poured over the top of semola couscous and served with a side of fish or seafood. Try it at **Salamureci Ristorante** (page 106) in Trapani or go to San Vito Lo Capo's **Cous Cous Fest** in September (page 101).

Street Food

Street food is a serious business in Palermo, from irresistible **panelle** (fried chickpea fritters) to the more adventurous **pani cà meusa** (spleen and lung sandwich) (page 58). Across the island, Catania has its own street food specialties, including **arancini** (fried rice balls) and **cipollina,** a pastry stuffed with onions, mozzarella, ham, and tomatoes (page 206).

granita

Regional Specialties
Pasta alla Norma
Named after Vincenzo Bellini's opera, Catania's famous dish is made with tomato sauce, fried eggplant, fresh basil, and grated ricotta salata cheese on top (page 206).

Pane Cunzatu
Translating to "seasoned bread," this sandwich packed with anchovies, olives, oregano, tomato, and cheese is typical around Trapani and can be found around the island. Try it in San Vito Lo Capo at **Salumeria Enoteca Peraino** (page 101) or **Malvasia Pane Cunzatu & Restaurant,** which has locations in Milazzo and Vulcano (pages 149 and 176).

Wine
Mount Etna
Wine is grown throughout Sicily, but perhaps the most unique place to taste vino is on the slopes of Mount Etna, where the volcanic soil and high elevation lends unique ash, sand, and minerals to the grapes (page 228).

Marsala
To the west, taste marsala in its namesake town, where this fortified wine is experiencing a resurgence (page 124).

Malvasia
The local malvasia Sicilian wine is known for its honeysuckle aroma and pear notes. Visit wineries and vineyards in the Aeolian islands of **Lipari** (page 155) and **Salina** (page 162).

Sweets and Baked Goods
Bakeries
In Sicily, many bakeries keep alive centuries-old recipes perfected by nuns cloistered in convents; give them a try at Palermo's **I Segreti del Chiostro** (page 57) or Erice's **Pasticceria Maria Grammatico** (page 106).

Chocolate
The southeastern town of **Modica** is famous for its chocolate, a legacy of Spanish rule in Sicily. The texture makes Modica chocolate stand out: Sugar crystals can be felt in each bite of chocolate, a result of the unique production process (page 292).

Granita
A specialty of the provinces of Messina and Catania, granita is a semi-frozen Italian ice served with whipped cream and a brioche on the side for dipping. Flavors range from fruity (lemon, orange, strawberry) to nutty (pistachio, almond), as well as chocolate and coffee. Go to **Washington Bar** (page 150) in Milazzo or **Antica Pasticceria Irrera** (page 242) to try it in its regional home. The seasonal granitas at **Bam Bar** in Taormina are also famous (page 219).

Palermo

No trip to Sicily is complete without a few days in the fascinating city of Palermo, a nucleus of art, culture, and gastronomy. Most travelers get their first taste of what makes Sicily unique wandering the streets of Palermo's historic city center, snacking their way through its outdoor markets, and enjoying the rowdy nightlife. You'll know right away that this is not Rome, Venice, or Milan: Palermo has its own lively flavor and old-world charm, thanks to the buskers in the piazzas, slow early evening passeggiata walks, spontaneous bursts of music from cars passing by, and cute old grannies providing an unofficial "neighborhood watch" from their balconies above.

Originally settled by Phoenicians in 734 BCE, Palermo has always been an important city, located in the center of the Mediterranean

Highlights

Look for ★ to find recommended sights, activities, dining, and lodging.

★ **Palazzo dei Normanni:** This monumental palace is a stunning hodgepodge of architectural styles emblematic of centuries of conquerors and cultures (page 43).

★ **Palermitan Street Food:** Test out traditional Palermitan snacks, like panelle chickpea fritters, crocchè fried potato dumplings, or sfincione, a fluffy focaccia-style pizza, many of them only made here in Palermo (page 58).

★ **Mondello Beach:** Head to the sea like the Palermitani in this charming beach town just northwest of Sicily's capital city (page 71).

★ **Wine Tasting in Camporeale:** Head out of town less than an hour to Palermo's wine country for tastings and vineyard visits in the DOC Monreale region (page 74).

and right along the Afro-European trade routes. When the Greeks conquered Palermo between the 8th and 7th centuries BCE, they renamed the city Panormos, meaning "all port." Through Roman, Byzantine, and Arab rule over the centuries, the city developed its distinctive layers of cultural and architectural history, visible in its churches, palaces, and monuments. The Palazzo dei Normanni is a perfect example, dating to the 8th century BCE and with Arab, Norman, and Spanish architectural elements.

Food and wine lovers will quickly settle into la dolce vita here. Treat yourself to affordable street food, gourmet restaurants, and bountiful homemade meals on vineyard visits. Sicily is a true melting pot of flavors. Each dish tells the history of the island, with ingredients brought here by way of Greece, Northern Africa, and Spain. Keep an eye out for can't-miss regional dishes that can't be found anywhere else, like sfincione (focaccia-style pizza).

ORIENTATION

In Palermo, the **Quattro Canti** ("Four Corners") crossroads at **Via Maqueda** (running northwest-southeast) and **Corso Vittorio Emanuele** (running southwest-northeast) should be the central point on your mental map, dividing the **centro storico** into four main neighborhoods. Starting in the northeast and moving clockwise, they are La Loggia (Vucciria), Kalsa, Albergheria (Ballarò), and Monte di Pietà (Capo).

La Loggia, also known as Castellammare, is home to Palermo's port and the Mercato Vucciria. To the south, **Kalsa** is home to some of the city's best green spaces: the extensive, historic Orto Botanico dell'Università di Palermo gardens, Villa Giulia park, and the Foro Italico seaside promenade. West of Kalsa, **Albergheria** is one of the city's oldest sections, home to many of Palermo's North African, Sri Lankan, and Bangladeshi

residents. Its main highlights are the Mercato di Ballarò, Palermo's oldest and largest market, and the ancient Palazzo dei Normanni. North of Albergheria, Monte di Pietà also has its own outdoor market from which the neighborhood takes its nickname of **Capo,** along with the Cattedrale di Palermo and the famous Teatro Massimo.

Palermo Centrale train station sits south of the Quattro Canti, wedged between Albergheria and Kalsa. Only a few main sights lie outside the city center: the **Giardino Inglese,** north of the city; and the 12th-century, Islamic-inspired **Castello della Zisa** and the **Catacombe dei Cappuccini,** both in the northwestern neighborhood of **La Zisa.**

It's worth noting that though Palermo boasts some lovely waterfront areas, the city's main beach is in **Mondello,** half an hour's drive northwest. Save time to round out your stay in Palermo with a half-day in the countryside for wine tastings in **Camporeale** or a full-day ferry trip to the marine-protected island of **Ustica.**

PLANNING YOUR TIME

Three to five days is a good amount of time to spend in western Sicily; an overview of **Palermo** requires at least two days. Sicily's capital is likely your best base for the region; from here, it's easy to take day trips to most of the highlights of the area by bus, train, or rental car.

Falcone-Borsellino (PMO) airport, formerly known as Punta Raisi, is the main hub for flights arriving in Sicily, located 19 miles (31 km) west of the Palermo city center on Sicily's northwestern coast. In Palermo proper, having your own car is not recommended or truly necessary. With accommodations in the centro storico, most of the sites you'll want to visit can be reached **on foot** or with a quick taxi ride. However, in the surrounding region's smaller towns, it's helpful and sometimes

---

Previous: Fontana Pretoria; Spiaggia di Mondello; Tenuta Sallier de La Tour.

Palermo and Vicinity

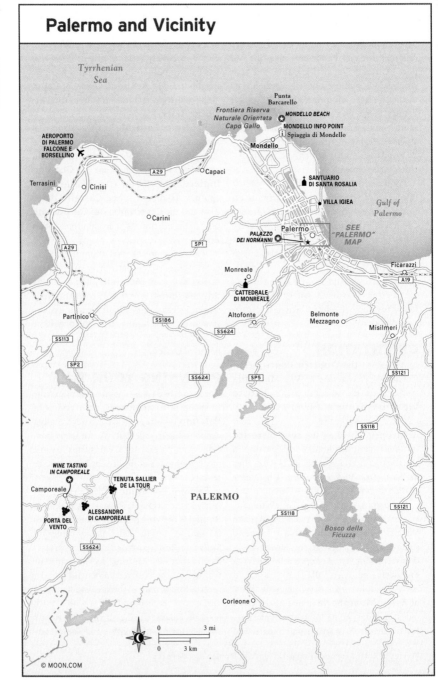

Tyrrhenian Sea

Punta Barcarello

Frontiera Riserva Naturale Orientata Capo Gallo

MONDELLO BEACH
MONDELLO INFO POINT
Spiaggia di Mondello

Mondello

AEROPORTO DI PALERMO FALCONE E BORSELLINO

A29

Capaci

Terrasini

Cinisi

SANTUARIO DI SANTA ROSALIA

VILLA IGIEA

Gulf of Palermo

Carini

A29

SP1

Palermo

SEE "PALERMO" MAP

Ficarazzi

A19

Monreale

CATTEDRALE DI MONREALE

Belmonte Mezzagno

Partinico

SS186

SS624

Altofonte

Misilmeri

SS113

SP2

SS624

SP5

SS121

SS118

WINE TASTING IN CAMPOREALE

TENUTA SALLIER DE LA TOUR

Camporeale

PALERMO

PORTA DEL VENTO

ALESSANDRO DI CAMPOREALE

SS118

SS121

Bosco della Ficuzza

SS624

Corleone

0   3 mi
0   3 km

© MOON.COM

necessary to **rent a car** to get around. **Trains** and **buses** connect Palermo to most of the main towns and cities in the region, but service can be infrequent or delayed, and having your own rental car can offer more flexibility.

Sicily's subtropical Mediterranean climate, with **mild winters** and **hot, dry summers,** makes it an ideal destination all year round, with the exception of a few weeks in August when the island becomes crowded with tourists on their summer holidays.

Safety

Overall, Palermo is a safe place to travel, but you should be smart about not flashing valuable jewelry or cameras and always keeping an eye on your bags and backpacks while moving through more crowded areas like the markets. Main squares remain populated and safe well into the evenings, but visiting the areas around the **Ballarò** and **Capo Markets** in the late night is not recommended.

Itinerary Ideas

THREE DAYS IN PALERMO

Guided tours, vineyard visits, accommodations, and car rentals should be reserved in advance to avoid disappointment, and restaurant reservations are recommended.

Day One: Palermo

1 Start your day with an espresso on the panoramic rooftop bar of the **Rinascente** luxury department store on Via Roma.

2 At 10am, meet up with your guide from Palermo Street Food at the **Teatro Massimo** for a walking tour of Palermo and a grazing street food lunch of Sicilian specialties.

3 Walk 15 minutes south along Via Porta di Castro to spend a few hours inside Europe's oldest royal residence, the **Palazzo dei Normanni.** Save time to admire the Byzantine mosaics inside the Cappella Palatina chapel.

4 When it's just about that time for a classic Sicilian midday nap, head back to the convenience of your luxury apartment at **Palazzo Sovrana,** a 20-minute walk northeast via Via Vittoria Emanuele and Via Maqueda.

5 Refreshed, stop for an aperitivo at **Enoteca Picone** wine bar, just a few blocks off the high-end shopping area of Via della Libertà. It's a 15-minute walk northwest on Via Messina.

6 Just across the street, enjoy a seafood-centric dinner at **Corona Trattoria.** Soak in the Sicilian hospitality of the cheerful Corona family in their modern trattoria, before returning to your apartment for a peaceful rest after all that walking.

Day Two: Palermo and DOC Monreale Wine Country

1 Start your day at the **Quattro Canti,** meeting up with the best guide in town to discover Palermo's noble palaces on a tour with native Palermitana Marcella Amato. She's your hookup for a private glimpse into the city's luxurious aristocratic past that a typical tourist would never get to see on their own.

Itinerary Ideas

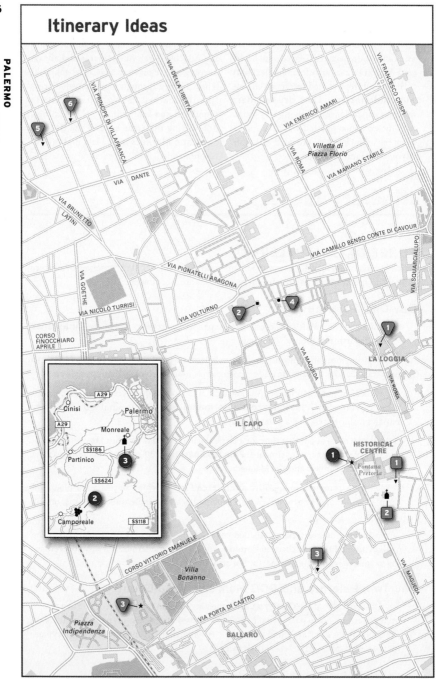

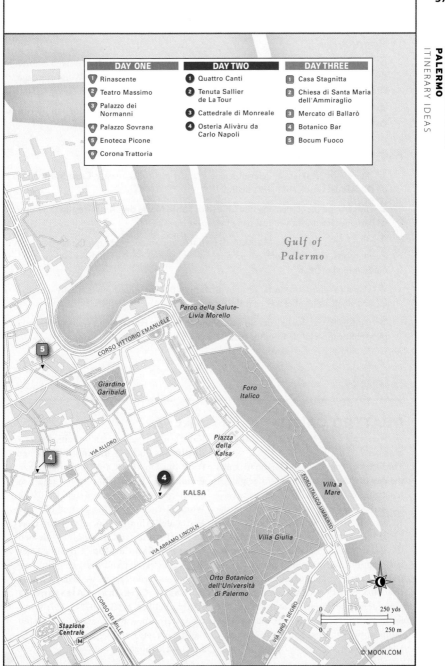

DAY ONE	DAY TWO	DAY THREE
1 Rinascente	1 Quattro Canti	1 Casa Stagnitta
2 Teatro Massimo	2 Tenuta Sallier de La Tour	2 Chiesa di Santa Maria dell'Ammiraglio
3 Palazzo dei Normanni	3 Cattedrale di Monreale	3 Mercato di Ballarò
4 Palazzo Sovrana	4 Osteria Alivàru da Carlo Napoli	4 Botanico Bar
5 Enoteca Picone		5 Bocum Fuoco
6 Corona Trattoria		

Gulf of
Palermo

Parco della Salute-
Livia Morello

CORSO VITTORIO EMANUELE

Giardino
Garibaldi

Foro
Italico

VIA ALLORO

Piazza
della
Kalsa

Villa a
Mare

KALSA

VIA ABRAMO LINCOLN

Villa Giulia

CORSO DEI MILLE

Orto Botanico
dell'Università
di Palermo

Stazione
Centrale
Ⓜ

0   250 yds
0   250 m

© MOON.COM

2 After the tour, pick up your rental car to head out of Palermo for the day. Spend the afternoon in the vineyards with Costanza Chirivino at **Tenuta Sallier de La Tour** for a wine tasting and lunch in Camporeale, a 45-minute drive south on SS624 into the DOC Monreale region.

3 On the way back from Camporeale, stop by the **Cattedrale di Monreale** to admire the Norman architecture and Byzantine-style mosaics of this UNESCO World Heritage Site before driving back to Palermo.

4 Back in Palermo, treat yourself to a traditional Sicilian dinner at the family-run **Osteria Alivàru da Carlo Napoli,** in the Kalsa neighborhood.

Day Three: Palermo Like a Local

1 Start with breakfast at Palermo's oldest family-run coffee roaster, **Casa Stagnitta,** on Discesa dei Giudici in Piazza Bellini.

2 Just around the corner, pop into **Chiesa di Santa Maria dell'Ammiraglio** to admire its Baroque facade and awe-inspiring Byzantine mosaics.

3 Make your way to the **Mercato di Ballarò,** and wander through the labyrinth of greengrocers, mountains of fresh produce, and boisterous vendors in this 1,000-year-old outdoor food market.

4 After an afternoon siesta, drop by **Botanico Bar** for a pre-dinner aperitivo drink, located along a slim alleyway near the Piazza Sant'Anna.

5 Finish off your day in Palermo with dinner at **Bocum Fuoco** with a series of elegantly plated bites and a bottle from the natural-focused wine list.

Sights

QUATTRO CANTI

Via Maqueda and Corso Vittorio Emanuele; open 24 hours; free

The historic "Four Corners" landmark splits the city of Palermo into its main neighborhood quarters, or quartieri. Built in the classic Sicilian Baroque style developed in the 1600s, this early example of city planning lies at the cross streets of Via Maqueda and the Corso Vittorio Emanuele. At each corner, beautiful, nearly identical curved facades feature a quartet of fountains portraying the rivers that once flowed through the city and sculptures representing the four seasons, the Spanish kings of Sicily, and the main patron saints of the Palermo: Ninfa, Oliva, Agata, and Cristina.

KALSA

Kalsa's main pedestrian square, **Piazza Bellini,** is located around the corner from the Quattro Canti and the Piazza Pretoria. In Piazza Bellini, you'll find two of Palermo's Arab-Norman-style UNESCO World Heritage Sites: the Church of Santa Maria dell'Ammiraglio, also known as **La Martorana,** and its adjoining domed **Chiesa di San Cataldo.** On the corner of Piazza Pretoria and Piazza Bellini, the garden and rooftop views from **Chiesa di Santa Caterina d'Alessandria** (Piazza Bellini, 2; tel. 091/2713837; www.monasterosantacaterina.com; 10am-6pm daily; €3), famed for the pastry shop inside, are also a highlight.

This popular meeting point is used for tour groups, as well as those who are meeting for a coffee at the landmark torrefazione (coffee roaster) **Casa Stagnitta.** Here, you can also access the city's free Wi-Fi or stop by the **Tourist Information Point** (Via Maqueda; www.visitpalermo.it; 9am-8pm Mon.-Sat.). On summer evenings, the square is filled with groups who organize meetups for dancing, friends meeting for an aperitivo, or, if you're lucky, a street-busking accordion player.

Fontana Pretoria

Piazza Pretoria; open 24 hours; free
Especially given its location just across the street from a church, the 16th-century citizens of Palermo were shocked by the 48 nude statues that adorn this fountain, representing the 12 Olympians of Greek mythology among other figures. The citizens referred to it as "the fountain of shame." With the fountain located right in front of the **City Hall** (Palazzo Pretorio, Piazza Pretoria, 1; tel. 091/326056; www.comune.palermo.it), the nickname also applies to the unsavory corruption of Palermitan government throughout the 18th and 19th centuries.

What has become one of the city's most recognizable landmarks was not originally designed for this location. The Praetoria Fountain was built in 1554 by Francesco Camilliani, a Tuscan Renaissance sculptor, to be placed in the Florentine garden of Luigi de Toledo. Twenty years later, after de Toledo passed away, his son decided to sell the masterpiece to the Senate of Palermo. The fountain had to be dismantled into over 600 pieces and moved down to Sicily by ship, and the surrounding buildings had to be torn down to create a space for this massive structure.

La Martorana
(Chiesa di Santa Maria dell'Ammiraglio)

Piazza Bellini, 3; tel. 345/8288231; www.arcidiocesi.palermo.it; 9:45am-1pm Mon.-Sat.; €2 entrance fee
The Chiesa di Santa Maria dell'Ammiraglio, better known as La Martorana, was built in 1143 and underwent extensive modification between the 16th and 18th centuries. Although only a handful of the original iconographic mosaics remain, this church is characterized by its overlapping ornate Baroque decorations, Islamic inscriptions, Byzantine dome, and Norman columns. It was given to a Benedictine monastery and became known as La Chiesa della Martorana for its noble founder, Eloise Martorana. Following along with Sicily's history of pastry making, the nuns of this convent were famous for their sculpted marzipan fruit- and vegetable-shaped sweets known as frutta di Martorana, which they say originated right here.

This church is the seat of the Greek Orthodox parish of San Nicolò dei Greci as well as the Italo-Albanian Catholic community. Since 2015, it has been included in the Arab-Norman UNESCO World Heritage Sites of Palermo. Adjoining Santa Maria dell'Ammiraglio is the Catholic **Chiesa di San Cataldo** (Piazza Bellini, 1; https://arabo-normannaunesco.it; 10am-6pm daily; €2.50), another prime example of Arab-Norman architecture easily recognizable by three red domes on the roof.

Galleria d'Arte Moderna Palermo

Via Sant'Anna, 21; tel. 091/8431605; www.gampalermo.it; 9:30am-6:30pm daily; general admission €7
Located on a pedestrian street just off Via Roma, Palermo's GAM, or Gallery of Modern Art, is housed in a 15th-century palazzo and Franciscan convent. The museum holds over 200 works of art, including paintings by Giuseppe Sciuti, Francesco Lojacono, Giovanni Boldini, and Ettore de Maria Bergler. Sicilian art buffs will recognize pieces by Renato Guttuso, a 20th-century expressionist and social realist painter from Bagheria, and Antonio Leto, a top impressionistic-style landscape painter from Monreale. Even if these names don't ring a bell, guests will enjoy browsing through the gallery's extensive works featuring Sicilian landscapes. Entrance to tour the permanent

Palermo

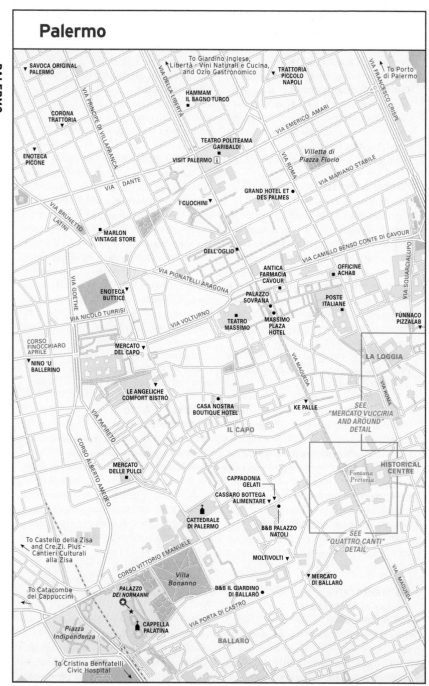

SAVOCA ORIGINAL PALERMO

To Giardino Inglese, Libertà · Vini Naturali e Cucina, and Ozio Gastronomico

TRATTORIA PICCOLO NAPOLI

To Porto di Palermo

VIA FRANCESCO CRISPI

VIA DELLA LIBERTÀ

CORONA TRATTORIA

VIA PRINCIPE DI VILLAFRANCA

HAMMAM IL BAGNO TURCO

VIA EMERICO AMARI

ENOTECA PICONE

TEATRO POLITEAMA GARIBALDI

VISIT PALERMO ℹ

Villetta di Piazza Florio

VIA ROMA

VIA DANTE

GRAND HOTEL ET DES PALMES

VIA MARIANO STABILE

VIA BRUNETTO LATINI

I CUOCHINI

MARLON VINTAGE STORE

DELL'OGLIO

VIA CAMILLO BENSO CONTE DI CAVOUR

OFFICINE ACHAB

VIA SQUARCIALUPO

ANTICA FARMACIA CAVOUR

VIA PIGNATELLI ARAGONA

VIA GOETHE

ENOTECA BUTTICÈ

PALAZZO SOVRANA

POSTE ITALIANE

VIA NICOLÒ TURRISI

VIA VOLTURNO

TEATRO MASSIMO

MASSIMO PLAZA HOTEL

FÙNNACO PIZZALAB

CORSO FINOCCHIARO APRILE

MERCATO DEL CAPO

LA LOGGIA

NINO 'U BALLERINO

VIA MAQUEDA

VIA ROMA

VIA PAPIRETO

LE ANGELICHE COMFORT BISTRÒ

CASA NOSTRA BOUTIQUE HOTEL

KE PALLE

SEE "MERCATO VUCCIRIA AND AROUND" DETAIL

CORSO ALBERTO AMEDEO

IL CAPO

MERCATO DELLE PULCI

HISTORICAL CENTRE

CAPPADONIA GELATI

CASSARO BOTTEGA ALIMENTARE

Fontana Pretoria

CATTEDRALE DI PALERMO

B&B PALAZZO NATOLI

SEE "QUATTRO CANTI" DETAIL

To Castello della Zisa and Cre.Zi. Plus · Cantieri Culturali alla Zisa

CORSO VITTORIO EMANUELE

MOLTIVOLTI

VIA MAQUEDA

To Catacombe dei Cappuccini

Villa Bonanno

MERCATO DI BALLARÒ

PALAZZO DEI NORMANNI

B&B IL GIARDINO DI BALLARÒ

Piazza Indipendenza

CAPPELLA PALATINA

VIA PORTA DI CASTRO

BALLARÒ

To Cristina Benfratelli Civic Hospital

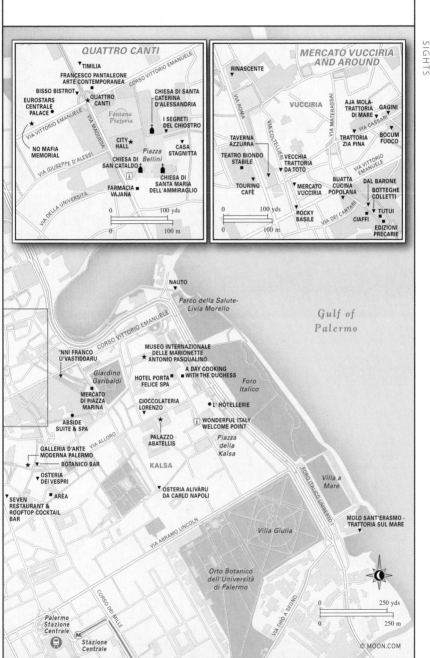

QUATTRO CANTI

TIMILIA
FRANCESCO PANTALEONE ARTE CONTEMPORANEA
BISSO BISTROT
EUROSTARS CENTRALE PALACE
QUATTRO CANTI
CORSO VITTORIO EMANUELE
CHIESA DI SANTA CATERINA D'ALESSANDRIA
I SEGRETI DEL CHIOSTRO
VIA MAQUEDA
Fontana Pretoria
CITY HALL
Piazza Bellini
CASA STAGNITTA
NO MAFIA MEMORIAL
VIA VITTORIO EMANUELE
CHIESA DI SAN CATALDO
CHIESA DI SANTA MARIA DELL'AMMIRAGLIO
VIA GIUSEPPE D'ALESSI
FARMACIA VAJANA
VIA DELLA UNIVERSITÀ

0   100 yds
0   100 m

MERCATO VUCCIRIA AND AROUND

RINASCENTE
VIA ROMA
VUCCIRIA
VIA MATERASSAI
AJA MOLA-TRATTORIA DI MARE
GAGINI
VIA COLTELLIERI
TRATTORIA ZIA PINA
BOCUM FUOCO
VIA CASSARI
TAVERNA AZZURRA
TEATRO BIONDO STABILE
VECCHIA TRATTORIA DA TOTÒ
VIA VITTORIO EMANUELE
TOURING CAFÈ
MERCATO VUCCIRIA
BUATTA CUCINA POPOLANA
DAL BARONE
BOTTEGHE COLLETTI
ROCKY BASILE
VIA DEI CARTARI
TUTUI
CIAFFI
EDIZIONI PRECARIE

0   100 yds
0   100 m

NAUTO
Parco della Salute-Livia Morello
Gulf of Palermo
CORSO VITTORIO EMANUELE
'NNI FRANCO U'VASTIDDARU
MUSEO INTERNAZIONALE DELLE MARIONETTE ANTONIO PASQUALINO
A DAY COOKING WITH THE DUCHESS
Giardino Garibaldi
HOTEL PORTA FELICE SPA
Foro Italico
MERCATO DI PIAZZA MARINA
CIOCCOLATERIA LORENZO
L' HÔTELLERIE
ABSIDE SUITE & SPA
WONDERFUL ITALY WELCOME POINT
GALLERIA D'ARTE MODERNA PALERMO
VIA ALLORO
PALAZZO ABATELLIS
Piazza della Kalsa
BOTANICO BAR
OSTERIA DEI VESPRI
KALSA
Villa a Mare
SEVEN RESTAURANT & ROOFTOP COCKTAIL BAR
ARÈA
OSTERIA ALIVÀRU DA CARLO NAPOLI
FORO ITALICO UMBERTO I
VIA ABRAMO LINCOLN
MOLO SANT'ERASMO - TRATTORIA SUL MARE
Villa Giulia
CORSO DEI MILLE
Orto Botanico dell'Università di Palermo
VIA TIRÒ A SEGNO

0   250 yds
0   250 m

Palermo Stazione Centrale
Stazione Centrale

© MOON.COM

collection is free on the first Sunday of the month, and guided tours of the repositories of art hidden behind the scenes are available on the second Sunday of each month.

Palazzo Abatellis

Via Alloro, 4; tel. 091/6230011; www.regione.sicilia.it/ beniculturali/palazzoabatellis/home.htm; 9am-6:30pm Tues.-Fri., 9am-1pm Sat.-Sun. and holidays; general admission €8, reduced rates €4, free first Sun. of each month

A masterpiece of Catalan-Gothic architecture, dating back to the 15th century, this palace was originally built as the residence of Francesco Abatellis, the port master of the Kingdom of Sicily. It has since acted as an ancient noble home, a cloistered monastery for nuns, and now as the location of the Regional Gallery of Sicily, restored by the Venetian architect Carlo Scarpa to exhibit the largest collection of Sicilian works from the Romanesque to Baroque periods. Highlights of the museum include 12th-century wooden artifacts, 14th- and 15th-century sculptures, and tiles from the 14th to 17th centuries. The gallery also features Francesco Laurana's 15th-century bust of Eleanor of Aragon and the 15th-century *Virgin Annunciate* painting by Antonello da Messina. **Guided tours** are available upon request.

Museo Internazionale delle Marionette Antonio Pasqualino

Piazza Antonio Pasqualino, 5; tel. 091/328060; www. museodellemarionette.it; 10am-2pm Sun.-Mon., 10am-6pm Tues.-Sat.; general admission €5, students and children €3, performances €12

Up until the introduction of the television, puppet shows were a traditional form of entertainment here in Sicily. Located on a small street in the Kalsa quarter, just one block from the sea, Antonio Pasqualino's International Marionette Museum is an incredible collection of handmade theater puppets and home to the theater for the Sicilian puppeteering troupe Fratelli Napoli.

Orto Botanico dell'Università di Palermo

Via Lincoln, 2; tel. 091/23891236; www.ortobotanico. unipa.it; 9am-6pm daily Mar. and Oct., 9am-7pm daily Apr. and Sept., 9am-8pm daily May-Aug., 9am-5pm daily Nov.-Feb.; general admission €5, children ages 6-17 and seniors €3, less abled guests and their companions and children under 5 free, family ticket (2 adults, 2 children) €10

The University of Palermo's Botanical Garden, an enormous outdoor museum, has been around for nearly 200 years. The Herbarium Mediterraneum was founded at the beginning of the 19th century and hosts a collection of Sicilian plants, ferns, mosses, mushrooms, a diverse selection of preserved and dried fruit, and seeds dating back to the early 20th century, as well as thousands of exotic plant species. Palermo's favorable climate has allowed many exotic tropical plants to thrive here, making this an important point of reference for other large botanical gardens around Europe. During the summer season, the garden staff collects plants and seeds throughout Sicily that will be identified and stored in the botanical garden's seed bank. It's a great place to spend an afternoon, especially during the spring and fall **Zagara Festival,** a market exhibition dedicated to biodiversity and rare collectible plants.

BALLARÒ (ALBERGHERIA)
★ Palazzo dei Normanni

Piazza Indipendenza, 1; tel. 091/6262833; www.ars. sicilia.it/visita-il-palazzo-reale; 8:15am-5:40pm Mon.-Sat., 8:15am-1pm Sun. and holidays; Royal Palace, special exhibition, Royal Apartments, and Palatine Chapel combination ticket €14.50, additional access to the Royal Gardens €2, reduced rates available for seniors, children, and students, children under 13 accompanied by an adult free

Discover the complex beauty of Sicily's history in the Palazzo dei Normanni, where layers of architectural styles are piled on top of one

---

1: Piazza Bellini at golden hour 2: Quattro Canti

another, one for each of Sicily's rulers over time. The palace was originally constructed on what was the highest point of the ancient city; the remains of 8th-century BCE Punic construction can still be found in the basement. When Arabs conquered Sicily in the 9th century CE, the first portion of the current complex was built as a military fortress. In 1072, when the Normans arrived in Palermo, the castle was expanded into a royal palace, then known as Palazzo Reale. In turn, the Spanish Bourbons renovated and beautified their kings' home with additions that include a room of frescoes dedicated to the Greek god Hercules.

Entrance to the palace includes access to the sumptuous, richly furnished Royal Apartments, decorated with murals of angels and mythological allegories; lovely gardens designed in the 17th century; appropriately austere dungeons; a tower built as an astronomical observatory in the 18th century; and rooms still used by legislators of the Sicilian government, including the Salone d'Ercole, with its frescoes of Hercules painted by Velazquez. Because parts of the palace are still in use by the Sicilian parliament, it's important to note that the Royal Apartments are closed to the public Tuesday-Thursday.

But perhaps the most important stop on your visit is the famous **Cappella Palatina,** the royal chapel added by King Roger II in 1132. This precious chapel is completely covered from top to bottom in golden Byzantine mosaics depicting Christ and biblical scenes including Adam and Eve, as well as wooden ceilings masterfully carved by Egyptian artisans. In the chapel, Norman and Northern African Fatimid architecture styles, Byzantine domes, Arabic arches, and eight-pointed stars are mixed with Christian crosses in a structure that could only exist in a place like Sicily.

IL CAPO (MONTE DI PIETÀ)
NO Mafia Memorial

Via Vittorio Emanuele, 353; tel. 347/9673896; www. nomafiamemorial.org; 11am-6pm daily; free entrance or a requested donation

This narrative museum and exhibition area recounts how the history of Palermo is intertwined with the mafia. Supported by former Mayor Leoluca Orlando, the NO Mafia Memorial is a journey through important stories, often untold or misinterpreted. The museum strives to be a space to explore and understand the reality of organized crime and the anti-mafia movements here in Sicily.

Cattedrale di Palermo

Corso Vittorio Emanuele; tel. 091/334373; www. cattedrale.palermo.it; 7am-7pm Mon.-Sat., 8am-1pm and 4pm-7pm Sun.; entrance fees €5-10, reduced rates available for children and seniors

The city's main cathedral, located on Corso Vittorio Emanuele west of the Quattro Canti and dedicated to the Virgin Mary, was reconstructed several times between 1185 and 1801, but it was originally built on the site of Roman and Carthaginian temples dating back to 400 BCE. The temples became a Byzantine basilica, then a mosque, and finally the current Christian cathedral. The cathedral you see today is a real masterpiece, covered in countless columns, arches, and elaborate geometric carvings. The interior, though massive, is perhaps a bit less impressive, almost completely white marble, though it's worth a trip inside to visit the tombs, treasury, and panoramic rooftop for an extra €8.

OUTSIDE CITY CENTER
Catacombe dei Cappuccini

Piazza Cappuccini, 1; tel. 091/6527389; www. catacombepalermo.it; 9am-1pm and 3pm-6pm daily, closed Sun. afternoons Oct.-Mar.; general admission €3

The remarkably creepy Capuchin Catacombs display thousands of mummified remains of Palermitani from the 17th to 19th centuries. Originally used as a burial ground for the monks of the Capuchin monastery, the catacombs were eventually expanded to include the remains of secular citizens, as it became a status symbol to be buried here. This

1: Orto Botanico dell'Università di Palermo
2: Cattedrale di Palermo 3: street in front of Teatro Massimo 4: Palazzo dei Normanni

mysterious museum of the dead is certainly not for the faint of heart: The walls are covered with skeletons, some of which are extremely well-preserved, mummified fully dressed and even retaining some of their hair. The catacombs can be reached on a 20-minute (1.1-mi/1.8-km) walk from the Cattedrale di Palermo along Via Cappuccini, located outside of the historic center of Palermo in the western neighborhood of La Zisa.

Castello della Zisa

Piazza Zisa; tel. 091/6520269; www. arabonormannaunesco.it; 9am-6:30pm Mon.-Sat., 9am-1pm Sun. and holidays; €6, reduced rates €3, under 18 free

Located near the Capuchin Catacombs, the Zisa castle is recognized as a UNESCO World Heritage Site for its unique Arab-Norman heritage. Built in the 12th century as the summer home and hunting lodge of King William I of Sicily, it was ultimately finished by his son, William II. Norman rule of the Kingdom of Sicily was characterized by what was, for the time, a remarkable level of respect for the Muslim, Roman, and Byzantine people who lived there, visible in the obvious influence of North African royal residences on Castello della Zisa's architecture. Arab craftsmen were employed to build the castle's typically Arab courtyard cooled by a fountain, mosaics, and muqarnas, or vaulted, ornamented ceilings.

Though it was used 1808-1950 as a private residence of the Princess Notarbartolo di Sciara, the castle stood abandoned for some time until restoration began in 1991. Today, a visit to the Castello della Zisa is an important journey through the influence of Islamic art and artifacts on the city of Palermo.

Sports and Recreation

PARKS

Villa Giulia

Via Lincoln; tel. 091/7404028; 8am-sunset daily; free

This tranquil, square 18th-century city garden was built in 1777 for the viceroy's wife, Giulia d'Avalos. Located right next to the University of Palermo's Botanical Garden and across the street from the sea, this park is a perfect place to peacefully read a book or take a stroll. Highlights within the park include the neoclassical entrance, the central 12-sided sundial clock, and various marble sculptures including the Fontana del Genio, a fountain depicting "The Genius," a protective spirit and symbolic patron of Palermo.

Foro Italico

Foro Italico Umberto I, 1; tel. 091/7401111; open 24 hours; free

The panoramic promenade here was commissioned in 1582 by the viceroy Marco Antonio Colonna. Now this popular park is open to runners, sunbathers, athletes, and all city dwellers who need a little bit of space to stretch out. The open lawn spans from Via Cala to Piazza Vincenzo Tumminello along a 0.6-mile (1-km) coastal **walking trail and bike path.** The newly constructed wellness area, known as **Il Parco della Salute,** includes a multipurpose sports pitch for soccer and basketball, a children's play area, and a landscaped garden filled with native Mediterranean tree species.

Giardino Inglese

Via della Libertà, 63; tel. 091/7406790; 8am-8pm daily; free

This 646,000-square-foot (60,000-sq-m) historic garden was built in 1850 by G. B. Filippo Basile, one of the most famous Sicilian architects of the 19th century. The geometric green garden includes the central fountain, walking paths lined with exotic plants, a skating rink, children's amusement park, and numerous statues of famous personalities of the period. The entire garden spans various hills and valleys that now host seasonal concerts, festivals, and sports events. The gardens can be reached on foot with a straight shot up Via Maqueda, which turns into Via Ruggero Settimo and then Via della Libertà, a 30-minute (1.5-mi/2.5-km) walk.

WALKING TOURS

Palermo Street Food

www.palermostreetfood.com; group tours available
daily; €30-45 plus the cost of tastings

Palermo Street Food just might be the very first tour organization dedicated to street food in Palermo. This little company was founded in 2012 by Salvatore Agusta and Danielle Aquino Roithmayr. Tours are managed by Giorgio Flaccavento, one of their best and most knowledgeable guides.

Don't expect a watered-down, G-rated street food experience here. All the tours are hosted by licensed local Palermitani. They know the city like the backs of their hands and have grown up with these foods. Some of the city's most typical street foods will be tasted on this tour, including panelle, crocchè, arancine, and cannoli. While respecting the guests' special tastes and food restrictions, the selection of street food samples will vary depending on the season and even the day of the week. What makes the folks at Palermo Street Food special is their passion for authenticity and their pure excitement in sharing their city with you.

Walking tours last 2.5-4 hours and can be offered in Italian, English, Spanish, or French. Expect around 6-8 stops to sample street food while walking through the historic center of town and deep into the **Mercato Vucciria.** Your guide will also point out art and architecture, while describing the history behind each snack. Make sure to bring coins and small bills; food is not included in the cost of the tour, and the vendors will appreciate the correct change. Email for reservations and availability.

Palermo Market Tours

Mercato di Ballarò; tel. 338/4269041; www.lindasarris.
com; 10am Tues.-Sat. (must book in advance)

The best way to understand a culture is to dive deep into its food, and the quickest way is to head straight into the market. This walking tour introduces food lovers to Palermo's oldest outdoor market: **Ballarò.** Guests have the opportunity to chat with trusted purveyors while wandering through a labyrinth of hollering vendors, vibrant seasonal colors, and the delicious aromas of fried Sicilian snacks.

mountains of ready-to-eat prepared local dishes in Palermo's markets

The classic samples usually include sfincione, panelle, baked ricotta, and Sicilian almonds. Depending on the season and the gumption of the guests, the tour can swing more toward desserts or to more extreme snacks like babbalucci snails, the famous spleen sandwich, or charcoal-grilled stigghiole. This private, two-hour, chef-led experience includes street food tastings along the way. Email for reservations, pricing, and availability.

Marcella Amato: Unique Luxury Experiences

tel. 347/480-9632; www.marcellaamato.it; by appointment only; two-hour tours start at €200

Palermo native Marcella Amato has been working in the tourism industry since 1996 and has become the go-to reputable guide for luxury experiences, from meeting small artisans to discovering noble palaces and magnificent, often-overlooked city sights. She offers private guided tours of the city in English, Spanish, or Italian, always with an extremely kind and knowledgeable approach.

COOKING CLASSES

A Day Cooking with the Duchess

Via Butera, 28; tel. 333/3165432; www.butera28.it/palermo-cooking-classes-sicily; 8:30am-3:30pm daily by reservation; group lessons €160 per person

Spend a day with the duchess for a true authentic Sicilian experience and a glimpse into Palermo's noble history. In the former home of the late Prince Giuseppe Tomasi di Lampedusa (author of the novel *The Leopard)*, Nicoletta, the Duchess of Palma, begins by escorting guests through the vibrant **Mercato del Capo** to select seasonal ingredients before heading back to the beautiful 18th-century palazzo by the sea for a hands-on cooking lesson. She highlights typical Sicilian dishes like perfectly fried panelle or a summer gelo di melone watermelon pudding decorated with fresh jasmine flowers from the garden, along with many of her own family specialties. Working around her blue and white majolica ceramic-tiled kitchen, guests roll up their sleeves and get

cooking to prepare a full meal to be shared in the formal dining room or on the lush garden terrace. A truly memorable experience not to be missed.

Garajo Tailor-Made Chef

Various locations around the city depending on the number of guests; tel. 320/5593008; www. gabriellagarajo.it; cooking lessons for 2-6 guests €135-180 per person

For the simplicity of traditional and genuine cooking with a pinch of personality, take a cooking lesson with Palermitan chef Gabriella Garajo in a relaxing, convivial, and friendly environment. Her classic recipes are often drawn from her nonna's cookbooks, revisited in a modern way. Gabriella offers a "home restaurant," where guests are welcomed with an aperitivo or a traditional meal; various options for hands-on cooking lessons in select locations around the city; or a special lesson and meal for groups of 12 or more in Palazzo Francavilla, in front of Teatro Massimo. Email for reservations, pricing options, and availability.

SPAS AND RELAXATION

Hammam Il Bagno Turco

Via Torrearsa, 17/d; tel. 091/320783; hours for women 3pm-8pm Mon.-Wed., 11:30am-8pm Fri., hours for men 4pm-8pm Tues., mixed hours 3pm-8pm Thurs., 11:30am-8pm Sat.; Turkish bath from €40, massages from €30

In the heart of the busy city center, discover a place of relaxation at Palermo's Turkish bathhouse. This spa offers massages, body scrubs, nourishing masks, facials, and traditional Turkish bath treatments. Treat yourself and cleanse your body from impurities in an atmosphere of pure tranquil luxury.

Hotel Porta Felice Spa

Via Butera, 45; tel. 091/6175678; www.hotelportafelice.it; 1pm-9pm daily with reservations only; foot massage €41, hot stone massage €62, mini facials €35, body waxing from €8

Find a little oasis in the middle of the city. The wellness center at the Hotel Porta Felice features a steam bath, sauna, and Jacuzzi.

Personalized anti-stress, deep tissue, and stone massages or body scrubs can be organized for guests of the hotel and others who wish to rejuvenate and beautify their body in the midst of a busy travel schedule. Their base package (€31) includes access to the sauna, steam bath with aromatic essences, showers, Jacuzzi, and complimentary herbal tea.

Entertainment and Events

PERFORMING ARTS

Palermo has always been the cultural hub of Sicily, especially for the aristocratic upper class. It was recognized as the 2018 Italian Capital of Culture, which stimulated a positive insurgence of cultural events, performances, and art exhibitions within the city. The **Museo Internazionale delle Marionette Antonio Pasqualino** is another great place to check out an artform truly unique to Sicily, with frequent puppet shows.

Vucciria (La Loggia)
Teatro Politeama Garibaldi

Via Filippo Turati, 2; tel. 091/6072532; www. orchestrasinfonicasiciliana.it; ticket office 9:30am-4:30pm Mon.-Sat., 9:30am-1:30pm Sun.; tickets €6-35

One of Palermo's main opera houses and home of the Sicilian symphony orchestra (the Orchestra Sinfonica Siciliana), the Politeama Garibaldi was built in 1865 to satisfy the needs of aristocratic society while the Teatro Massimo was still under construction. Check the website for the schedule of regular seasonal concerts November-June.

Teatro Biondo Stabile

Via Roma, 258; tel. 091/7434302; www.teatrobiondo. it; ticket office 9am-1pm and 4pm-7pm Tues.-Sat., 9am-noon and 4pm-7pm Sun.; from €45

Located on Via Roma just across from the Vucciria Market, Teatro Biondo is one of Palermo's main theaters. It was built in the early 1900s and is recognized by the Ministry of Cultural Heritage and Tourism as "a theater of significant cultural interest." Teatro Biondo houses theatrical and dance performances as well as a concert hall for mainstream Sicilian performing artists.

Teatro Massimo

Teatro Massimo

Piazza Verdi; tel. 091/6053580; www.teatromassimo. it; guided visits every hour 9:30am-6pm Tues.-Sun.; performance tickets €25-125

Teatro Massimo is one of Palermo's most iconic landmarks, Europe's third largest opera house after Paris and Vienna. The theater was built at the end of the 19th century, its facade an homage to classic Greek temples. Following the passing of its original architect, Giovani Battista Basile, construction was completed by his son Ernesto in the neoclassical style. Opened in 1897, it was dedicated to King Victor Emanuel II. You might recognize it from Francis Ford Coppola's 1990 film *The Godfather Part III*. The acoustically perfect, horseshoe-shaped auditorium can host up to 1,250 guests in gallery seating along with its five floors of box seats. Seasonal opera, ballet, concerts, and recital performances run consistently September-June; visit the theater's website for more details.

Although not otherwise open to the public outside of performances, 30-minute **guided visits** (www.ticketone.it; from €8) allow visitors to admire the theater's graceful stuccoes, Baroque-style deep garnet velvet and gold seating areas, wooden and glass decorations, and the intricate flower-wheel ceiling, created by Palermitan painter Rocco Lentini, featuring petals that open up to control the temperature of the theater.

ART GALLERIES
Vucciria (La Loggia)
Francesco Pantaleone Arte Contemporanea

Via Vittorio Emanuele, 303; tel. 091/332482; www.fpac. it; 10am-1pm and 4pm-7pm Tues.-Sun.; free

The Francesco Pantaleone Arte Contemporanea, or FPAC, was founded in 2013 in the Vucciria Market area before moving to a new space at the corner of Palermo's Quattro Canti. Curator Francesco Pantaleone continues his original goal of representing established contemporary artists as well as opening up his space to emerging local talent. Each carefully curated exhibition features a story of the artist's home territory that conveys a deep personal connection to their natural landscapes.

Outside City Center
Cre.Zi. Plus - Cantieri Culturali alla Zisa

Via Paolo Gili, 4, Cantieri Culturali alla Zisa 10/11; tel. 334/1520175; www.creziplus.it; 8:30am-9:30pm Mon.-Thurs., 8:30am-midnight Fri.-Sat.; free

Within the Cantieri Culturali alla Zisa complex, in a former industrial area behind the Castello della Zisa, this art center is a recent addition to the city's cultural footprint. Cre. Zi. Plus's creative projects intersect culture with social innovation, with co-working and special-event spaces. The innovative Social Kitchen project brings people together to share ideas and values through food. Check out the **bistro** or the ongoing schedule of community programs, art exhibitions, food and wine festivals, and special events.

FESTIVALS AND EVENTS

Palermo is a warm and vivacious city, where any given day can turn into a celebration, from busking street performers to the songs of fishmongers promoting goods from their market stalls. There isn't a "festival season" per se, but when the weather is nice (which is nearly all year long), people gather in the streets for any reason possible to celebrate la dolce vita.

Zagara Festival

Orto Botanico dell'Università di Palermo, Via Lincoln, 2; tel. 091/23891236; www.ortobotanico.unipa.it/zagara. html; 9am-7pm, spring festival in Mar., fall festival in Oct.; entrance fee €6

This three-day, semiannual festival of the zagara citrus flower has been running for the last 25 years at the University of Palermo's Botanical Garden. The festival was created by botanical experts to highlight plant nurseries from all around Italy and educate attendees on gardening, ecology, and horticulture. The paths through the botanic gardens are filled

Le Vie dei Tesori

Via E. Amari, 38; tel. 091/7745575; www.leviedeitesori.com; weekends late Sept.-Nov. and around Christmas; €12 for 10 visits, €6 for 4 visits, €2.50 for single entrance
Le Vie dei Tesori is an islandwide cultural heritage festival, transforming each participating city into an open-air museum. Discover hidden secrets with guided visits to palaces, terraces, monasteries, churches, and gardens that are usually closed to the public. In the city of Palermo, visitors can obtain access to private locations such as **Villa Pottino** and **Palazzo Ajutamicristo,** both sumptuous private residences, the former built in the early 20th century in the art nouveau style, the latter built for a 15th-century merchant to display his newfound wealth. As part of the holiday festivities, **Christmas concerts** are scheduled annually at the end of December in Palermo, Catania, Marsala, Ragusa, and Naro/Agrigento.

Outside Palermo, additional participating cities include:

- **Western Sicily:** Trapani, Marsala, Sambuca di Sicilia, Naro, Sciacca, and Caltanissetta

- **Eastern Sicily:** Acireale, Catania, and Messina

- **Southeastern Sicily:** Modica, Noto, Ragusa, Scicli, and Syracuse

with educational programs, tented booths, and an extensive offering of plants, flowers, bulbs, seeds, and trees for sale. The festival highlights include special guided tours of the garden, themed exhibitions, gardening workshops, and children's programs.

Festa di Santa Rosalia

Cattedrale di Palermo; tel. 338/4954084; www.facebook.com/FestinoDiSantaRosaliaPalermo; July 10-14; free
This annual five-day celebration for the patron saint of Palermo has been going on for 400 years. The multiday festival, known in the Sicilian dialect as "u fistìnu," includes a traditional historical procession—a mix of folklore and religion—that culminates with a fireworks display over the Foro Italico seaside park. The great procession on July 14 includes a solemn parade for Santa Rosalia's triumphant chariot, carrying her relics through the city streets to celebrate Palermo's liberation from the plague of 1624.

This event attracts tens of thousands of tourists to the city every year. Traditional culinary specialties are served in honor of the patroness, including pasta con le sarde, garlic babbalucci snails, and fresh wedges of summer watermelon. It's a great time to visit Palermo and see the town at its liveliest.

Ballarò Buskers

Mercato di Ballarò; www.ballarobuskers.it; late Oct.; free
During this annual international celebration, artists, bands, clowns, acrobats, jugglers, and dancers take to the streets of the Ballarò neighborhood, whose main feature is its vivacious outdoor food market. The festival aims to create a sense of community with colorful festivities including circus arts, music, parades, performances, and workshops for children throughout the neighborhood.

Shopping

Palermo is a great place to shop for Sicilian souvenirs, antiques, food, and home goods. Prominent shopping areas are concentrated in the historic city center around the three main outdoor food markets (Capo, Ballarò, and Vucciria), or along **Via della Libertà** and **Via Ruggero Settimo.**

VUCCIRIA (LA LOGGIA)
Clothing and Accessories
Officine Achab

Via Roma, 340; tel. 091/6161849; www.facebook. com/OfficineAchab; 9:30am-1pm and 4pm-7:30pm Mon.-Sat.

This boutique concept store offers quality clothing, artisan jewelry, children's toys, and books from select artists and designers. It's a great place to pick up a few unique gifts before leaving Palermo.

KALSA
Markets
Mercato di Piazza Marina

Piazza Marina, 22; 9am-1pm Sun.

Stroll down to Piazza Marina, located in the Kalsa district, for the Sunday morning flea market. Search through 20th-century memorabilia, old vinyl and cassettes, wooden toys, books, paintings, and art prints. It's the perfect place to track down hard-to-find items like vintage kitchen utensils, antiques, jewelry, watches, and Sicilian puppets. While you're there, check out **Giardino Garibaldi,** the piazza's small public park, to see the famous *Ficus macrophylla* tree; it's the largest in all of Europe!

Souvenirs
Edizioni Precarie

Via Alessandro Paternostro, 75; tel. 320/0141065; www. edizioniprecarie.it; 10:30am-2:30pm and 4:30pm-8:30pm Mon.-Sat.

This printmaking workshop and paper store sells handmade screen-printed art pieces, precious ceramics, and unique notebooks made from the traditional papers used in butcher shops and vegetable stands.

Tutui

Via Alessandro Paternostro, 75; tel. 333/3601554

Take a break from barhopping in this busy area and stop by Daniela Sucato's shop, sometimes open into the evening, to browse through her charming selection of colorful printed dresses and beautiful costume jewelry. You'll be sure to find something small that will sneak its way into your suitcase.

Ciaffi

Via Alessandro Paternostro, 82; tel. 345/5298459; www.instagram.com/ciaffibijoux; 3pm-8pm Mon.-Wed., 11am-9pm Thurs., 11am-11:30pm Fri.-Sat., 11am-10pm Sun.

This tiny jewelry shop, hidden among the bars of Via Alessandro Paternostro, also sells a line of Sicilian-inspired perfumes—a perfect memory from your time spent on this magnificent island.

Arèa

Piazza Rivoluzione, 1; tel. 338/8887303; www.facebook. com/areapiazzarivoluzione; 5:30pm-2am daily

This art gallery offers a public exhibition of local artisan works along with the option to purchase pieces made here in Palermo. From paintings to hand-carved wooden tableware, limited-edition prints, and pottery, Arèa is a great stop for those looking to take an original piece of artwork home with them.

IL CAPO (MONTE DI PIETÀ)
Markets
Mercato delle Pulci

Piazza Domenico Peranni, 2; www.antiquariatoantico.it; morning-sunset daily, including holidays

Bring a little piece of Sicily home with you. Interior designers, decorators, art collectors, and tourists alike flock to this street market located between Piazza Peranni and Piazza del Papireto behind Palermo's main cathedral. The garage-style kiosks are filled with all kinds of antiques, treasures, vintage and upcycled goods, and period furniture. This flea market opened immediately after World War II, playing an important role in the economic revitalization of the city. Today, it has become a crossroads of past and present filled with bargain deals on colorful ceramics as well as paintings and silverware.

Clothing and Accessories
Marlon Vintage Store
Via Paolo Paternostro, 41A/41B; tel. 335/458025; www. marlonvintagestore.business.site; 10:30am-1pm and 4pm-8pm Mon.-Sat.

Just a short walk from the Mercato del Capo and the Teatro Massimo opera house, Marlon offers unique vintage clothing for men and women, accessories, footwear, handbags, and vinyl records.

Dell'Oglio
Via Ruggero Settimo, 26b; tel. 091/320238; www. dellogliostore.com; 4pm-8pm Mon., 10am-1:30pm and 4pm-8pm Tues.-Fri., 10am-1:30pm and 4:30pm-8pm Sat.

Tap into Palermo's rich aristocratic past with a few finely tailored pieces from Dell'Oglio. This boutique family-run clothing store offers mens- and womenswear right on the main shopping avenue in Palermo. Dress to the nines with top-notch garments and live your best dolce vita, dressed like a real Italian.

Food

The culinary scene in Palermo accommodates all kinds of food lovers, with dishes from affordable and filling street food snacks to fresh seafood, fine dining, simply prepared and abundant plates of pasta, and decadent sweets. Compared to other major cities in Italy and Europe, the cost of food here is extremely inexpensive, and there is a huge variety of dishes. You'll find French-influenced, aristocratic family recipes drenched with bechamel and luscious flavors that date back to the Normans, who came to the Kingdom of Sicily with their own in-house family chefs, as well as **cucina povera,** the art of making delicious food with cheap ingredients. The layers of Sicily's cultural heritage shine through in the sweet-and-sour flavorings known as agrodolce, thought to be influenced by Arab cuisine, and over-the-top decorated desserts, remnants of the decadent Baroque era. No matter what you're eating, dried citrus and candied fruit, as well as locally grown almonds and pistachios, are ubiquitous.

VUCCIRIA (LA LOGGIA)
Pizzerias
Timilia
Via Maqueda, 221; tel. 091/7846088; www.pizzatimilia. it; 11:30am-12:30am daily; slices €2-5

A rarity on this major pedestrian street, where most of the souvenir shops, bars, and restaurants are not worth your while, this is a great option for a slice of pizza on the go. The selection changes daily, the pizzas are always made with top-quality flour, and the prices are extremely affordable. There are a few high-top tables out front where you can sit with a cold beer and slice of pizza to people-watch while the locals enjoy an evening passeggiata walk.

★ Fúnnaco PizzaLab
Via Pantelleria, 19; tel. 351/8767650; www.funnaco.it; 7:30pm-midnight Tues.-Thurs., 7:30pm-12:30am Fri.-Sat., 7:30pm-midnight Sun.; pizzas €8-15

Pizza is traditionally only served at dinnertime in Italy. Here at Fúnnaco, guests can feast on Neapolitan personal pies made with the best high-quality ingredients from Sicily. The signature namesake pizza is made with a sauce from yellow grape tomatoes, slow-cooked red cherry tomatoes, DOP buffalo mozzarella, and caviar-pearls of extra virgin olive oil and arrives with a dome-shaped cover filled with olive wood smoke that the servers release at the table. The menu clearly notes any ingredients that may alert guests with intolerances. There are also lactose-free and gluten-free options available. Pizza doughs can be selected individually depending on the diner's flour, style, or levitation preference. Reservations are highly recommended and can be easily booked through its website or by sending a text message through WhatsApp.

Markets
Mercato Vucciria

Via dei Frangiai, 50; market hours 8am-1pm Mon.-Sat., nightlife center and street food after 9pm Mon.-Sat.

Once one of the most important food markets in the city, nowadays La Vucciria has dwindled to just a handful of fishmongers and street food vendors. It can be a nice stop on an early morning walk, but is more frequented in the evenings, when the square and its surrounding alleyways become completely packed with young people standing outside drinking, dancing, and snacking on Palermo's famous street food like sfincione, boiled octopus, and panelle.

Restaurants
★ Bocum Fuoco

Via dei Cassari, 6; tel. 091/332009; www.bocum.it; 6:30pm-1:30am Tues.-Sun.; plates €6-18

Born as the first "mixology" bar in Palermo, Bocum has evolved into an approachable but high-end restaurant, while still staying true to its roots of serving up some of the very best drinks in town. Bocum Fuoco has an open kitchen on the first floor where many of the dishes are prepared over an open-fire grill. There are cozy seating areas upstairs near the bar and outdoor tables on the side street. Small plates can be shared, and the customer service is absolutely superb. Chef Andrea Vitale transforms local ingredients

with a fresh and finely tuned flair. The long wine list features only organic and natural wines, mainly from Sicily.

Vecchia Trattoria da Totò

Via Coltellieri, 6; tel. 333/3157558; 9am-midnight daily; €10-18

Perfect for a hearty plate of pasta and a half-liter of house wine, in the heart of the Vucciria, this simple trattoria is the real deal, with affordable prices and authentic fare. Try the fried sarde allinguate appetizer or a portion of fried calamari before diving into the pasta dishes. It's a great spot for sharing plates since the portions are bountiful. For two or three people, start with an appetizer and a carafe of house wine and then split one or two plates of pasta and one secondo piatto of grilled or fried fish.

Aja Mola - Trattoria di Mare

Via dei Cassari, 39; tel. 091/7296599; www. ajamolapalermo.it; 12:30pm-2:30pm and 7:45pm-11pm Tues.-Sun.; €12-24

Check out one of the freshest seafood spots in town, located on a back street between the Vucciria market square and La Cala harbor. The restaurant is named for an old Sicilian song from the centuries-old tradition of tuna fishing. The front-of-house staff confidently pairs meals with a long list of Italian natural wines. The raw seafood dishes, such as tuna tartare with zucchini blossoms and sesame or the thinly sliced sashimi with burnt milk and almonds, are just as delightful to taste as they are to look at. Like most savvy seafood restaurants, Aja Mola is closed on Mondays to mirror the fish market schedules.

Trattoria Piccolo Napoli

Piazzetta Mulino a Vento, 4; tel. 091/320431; www. trattoriapiccolonapoli.it; 12:30pm-3:30pm and 7:30pm-11pm Mon.-Sat.; €14-25

This long-running family trattoria, specializing in seafood and typical Sicilian cuisine, is located not far from the port of Palermo. With friendly hospitality in a very casual setting, it's the perfect place for an introduction to the home cooking of Sicily. Fresh local fish comes in daily, and dishes feature classics like fried panelle or artichokes, pasta con le sarde, local marinated raw white or red shrimp, and typical desserts like cannoli, biancomangiare, and cassata.

Trattoria Zia Pina

Via dei Cassari, 69; tel. 327/0862709; noon-3pm Mon., noon-3pm and 7pm-1am Tues.-Sat., 7pm-midnight Sun.; €20-25

Always a favorite for freshly grilled seafood and simple pasta dishes, Trattoria Zia Pina is not a fancy restaurant; think paper tablecloths and plastic water glasses. There is no set menu, and staff will bring you a handwritten check at the end of the meal. The two brother-in-law owners put out a large daily buffet of self-serve hot and cold antipasti, and guests can select their own seafood to order fried, grilled, or tossed with pasta. Just point to what you want, from swordfish steaks, big prawns, fresh calamari, whole sardines, and bite-size anchovies. Get a table outside to enjoy the full experience. Zia Pina is best enjoyed at lunchtime. The staff is very friendly, but for the most part nobody speaks English here, so get ready to gesture and smile your way through it.

Cafés and Light Bites
Rinascente

Via Roma, 289; tel. 391/3771774; www.rinascente.it; 11am-3:30pm and 6pm-11:30pm daily

The rooftop of this high-end department store is a perfect place to sip your afternoon coffee with a panoramic view of the city. Stop by just to snap a few photos or reserve ahead to enjoy an evening al fresco at aperitivo time overlooking the Piazza San Domenico square on Via Roma.

Fine Dining
Gagini

Via dei Cassari, 35; tel. 091/589918; www. gaginirestaurant.com; 12:30pm-3pm and 7:30pm-11:30pm daily; tasting menus €45-85

Named for Antonello Gagini, an Italian Renaissance sculptor from Palermo, Gagini

is a luxurious culinary experience highlighting top-quality products with the creative touch of one of the city's top chefs. The series of four-, six-, or eight-course tasting menus combine seasonal produce with Sicily's best "materie prime"—natural raw ingredients like almonds and pistachios, lumache snails, Slow Food Presidium garlic, sesame seeds, and capers. Its exceptionally curated wine list includes international, Italian, and Sicilian labels made with classic, organic, and natural practices.

KALSA
Restaurants
★ Osteria Alivàru da Carlo Napoli

Via della Vetriera, 1; tel. 340/3081048; www.alivaru. com; 1pm-3pm and 7pm-10pm daily; substantial dishes €5-15

Taste your way through Sicily's best products in a warm and inviting atmosphere in Piazza Magione in the Kalsa neighborhood of Palermo's historic center. From charcuterie boards to homemade traditional Palermitan specialties and Sicilian wines, this small family-run restaurant offers delicious and authentic food at exceptionally affordable prices. Chef/owner Carlo Napoli was born and raised in the Ballarò neighborhood, famous for its bustling food market. This osteria, open since 2022, features simply made recipes inspired by the market's seasonal ingredients and dishes you'd find on the table in a Palermitan's home kitchen.

Molo Sant'Erasmo - Trattoria sul Mare

Caletta Sant'Erasmo; tel. 388/7892914; www. molosanterasmo.it; noon-2am daily; dishes €11-28

On the seafront promenade of Foro Italico and across the highway from the Villa Giulia park, Molo Sant'Erasmo offers indoor and outdoor dining spaces serving fresh Sicilian creations and almost exclusively fish-based dishes, with just a handful of non-fish items on the menu. While the seafood plates will run your bill up much higher than planned (ranging €30-90), these towering platters are filled with

raw seafood, shucked shellfish, tartare, and sashimi good enough to rival your local oyster bar back home.

Buatta Cucina Popolana

Via Vittorio Emanuele, 176; tel. 091/322378; www.buattapalermo.it; 12:30pm-2:30pm and 7:30pm-10:30pm daily; €23-36

This perfect small bistro, awarded Michelin's "Bib Gourmand" award, highlights top-quality ingredients and typical Sicilian fare. It's one of the only places in town with an exceptional natural wine list. Daily rotating specials are usually the highlight of a meal here. The chef's personal recipe for Palermitan sfincione pizza rivals the best street food stalls around town. With a rounded menu of vegetarian, fish, and meat dishes, there's something for everyone at Buatta. Reservations are recommended.

Cafés and Light Bites
Cioccolateria Lorenzo

Via del Quattro Aprile, 7; tel. 091/549486; www.instagram.com/cioccolaterialorenzo; 8:30am-8pm Tues.-Fri., 9:30am-8pm Sat., 9:30am-1:30pm Sun.

Just around the corner from the Piazza Marina square and the towering ficus trees in the Garibaldi Garden, Cioccolateria Lorenzo is a charming coffee and sweets shop where guests can enjoy a midday treat in a relaxing café atmosphere. Bite-size bonbons or homemade cakes pair perfectly with a coffee or tea. Stop by after a browse through the Sunday flea market in the square, or pop in for a glass of wine in the late afternoon. Great music and friendly service await.

★ Casa Stagnitta

Discesa dei Giudici, 46; tel. 091/6172819; www.casastagnitta.it; 6:30am-7pm Mon.-Sat.; under €5

Ideal Caffè Stagnitta has been around since 1928 and is the oldest torrefazione (coffee roaster) in the city still in its original location.

Overseen by fourth-generation brothers Massimo and Gianfranco Marchese, it produces coffee for many restaurants and bars in town and also sells directly at the store and online. Casa Stagnitta opened next door to the roasting shop when the street became a pedestrian zone, of course serving its own coffee, but also preparing gelato and typical pastries. It's a special little place in the historic center of Palermo, tucked away next to Piazza Bellini and around the corner from the famous fountain of Piazza Pretoria.

★ I Segreti del Chiostro

Chiesa di Santa Caterina, Piazza Bellini, 33; tel. 327/5882302; www.isegretidelchiostro.com; 10am-6pm daily; €5

I Segreti del Chiostro (Secrets of the Cloister) is a pastry shop hidden away inside the **Chiesa di Santa Caterina** near the famous Fontana Pretoria between Piazza Pretoria and Piazza Bellini. Look for a small sign and an attendant outside, who will direct you upstairs to a small indoor garden and this very special shop, where long-lost Sicilian pastry recipes have been preserved from many of the city's monasteries. Pick up a few almond biscotti, frutta di martorana marzipan fruits, or a pack of cannoli to take home with you—if you can resist eating them all on the spot.

Fine Dining
Osteria dei Vespri

Piazza Croce dei Vespri, 6; tel. 091/6171631; www.osteriadeivespri.it; 12:30pm-2:30pm and 7:30pm-10:30pm Mon.-Sat.; tasting menus €35-95

Chef Alberto Rizzo's innovative and modern way of working with Sicilian ingredients is one of the dining highlights of Palermo. By transforming traditional flavor combinations, he brings a fresh outlook to Sicilian cuisine. Authentic Palermitan dishes like pasta con tenerumi are revisited with the addition of ginger and house-smoked mackerel. The seasonal menu is surprising and always satisfying. The carte dei vini (wine list) of Chef Alberto, a wine connoisseur, arrives at the table like a thick encyclopedia and is, as to be

---

1: view from the Rinascente department store's rooftop lounge 2: dish at Osteria Alivàru da Carlo Napoli 3: people strolling through Mercato di Ballarò

☆ Street Food in Palermo

pane panelle e crocchè, a sandwich stuffed with chickpea fritters and potato dumplings

As Anthony Bourdain said, "In Palermo, street food is deadly serious." Although street food has become internationally trendy, the original place to try it is truly in the streets of Palermo, from vendors who have been making these items their entire lives.

The best way to experience Palermo's street food scene is with a trusted guide. There are several options for food market tours and tastings that include street food samples, but the most authentic experience will be with a local culinary expert from **Palermo Street Food.** Here is a rundown of the top can't-miss Palermitan street foods.

ARANCINE

It's debated whether to call these breaded and fried rice balls arancine (feminine) or arancini (masculine), but here in Palermo, they are always referred to as arancine (derived from the name of a small orange). These deep-fried treats are typically made with bright yellow saffron risotto, filled with a tomato-based meat ragù and green peas. Extremely large "arancine bombe" are served at **Touring Cafè** (Via Roma, 248; 6:30am-9pm daily), not far from Mercato Vucciria, and more creative fillings like pumpkin with pork sausage or sweet pistachio pesto are sold from street food kiosks like **Ke Palle** (Via Maqueda, 270; tel. 091/6112009; 10:30am-midnight daily) in Mercato del Capo. For a real treat, head over to **Donnafranca** (Via Maqueda, 292; tel. 091/8434502; 7am-1am daily) for crispy, freshly fried arancine on the main avenue, just steps from the Teatro Massimo.

BABBALUCCI

Babbalucci are small land snails sautéed with olive oil, whole cloves of garlic, parsley, and black pepper. Typically served for the **Festa di Santa Rosalia,** they can be found through most of the summer. The trick to eating them is to pick up one at a time with your fingers and suck the snail out from the shell. They are often served with toothpicks to help get the trickly little guy out of there. The very best ones are sold in **Piazza della Kalsa,** not far from Palazzo Abatellis.

CROCCHÈ

Sometimes referred to as cazzilli, these deep-fried potato dumplings are made with onion and parsley, often served in a panino along with panelle and a squeeze of fresh lemon juice. Find them in the **Mercato di Ballarò** during the day and in **Mercato Vucciria** at night.

FRITTOLA

Walking through the ancient markets of the **Capo** and **Ballarò,** you'll find frittola vendors carrying baskets filled with steaming pieces of fried veal, seasoned with bay leaf and lots of black pepper. Originally a way to use up the leftovers that the butchers could not sell in their shops, these crispy, chewy, and tender bites—when served on a sesame bun with a heavy dose of salt, black pepper, and fresh lemon juice—are completely divine.

PANELLE

Naturally gluten-free Sicilian chickpea crisps, deep-fried and seasoned simply with fresh parsley and a squeeze of lemon. This is a typical afternoon snack for schoolchildren or workers before or after a long day. The pane e panelle is a sandwich roll stuffed with panelle and a few crocchè potato croquettes.

PANI CÀ MEUSA

Also known as a panino con la milza, this hard-core street food sandwich is filled with thinly sliced cuts of spleen and lung that are boiled and then slowly cooked in lard, and served on a traditional "vastedda" sesame seed bun. You get to decide if you want it schietta (single—only with lemon and salt) or maritata (married—with shredded caciocavallo cheese or fresh ricotta). Try it at **Rocky Basile** (Via Vittorio Emanuele, 211; 11:30am-4am daily) near Vucciria, or **Nino U' Ballerino** (Corso Camillo Finocchiaro Aprile, 76/78; open 24 hours) near Mercato del Capo.

SFINCIONE

A fluffy focaccia-style Sicilian "pizza" topped with tomato sauce, breadcrumbs, onion, and anchovies. It's traditionally served as street food and only found in the city of Palermo. Most **food carts** selling sfincione pick it up from the same late-night bakery, so the quality will only vary depending on how fresh they are. Ask the "sfinciunaru" vendor to toast it inside their hidden griddle and enjoy it warm.

STIGGHIOLE

With roots from the Latin word "extilia," meaning intestines, this dish actually has Greek origins, and you'll even find something very similar in Turkey. Stigghiole is made with lamb, veal, and sometimes goat intestines that have been wrapped around green spring onion with a few sprigs of fresh parsley. It's the perfect balance of fat, salt, and bite. Find them in the **Vucciria** Market at night or in the **Ballarò** Market in the morning.

expected, extensive and carefully curated. The small dining room is comfortable and cozy with a knowledgeable front-of-house team. Tables are moved outside into the piazza in summertime.

Street Food
'Nni Franco U'Vastiddaru

Via Vittorio Emanuele, 102; tel. 091/325987; 9am-1am daily; €2-8

A classic stop on a late-night street food tasting tour of the city, Franco's small fast-food corner is best known for its plates of fried chickpea panelle and mini arancinette rice balls, as well as the most popular panino con la milza sandwich, made with slow-cooked slices of spleen and lungs topped with caciocavallo or ricotta cheese.

BALLARÒ (ALBERGHERIA)
International
Moltivolti

Via Giuseppe Mario Puglia, 21; tel. 091/2710285; www.moltivolti.org; 9am-11pm Sun.-Thurs., 9am-midnight Fri.-Sat.; entrées €7-14

Moltivolti is a melting pot bistro and co-working space in the Ballarò neighborhood. Still unfortunately rare in Palermo, this special kitchen staff is led by chefs of multiple nationalities—from Italy, Greece, Senegal, Gambia, and Afghanistan—working in harmony together. Their trademark phrase, "La mia terra è dove poggio i miei piedi" ("My land is where I rest my feet") clearly conveys their core mission of inclusivity. The menu ranges from dishes like pasta alla Norma, lasagne, and Sicilian couscous to lamb meatballs, Tunisian brik, and mafè, a Senegalese meat stew with peanut sauce. Everyone is welcome to work, drink, and eat here.

Markets
★ Mercato di Ballarò

Via Ballarò, 1; 8am-5pm daily

This 1,000-year-old market in the historic Ballarò neighborhood is the largest and oldest open-air food market in the city. Locals and tourists alike weave through the winding labyrinth of stalls to purchase fresh fruit, vegetables, cheese, fish, meat, and local street food. Prices are truly up for debate here, with vendors singing and shouting out deals. All purchases must be made in cash, and the products found here are among the cheapest of all the markets. Ballarò is one of the only places in the city where you'll see Palermo's Sri Lankan, North African, Bangladeshi, and Italian purveyors selling specialties side by side.

IL CAPO (MONTE DI PIETÀ)
Bistros
Bisso Bistrot

Via Maqueda, 172A; tel. 328/1314595; www.bissobistrot.it; 9am-11pm Mon.-Sat.; €12-20

Located on the corner of Palermo's Quattro Canti in the former premises of a bookstore, this is a favorite spot for a quick lunch, with heaping portions of pasta or simple Sicilian soups like macco di fava or minestra di tennerumi for under €7. At night, Bisso becomes very busy, so it's best to put your name on the waiting list and grab a glass of wine while you wait outside.

★ Le Angeliche Comfort Bistrò

Vicolo Abbadia, 10, Mercato del Capo; tel. 091/6157095; www.leangeliche.it; noon-7pm Mon., 9am-7pm Tues.-Thurs., 9am-11pm Fri.-Sat.; granita and gelato €6-8, main dishes €16

This spot is a joyful success story of a group of four young entrepreneurs, Floriana, Veronica, Chiara, and Barbara, who came together to build this dreamy Sicilian bistro-café and backyard garden patio with lounge chairs and hammocks. Hidden on a side street within the Capo Market, the restaurant focuses on specialized pastries and the old recipes of great-grandmothers that have nearly been forgotten. In summertime, the women rotate a daily list of granita made from seasonal fruit, from kiwi to strawberries and prickly pear, that pair perfectly with fresh-from-the-oven almond or orange brioche buns. While sporadically open for breakfast time, the bistro is mainly open for lunch, dinner, and special events featuring local natural winemakers. The main goal here is to make customers feel at home.

Cafés and Light Bites
Cassaro Bottega Alimentare
Via Vittorio Emanuele, 415; tel. 320/9281178; www. botteghealimentari.com; 10am-8pm daily

Hidden among an entire avenue of souvenir shops, this small bottega has a carefully selected collection of Sicilian food products that can be purchased to take home in your suitcase, from dry pastas to honey, tinned tuna, or small jars of pestos and pâtés. In the back of the shop, there is a quiet outdoor garden space where the in-house salumiere prepares salads, charcuterie platters, sandwiches, and small plates perfect for a lunch break or aperitivo snack.

Cappadonia Gelati
Via Vittorio Emanuele, 401; tel. 392/5689784; www. cappadonia.it; noon-6pm Mon.-Fri., noon-8pm Sat.-Sun.; €5

Since July 14, 2018 (the day of the Santa Rosalia Festival in Palermo), master ice cream maker Antonio Cappadonia has maintained his prices as well as unparalleled quality in his precious gelato shop. The fruit-based flavors change according to the seasons. Each batch uses the same recipe, with the addition of flavors like strawberry, lemon, coffee, and Slow Food Presidium Trapani sea salt caramel. This incredible gelateria has a second location near the Teatro Politeama Garibaldi (Piazzetta Francesco Bagnasco, 29).

Markets
Mercato del Capo
Via Cappuccinelle; 8am-1pm Mon.-Sat.

Situated behind the Teatro Massimo, the Capo Market is part of the heart and soul of the city, a place for grocery shopping, local food tastings, and picking up typical products like capers, tomato paste, Sicilian oregano, vacuum-sealed sun-dried tomatoes, olives, pistachios, and pasta to take home in your suitcase. As market tourism has become more popular in the last decade, the vendors and restaurants have adapted to offer ready-to-eat options for guests who might not be purchasing ingredients to cook for themselves. Small kiosks provide fresh-squeezed orange and pomegranate juices, fried street food treats, and even simple traditional plates of sarde a beccafico, parmigiana di melanzane, stuffed artichokes, and caponata, along with a glass of wine or a sparkling spritz cocktail.

Street Food
Savoca Original Palermo
Via Sammartino, 103; tel. 091/341228; 5pm-10:30pm daily; €0.80/piece

This typical Sicilian rosticceria takeout counter offers hot snacks like pizzette, arancine, timballi, baked calzone, and roast chickens. Perfect for a quick stop before a night out. Taste your way through the city's specialties with its fast-casual buffet of savory bites.

I Cuochini
Via Ruggero Settimo, 68; tel. 091/581158; www. icuochini.com; 8:30am-2:30pm Mon.-Fri., 8:30am-2:30pm and 4:30pm-7:30pm Sat.; €5

I Cuochini is the ultimate antica rosticceria in Palermo, tucked away, but not forgotten, for nearly 200 years! In Sicily, a rosticceria is a place to buy hot food to be quickly eaten on the spot at the banco counter or taken away. This hidden gem is located in a small courtyard a bit north of the city center, not far from Teatro Politeama Garibaldi. Still in its original location, I Cuochini is a savory bakery that has been serving small pezzi (bites) in classic Palermo-style since 1826. Don't expect sit-down service or even proper plates and cutlery; most of the bites are served in a napkin or on a plastic plate. It's cheap, high quality, and the kitchen is spotless. Wash it all down with a cold Partannina citrus soda. It's a simple, quick stop for a savory breakfast or lunchtime snack.

Trattoria

★ Corona Trattoria

Via Guglielmo Marconi 9; tel. 091/335139; www. coronatrattoria.it; 12:30pm-3pm and 8pm-11pm Tues.-Sat., 12:30pm-3pm Sun.; €20-30

The Corona family brings a cheerful, loving vibe to their chic trattoria. Daily offerings feature local seafood and traditional Sicilian specialties like spaghetti with squid ink and bottarga, sweet-and-sour caponata, a raw plate of local gamberi rossi, or fried calamaretti. Top-notch service and exceptional high-quality ingredients make this place shine. The extensive wine list, curated by Orazio Corona, features hard-to-find natural and traditional wines from all around Sicily. Get a reservation because this small trattoria books up fast.

OUTSIDE CITY CENTER
Pizzeria

★ Ozio Gastronomico

Via di Blasi Francesco Paolo, 2; tel. 091/346306; www. oziogastronomico.com; 1pm-3pm and 6:30pm-midnight daily; €18-30

Although it's a long walk north of city center (1.9 mi/3 km; 40 minutes via Via Maqueda/Via della Libertà), pizza lovers flock to Ozio Gastronomico for the best pie in town. Friendly and knowledgeable owner Dario Genova is a Palermitan who brought real Neapolitan pizza to his hometown. Working with small food producers and the highest-quality ingredients possible, this upscale pizzeria is definitely worth the trek. Enjoy the greatest hits like a pizza margherita or test out some of Dario's original creations like his version of sfincione topped with slow-cooked red onions, citron zest, and grated tuna bottarga.

Bars and Nightlife

If you're ready to take the city by storm, the nightlife in Palermo has a lot to offer, from small casual bars to chic cocktail spots, and of course lots of delicious street food for a late-night bite.

VUCCIRIA (LA LOGGIA)
Taverna Azzurra

Via Maccherronai, 15; tel. 091/304107; 9am-5am Mon.-Sat.

Stay out all night with the locals at Taverna Azzurra in the vivacious Vucciria Market. This no-fuss pub is the meeting point for young locals looking for a cheap night out with great music. Mixed drinks are served in plastic cups to take outside into the street, the beers are cheap, and the atmosphere is perfectly Palermitan.

Nauto

Piazzetta Capitaneria di Porto; tel. 366/5409382; www.facebook.com/nautoscopioarte; 9am-2am daily June-Sept.

Created as Nautoscopio Arte for an installation by Giuseppe Amato, this summer beach bar near the port of Palermo has developed into a casual setting for art, music, and theater performances. Although Palermo is not technically a beach town, Nauto brings a seaside vibe to the city. Enjoy a cocktail overlooking the sea at sunset or cozy up on the upcycled wooden pallet couches in the evening. Follow its calendar for special events and parties throughout the high season.

KALSA
Botanico Bar

Vicolo dei Corrieri, 38; tel. 389/6892503; www.facebook.com/botanicobarpalermo; 6pm-2am Tues.-Sat., 6pm-1am Sun.; €6-10

Palermo's nightlife happens out in the streets or in the main piazza squares. Here at Botanico Bar, just off Piazza Sant'Anna, this top cocktail bar offers great drinks and groovy playlists to enjoy on the benches along a slim alleyway decorated with plants and succulent-covered balconies above. Mini schoolhouse chairs and low wooden furniture surround coffee tables where drinks can be perched, and when it's crowded, the entire vicolo alley fills up with young clientele elbow to elbow. Stop by on the early side for a low-key crowd, and enjoy the aperitivo box filled with puff pastry savory snacks, olives, hummus, and focaccia bites. The bar even serves brunch on the weekends in autumn and winter (10:30am-2:30pm Sat.-Sun.).

Botteghe Colletti

Via Alessandro Paternostro, 79; tel. 091/7815000; 6:30pm-2am daily

A truly fantastic cocktail bar with talented top-notch bartenders just off of Corso Vittorio Emanuele. Colletti is a tiny vintage spot decked out with antique furniture, deep green walls, exposed wood ceilings, and sexy mood lighting. Pop in for one of their famous smoked negroni and order a platter of simple small bites like crostini, panelle, chips, and mini sandwiches.

Dal Barone

Via Alessandro Paternostro, 87; tel. 349/5084347; www.dalbaronevino.it; 6pm-midnight Mon.-Sat.; glasses €6-8

With only three tables inside and a handful on the street side, Dal Barone fills up quickly. This original wine bar is one of the only places in town where you can get an all-organic and natural wine list, with various options for pours by the glass as well. It serves classic potato chips for aperitivo, or can make a cestino del contadino (farmers basket) with toasted bread, grapes, cheese, and olives.

Seven Restaurant & Rooftop Cocktail Bar

Hotel Ambasciatori, Via Roma, 111; tel. 333/3613985; www.sevenrestaurantpalermo.it; aperitivo 6pm-8pm and dinner service 8pm-midnight Tues.-Sun.; drinks €10-15

Reserve ahead for a sunset view from the best rooftop cocktail bar in town. Take the small elevator to the top floor and follow the steps up to the terrace rooftop, where the hostess will escort you to your table on one of the three terraced floors overlooking the sea and the historic center of Palermo. Along the horizon, the bird's-eye view of Palermo includes the main sights of the Teatro Massimo, Palermo Cathedral, Santa Caterina Monastery, and the Norman Palace. Classic cocktails, non-alcoholic mocktails, and signature drinks are available during aperitivo

Seven Restaurant & Rooftop Cocktail Bar

hours, or plan to stay for dinner to taste the unique house specialties like risotto with calamari, provolone, mustard greens, and tuna roe bottarga.

IL CAPO (MONTE DI PIETÀ)

Enoteca Butticè

Piazza S. Francesco di Paola, 12; tel. 091/2515394; www. enotecabuttice.it; 12:30pm-3pm and 5pm-11:30pm Mon.-Sat.

Originally opened in 1936 by Giuseppe Butticè as a salumeria deli and wine shop just behind Teatro Massimo, Enoteca Butticè is now known as one of the best wine bars in the city. Stop by for a glass of wine and its plentiful aperitivo platters 5pm-8:30pm, or make a reservation for dinner in the small dining room. The wine list includes over 700 Sicilian, Italian, and international labels.

Enoteca Picone

Via Guglielmo Marconi, 36; tel. 091/331300; www. enotecapicone.com; 9:30am-1:30pm and 5pm-11:30pm daily

After a day of touring the city, it's time to treat yourself. Meet up for aperitivo time at Enoteca Picone, a historic wine bar open since 1946. Picone's whip-smart sommelier, Vera Bonanno, is one of the top wine experts in the city. Its selection of over 7,000 international, Italian, and Sicilian wines can be served with a mixed meat-and-cheese platter or enjoyed with a basket of fresh bread and electric-green extra virgin olive oil. Sit outside for an hour or two with a bottle of wine or sip on a cognac, whisky, or grappa.

OUTSIDE CITY CENTER

Libertà - Vini Naturali e Cucina

Via della Libertà, 93d; tel. 091/9102341; 10am-3pm and 6pm-11pm Tues.-Sun.

This newly opened natural wine bar is located in Palermo's upper-class neighborhood on Via della Libertà, north of the city center. Restaurateurs Stefania Milano and Franco Virga created a chic local haunt for wine lovers. Their young chefs, Alessandro Fanara and Francesco Mango, pair contemporary Sicilian dishes with top-quality bottles from hard-to-find producers.

Accommodations

When looking for accommodations in Palermo, the most convenient will be located within walking distance from the **Quattro Canti.** Additional apartment rentals are available through websites such as Airbnb, but as Palermo is relatively affordable, basing yourself in a hotel or resort can be a great choice to ensure you have the additional service and guidance of a hotel concierge.

VUCCIRIA (LA LOGGIA) €100-200

Massimo Plaza Hotel

Via Maqueda, 437; tel. 091/325657; www. massimoplazahotel.com; from €118

Right in front of the Teatro Massimo, the four-star Massimo Plaza Hotel is in the middle of all the action. Family-owned since 1921, this 11-room hotel offers simple and convenient accommodations with the centro storico of Palermo right at your fingertips.

★ Palazzo Sovrana

Via Bara All'Olivella, 78; tel. 351/5615444; www. palazzosovrana.it; €150-300

Make yourself at home in the historic city center of Palermo. The luxury apartment rentals at Palazzo Sovrana, located right in front of the Teatro Massimo, have the best view in town. This historic palace was recently renovated, and each of the spacious and modern apartments are at least 430-750 square feet (40-70 sq m), to ensure peace and quiet in the comfort of your home away from home.

Each apartment has two or three balconies, a queen-size bed, television, and private bathroom. Enjoy top-tier Sicilian hospitality from a friendly English-speaking concierge staff who can organize stress-free airport transfers, offer free parking, and arrange guided itineraries around Palermo.

€200-300

Grand Hotel et des Palmes

Via Roma, 398; tel. 091/8048800; www.grandhotel-et-des-palmes.com; starting at €279

This art nouveau (Liberty)-style palace is one of Palermo's most exquisite five-star hotels. It was built in 1874 and renovated in 1907 by Palermo's finest architect, Ernesto Basile, who also finished his father's Teatro Massimo opera house. It is also where composer Richard Wagner finished writing *Parsifal*. The Grand Hotel et des Palmes was given a facelift and reopened after the COVID-19 pandemic. The grand lounges and luxurious suites of this hotel fully encapsulate the elegance of old-world Palermo. Ouverture Terrace is its sushi restaurant on the fifth floor with spectacular views of the city, while the Neobistrot & Mixology Bar offers high-end dining and a lush cocktail lounge decked out with burgundy velvet sofas and stained-glass windows.

KALSA

€100-200

Abside Suite & Spa

Via Merlo, 15; tel. 338/8790226; www.absidesuite.it; €142

This luxury guesthouse is conveniently located right in the heart of Palermo's city center between Piazza Marina and Piazza Bellini. There is garden space, a shared lounge, private parking, and a terrace available for overnight guests to enjoy. Air-conditioned rooms and suites are equipped with a private bathroom, desk, kettle, minibar, safety deposit box, flat-screen TV, and Wi-Fi service. For families, the standard double room has a double bed and double sofa bed with views of the nearby Basilica of St. Francis of Assisi. Couples might opt for either the standard suite with a mini pool inside the room, the Hydromassage Suite with an indoor Jacuzzi and its own sauna along with a private outdoor terrace seating area, or the Junior Suite with its own terrace and outdoor hot tub.

L'Hôtellerie

Foro Italico Umberto I, 13; tel. 339/5898058; www. lhotellerie.it; €155

Located near the botanical garden and the city's waterfront promenade, L'Hôtellerie is one of the very few design hotels in Palermo. This 16th-century palace has rooftop views of the city along with stylish rooms equipped with Wi-Fi service, flat-screen televisions, coffee machines, private bathrooms with bidets and complimentary toiletries, and on-site breakfast service. Pets are welcome and airport transfers can be organized (both with advance notice).

BALLARÒ (ALBERGHERIA)
€100-200

B&B Il Giardino di Ballarò

Via Porta di Castro, 75/77; tel. 091/212215; www. ilgiardinodiballaro.it; from €100

Located in a restored 18th-century palazzo on a residential street connecting the Ballarò outdoor food market and the Norman Palace, this quaint, family-run bed-and-breakfast offers understated rooms and a beautiful hidden garden, rooftop courtyard, guest kitchen, and outdoor hot tub.

B&B Palazzo Natoli

Via Santissimo Salvatore, 6; tel. 091/7780666; www. palazzonatoli.com; €190

Perfectly situated just off the main avenue of Corso Vittorio Emanuele near the picturesque Quattro Canti intersection, Palazzo Natoli offers bright and modern four-star accommodations along with 24-hour front desk service, Wi-Fi connection, air-conditioning, and optional room service.

IL CAPO (MONTE DI PIETÀ)
Under €100
Eurostars Centrale Palace
Via Vittorio Emanuele, 325; tel. 091/336666; www. eurostarshotelcompany.com; from €65

A four-star hotel centrally located in the heart of Palermo's historic center right next to the Quattro Canti, the Palermo branch of the Eurostars hotel group features bright air-conditioned rooms, a private terrace with views of the city, and a grand continental breakfast.

€200-300
Casa Nostra Boutique Hotel
Via Sant'Agostino, 134; tel. 091/327003; www. casanostrapalermo.com/boutique-hotel; €210

This boutique hotel is located in the heart of Palermo's city center, near the Teatro Massimo theater and the Mercato del Capo outdoor food market. Built in a historic palace, the 12 carefully renovated rooms and suites are equipped with Wi-Fi service, smart televisions, coffee machines, and minibars. The common spaces include a fitness center, small bistro, garden, outdoor courtyard, and Jacuzzi pool. For a budget-friendly option, try its bed-and-breakfast on Vicolo Maestro Cristofaro, 2.

OUTSIDE CITY CENTER
€300 and up
★ Villa Igiea
Via Belmonte, 43; tel. 091/6312111; www. roccofortehotels.com; starting at €300 in the winter season

This historic turn-of-the-century Liberty-style villa opened in 1900 as a hotel in the former home of the Florio family. Known for hosting the crème de la crème of high society during the Belle Époque, it was then taken over in 2019 by the Rocco Forte Hotel group to be fully refurbished, reopening as a five-star luxury hotel in June of 2021. On the outskirts of Palermo, overlooking the sea and the yacht harbor, Villa Igiea has always been a destination for a high-end stay in the capital city. Several in-house restaurants and bars, an outdoor pool, and top-notch spa services are available for guests. Multiday room packages can be upgraded to include excursions around the city in addition to the high-end amenities and spacious suites with sea-facing terraces. Carrara marble bathrooms, king-size beds, Irene Forte toiletries, complimentary Wi-Fi, television, and cozy bathrobes and slippers certainly sweeten the deal. This is far and away the place to treat yourself in Palermo, although you might never want to leave the property.

Information and Services

TOURIST INFORMATION
Visit Palermo (www.visitpalermo.it) information desks can be found at the harbor, Piazza Bellini, and the Teatro Politeama Garibaldi. In addition to distributing information and tourist materials, the **Wonderful Italy Welcome Point** (Via Torremuzza, 15; tel. 02/8088-9702; www.visitpalermo.it; 10am-1pm and 5pm-7pm Mon.-Sat., 10am-2pm Sun.) can help tourists with printing boarding passes and booking tour guides, taxis, excursions, wine tastings, tours, and restaurant reservations.

OTHER SERVICES
- **Poste Italiane:** Via Roma, 320; tel. 091/7535392; www.poste.it; 8:20am-7pm Mon.-Fri., 8:20am-12:30pm Sat.
- **Antica Pharmacy Cavour:** Via Camillo Benso Conte di Cavour, 96; tel. 091/6119419; open 24 hours
- **Pharmacy Vajana:** Via Maqueda, 189; tel. 091/6162769; 8:30am-1:15pm and 4pm-8pm Mon.-Fri.
- **State Police:** Polizia di Stato/Questura

Palermo, Piazza della Vittoria, 8; tel. 091/210111; www.questure.poliziadistato.it

- **Cristina Benfratelli Civic Hospital:** Ospedali Civico Di Cristina Benfratelli, Via Ernesto Tricomi; tel. 091/6661111; www.arnascivico.it; open 24 hours

- **United States Consulate:** Conosolato Stati Uniti D'America, Via Giovan Battista Vaccarini, 1; tel. 091/305857; www.it.usembassy.gov/embassy-consulates/naples/consular-agency-palermo; 9am-12:30pm Mon.-Fri.

Getting There

Most international visitors arrive to Palermo with a connecting flight via a larger Italian city, like Rome or Milan. Palermo can also be reached on an overnight ferry from Naples. Though it is possible to drive to Sicily from mainland Italy, it will take the better part of a day and is not recommended. To make the best use of your time, take advantage of quick flights on budget airlines.

BY AIR

Aeroporto di Palermo Falcone e Borsellino

Località Punta Raisi, Cinisi; tel. 800/541880; www.aeroportodipalermo.it

Still often referred to by its original name, **Punta Raisi,** the airport in Palermo was renamed to commemorate two Italian judges who were assassinated in 1992 for their efforts to take down the Sicilian mafia. The airport is located in the seaside town of Cinisi, 19 miles (31 km) west of Palermo city center, with a runway that seems to head straight into the deep blue sea. Two currency exchange desks are available for international travelers (Check-in Area A and in the Departures Hall). Free Wi-Fi is accessible in the terminal. Wheelchair-accessible elevators, restrooms, and the Sala Amica Lounge are available for guests who require additional assistance. Shops, cafés, a post office, and pharmacy are conveniently located throughout the airport.

Several major airlines offer daily/weekly service to several top Italian and European destinations, including **Rome** (1 hour 15 minutes; €25), **Naples** (1 hour 5 minutes; €50), and **Bari** (1 hour 15 minutes; €100).

Rental cars can be picked up at the Palermo airport from **Avis** (tel. 091/591684; www.avisautonoleggio.it), **Budget** (tel. 06/65010678; www.budgetautonoleggio.it), **GoldCar** (tel. 06/45209634; www.goldcar.es/it), and **Sicily by Car** (tel. 091/591250; www.sicilybycar.it). Additional small autonoleggio providers are available with a navetta shuttle bus service off-site. It's a 30-minute (19 mi/31 km) drive to Palermo's historic center from the airport, mostly on the **E90** coastal highway.

Shuttle bus service from the airport to Palermo's city center is provided by **Prestia e Comandè** (www.prestiaecomande.it; €6 one-way). Tickets can be purchased in advance online, at the arrivals gate inside the airport, or on-site directly from the bus driver. Buses from the city run every 30 minutes 4am-11pm; buses from the airport run 5am-midnight. Departing from the bus terminal in the central station, along Via Roma and Via Libertà, the bus ride takes approximately 45 minutes to 1 hour.

Train service from the airport to the Palermo Centrale station is provided by **TrenItalia** (www.trenitalia.it; €6.50 one-way). Tickets can be purchased in advance online or from an automated kiosk in the basement level of the airport. This trip takes 50 minutes, making several stops in various residential areas of the city before arriving at the main station, Palermo Centrale. Tickets must be time-stamped at the station before boarding. Bathrooms are available on the train.

Taxis are available outside the arrivals gate at the airport. The ride to downtown Palermo takes about 30 minutes and costs around €50. Shared taxi vans can be utilized when guests are headed to main locations in the city, such as the Palermo Centrale train station. Shared taxis are located just to the right of the main exit near the shuttle buses and cost €8 per person.

BY TRAIN

Palermo Stazione Centrale

Piazza Giulio Cesare; www.trenitalia.com

The main train station in the historic center is Palermo Stazione Centrale, located at Via Roma and Via Lincoln. Tickets can be purchased in advance online or from an automated kiosk at the train station entrance. Tickets must be time-stamped at the station before boarding the train. Palermo is well connected by train to **Agrigento** (2 hours; from €10.90), **Cefalù** (1 hour; from €6.80), and **Milazzo** (2 hours 30 minutes; from €13.60), gateway to the Aeolian Islands. From **Catania** (3 hours 30 minutes; from €16.40), you can connect to various points on Sicily's eastern coast. If traveling all the way from the Italian mainland, there are trains available to **Napoli Centrale** (9 hours 30 minutes; from €35), but this is by no means the fastest way to travel, and is often not even the cheapest.

BY FERRY

Porto di Palermo

Molo Santa Lucia; www.adsppalermo.it

Ferries and cruise ships arrive in the ferry terminal in the port of Palermo. Guests traveling from the Amalfi Coast to Sicily can take advantage of the year-round, overnight ferry from Napoli to Palermo, organized by **Traghetti Lines** (www.traghettilines.it; seats €31, cabins €67, car transport €14-30). Tickets for the 11-hour trip can be reserved in advance online or in the Massa port of Naples ticket counter. This can be a good option for some, as it saves the cost of a hotel for the night.

In summer (June-Sept.), it's also possible to travel from Palermo to the Aeolian Islands via hydrofoils operated by **Liberty Lines** (tel. 0923/873813; www.libertylines.it).

Palermo is also a port of call for cruise lines visiting the Mediterranean, including itineraries from **Norwegian Cruise Line** (www.ncl.com), **Royal Caribbean** (www.royalcaribbean.com/cruise-to/sicily-palermo-italy), **Costa Cruises** (www.costacruises.com), and **MSC Cruises** (www.msccruises.com).

BY CAR

Palermo's infamous reputation for bad traffic precedes it—this is probably not a place you'll want to be navigating with your own car, so if you're traveling Sicily on a road trip, it may be best to find a way to drop your car off before you get to the capital city. That said, Palermo is a fairly easy drive from **Catania** (2.5 hours; 120 mi/193 km) and points on the eastern coast through the island's mountainous interior (though do be prepared for construction and detours), and is no more than 2 hours from any of the highlights on the western coast.

Getting Around

Palermo's centro storico is very walkable, making cars, motorbikes, and public transportation in many cases unnecessary for tourists.

BY BUS

The **AMAT** (www.amat.pa.it) bus system within the city of Palermo is truly a local's public transportation system, mostly utilized by commuters, but it can be useful for travelers who want to save time instead of walking. Timetables are posted at each bus stop, but make sure you plan for extra travel time, as buses often run on "Sicilian time." **Bus 101** runs from Stazione Centrale to the Teatro Politeama Garibaldi and Giardino Inglese. **Bus 806** (leaving from Piazza Francesco Crispi at the western end of the Giardino Inglese) connects to the beach town of Mondello. A single-ride ticket costs €1.40 and can be purchased ahead of time at any tabacchi shop, newsstand, or AMAT bus office. Bus tickets should be time-stamped with a small machine near the driver upon boarding. City buses are often patrolled by the municipal police, and you risk a €54 fine if you do not have a ticket or if it has not been properly time-stamped.

BY TAXI

For a few important city sights that are a bit farther from the centro storico, such as the Catacombe dei Cappuccini and Castello della Zisa, it can be helpful to take a taxi, which are usually fairly reasonably priced. A one-way taxi to the Castello della Zisa, for example, costs €20, while a lift up to the Sanctuary of Santa Rosalia is €30. Local taxi services are provided by **Radio Taxi Trinacria** (tel. 091/6878) and **Autoradio Taxi** (tel. 091/8481). Taxi stands are located in Piazza Giuseppe Verdi by the Teatro Massimo, Piazza Castelnuovo near the Teatro Politeama Garibaldi, in front of the Stazione Centrale train station, and on Corso Vittorio Emanuele by the Fontana Pretoria.

BY CAR OR PRIVATE DRIVER

Driving a car around Palermo is not generally recommended. Tricky ZTL restrictions in the historic center (regulations to limit traffic), limited secure places to park, and undeniably fearless Sicilian drivers are best avoided if at all possible. To drive in the centro historico, daily **ZTL passes** must be purchased at a tabacchi shop, or you'll risk a fine of at least €150. Renting a car when you plan to leave Palermo and venture off to other parts of the island can be a great option, but a car for your days in Palermo is not necessary. Rental agencies in Palermo include **Hertz** (Via Messina, 7E) and **Sicily By Car** (Via Mariano Stabile, 6A). If you choose to park a car in Palermo, expect guarded parking lots to cost €12-20 per day, or inquire with your hotel about parking.

Vicinity of Palermo

Within the province of Palermo, hit the road to relax on the sandy beaches of Mondello or Cefalù. If you're looking for the best quality accommodations, restaurants, and nightlife, plan to stay in the city of Palermo and take quick day trips outside town with your own rental car or the train when possible. Be sure to explore the peaceful Sicilian countryside with a vineyard visit and wine-tasting experience in Camporeale, and pencil in a few hours to see the Cattedrale di Monreale, a UNESCO World Heritage Site and extraordinary example of Norman-Arab-Byzantine architecture.

MONDELLO

A 20-minute bus ride from the center of Palermo is the seaside village of Mondello, where you can enjoy a gelato on the beach or relax under an umbrella at a lido beach club. Once only a swampy hunting reserve plagued by malaria, Mondello has become one of the busiest beaches in Sicily. Its close location to the capital city makes it a popular location for second homes for Palermo's upper class. In the late 19th century, the art deco-style villas that were built here began the town's transformation into the quaint seaside village it is today. Mondello has become the heart of Palermo's summer beach scene from June through September. The village becomes a ghost town in winter, except for the residents who live here year-round and the active locals who enjoy exercising along the lungomare.

Sights
Santuario di Santa Rosalia

Via Bonanno Pietro; tel. 091/540326; www.
santuariosantarosalia.it; 7:30am-1pm and 1:30pm-
6:30pm daily, 7am-1pm and 3pm-6:30pm Easter and
Christmas; free

Located between the city of Palermo and Mondello, the Sanctuary of Santa Rosalia sits at the top of Monte Pellegrino overlooking the bay of Palermo. If you can't make it during the annual July 14 **Festa di Santa Rosalia,** simply drive up to the sanctuary to pay respect to Palermo's patron saint at her final resting place. It's a unique chance to see a lovely church built deep into a cave. According to tradition, she belonged to the 12th-century noble Sinibaldi family from the province of Agrigento. After retiring to her cave to live as a hermit, she appeared to a hunter in a dream in 1624, nearly 500 years after her death, indicating where he could find her remains, which she told him should be carried in a procession through the city in order to save it from the plague.

Nestled at the top of the mountain, the church and the cave sanctuary are traditionally visited by local families praying for the health of their loved ones. During the COVID pandemic, Palermitans looked to Santa Rosalia to help overcome the virus and protect their citizens. The 7-mile (11.3-km) drive from the port of Palermo via SS113 will take about 25 minutes. The sanctuary is located 25 minutes from the beach in Mondello, following Via Monte Ercta northwest to the Viale Margherita di Savoia. The number 812 AMAT city bus (www.amat.pa.it; 35 minutes; €2) to Montepellegrino departs every two hours from the Libertà/Archimede bus stop on Via Libertà and Via Archimede, in front of the Hermès store; guests should get off at the Santuario stop (number 1904) right in front of the entrance to the shrine of Santa Rosalia. For those driving up to Monte Pellegrino, parking is available at the Stele Croce di Via al Santuario Santa Rosalia (Via Santuario Monte Pellegrino), a 4-minute walk from the entrance. A taxi ride will cost €30 each way; however, the local drivers offer a package for €70 that includes a round-trip ride including the time they will wait while you tour the sanctuary.

★ Beaches

Mondello's mile-long (1.6-km) sandy stretch of golden beach, the closest beach to the city of Palermo, gets busy quick when summer hits. More isolated and rocky, the **Riserva Naturale di Capo Gallo** (www.riservacapogallo.it) begins at the northwestern end of town, a good option to avoid the summer crowds in Mondello or a quiet place to explore on foot any time of year.

Spiaggia di Mondello

Viale Regina Elena, Mondello; open 24 hours; free
Just 20 minutes northwest of Palermo's city center, the Spiaggia di Mondello is a long, golden-sand beach frequented by travelers, local beachgoers, and windsurfers. Sections of the beach are free and open to the public while other areas, like **Italo-Belga** (Viale Regina Elena, 59a; www.mondelloitalobelga.it) and **Lido Onde** (Viale Regina Elena, 53; tel. 091/450436; €16-25), are accessible only to those who pay the daily beach club fee, which conveniently includes bathrooms and outdoor showers. Beach beds and umbrellas can be rented daily at the ticket booths on the Viale Regina Elena beachfront or reserved in advance online (www.mondello.marcomedia.it; €11-20). The beachfront runs along the Viale Regina Elena road and is easily reached by car, taxi, or city bus. This main road is filled with bars, cafés, and ice cream shops. For those using the free beach areas, there are unfortunately no public restrooms available except at the cafés and bars that offer these services to paying customers only.

Punta Barcarello

Capo Gallo Nature Reserve, Via Barcarello, 31; www.parks.it/riserva.capo.gallo
Located at the west end of Mondello in the Capo Gallo Nature Reserve, this secluded rocky beach coast is a great place to escape the crowds at the Spiaggia di Mondello. There are no amenities or beach services here, just a wild natural place to enjoy a walk or a relaxing swim. The current can be rougher than in the protected bay in Mondello, and accessing the water requires climbing over large rocks. Make sure to bring along your own towels, umbrellas, and water shoes to make the most of your day.

Water Sports

Albaria Club

Viale Regina Elena 89/a; tel. 091/453595; www.albaria.org; 9am-6pm daily; windsurfing rentals €25 per hour, SUP rentals €16 per hour
For those looking to soak up the sun while getting in their exercise, Albaria offers walk-in rentals for stand-up paddleboards (SUP), wind surfboards, and canoes. Albaria also offers private and group **lessons** for SUP, windsurfing, and sailing.

Boat Service Mondello

Via Piano di Gallo; tel. 327/5618175; www.boatservicemondello.it; 8am-7pm daily; rentals from €80
Boat Service Mondello offers half- and full-day gommone and motorboat rentals for up to six people (from €80). A nautical license is not required. If you would prefer to have a skipper on board, this can be added to your reservation (additional €40 half day, €70 full day). It also offers a guided half-day boat excursion, again for a maximum of six, leaving at 9am from the Mondello tourist marina (€220 fee includes 3-hour 30-minute excursion, boat rental, skipper, snorkeling kit, and fuel).

Food

Baretto

Viale Regina Elena, 83; tel. 335/6774759; www.barettomondello.it; 8am-8pm daily Apr.-Oct.; €5
The Schillaci family has been serving gelato from this tiny green beach shack since 1957. Seasonal specialties include mulberry, strawberry, prickly pear, and lemon as well as classic Italian flavors like hazelnut, pistachio, and stracciatella. Try their famous coffee-flavored caffè gelato; ask for it "con panna sotto" to have freshly whipped cream added to the bottom of your cone. Make sure to stop by to enjoy a treat at the end of a beach day before heading back to Palermo.

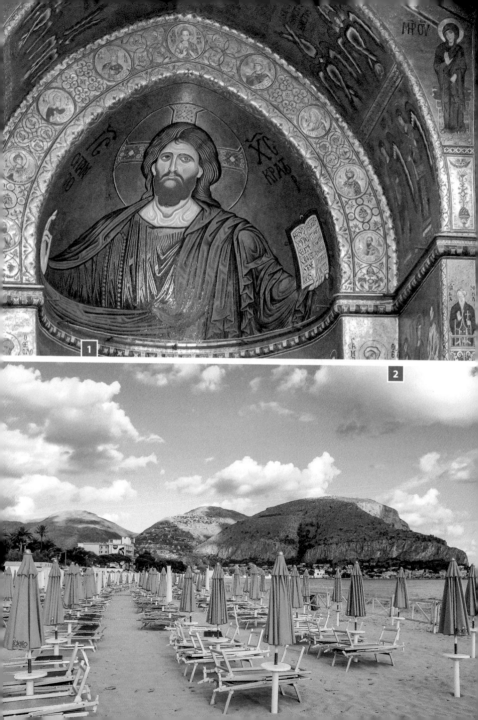

Information and Services

Mondello Info Point: Piazza Mondello, 2; www.visitpalermo.it; 8am-2:30pm and 3:30pm-7pm daily

Getting There

From central **Palermo,** Mondello is a 15-minute drive; pass the Stadio Renzo Barbera on Viale Diana, which becomes Viale Margherita di Savoia. This will take you directly to Viale Regina Elena/SS113 for Mondello. Paid parking spots (€1 per hour) are marked with a blue stripe and will need to be paid with a ticket from a nearby blue kiosk machine. There are a few private parking lots (from €2 per hour) near the beach, but make sure to check their closing times so your car does not get locked in the gate for the night. A taxi ride from Palermo to Mondello will cost approximately €25.

The number **806 bus** (www.amat.pa.it) is scheduled to run approximately every 20 minutes from Palermo's centro storico, but be prepared for the wait time to be longer than expected. Check the signs posted at the bus stop and confirm with the driver for daily timetables and when the last return bus will depart. The 806 bus leaves from the Piazza Francesco Crispi square at the western end of the Giardino Inglese and takes about 25 minutes to arrive in Mondello. A one-way ticket costs €1.40 and can be purchased ahead of time at any tabacchi shop, newsstand, or AMAT bus office.

CATTEDRALE DI MONREALE

Piazza Guglielmo II, 1; tel. 091/6404413; www. monrealeduomo.it; 9:30am-12:30pm and 3pm-4:30pm Mon.-Fri., 8:30am-9:30am and 3pm-4:30pm Sat.-Sun. and holidays, open only for personal prayers during Easter season (Mar.-Apr.); free, €4 for treasury and roof access

In the small hillside town of Monreale, overlooking Palermo, is the astonishing Cattedrale di Monreale, one of Sicily's treasured UNESCO World Heritage Sites. Thought of as one of the best existing examples of Norman architecture, this 12th-century masterpiece is one of the island's most-visited attractions.

The history of the cathedral dates back to the 12th century, when the Normans seized Palermo and its surrounding area from Arab rule. Despite the conflict, the Norman ruler at the time, William II or William the Good, was famed for being open-minded and tolerant, and when he set about building a new church (in competition with the Palermo Cathedral down the hill), he incorporated many North African and Middle Eastern artistic and architectural influences. Construction, blessed by the pope, began in 1174 and was finished in an impressive 11 years. William II lived just long enough to see it completed and was buried within, alongside his father William I.

The duomo is stunning even before you walk through its bronze doors, green with age and decorated with biblical scenes, griffins, and floral motifs. The interior is covered in spectacular gilded mosaics, with a Middle Eastern-style triple-apsed choir and a layout that's part-Roman Catholic, part-Orthodox—another complex depiction of Sicily's layered history. The geometric marble flooring, Baroque chapels, Byzantine stained glass, and intricate woodworked rooftops will take your breath away. Don't neglect to visit the adjacent cloister, with its marble column and arched Arabic arcade containing a lush, contemplative garden. For an additional fee, you can visit the treasury and get access to the panoramic rooftop terrace.

Getting There

From the center of Palermo, the Monreale Cathedral can be reached in 25 minutes with a straight route from the Cattedrale di Palermo along Corso A. Amedeo. The road will veer right then become Corso Calatafimi. Continue on SP69 and drive to Via Arcivescovada in Monreale. There are parking lots near the Cattedrale di Monreale where you can leave the car while touring the

1: inside the Cattedrale di Monreale **2:** Spiaggia di Mondello

church. A taxi will cost around €30 each way. It's also possible to take AMAT **bus 389** (35 minutes; €1.40), which runs about every hour from Piazza Indipendenza near Palazzo dei Normanni.

★ CAMPOREALE AND MONREALE WINE COUNTRY

In the town of Camporeale, a 45-minute drive from Palermo in Sicily's Monreale DOC wine-making region, the local economy is very closely linked to agriculture and the production of its main products: grapes, wheat, and olives. The hills of Camporeale are famous for their exceptional production of syrah. The medieval town was founded in 1452, and has a charming historic center. For three days at the beginning of October, the town celebrates **Camporeale Day,** a festival of food, wine, and music that highlights ancient crafts such as pottery and textile embroidery. During the festival, the town organizes shuttle bus services to take guests to the nearby vineyards. A half-day vineyard visit and wine tasting in Camporeale can be an easy break during your Palermo-based travels.

Vineyard Visits and Wine Tasting

Many of the vineyards here in Monreale are around 1,600 feet (500 m) above sea level, with a sandy soil that cannot retain too much water, keeping winemakers extremely busy all year long. Most of the cantinas you'll see in this part of Sicily are housed in renovated country homes nestled among the rolling hills, rows of vineyards, olive orchards, or wheat fields.

Alessandro di Camporeale

Contrada Mandranova, Camporeale; tel. 0924/37038; www.alessandrodicamporeale.it; by appointment only, 10:30am, 12:30pm, and 3pm Mon.-Fri., 10:30am Sat.
Winery tours, tastings, and lunch options are available at this family winery in the town of Camporeale. Options range from 90-minute basic wine tastings (€12 per person) to 2-hour food-and-wine tastings, including samples of five wines (€25 per person). A full lunch following your winery tour and tasting can also be organized for €40 per person. Call ahead to schedule a visit. Alessandro di Camporeale can be reached via a 45-minute drive from Palermo, exiting at the Camporeale–San Cipirello turnoff from SS624.

countryside outside Palermo

Tenuta Sallier de La Tour

Viadotto Pernice, Camporeale; tel. 091/6459711;
www.tascadalmerita.it/tenuta/sallier-de-la-tour; by
appointment only; €40 per person for a tour and
tasting of 3 wines

Within the Monreale DOC winemaking region, with vineyards spread across rolling hills, this wine estate is one of five properties under the umbrella of Tasca d'Almerita, one of the top winemaking families in Sicily. Since the 1950s, they have been cultivating mainly syrah grapes, an international varietal that grows extremely well in the Camporeale area, as well as Grillo, Inzolia, and Nero d'Avola. Call ahead to schedule a visit or tasting. Sallier de La Tour can be reached with a 40-minute drive from Palermo, exiting at the Camporeale–San Cipirello turnoff from SS624.

Porta del Vento

Contrada Valdibella, Camporeale; tel. 335/6692875;
www.portadelvento.it; by appointment only; €15 per
person

The certified biodynamic and organic property of Marco Sferlazzo spans 44 acres (18 ha) in the DOC Alcamo and DOC Monreale winemaking regions alongside Camporeale. The vines are trained with an alberello system, meaning they are pruned to grow freestanding like a small tree, and most of them are over 50 years old. Ninety-minute vineyard visits and wine tastings can be scheduled for groups of 4-20 people. Smaller tastings can be organized for a minimum of €60. Call to schedule an appointment. Porta del Vento can be reached with a 50-minute drive from Palermo, exiting at the Camporeale–San Cipirello turnoff from SS624.

Getting There

From central **Palermo,** Camporeale is a 45-minute drive on the **SS624** toward Sciacca. The town of Camporeale does not have many sightseeing options, and most visits to this area will be focused on visiting wineries. For winery visits outside Palermo, guests will have to provide their own transportation or hire a private driver.

Western Sicily

Western Sicily has an incredible mix of natural landscapes, charming towns and seaside villages, extremely important archaeological sites, and of course top food and wine. Often overlooked by foreign tourists, the west coast, including Trapani, Marsala, and the Aegadian Islands, can offer an authentic Sicilian travel experience enjoyed from an insider's point of view by way of beaches with smaller summertime crowds, undiscovered islands, and plentiful vineyards and small-scale wineries to visit.

Heading southwest, most likely with one's own car, the coastlines range from pristine golden-sand beaches in protected nature reserve areas to rocky coves and smooth, white limestone shores in the province of Agrigento. The volcanic island of Pantelleria merits its own trip,

Highlights

Look for ★ to find recommended sights, activities, dining, and lodging.

© MOON.COM

★ **Saline di Trapani e Paceco:** Watch as sea salt is extracted using traditional methods. Shallow seawater ponds and heaping mountains of white salt line the World Wildlife Fund-protected coastal road from Trapani down to Marsala (page 103).

★ **Aegadian Islands:** At this tropical paradise just 9 miles (14.5 km) off the coast of Trapani and Marsala, you can swim through clean, crystal blue waters, discover ancient caves dating back to the Neolithic Age, and explore sleepy fishing villages on three tiny isles (page 108).

★ **Tasting Marsala:** Experience the resurgence of one of Italy's unique winemaking styles, honed and perfected in the city of Marsala since the 1770s (page 124).

★ **Scala dei Turchi:** A breathtaking natural wonder, this terraced beach is made from white marl stone that has been sculpted into a smooth "staircase" by the strong wind and waters of the Mediterranean coast near Agrigento (page 130).

★ **Valle dei Templi:** Take a trip back in time to ancient Magna Graecia at the well-preserved remains of seven Doric-style temples, dating all the way back to the 6th century BCE in Agrigento (page 132).

Western Sicily

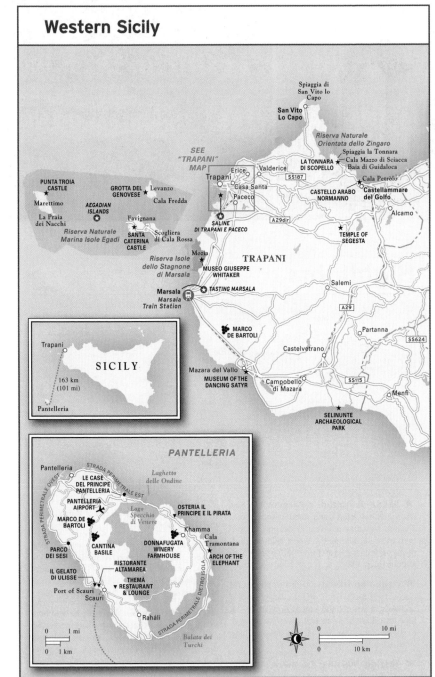

Spiaggia di
San Vito lo
Capo

**San Vito
Lo Capo**

*Riserva Naturale
Orientata dello Zingaro*

Spiaggia la Tonnara
LA TONNARA ★ ─ Cala Mazzo di Sciacca
DI SCOPELLO ─ Baia di Guidaloca

*SEE
"TRAPANI"
MAP*

Valderice

Cala Petrolò

Erice

Trapani

SS187

**Castellammare
del Golfo**

Casa Santa

**CASTELLO ARABO
NORMANNO**

**PUNTA TROIA
CASTLE**

**GROTTA DEL
GENOVESE** ★ Levanzo

Paceco

A29dir

Alcamo

Marettimo

Cala Fredda

**AEGADIAN
ISLANDS**

La Praia
dei Nacchi

Favignana

*Riserva Naturale
Marina Isole Egadi*

**SANTA
CATERINA
CASTLE**

Scogliera
di Cala Rossa

**SALINE
DI TRAPANI E PACECO**

**TEMPLE OF
SEGESTA** ★

TRAPANI

Salemi

Mozia

*Riserva Isole
dello Stagnone
di Marsala*

**MUSEO GIUSEPPE
WHITAKER**

A29

Marsala
Marsala
Train Station

TASTING MARSALA

Partanna

SS624

**MARCO
DE BARTOLI**

Castelvetrano

Mazara del Vallo

SS115

Menfi

**MUSEUM OF THE
DANCING SATYR**

Campobello
di Mazara

**SELINUNTE
ARCHAEOLOGICAL
PARK** ★

Trapani

SICILY

163 km
(101 mi)

Pantelleria

PANTELLERIA

Pantelleria

STRADA PERIMETRALE OVEST

STRADA PERIMETRALE EST

*Laghetto
delle Ondine*

**LE CASE
DEL PRINCIPE
PANTELLERIA**

**PANTELLERIA
AIRPORT**

**MARCO DE
BARTOLI**

*Lago
Specchio
di Venere*

**OSTERIA IL
PRINCIPE E IL PIRATA**

Khamma

Cala
Tramontana

**PARCO
DEI SESI**

**CANTINA
BASILE**

**DONNAFUGATA
WINERY
FARMHOUSE**

**ARCH OF THE
ELEPHANT**

**RISTORANTE
ALTAMAREA**

**IL GELATO
DI ULISSE**

**THEMÁ
RESTAURANT
& LOUNGE**

Port of Scauri

Scauri

STRADA PERIMETRALE DIETRO ISOLA

Raháli

*Balata dei
Turchi*

0   1 mi

0   1 km

0   10 mi

0   10 km

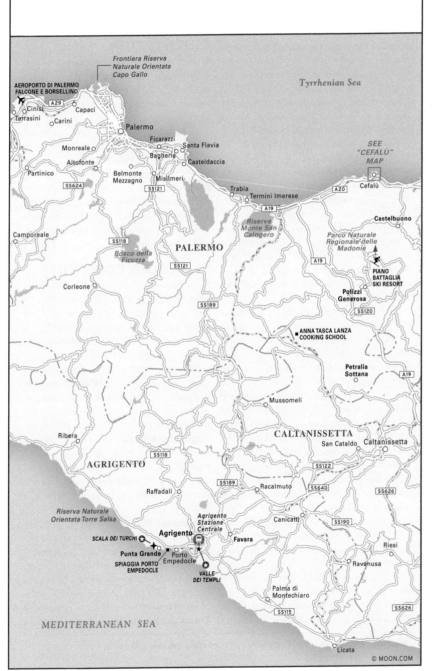

or can be visited in as little as three days with a flight from Palermo or Trapani.

With a shorter period to explore, the three Aegadian Islands off the coast of Trapani and Marsala can be reached by ferry for a day trip. At the center of the northern coast, between Palermo and Messina, Cefalù and its long stretch of sand beach right in the midst of the town center and its UNESCO World Heritage Site duomo have been a top destination in Sicily for at least the last 15 years.

A Sicilian holiday doesn't need to be restricted to only a summertime trip. The other seasons are a great time to explore the Madonie Mountains and visit Greek ruins like the Valley of the Temples, Segesta and Selinunte, or the Phoenician island of Mozia without the fierce sun of a summer afternoon. In these periods, you can almost have an entire archaeological park to yourself. Most beaches are scenic enough to merit a stop even in the off-season.

The local dishes take a culinary twist from the rest of the island due to western Sicily's proximity to Northern Africa, influencing the now traditional dishes with flavors and techniques of the past from the period of Arab domination in 827-1061. While traveling in this part of the island, look for handmade semola couscous with rich broths poured over the top and seafood garnishes including fish, red prawns from Mazara del Vallo, and squid; eggplant caponata topped with toasted almonds; the tomato-based red pesto Trapanese sauce for pasta, and various sweet-and-sour flavor profiles. The west side of the island is also known for marsala, a fortified wine made in its namesake town of Marsala, and traditional wines made from white grapes including local varietals such as grillo, inzolia, and zibibbo.

While it may not be the first place visitors to Sicily go, the "occidentale" (west) is a destination for those looking for a reason to slow down and disconnect. Discover an ancient and authentic side of Sicily—before it becomes the next big thing.

ORIENTATION

Outside Palermo, you'll find more beaches, including the picture-perfect sandy stretch of Cefalù, an hour east of the city, and several less developed ones heading west or south along the coast.

Continuing west, you'll find the larger towns of Trapani and Marsala, gateways to the Aegadian Islands of Favignana, Levanzo, and Marettimo, and eventually curving southeast along Sicily's southern coast toward Agrigento, the home of the spectacular Valle dei Templi Greek temples. Along the way, you'll find even more archaeological treasures at Segesta and Selinunte.

PLANNING YOUR TIME

From Palermo, it's easy to take day trips to most of the highlights of the area either by bus, train, or rental car. That said, if you prefer a quieter, more pastoral setting for your vacation, there are lovely accommodations throughout the southern coastal region, or you could opt to stay the night in a smaller seaside town like **Castellammare del Golfo** or **San Vito lo Capo.** Trapani or Marsala are equally great options on the west coast to use as a base for exploring the **Aegadian Islands,** while visitors who are interested in history should consider saving one full day to stay closer to Agrigento for time to visit the **Valle dei Templi.** Overall, this part of Sicily can be enjoyed fully with at least 5-7 days.

Falcone e Borsellino (PMO) airport, formerly known as Punta Raisi and the main airport for accessing western Sicily, is located 19 miles (31 km) west of the Palermo city center on Sicily's northwestern coast. In western Sicily's smaller towns, it's helpful and sometimes necessary to rent a car to get around. **Trains** and **buses** connect Palermo to most

---

Previous: windmill near Trapani; Valle dei Templi; coast of the Aegadian island of Levanzo.

of the main towns and cities in the region, but service can be infrequent or delayed, and having your own **rental car** can offer more flexibility. The main coastal cities of Cefalù, Trapani, and Marsala are effortlessly accessible by public transportation from Palermo and simply explored on foot, while the smaller seaside towns of Castellammare del Golfo, Scopello, the Madonie Mountains, and the southern coast surrounding Agrigento are more easily discovered when driving your own car.

Sicily's subtropical Mediterranean climate, with **mild winters** and **hot, dry summers,** makes it an ideal destination all year round, except for a few weeks in August when the temperatures skyrocket and the beaches become overly crowded.

Itinerary Ideas

DAY ONE: WEST FROM PALERMO

Pick up a rental car upon arrival at the Palermo Falcone e Borsellino airport and let the Sicilian adventures begin.

1 Drive 40 minutes west to the seaside village of Scopello to visit **La Tonnara di Scopello,** the town's old tuna fishery.

2 Just in front of the tonnara, a small beach, **Spiaggia la Tonnara,** looks out to picturesque faraglioni stone stacks and is a scenic spot for an afternoon of sunbathing.

3 Backtrack 20 minutes to spend the evening in Castellammare del Golfo's central harbor. Relax with an aperitivo drink followed by dinner at **Ristorante Cumpà** for local Sicilian specialties and mouthwatering seafood dishes.

DAY TWO: TRAPANI AND ERICE

1 Get ready to hit the road with a sack lunch of pane cunzatu or arancini and spend the morning at the 5th-century BCE Greek ruins at the **Temple of Segesta,** a 40-minute drive inland. Take a few hours to explore the Doric temple and the remains of a Greek theater.

2 Head west 45 minutes to reach Trapani. Park the car and ride the **cable car** from Trapani to Erice.

3 Walk through the medieval village of Erice to **Pasticceria Maria Grammatico** for the area's best desserts.

4 Spend the evening in Trapani, wandering through the charming historic center and dining at **Salamureci Ristorante.**

DAY THREE: AGRIGENTO AND THE VALLEY OF THE TEMPLES

1 Depart for Agrigento, breaking up your drive after about two hours with a seafood lunch at beachfront **Ristorante La Scogliera,** in Siculiana Marina.

2 After a 20-minute drive to the east, you'll arrive at the stunning **Scala dei Turchi.** These dramatic white limestone rock formations are scenic year-round; prepare to bring everything you need for a swim in summertime.

Itinerary Ideas

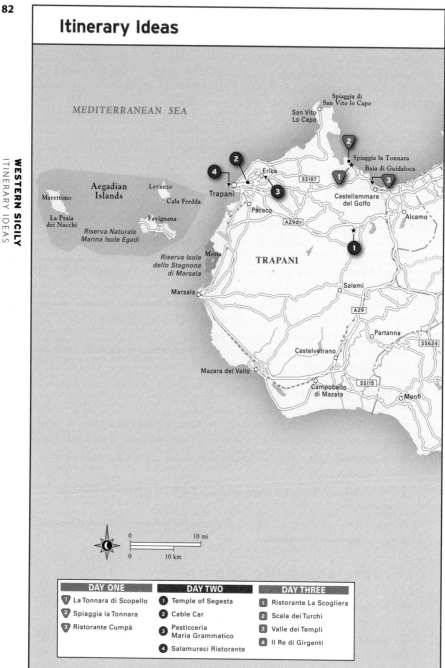

MEDITERRANEAN SEA

Spiaggia di
San Vito lo Capo

San Vito
Lo Capo

Spiaggia la Tonnara
Baia di Guidaloca

Erice

SS187

Castellammare
del Golfo

Alcamo

Aegadian
Islands

Levanzo

Cala Fredda

Trapani

Paceco

A29dir

Marettimo

La Praia
dei Nacchi

Favignana

Riserva Naturale
Marina Isole Egadi

Riserva Isole
dello Stagnone
di Marsala

Mozia

TRAPANI

Salemi

A29

Marsala

Partanna

SS624

Castelvetrano

Mazara del Vallo

Campobello
di Mazara

SS115

Menfi

0   10 mi

0   10 km

DAY ONE	DAY TWO	DAY THREE
1 La Tonnara di Scopello	1 Temple of Segesta	1 Ristorante La Scogliera
2 Spiaggia la Tonnara	2 Cable Car	2 Scala dei Turchi
3 Ristorante Cumpà	3 Pasticceria Maria Grammatico	3 Valle dei Templi
	4 Salamureci Ristorante	4 Il Re di Girgenti

Tyrrhenian Sea

AEROPORTO DI PALERMO
FALCONE E BORSELLINO

A29

Terrasini

Capaci

Frontiera Riserva
Naturale Orientata
Capo Gallo

Palermo

Ficarazzi

Santa Flavia

Monreale

Altofonte

Partinico

SS624

Belmonte
Mezzagno

SS121

Misilmeri

Trabia

Cefalù

Termini Imerese

A20

A19

Camporeale

SS118

PALERMO

Riserva
Monte San
Calogero

Bosco della
Ficuzza

SS121

A19

Corleone

SS189

SS120

Mussomeli

CALTANISSETTA

Ribera

SS118

San Cataldo

Caltanissetta

AGRIGENTO

SS189

Raffadali

Racalmuto

SS122

SS640

SS626

Riserva
Naturale
Torre Salsa

Agrigento
Stazione
Centrale

SS190

Riesi

1 **2** Agrigento **4**

Punta Grande Porto
Empedocle

3

Ravanusa

Palma di
Montechiaro

SS115

SS626

MEDITERRANEAN SEA

Licata

© MOON.COM

3 In the late afternoon, visit the **Valle dei Templi;** you'll need a few hours to get the most out of this 8-square-mile (21-sq-km) site, dotted with ancient Greek temples and surrounded by olive and almond groves.

4 After taking in all that history, it's time to refresh at your hotel and enjoy a well-deserved dinner at **Il Re di Girgenti,** still in view of the archaeological site.

Cefalù

If you've seen promotional photos of sandy beaches in Sicily, more often than not they have been taken in the picturesque town of Cefalù, located east of Palermo. Situated at the foot of a dramatic promontory, today known as La Rocca, this has been a desirable site of strategic importance and trade since even before Greek settlement. Like Palermo, Cefalù was ruled in turn by the Byzantines and then the Normans, who left their mark on the city with the Norman-style Duomo di Cefalù in the main **Piazza del Duomo** square. An ancient Greek temple and what was once a Norman castle dominate the towering La Rocca cliffs, offering breathtaking views. Mosey along the gorgeous beachfront and old port; the golden shoreline includes a large stretch of free public beach space as well as private lido clubs where you can spend the day relaxing under an umbrella.

This is by far one of the most popular destinations for a Sicilian summer beach day, but it's equally enjoyable in winter, when you can peruse the city sights and stroll along the serene beach without the usual crowds. It makes for a great break from the hustle and bustle of Palermo. There's nothing better than sitting in the main piazza while enjoying a gelato or aperitivo cocktail in front of the cathedral and the towering Rocca di Cefalù mountain.

SIGHTS
Duomo di Cefalù

Piazza del Duomo; tel. 0921/922021; www. cattedraledicefalu.com; 8:30am-closing (varies by season) daily; €3 general entrance, reduced rates for groups of 10 and guests over 65 €2, students €1
The landmark Roman Catholic basilica in the heart of Cefalù's Piazza del Duomo is a UNESCO World Heritage Site. Sitting just below the La Rocca mountain, the 12th-century cathedral features the mixture of Norman, Arab, and Byzantine styles of architecture that is typical to the area. A popular location for grand Sicilian weddings and film shoots, it's a perfect place for people-watching.

Museo Mandralisca

Via Mandralisca, 13; tel. 0921/421547; www. fondazionemandralisca.it; 9am-7pm daily Sept.-July, 9am-11pm daily Aug.; adults €6, students €2
The Mandraliscas were a noble Sicilian family that was well connected with the Italian government during the early 1800s. The Mandralisca museum art gallery is located on the street where the family once lived. The family's personal collection includes archaeological treasures, ancient furniture, and most importantly the petite, smirking *Portrait of an Unknown Sailor* by Antonello da Messina, one of Sicily's foremost Renaissance painters.

Cefalù Medieval Laundry
(Lavatoio Medievale Fiume Cefalino)

Via Vittorio Emanuele; open 24 hours; free
Tucked away in a small courtyard in the center of Cefalù, lava-stone steps lead down to the centuries-old site of the public laundry. Built in the Middle Ages, it was a place for women to meet, wash their clothes, and bathe in the health-giving, ice-cold water.

Temple of Diana

Via Passafiume, Salita Saraceni; open 24 hours; €5 entrance fee to La Rocca Park
The ancient temple of this 4th-century BCE

Cefalù

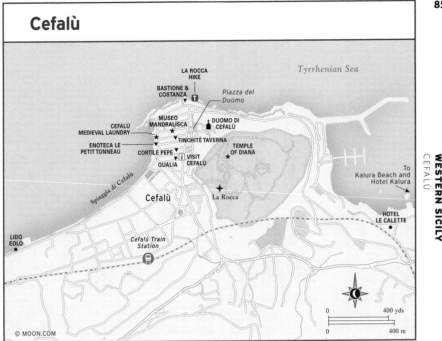

megalithic stone landmark was built in dedication to the Greek goddess Artemis, or Diana to the Romans. Sacredly linked to the worship of water, the ruins of small chapels and barracks here were probably originally intended for the cult of pagan divinities, but were later replaced with a Christian church dedicated to Santa Venera. Visit the temple on a hike along the La Rocca cliffs for panoramic views of Cefalù.

HIKING

La Rocca Hike

Distance: *2 miles (3.2 km) round-trip*
Time: *1 hour round-trip*
Trailhead: *End of Corso Ruggero and Via Carlo Ortolani di Bordonaro, near the lungomare beach promenade*
Information and Maps: *Local tourism office*

A one-hour hike leads up to La Rocca, where the ruins of its former Norman castle and surrounding medieval walls dramatically overlook the beach below. On the west side of La Rocca, you'll find the remains of the Temple of Diana, dating back to the 4th century BCE. This hike can be extremely hot in summertime; bring along a hat and a few bottles of water.

BEACHES

Spiaggia di Cefalù

Lungomare Giuseppe Giardina; open 24 hours; free

The golden sands of Cefalù's public beach are one of Sicily's top destinations in summer. Free showers are available along the coastline, and the warm, still waters of the sea here are perfectly suited for families and small children. The mountain spring water that streams out just behind the medieval wash house offers a chilling refreshment for beachgoers in the height of summer.

An affordable option for visitors who want the amenities of a beach club is **Lido Eolo** (Lungomare Giuseppe Giardina, 11; tel. 338/5237623; www.lidoeolo.business.site; 9am-7pm daily; €15 per day). Daily umbrella

and beach bed rentals are available in summer. A restaurant, bathrooms, and bar service can be used by guests of the club.

Kalura Beach

Via Cavallaro; open 24 hours; free

Pack all your beach supplies and an umbrella for shade and head to the other side of town for a dip on the quieter side of Cefalù. The small, pebbled beach is a great option for those looking to get away from the crowds on the sandy shores near the historic center.

FOOD AND BARS
★ Bastione & Costanza

Piazza Francesco Crispi, 13; tel. 0921/571222; www. bastionecefalu.com/bastione-costanza; 11am-3pm and 5pm-11:30pm daily; pizzas €6-12

This restaurant serves up fresh fish and top-quality pizza using a natural lievito madre yeast starter and the best local ingredients from farms around Sicily. The extensive Sicilian wine list includes traditional and natural bottles at affordable rates.

Tinchité Taverna

Via XXV Novembre, 37; tel. 0921/421164; www. tavernatinchite.com; 12:30pm-3pm and 7pm-11:30pm daily; entrées €10-20

This small bar and restaurant is located just one block from the beach. It's a perfect spot for a quick lunch featuring antipasti, octopus salad, fried salt cod fritters, pasta, and main dishes, as well as great craft Sicilian beers.

★ Qualia

Via G. Amendola, 16A; tel. 0921/820104; https://qualia. superbexperience.com; 7:30pm-10:30pm Mon. and Wed., 12:30pm-2pm and 7:30pm-10:30pm Thurs.-Sun.; tasting menus or à la carte dishes €16-24; reservations necessary and credit card deposits required through the site when booking

This small 12-table restaurant, with indoor and outdoor dining, offers a revisitation of local flavor pairings and homestyle nonna dishes like roasted octopus or pasta with cuttlefish prepared with the fine-dining finesse of chef Davide Catalano. The wine list includes many hard-to-find natural wines from around Sicily, selected by co-owner Marilena Garbo. Book your reservation in advance through its website to snag a highly coveted table at Qualia, open since 2017 in the center of Cefalù's historic center.

Enoteca Le Petit Tonneau

Via Vittorio Emanuele, 49; tel. 0921/421447; www. lepetittonneau.it; 9:30am-1am Sun.-Thurs., 9:30am-1:30am Fri.-Sat.; €25

This uber romantic enoteca has private tables for two, each overlooking the sea from its own little stone cave balcony. The wine list features traditional and natural wines from all around Sicily. Reservations are required.

Cortile Pepe

Via Nicola Botta, 15; tel. 0921/421630; www. cortilepepe.it; 7:30pm-11pm Thurs., 12:30pm-2:30pm and 7:30pm-11pm Fri.-Tues.; 4-course tasting menu €39, 6-course chef's tasting menu €65, entrées €16-20

Dine under the stars at Cortile Pepe's beautiful outdoor space in the center of town. Restaurateur Toti Fiduccia and chef Giovanni Lullo have created a space that combines modern dining with traditional, top-quality, local ingredients. Lullo's fresh pasta spaghettone with pressed Swiss chard, red shrimp, sea urchin, and tuna bottarga is a complex and satisfying dish to follow a long day at the sea.

ACCOMMODATIONS

Many visitors heading to Cefalù will go for a day trip from Palermo, spending their nights back in the capital city. There are also plenty of small bed-and-breakfasts as well as Airbnb apartments available within walking distance from the town and the sea. Families might opt to stay in a hotel with a pool and take short day trips from Cefalù to surrounding areas like the villages in the Madonie Mountains.

1: Duomo di Cefalù **2:** beach day in Cefalù **3:** view of Cefalù

★ Hotel le Calette

Via Cavallaro, 12; tel. 0921/424144; www.lecalette.it; from €198

On the quieter side of the gulf of Cefalù, this five-star hotel can be a great place to spend the night after a long beach day or to base yourself for a few days of exploring the nearby Madonie Mountains. The luxurious gardens lined with flowers, on-site dining options, spa services, private lido deck, and pool overlooking the sea are among the many perks of this gorgeous resort.

Hotel Kalura

Via Cavallaro, 13; tel. 0921/421354; www.hotelkalura. com; from €200

This three-star hotel is also located in the less touristic part of the city and is fully equipped with rooms and apartments for rent, and a bar and restaurant on-site. The pool is open March-November, which can be a perk for those traveling in the shoulder seasons. The nearby Kalura Beach is a prime destination for those looking to escape the crowds of the main beach in Cefalù. Yoga classes are offered to guests of the hotel upon request.

INFORMATION AND SERVICES

- **Visit Cefalù:** Corso Ruggero, 77; www.visitcefalu.com

GETTING THERE

From Palermo, you can drive the 47 miles (76 km) to Cefalù in under 1 hour via the E90 highway. Street parking in Cefalù is available, but keep a close eye on the signage and parking grid colors. Parking spaces marked with a blue outline on the street require paid hourly (€1 per hour) tickets purchased from a nearby parking kiosk. White parking spaces are free, but make sure to check all nearby signs before leaving your car. Yellow spots are restricted and generally used only by town residents. There is a parking lot at the train station and paid parking spaces along the beachfront or at the 24-hour **Parcheggio Coco** parking lot (Lungomare Giuseppe Giardina). Once guests arrive in Cefalù by car, train, or private driver, the city center is small enough to explore on foot in a half or full day.

Cefalú Train Station

Via Passafiume, 40; www.trenitalia.com

The train station in Cefalù is just a 10-minute walk from the beach. Tickets can be purchased in advance online or from an automated kiosk at the train station entrance. The train from Palermo Centrale to Cefalù takes one hour and costs €6.80. Tickets must be time-stamped at the station before boarding the train.

1: dining room at Qualia **2:** pizza at Bastione & Costanza

Madonie Mountains

This is a territory in the central-northern part of Sicily, scattered with high peaks, mountains facing the sea, lush vegetation, valleys, plateaus, cliffs, and gentle hills filled with unique flora and fauna. Tourism in this area is made up mainly of Sicilians or Italians and a small percentage of foreign outdoor adventurers. The main highlights of the region are far and away the quaint mountain villages, the ski resort on Piano Battaglia in Petralia Sottana, and the Parco Naturale Regionale delle Madonie. Culinarily speaking, the area is known for its stretched cow's milk provola cheeses, wild mushrooms, manna (ash tree sap) from Pollina and Castelbuono, wild pork, peppers and Badda beans from Polizzi Generosa, and wild bitter greens. Most of the restaurants in this area focus on rustic traditional recipes using local ingredients from the mountains.

The villages in the Madonie mountain range are speckled around the central Parco delle Madonie nature reserve. Of particular note are Castelbuono, which is on the north side of the park; Gangi, located southeast of the park; Petralia Sottana and Polizzi Generosa, which lie along the south side of the park; and Sclafani Bagni, near the western end of the park.

RECREATION
Parco Naturale Regionale delle Madonie
tel. 0921/684011; www.parcodellemadonie.it
This park spans an area of 40,000 acres (16,190 ha) from the coast to the mountains nearly 6,560 feet (2,000 m) above sea level in the province of Palermo. The **Qui Parco** (Piazza San Mamiliano, 5, Gratteri; tel. 0921/431104) information center provides helpful tourism assistance, itineraries, and nature excursion details, as well as printed guidebooks.

Skiing
Piano Battaglia Ski Resort
Strada Provinciale 54, Petralia Sottana; www. madoniesci.it; daily 9am-4pm; day tickets adults €30, children €24
Piano Battaglia is the only ski resort in western Sicily featuring seven trails spread over 2.8 miles (4.5 km) with two chairlifts. Set among a beech tree forest between the mountain range of Pizzo Carbonara (6,492 ft/1,979 m above sea level) and Monte Mufara (6,119 ft/1,865 m), this is a popular destination for skiing and snowboarding December-March. The Apennine climate boasts intense, snowy Mediterranean winters with an average temperature of 31°F (-1°C) as well as mild and dry summers with an average temperature of 63°F (17°C). In summertime it becomes an ideal destination for hiking. Bus services from Palermo are available through Piana Battaglia da Palermo (tel. 091/7848420; www. pianobattagliadapalermo.it; 1 hour 30 minutes; €15).

Tours
The Heart of Sicily
www.theheartofsicily.it
Just due south of Cefalù, the Madonie Mountains between the Imera and Pollina rivers can be best explored through this new association, launched in 2022. They focus on bringing attention to the nearly forgotten culinary, cultural, and naturalistic aspects of small villages such as Polizzi Generosa and Petralia Sottana. From a visit to a cheesemaker, tomato factory, an artisan ceramic producer, the Parco Naturale Regionale delle Madonie, or vineyards in Valledolmo, The Heart of Sicily has carefully researched just how to explore this region and dive deeper into the history and rich biodiversity of this

1: Madonie Mountains **2:** Parco Naturale Regionale delle Madonie

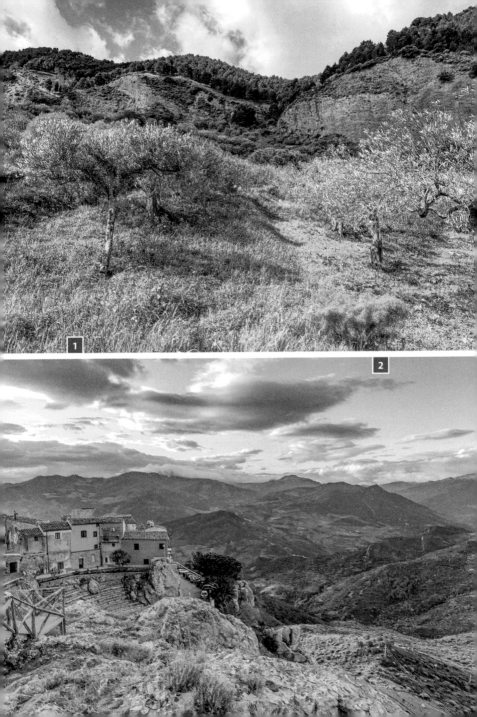

part of Sicily's entroterra inland. Visit their website to learn about offerings and pricing for multiday itineraries or reach out to their team for availability options.

FESTIVALS AND EVENTS

Ypsigrock Music Festival

Castelbuono; www.ypsigrock.it; €35-60 per day

This highly celebrated three-day indie music festival has been hosted annually each August in Castelbuono since 1997. It hosts nearly 3,000 guests each day and has featured huge, internationally known artists such as The National, Belle & Sebastian, Mogwai, and Caribou. Shows have been performed in various picturesque locations around Castelbuono, including a deconsecrated Baroque church, an 18th-century cloister, and a natural amphitheater. The festival offers add-on options to camp out at one of its forest sites, or guests often organize their own accommodations in small B&Bs or agriturismi farmstays nearby.

Castelbuono Jazz Festival

Castelbuono; www.facebook.com/ CastelbuonoJazzFestival; tickets from €17

The Castelbuono Jazz Festival takes place annually in mid-August. Centered around the Piazza Castello, this three-evening festival hosts the great protagonists of Italian jazz, bringing thousands of music lovers to this charming mountain town each year. Concerts have featured top performers including James Senese, Richard Galliano, Peppe Servillo, and Stefano Di Battista.

FOOD

Palazzaccio Ristorante

Via Umberto I, 23, Castelbuono; tel. 0921/676289; www.ristorantepalazzaccio.it; 9am-3pm and 7pm-midnight Mon., 12:30pm-3pm and 7pm-midnight Tues.-Sun.

Chef Sandro Cicero's rustic cuisine is made with the goal of highlighting the best raw materials of the area. Dishes feature mostly meat (fish dishes only in summertime) with wild porcini and ferla mushrooms, local vegetables,

and refined mountain cheeses. The restaurant, awarded with a Bib Gourmand mention by the *Michelin Guide,* has been known to offer a drinking water menu along with a prestigious wine list of over 300 labels. It also has a wine bar nearby, **Quaranta Cantina Palazzaccio** (Cortile Venere Ciprea, 2; tel. 0921/443512; 11:30am-2:30pm and 6:30pm-midnight Wed.-Mon.).

Il Castello Ristorante

Via Generale di Maria, 27, Petralia Sottana; www. il-castello.net; tel. 0921/641250

The homestyle madonita dishes here are made with traditional local recipes. This casual restaurant also specializes in sourdough pizza made with mountain water, natural yeast starter, and 48-hour levitation. Try the meat dishes and a wide selection of wine from its underground stone cellar.

★ Trattoria Sant'Anna

Via Sant'Anna, 2, Gangi; tel. 0921/602422; www. trattoriasantanna.it; 12:30pm-3pm and 7:30pm-10:30pm Sun.-Tues. and Thurs.-Fri., 12:30pm-3pm and 8pm-10:30pm Sat.; €10-20

Gangi is a town known for its amazing ingredients, and Trattoria Sant'Anna lives up to the reputation. Inside the historic Palazzo dei Bongiorno, owners Santo Spitale and Antonio Mocciaro have created a casual restaurant celebrating their town's gangitana cuisine. Freshness and quality are their highest priorities. Local mountain dishes include fava bean soup, maccheroni with wild fennel, sausage, and ricotta, as well as pork roasts and raw beef carpaccio. Outdoor seating is available in spring and summer.

★ Terrazza Costantino

Rione Sant'Antonio, 24, Sclafani Bagni; tel. 339/1155915; www.terrazzacostantino.com; 7:30pm-10pm Mon.-Tues. and Thurs.-Fri., 12:30pm-2pm and 7:30pm-10pm Sat.-Sun.; €45 tasting menus only; reservations must be made in advance

Stunning plates are developed with precision and special attention to elevate local raw ingredients. The gnocchi with sumac, Madonie truffles, and mint or the lamb loin with sunchokes, foie gras, and artichokes delight all the senses. Most likely if you find yourself in the small town of Sclafani Bagni, it's because you've already heard of chef/owner Giuseppe Costantino's brilliant 16-seat fine-dining restaurant. He is on the right track to earn his first Michelin star, now mentioned with the Bib Gourmand award.

ACCOMMODATIONS

★ Gratteri Resort

Via Parisea, Gratteri; tel. 377/3739549; www. gratteriresort.com; from €140

Gratteri Resort provides a unique upscale option for travelers visiting the Madonie Mountains area or for those who want to be out of the town center of Cefalù, just 30 minutes away. Services include local touring information, Wi-Fi service, indoor and outdoor common areas, doorman, and 24-hour reception. Small pets are allowed too. A Turkish bath, Finnish sauna, and heated outdoor pool are available to guests of the resort. The spa, as well as the solarium and swimming pool, are also available to nonguests, with a reservation (daily rate adults €15, children €10).

Relais Santa Anastasia

Contrada Santa Anastasia, Castelbuono; tel. 0921/672233; www.abbaziasantanastasia.com; rooms from €155

This hotel and eco-resort is less than 6.2 miles (10 km) from the seaside, just south of the village of Sant'Ambrogio. Guests get treated to the service of a resort in this simple countryside inn. It was converted from a medieval Benedictine abbey and now includes rooms and suites of various categories, all named for grape varietals, surrounded by a central stone courtyard, a sun terrace, an in-house restaurant, and an outdoor swimming pool and Jacuzzi. Make sure to try its house wines, made biodynamically nearby.

Susafa

Contrada Susafa, Polizzi Generosa; tel. 338/9608713; www.susafa.com; from €215

Set between Polizzi Generosa and the small village of Vallelunga, Susafa is a four-star boutique hotel in a fully renovated 200-year-old farmhouse. It's hidden away in the middle of nowhere, and that is precisely its charm. From the tree-lined swimming pool to the in-house fine-dining restaurant service, guests spending a night or two in the countryside of the Madonie Mountains can fully relax in the peace and quiet of this little oasis. Simply appointed and climate-controlled, neutral-toned rooms are equipped with a security safe, bathrobes, and slippers.

★ Happy Glamping Madonie

Contrada Piscazzi, Polizzi Generosa; tel. 328/2772541; www.happyglampingmadonie.com; from €30-65

On the southern side of the Parco delle Madonie, luxury campsites and tents pique the interest of adventurous travelers, couples, and families coming to this part of Sicily. They have five heated accommodations, including a yurt, and three waterproof canvas tents, all with their own small outdoor spaces to enjoy. All guests have access to a shared heated bathroom with a shower as well as a common area with free Wi-Fi, charging stations, and a place to cook. Communal and cozy, it's ideal for hikers, budget travelers, and outdoor aficionados.

GETTING THERE AND AROUND

All these towns are best reached only by car or private driver and require your own means of transportation for exploring freely throughout the day. Give yourself plenty of time to enjoy the small mountain roads when arriving in this area from bigger cities such as Palermo, Milazzo, Messina, or around Mount Etna.

A Destination Cooking School

Forward thinking and ahead of her time, Marchesa Anna Tasca Lanza founded a cooking school on her family vineyard property in 1989, way before anyone else was thinking about culinary travel. With her intensive promotional travels and series of cookbooks on Sicilian ingredients, family stories, endangered fruits and herbs, she became the utmost authority on Sicilian cuisine, sharing the recipes of her family's homeland with an international audience. Located in Case Vecchie in Regaleali, the school was handed down to Anna's only daughter, Fabrizia Lanza. Her treasured rose gardens, cozy kitchen, and vegetable patches flourished, always staying true to the seasonal farm-to-table values and authentic culinary traditions of Sicily. With weeklong workshops and intensive programs, Anna Tasca Lanza Cooking School is a top destination for food and wine lovers.

Anna Tasca Lanza Cooking School

ANNA TASCA LANZA COOKING SCHOOL

Contrada Regaleali, Case Vecchie; tel. 380/7541365; www. annatascalanza.com; 2-night all-inclusive packages start at €1,275 per solo traveler or €1,975 per couple, lesson and lunch programs available for groups of 4 or more for €190 per person
Hands-on cooking lessons feature historical Sicilian family recipes and traditional local dishes from the island, always using as many products as possible harvested directly from the school's gardens or prepared in the cooking school kitchen. Options are available for multi-night stays, weeklong workshop programs, or the annual intensive 10-week academic food systems winter program starting in January.

Gulf of Castellammare

Outside the hustle and bustle of the capital city of Palermo, the Gulf of Castellammare offers a series of small destinations for visitors looking for a bit more rest and relaxation. From the striking beachfront in Scopello in front of the faraglioni rock formations, to the wide-open bay surrounding the town of Castellammare del Golfo to the pristine landscapes of the Lo Zingaro Nature Reserve, this area of Sicily is great for those exploring beyond Palermo or Trapani.

Though the quickest route between Palermo and Trapani takes you inland, traveling along the coast of the Gulf of Castellammare will take you past some of western Sicily's best beaches, some quirky cultural attractions, and unspoiled nature to boot. The best way to tour this coastal region is to rent a car.

CASTELLAMMARE DEL GOLFO

Castellammare del Golfo is a great place to stop on a coastal drive between Palermo and Trapani. As the name suggests, the landscape is defined by the "sea fortress on the gulf," where the medieval Arab-Norman castle presides over the bay. This fairly small Sicilian town of about 15,300 residents is most popular in summertime, when visitors come here to slow down and enjoy long days at the beach. The town center of Castellammare del Golfo and its harbor are easily explored on foot and can be visited on a short day trip from the surrounding areas. This is a strolling town, not one to rush in and out of just to check the main sites off a travel list. Take a leisurely stroll through Castellammare on what the Italians refer to as a "passeggiata," walking and wandering with no agenda other than being outside, having a look around, people-watching, and enjoying time pass in a beautiful place.

Sights and Beaches
Belvedere Castellammare del Golfo
Località Belvedere, 53; open 24 hours; free

This scenic overlook off the SP187 offers a bird's-eye view of the seaside town, the azure waters, its beaches, and the Castello Arabo Normanno. Stop off for a few photos from above and breathe in that pure mountain air. You're in Sicily after all; take time to soak it all in and enjoy the view.

Castello Arabo Normanno
Piazza Castello; 0924/592555; 9am-1pm and 3pm-7pm daily; free entry, donations appreciated

The medieval castle that stands guard over it all tells the story of the conquests of Castellammare del Golfo. Built in the 9th century by the Arabs, expanded and renovated by the Normans, and then built up and protected with the outer fortress walls by the Swabians, this castle includes layers of architectural and cultural significance with its signature blend of Arab-Norman design. Inside, it currently hosts a dynamic museum complex known as La Memoria del Mediterraneo. The Memory of the Mediterranean depicts the history of the town in four main sections: water and mills, production (including the crafts of farmers, blacksmiths, cobblers, masons, carpenters, coopers, and tanners), archaeology (including Roman amphorae), and marine activities such as tuna fishing.

Cala Petròlo Beach
Largo Petrolo; 9am-5pm daily

The sand beach, flanked by high stone walls, at Cala Petròlo is conveniently situated close to the town's traditional restaurants, bars, gelaterias, and pizzerias. There are free beach areas as well as private clubs where visitors can rent beach loungers and umbrellas. This is a great option for traveling to the seaside with small children. During the high season, Cala Petròlo will also have lifeguards on duty.

Castellammare del Golfo

Food

L'Antico Granaio

Corso Giuseppe Garibaldi, 20; tel. 0924/511150; www.
facebook.com/l.antico.granaio.ristorante; 7pm-11:30pm
daily; €20-35

Just a few blocks from the harbor, L'Antico Granaio offers indoor and outdoor seating at its welcoming locale in the lively pedestrian zone of Castellammare del Golfo. Here, third-generation chef/owner Rosario Ventimiglia serves up straightforward seafood dishes and a notable wine list. Specialties include tagliatelle pasta with red mullet and squash blossoms, paccheri with octopus ragù, and busiate alla Norma.

★ Ristorante Cumpà

Via Don Leonardo Zangara, 3; tel. 388/3860253; www.
ristorantecumpa.it; noon-3pm and 7pm-11:30pm Mon.
and Wed., 7pm-11pm Tues., noon-3pm and 7pm-11pm
Thurs.-Sun.; €25-35

Sicilian food lovers flock to the waterfront of Castellammare del Golfo's harbor to dine at Cumpà. Elegantly plated and well-composed dishes feature flavors from the sea, straight from its trusted purveyor, a man referred to as "Zù Pitrinu." This charming restaurant offers an authentic experience with delicious food and wine, where you're treated as a friend, or cumpà, as they say here in the south. Request a table out front for the best view of the sea.

Gelateria Vernaci

Corso Bernardo Mattarella, 40; tel. 334/3422106;
www.vernaci.it; 10am-3am daily; €3-5

Finding a gelateria to get a quick ice cream fix, simple. Finding that one artisanal gelateria in town that uses all-natural ingredients, priceless. Here at Vernaci, you can taste gelati and granita handcrafted with fresh fruit, no preservatives, and the highest-quality local ingredients such as Sicilian lemons, pistachios from Bronte on Mount Etna, strawberries from Marsala, peaches from Bivona, and almonds from Agrigento—all while supporting a small, family-owned business.

Accommodations

Residence Itaca

Largo Petrolo, 1; tel. 320/6289651; www.residenceitaca.
net; from €90

The eight mini apartments at the Residence Itaca are conveniently located just steps away from the Cala Petròlo beach, the main harbor, and the Arab-Norman castle. Each apartment has its own bedroom, bathroom, and kitchen with oven and refrigerator, a small balcony, heating and air-conditioning, TV, and Wi-Fi service. Breakfast is served on the main sun terrace, and staff can help organize paid parking in the private garage, bicycle rentals, room service, tourism suggestions, and airport transportation from Trapani or Palermo upon request. It's a charming place to stay for a beach holiday in Castellammare del Golfo. It also offers weeklong rates for those looking to explore the surrounding areas for a bit longer.

Getting There

Castellammare del Golfo is an hour-long drive (40 mi/64 km) west on the E90 highway from Palermo and 50 minutes (23 mi/37 km) east of Trapani along the SS187 state road. For extended travel in this area, reach out to **Authentic Italy** (www.authenticitaly.com) to help with your holiday planning. Founder Gary Portuesi creates tailor-made travel experiences in his hometown of Castellammare del Golfo and beyond. Bus services are available from Palermo to Castellammare on **Russo Autoservizi** (www.russoautoservizi.it; 1 hour 40 minutes; €7).

SCOPELLO

The enchanting beach town of Scopello is one of the most romantic sites on the coast of northwestern Sicily. The central 17th-century baglio, a stone-walled piazza and historic village square, is the heart of the town, filled with souvenir shops, bars, and restaurants. Here, you can treat yourself to the local specialty, the pane cunzatu sandwich, a "seasoned bread" soaked in olive oil and topped with Sicilian oregano, olives, sliced tomatoes,

Temple of Segesta

Temple of Segesta

Contrada Barbaro, Calatafimi; tel. 0924/952356; www.parcodisegesta.com; 9am-6:30pm daily; €6 entrance fee

A trip to the Temple of Segesta is a great break from the nearby beaches of Castellammare del Golfo or a nice stop on the way to Trapani from Palermo; pack a picnic lunch and spend a few hours at this picturesque ruin set amid the tranquil countryside.

The Temple of Segesta (Tempio di Segesta) is a magnificent site: an unusually intact and expansive Doric temple, perfectly situated on 1,300-foot-high (400-m) Monte Barbaro, a 40-minute drive southeast of Trapani. This 85-foot-wide (26-m) ruin, with its dozens of solid Doric columns, is a complete masterpiece, known to have been built around 420 BCE. Though the Hellenistic influence of ancient Greece here is unmistakable, archaeologists believe it was built by an indigenous population known as the Elymians, though Greek colonists likely participated in the construction. There's also evidence that this extremely well-preserved temple was never finished; its columns lack the usual ornamentation, and the ruins have no roof. Still, the view from this monumental and statuesque temple is breathtaking and promotes meditative contemplation.

Higher up Monte Barbaro are the remains of a Greek theater, thought to have been built in the 3rd century BCE, with similarly sweeping views of the Gulf of Castellammare and surrounding windswept countryside. It's just over half a mile (1 km) up from the site's parking lot to tour both the temple and the theater; for those who would rather avoid a steep walk, a shuttle runs past both sites from the parking lot every 30 minutes (€1.50).

GETTING THERE

On the main road between Palermo and Trapani, it's a 40-minute drive from Trapani (19 mi/31 km) and an hour-long drive from Palermo (50 mi/81 km). From Castellammare del Golfo, the 13-mile (21 km) drive will take approximately 20 minutes along SP2 to SS113. To explore these areas without having to worry about your own transportation, consider hiring a private driver such as **Sunny Sicily** (http://sunnysicily.com; from €82 per person).

cured anchovies, and primo sale or pecorino sheep's milk cheese.

With fewer than 120 inhabitants, the small borgo (village) survives on tourism, especially during the summer season from May through September. Although the iconic faraglioni stone stacks eroded by the sea are visible for a quick photo snapped from above, it's worth the extra fee and time to head down the hill to the sea to see them up close, take a swim, and tour the old tonnara.

Sights and Beaches
La Tonnara di Scopello

Largo Tonnara; tel. 388/829-9472; www. latonnaradiscopello.it; 10am-6pm daily; €8

Scopello's main attraction is its old tuna fishery, La Tonnara di Scopello. Dating back to the 13th century, the tonnara sits on the edge of an emerald cove amid beautiful natural scenery. The facility is made up of two medieval watchtowers, fishing village housing units, and an old courtyard. Nowadays, the tonnara has been transformed into apartment rentals, a museum, and a special-event space, popular for photo shoots and destination weddings. Plan on spending at least 30 minutes here to see the old tuna fishing boats, nets, and equipment.

Spiaggia la Tonnara

Parking lot at the crossroads of Via Finanziere and Via Vincenzo Bellini; 9am-7pm daily; €4 beach access plus paid parking nearby

The most famous beach is set right across from the faraglioni rock stack formations, just in front of the old tonnara. It is referred to either as the Spiaggia la Tonnara or the Spiaggia dei Faraglioni, and rightfully so it has appeared in major film and television productions including *Ocean's Twelve, Inspector Montalbano,* and commercial shoots for Dolce & Gabbana and Guess. This spot is overly romantic, with calm, crystal clear water, making it a sought-after destination for sunbathing, a refreshing swim, and snorkeling.

Cala Mazzo di Sciacca

Contrada Mazzo di Sciacca; open 24 hours; free

Located between the town of Scopello and the beginning of the Lo Zingaro Nature Reserve, Mazzo di Sciacca cove is a popular free beach destination for a swim in summertime. Light refreshments and shaded tables are available at the small beach bar, Sorsi e Morsi. Pack along everything you'll need for the day, including sun protection, towels, water, snacks, and water shoes. To arrive, take SP63 to Contrada Cala Mazza and turn left onto Contrada Mazzo di Sciacca for parking near the beach.

Baia di Guidaloca

Contrada Ciauli; tel. 0924/592506; open 24 hours; free

The mixed sand, shell, and stone terrain of the Guidaloca beach, halfway between Scopello and Castellammare del Golfo, has two small bars nearby for refreshments. The calm waters are perfect for snorkeling. Bring along water shoes for small children for a more enjoyable experience. Head over to the Lido Dies Vaccus (Contrada Ciauli, 24; €20) to rent beach umbrellas and chairs for the afternoon, where there are showers, bathrooms, and a restaurant available.

Getting There

From Palermo, Scopello can be reached in about an hour (45 mi/72 km); from Trapani, it's a 45-minute drive (20 mi/32 km). It's a 15-minute (7 mi/11.3 km) drive from Castellammare del Golfo along the coastal road SS187 heading toward Scopello.

RISERVA NATURALE ORIENTATA DELLO ZINGARO

Via Salvo D'Acquisto, 1; tel. 0924/35108; www. riservazingaro.it; 7am-7pm daily Apr.-Sept., 8am-4pm daily Oct.-Mar.; €5 fee can be paid at the cabin kiosk at either entrance (includes trail map)

Practically around the corner from

1: Scopello's iconic faraglioni 2: Baia di Guidaloca 3: Riserva Naturale Orientata dello Zingaro

Castellammare del Golfo, this stunning coastal nature reserve includes several miles of hiking paths, including the 4-mile one-way (6.4-km) **Coastal Path** that passes the reserve's seven swimming coves. Unfortunately, in summer 2020, the nature reserve was severely damaged by a fire, but it reopened the following year and continues to thrive, growing back to the lush nature preserve it once was. Since the beaches here take a little extra work to get to, they're often less crowded. Plan on spending at least three hours each way to enjoy the entire coastal trail with time to stop for a swim or two. For a beach day, make sure to pack water for the whole day, a picnic, sun protection, and sturdy shoes for walking. The southern entrance is located on the Scopello side, which offers more parking spaces, while the north entrance is closer to San Vito lo Capo.

Beaches

All the pristine beaches, swimming areas, and coves within the Lo Zingaro Nature Reserve are accessible by the Coastal Path or by boat. Highlights within the reserve include the pebble beach of **Cala Capreria** (0.7 mi/1.2 km, 20 minutes from the south entrance); **Cala della Disa** (1.6 mi/2.6 km, 35 minutes from the south entrance; 2.3 mi/3.7 km, 50 minutes from the north entrance), a pebble-and-sand beach about midway along the path; and **Cala Dell'Uzzo** (1.1 mi/1.8 km, 20 minutes from the north entrance), the largest and most popular pebbled beach, located an easy walk from the north entrance of the reserve. Beach amenities are not available in these locations, and the trails are not very shaded; prepare to bring along everything you'll need for the day. Plan on stopping at no more than three coves on a day trip, leaving more to discover the next time you visit.

Hiking

There are two main hiking trails, marked on the trail map available at the park entrance. The **Mid-Coastal Route** (Il Percoso di Mezza Costa) is a challenging 5.6-mile (9-km,

4-5-hour) trail heading toward the upper part of the reserve, while the other, the **High Trail** (Il Sentiero Alto) is even more challenging and only recommended for experts, covering 10.6 miles (17 km, 7-9 hours; not recommended in summer heat). For those looking for an easier walk, take the **Coastal Path** instead.

Water Sports
Cetaria Diving Center Scopello

Via Marco Polo, 3, Scopello; tel. 368/3864808; www. cetaria.it

Take a deeper look at the underwater world of the nature reserve with a diving course or snorkeling boat adventure with the Cetaria Diving Center in Scopello. Guests may have the chance to spot grouper, bream, snapper, amberjack, sea sponges, anemones, gorgonian sea fans, and astroides corals, or even stenelle dolphins splashing about nearby (especially in spring or autumn). Equipment is provided, and groups are limited based on the guides available and size of boats needed.

Getting There

The Lo Zingaro Nature Reserve is located 45 minutes (25 mi/40 km) northeast of Trapani, between Scopello and San Vito lo Capo. There are two main entrances to access the reserve. The **north entrance** can be reached along the SS187 state road heading toward San Vito lo Capo, following signs for Villaggio Calampiso. The **southern entrance** is accessible from the A29 Palermo-Mazara del Vallo highway, exiting at Castellammare del Golfo and then following SS187 toward Trapani, passing Scopello and leaving your car in the parking lot a short walk away near Cala Mazzo di Sciacca. Keep in mind the only public bathrooms are located at the two entrances. From Palermo, the drive to the southern entrance will take approximately 1 hour 20 minutes; it's 2 hours to the north entrance.

SAN VITO LO CAPO

The soft, white-sand **beach in San Vito lo Capo** (Via Litoranea Lungomare; open 24 hours; free) makes this seaside town one of the most beautiful and popular summer destinations in Sicily. In addition to the beach, the town is known for its history of tuna fishing and its annual weeklong **Cous Cous Fest** (www.couscousfest.it), which takes place every September. The waterfront is lined with small restaurants, bars, and shops, perfect for a full beach day and long summer night. The crystal clear blue water, framed by mountains, is reminiscent of the Caribbean, and you might just forget you're in Italy for a little while. There are also several beach clubs that offer umbrella and lounge chair rentals. The nearby main strip along Via San Vito and the Via Litoranea Lungomare beachfront promenade both have several bars and cafés where paying customers can use the bathroom facilities in a pinch.

Food
Salumeria Enoteca Peraino

Via Camillo Benso di Cavour, 81/A; tel. 0923/972627; www.salumeriaperaino.it; 8:15am-9:30pm daily; panini starting at €3

This fantastic deli and wine shop is just a short walk from the shore in San Vito. It's the perfect spot to pick up a sandwich before heading to the sea for the day, and is much better quality than anything you will find on the main strip. Try the pane cunzatu, a typical sandwich from the province of Trapani seasoned with olive oil, oregano, tomato, cheese, olives, and preserved anchovies. Peraino also offers a great aperitivo in the evenings, with platters heaped with high-quality cured meats and cheeses and exceptional wines from all over Sicily.

★ Syrah Ristorantino

Via Savoia, 86; tel. 0923/972028; www.facebook.com/syrah.sanvitolocapo; 12:30pm-2pm and 7:30pm-11pm daily; entrées €14-35

Simply prepared, traditional Sicilian fare is served in an inviting small restaurant with indoor and outdoor seating. It's a convenient place to try the local specialty, fish couscous, right in the heart of the main strip in San Vito lo Capo. The menu is mainly seafood-focused, and although the plating is a bit retro, the flavors pack a punch.

Bar Gelateria la Sirenetta

Via Savoia, 2; tel. 0923/974386; www.gelaterialasirenetta.it; 8am-1am Tues., 6am-2am Wed.-Mon.; €3-10

La Sirenetta has been around since 1969. Just steps from San Vito's sand beach, this historic ice cream shop is known for its unique homemade gelsomino jasmine gelato and the town's specialty dessert, caldofreddo, an ice cream sundae with hot chocolate, whipped cream, and rum-soaked sponge cake.

Accommodations
Timbuktu Ostello

Via Piersanti Mattarella, 199; tel. 329/6170129; www.siciliantimbuktu.com; single beds from €24 per night

The Timbuktu hostel is a great option for solo travelers or students who don't want to spend a lot on accommodations. The hostel has hammocks in the garden and ample common area spaces, and can organize activities or Italian language lessons for guests during their stay. The friendly, local staff at Timbuktu have created a welcoming and affordable location for backpackers and budget travelers. It is located less than 20 minutes on foot from the sand beach in San Vito lo Capo.

★ B&B Baglio Giammaccaro

Via Frassino, 1, Custonaci; tel. 335/7065749; www.bagliogiammaccaro.it; from €145

Guests with their own mode of transportation will absolutely love staying at the Baglio Giammaccaro in Custonaci, just 15 minutes outside San Vito lo Capo. The nearby beaches at Cala Calazza, the Spiaggia di Màcari, and the Caletta del Bue Marino give you a taste of Sicily's wild, natural side with rocky sea access and smaller crowds. Hidden between the mountains of the Monte Cofano Nature Reserve and the sea, Baglio Giammaccaro offers luxurious country-style rooms and suites along with bike rentals, a barbecue area, terraces and gardens, an outdoor swimming pool, and spa services.

Hotel Mira Spiaggia

Via Litoranea, 6; tel. 0923/972355; www.miraspiaggia. it; rooms from €150

Although San Vito is not known for its luxury accommodations, this popular three-star hotel is a decent option for those looking for hotel amenities, restaurant, spa, and 24-hour concierge services, right on the beachfront of town.

Getting There

San Vito lo Capo is a 45-minute drive from **Trapani** (24 mi/39 km) on SP20 to SP18 and SP16. It is also accessible by car with a 1.5-hour drive from **Palermo** (67 mi/108 km) along the E90 highway to SS731 in Alcamo and SS187 to SP16.

Autoservizi Russo (www.russoauto-servizi.it) also offers bus service connecting Palermo's main terminal on Via Fazello (2 hours 35 minutes; €9.40 each way) or Piazza Repubblica in Castellammare del Golfo (1 hour; €6.40 each way) with San Vito lo Capo on Via Mattarella.

Trapani

According to Greek mythology, the sickle of the goddess Demeter fell into the sea to form the crescent-shaped city that is now known as Trapani. Located on Sicily's western coast, it's the sixth-largest port in Italy, important for salt production and tuna fishing and known for its sea salt flats, fresh seafood, and excellent white wines. Many people arrive here to embark on the ferry to the Aegadian Islands, off the coast. Trapani's beautiful, walkable city center has well-preserved architecture dating back to the 14th century, including palaces and churches with Gothic and Baroque influences. Just east of Trapani is its sister town of Erice, perched on its eponymous mountain. Take the funicular to the summit for a beautiful view of the city.

Around Trapani are more treasures to explore. The province is filled with small swimming coves, especially along the coast from Trapani to San Vito lo Capo, as well as unparalleled glimpses into Sicily's ancient Greek past. To the east, you'll find the Lo Zingaro Nature Reserve, a protected coastal paradise that was the first of its kind in Sicily, and the Temple of Segesta, a spectacularly well-preserved Doric temple from the 5th century BCE. Twenty miles (32 km) south of Trapani, plan a day in the beautiful city of Marsala to explore its famous vineyards and rediscover the long-lost history of marsala wine; continue southeast along the coast to the ancient ruins of the Greek settlement of Selinunte, the largest archaeological site in all of Europe.

SIGHTS

The historic center of Trapani is concentrated on a slender peninsula protruding west into the sea, with the port of Trapani in a sheltered cove to the south, and the Torre di Ligny tower and museum at the peninsula's western tip. Main road Corso Vittorio Emanuele runs from the tower through the center, with pedestrian areas that have myriad options for dining and drinking.

Museo Civico Torre di Ligny

Via Torre di Ligny, 37; tel. 333/8081462; 10am-1pm Mon.-Sat.; €2

This 17th-century tower, used as a watchtower and garrison to protect Trapani from the sea, sits at the very tip of a pier jutting off from the city's historic center. Today it houses an archaeological museum devoted to the history of Trapani, but the real highlight is the view you get from the top of the tower—especially at sunset.

Museo Regionale Conte Agostino Pepoli

Via Conte Agostino Pepoli, 180; tel. 0923/553269; 9am-5pm Tues.-Sat., 9am-noon Sun.; €6

Trapani

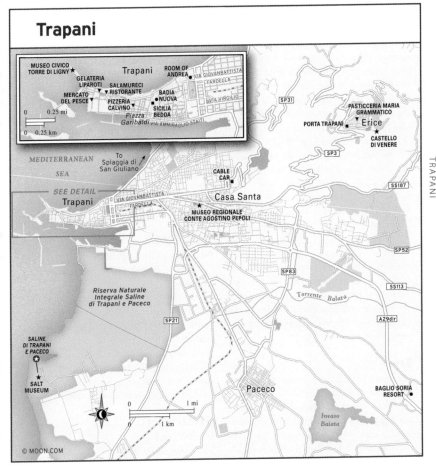

Check out the Museo Regionale Conte Agostino Pepoli to see the private collection of jewels, sculptures, paintings, coral, silver, and metalwork donated by the Pepoli, Fardella, and Hernandez noble families of Trapani and Erice. The museum also features historical exhibitions and archaeological findings discovered on-site, inside the convent of Padri Carmelitani, a structure that dates back to the early 1300s and today houses the museum.

★ Saline di Trapani e Paceco

Via Libica; tel. 092/3867700; www.wwfsalineditrapani. it; open 24 hours; free

Trapani is an ideal place for the extraction of sea salt. At the Saline di Trapani e Paceco, or Sea Salt Pans of Trapani and Paceco, the long, hot Sicilian summers, strong, dry winds coming off Northern Africa, humidity, and high salinity of the Mediterranean Sea are perfect for a love affair between sun, wind, and seawater. People have been producing sea salt in this area for centuries—the first written record dates back to the year 1,000. Artisanal Sicilian sea salt is world-renowned for being untreated, unrefined, and naturally rich in magnesium and potassium. Most gift shops and even grocery stores in Trapani and Marsala will sell local sea salt.

South of the port of Trapani, leaving the

city by the SP21, also known as the **Via del Sale** or Salt Road, the shores are lined with a patchwork of wide sea salt pans. Since 1995, almost 2,500 acres (1,000 ha) of this area have been protected by the World Wildlife Fund Italia through a partnership with the region of Sicily. This special terrain is a living, breathing ecosystem, continuously changing all year round, playing host to migrating birds like grey parrots, flamingos, wild ducks, and herons. You can simply pull off on the side of the road to take a look at the salt pans, colored in shades varying from white to lilac and pastel blue. Or, spend some time at the **Salt Museum** (Museo di Sale; Via Chiusa, Nubia; tel. 0923/867061; www.museodelsale. it; 9:30am-7pm daily; €2.50), housed in the former home of a salt worker built in the 16th century, where you'll learn about salt production and see traditional and modern tools used in the process. The entire landscape is dotted with some 50 medieval windmills, historically used to pump water through the salt pans and grind up the salt.

Erice

The medieval village of Erice, at the top of eponymous Monte Erice (2,500 ft/762 m), overlooks the city of Trapani, with views of the Aegadian Islands and San Vito lo Capo, a rocky cape protruding into the sea, to the west. Its labyrinthine layout of narrow, cobbled alleyways was actually built to slow down and trap invaders, but today it's a great place to get lost on purpose on a leisurely stroll. Erice has around 27,000 residents and extraordinarily includes over 60 churches. The village is accessible via a scenic 10-minute **cable car** ride on the Funivia Erice (Via Capua, 4; tel. 0923/569306; www.funiviaerice.it; €5.50 one-way, €9 round-trip). The valley station in Trapani is located on SP31 heading toward Erice on the corner of Via Capua, while the mountaintop station, Erice Vetta, is located on Via delle Pinete. Most tourists start their visit at the **Porta Trapani** village gate (Piazza Porta Trapani; www.comune.erice.tp.it), an impressive, arched entry into a tall stone wall.

The drive from Trapani takes at least 25 minutes, along SP31.

Castello di Venere
Largo Castello; tel. 329/7823035; 10am-6:30pm daily; €4

On the southeastern side of the outskirts of Erice, the Castello di Venere was built by the Normans in the 12th century, allegedly on the site of the ancient Temple of Venus, from which it gets its name. For a small fee, visitors can access an interior courtyard with a green lawn, with panoramic views (often through defensive arrow slits) of Trapani and the coast of western Sicily below.

BEACHES
Spiaggia di San Giuliano
Lungomare Dante Alighieri; www.trovaspiagge.it/ san-giuliano

On the northern outskirts of Trapani is the city beach, Spiaggia di San Giuliano. This 1-mile (1.6-km) stretch of fine, golden sand is equipped with lido beach clubs where you can rent umbrellas and lounge chairs, and there is also free public beach access. It's a popular and convenient destination for local Trapanese residents and surfers in summertime.

SHOPPING
Sicilia Bedda
Via Torrearsa, 66; tel. 0923/27509; www.sicilia-bedda. it; 9:30am-midnight Mon.-Sat., 10am-midnight Sun.

This hole-in-the-wall shop in Trapani's Old Town is positively packed with made-in-Sicily crafts and gourmet gifts, including world-famous Trapani sea salt. Grab some hand-painted ceramics or bring a taste of Trapani home with you in carry-on-friendly packages.

FOOD AND BARS

Trapani's local specialty is **fish couscous,** a steaming dish of couscous topped with fish and served with a seafood broth. Commonly eaten in countries in the Middle East and

1: cable car between Erice and Trapani **2:** Castello di Venere in Erice **3:** Saline di Trapani e Paceco

around North Africa, this dish was brought to Sicily by the Arabs and has kept its place in Trapani's cuisine. You won't find couscous in any other part of Italy, so take advantage while you're here! A **pane cunzatu** sandwich packed with anchovies, olive oil, oregano, tomato, cheese, and olives is a simple lunch to take with you for a beach day, available in most bakeries and bars. The traditional pasta to order here is the **busiate con pesto trapanese,** a twirled corkscrew-shaped noodle with a red pesto made from almonds, garlic, chili pepper, basil, and fresh tomato.

Trapani
Mercato del Pesce

Via Cristoforo Colombo, 3; 6am-2pm daily

Trapani does not have a central outdoor food market like other large Sicilian cities. Instead, there are vendors on most corners selling fruit and vegetables. The main event is the fish market, located near the port. Vendors sell just-caught Mediterranean fish like sardines, red tuna, mackerel, swordfish, and small red mullet. Squid, cuttlefish, and sea urchin come and go with the seasons, but you'll find that everything is extremely fresh.

Pizzeria Calvino

Via Nunzio Nasi, 71; tel. 0923/21464; 7pm-midnight Wed.-Thurs. and Sat.-Sun., 7pm-11pm Fri.; pizzas €6.50-13

Locals and tourists gather every night outside this brothel-turned-pizzeria waiting for a pie. You can peek into the kitchen to watch the pizzaioli quickly throwing dough while you wait. Tables are set in tiny alcove rooms, and the pizza arrives already cut into tiny squares for easy eating. The classic local pizza is the rianata, made with sliced cherry tomatoes (instead of tomato sauce), preserved anchovies, Sicilian pecorino cheese, and the namesake dried oregano. Expect casual pizzeria service, and order a few beers for the table while you enjoy a delicious pizza for a low-key night.

Salamureci Ristorante

Piazza Generale Scio, 17; tel. 0923/21728; www. salamureci.it; 12:30pm-2:30pm and 7:30pm-11pm Tues.-Sun.; main courses €15-24, tasting menu €50

Following in the footsteps of his father, young chef/owner Michele Bellezza offers innovative dishes focusing on local ingredients and fresh seafood from Trapani and Mazara del Vallo in this Trapanese restaurant dating back to 2011 in the historic center of town. There is seating available in its internal courtyard space or main indoor dining room. Chef Bellezza aims to redefine traditional flavors using Slow Food Presidium ingredients, ancient grains, strong Sicilian cheeses, and seasonal produce. Make sure to try his couscous, known in town as one of the very best.

★ Gelateria Liparoti

Viale delle Sirene, 21; tel. 389/2998096; 4pm-midnight Tues.-Sat., noon-2pm and 4pm-midnight Sun.; cones €1.50, cups €1.50-3.50, gelato with brioche €3.50

This artisanal gelato shop has unique flavors, like fig and walnut, peanut butter, ginger pear, licorice, watermelon, Sicilian mango, and mulberry.

Erice
★ Pasticceria Maria Grammatico

Via Vittorio Emanuele, 14; tel. 0923/869390; www. mariagrammatico.it; 9am-midnight daily May-Oct., 9am-9pm Tues.-Sun. Nov.-Apr.; under €5

The pièce de résistance of a visit to Erice is Pasticceria Maria Grammatico, where you can taste the handmade delicacies from the "pastry queen of Sicily." Maria Grammatico's incredible life story includes growing up in a Sicilian convent, where she "stole with her eyes" unwritten recipes by watching the nuns through a crack in the floor above the kitchen. At Pasticceria Maria Grammatico, stock up on almond pastries like belli e brutti, lingua di suocera, bocconcini, perfectly sculpted marzipan fruit, bucellati cookies stuffed with dried figs, and perhaps best of all, warm genovese—big, round, baked short-crust sweets filled with yellow pastry cream.

ACCOMMODATIONS

Badia Nuova

Via Badia Nuova, 33; tel. 0923/24054; www.
badianuova.it; from €75

The Badia Nuova hotel is centrally located in the pedestrian area of the city of Trapani, just 150 feet (46 m) from the beach. It has a beautiful rooftop bar and tastefully furnished suites and apartments with balconies and private terraces.

Room of Andrea

Palazzo Platamone, Viale Regina Margherita, 31; tel.
0923/365728; www.roomofandrea.it; from €148

This four-star hotel is located across from the Villa Regina Margherita park in Trapani's historic center, easily reachable by train, bus, car, or ferry. Guests can choose from the small selection of charming rooms with traditional tiled flooring and simple, elegant decor. An ample continental breakfast is served on the first floor each morning, and the concierge staff at the front desk can assist with recommendations and programming for your stay in Trapani. Paid parking is available in the large lot directly across the street.

Baglio Soria Resort

Contrada Soria; tel. 0923/861679; www.firriato-baglio-soria-trapani.it; €160

Located on the Firriato winery estate, only 20 minutes outside the city of Trapani, Baglio Soria is a charming 17th-century courtyard surrounded by vineyards and olive orchards overlooking the sea. Chef Andrea Macca's dishes are exquisitely plated, bringing together the natural flavors of the island in the resort's fine-dining restaurant. Wine tastings and cooking lessons are available upon request. Guests of the elegant resort can enjoy afternoons relaxing at the panoramic pool or in the wellness center.

GETTING THERE AND AROUND

To get to Trapani from Palermo, you'll have to either have your own rental car or take a bus; there is no direct train from Palermo.

Once you arrive, Trapani can easily be explored on foot. To get to the mountaintop village of Erice, you'll want to take the **Funivia Erice** (Via Capua, 4; tel. 0923/569306; www.funiviaerice.it; €5.50 one-way, €9 round-trip) funicular, with stations located on SP31 and Via Capua in Trapani and Via delle Pinete in Erice.

By Car

From **Palermo,** it's a 1-hour 15-minute drive to Trapani (about 60 mi/97 km) via E90 and A29dir/E933. Parking in Trapani is available in the Piazza Vittorio Emanuele, near the beach on the northern coast of the city, and within walking distance from the historic center of town. Paid parking spots (€1 per hour) are marked with a blue stripe and tickets will need to be purchased from a nearby blue kiosk machine.

By Train

The main train station is serviced by **TrenItalia** (Piazza Umberto I; www.trenitalia.com) with simple transfers available from **Marsala** (32 minutes; €3.30) or **Mazara del Vallo** (1 hour; €4.40). The train is not recommended for transportation from Palermo; in this case the bus is a faster option.

By Bus

The **Segesta Autolinee** (Via Fazello; tel. 06/164160; www.segesta.it) bus line has multiple daily services from Palermo to Trapani (2 hours; €9.60). Tickets can be purchased ahead of time online or at the Segesta ticket office in the Palermo bus station. Enter the Palermo Centrale train station, follow signs through the back of the station, and exit on the right side of the building to find the newly renovated bus terminal. The final stop on the bus line from Palermo to Trapani will leave you at the port of Trapani, exactly where you need to be if catching a ferry to the nearby Aegadian Islands or the overnight ferry to Pantelleria.

By Ferry

In the main port of Trapani, in front of Piazza

Garibaldi, guests can arrive/depart via hydrofoil with connections to the nearby Aegadian Islands (30 minutes to Favignana, €17; 25 minutes to Levanzo, €15; and 1 hour 20 minutes to Marettimo, €20) or Pantelleria (2 hours 30 minutes, €43, available only in summer) through **Liberty Lines** (Via Ammiraglio Staiti, 55/61; tel. 0923/873813; www.libertylines.it). Year-round ferry services connecting Trapani with the island of Pantelleria are available through **Siremar** (Viale Regina Elena, 12/30; tel. 090/5737; www.siremar.it) with the optional addition of a vehicle (€135). Pantelleria to Trapani ferries depart at noon (5 hours 45 minutes, €47 standard rate, €53 reserved chair seating, €84 overnight cabin) and from Trapani to Pantelleria at 11pm (7 hours 30 minutes).

★ The Aegadian Islands

The Aegadian Islands (Isole Egadi in Italian) archipelago, just 6 miles (9.7 km) off the coast of Trapani, are a west coast, low-key alternative to the Aeolian Islands between Sicily and Calabria. With three main inhabited islands—Favignana, Marettimo, and Levanzo—and two minor islands (Formica and Maraone between Levanzo and Sicily), these popular summer destinations turn back into sleepy fishing villages in the off-season (Nov.-Mar.) and are still relatively off international tourists' radars. Notable for the Battle of the Egadi in 241 BCE, which ended the First Punic War, the history of these islands runs deep with evidence of Neolithic and Paleolithic paintings, engravings, and graffiti in the caves of Levanzo, dating back at least 10,000 years.

The islands are also prime destinations for hiking, sailing, and other water sports including stand-up paddleboarding, scuba diving, and snorkeling. It is a small but mountainous archipelago covering a total area of only 15 square miles (39 sq km). Characterized by their uncontaminated nature, the waters are preserved as the largest Italian marine reserve (since 1991). The marine reserve is divided into four areas (zones A, B, C, and D), each with its own regulations on underwater excursions, bathing and diving, and sport and commercial fishing. The cuisine here is almost completely based on fresh seafood and fish, with local specialties including Trapanese couscous, sardine dishes, pasta with sea urchin or patella sea snails, and anything and everything made from Mediterranean red tuna.

If you have the time and need a vacation from your get-up-and-go Sicily vacation, a day trip to the Aegadian Islands is a great bet. The best beaches on the islands are mainly accessible by boat, and they vary from untouched, deep blue swimming holes to pebbled and rocky coasts. These islands are easily explored without the need for a car and can be reached by ferry from Trapani and Marsala.

Getting There and Around

Liberty Lines (tel. 0923/873813; www.libertylines.it) offers multiple crossings per day to the Egadi Islands from **Trapani** (Port of Trapani, Viale Regina Elena) and **Marsala** (Porto di Lylibeo, Lungomare Mediterraneo, 3). The most frequent crossings run to and from Favignana (30 minutes; €13-17), but you can also find transfers to continue on to Levanzo (25 minutes; €13) and Marettimo (1 hour 15 minutes; €23). One-way ferry service connects Favignana with Levanzo (10 minutes; €5.50) and Marettimo (45 minutes; €10.50), and Levanzo and Marettimo (30 minutes; €9.80).

Tours
Escursione Favignana

Via dei Ranucoli, 19, Trapani; tel. 350/1356353; www. escursionefavignana.com; starting at €75
Book your day trip (10am-6pm) to Favignana and Levanzo from the port of Trapani.

Motorboats equipped with awnings for shade will take you to Cala Azzurra, Bue Marino, and Cala Rossa with free time for swims throughout the day. Refreshments and fresh seasonal fruit are available on board. Pack your backpack, swimsuit, towels, and a light lunchbox to get ready for your adventure at sea.

FAVIGNANA

The butterfly-shaped island of Favignana is the largest (7.3 sq mi/19 sq km) and most popular destination of the three main Aegadian Islands, since it is the closest to mainland Sicily and offers the most nightlife and restaurant options. Easily reachable by ferry service from Marsala and Trapani, Favignana was once the prime producing region for tuna products and tinned bluefish. Surrounded by cliffs, the island's rocky beach destinations remain a bit off-the-radar for foreign tourists. The waters are prized for being crystal clear and ideal for snorkeling or diving because of the light-colored seafloor.

Orientation

On an island with only 4,300 inhabitants, the small town is concentrated at the center of the northern coast and can be explored on foot from the port where ferry boats arrive. The town of Favignana is filled with souvenir shops, boutiques, restaurants, cocktail bars, pharmacies, tourism booths, and the main sightseeing destination—where visitors can tour the old tuna factory.

Sights

Former Tuna Factory of Favignana e Formica
(Ex-Stabilimento Florio delle Tonnare di Favignana e Formica)

Via Amendola, 29; tel. 324/5631991; www.visitsicily. info/en/ex-stabilimento-tonnara-florio-di-favignana-e-formica; 10am-2pm daily; adults €6, reduced rates €3
This 19th-century tuna cannery was in operation until 1977, and similar to the tonnara in Scopello, it was owned by the affluential Florio family. A one-hour guided tour is

included in the entrance ticket price. The old tonnara currently hosts art exhibitions and special events.

Santa Caterina Castle
(Castello di Santa Caterina)

www.egadivacanze.it/favignana/castelli/il-castello-di-santa-caterina.html
Although this 9th-century Saracen castle has been completely abandoned and is deemed unsafe to visit, the panoramic views from this area give you a wonderful overview of the entire island and shores of Favignana. The limestone castle sits at 1,017 feet (310 m) above sea level on the top of Monte di Santa Caterina in the center of the island. It can be reached on a one-hour uphill trek via a cobblestone walking path off the Strada Sterrata road. It is recommended that you depart for this trip no later than 8am during summertime, or in the late afternoon, leaving enough time to make it back before dark.

Garden of the Impossible
(Giardino dell'Impossibile)

Villa Margherita Residence: Strada Comunale Corso, 10, Contrada Bue Marino; tel. 331/4601817; www. villamargherita.it/giardinodellimpossibile; reservations available May-Oct.; guided tours €20 per person
The Hypogeum Gardens are located on Maria Gabriella Campo's eden at Villa Margherita. The unfathomable breadth of calcarenite limestone quarries, botanical gardens, and "pirrere"-mined caves dating back to the 700s make up an oasis in a place where she was told that nothing could ever grow. Visits can be organized only with advance notice. Guided walking tours of the gardens last 2 hours 30 minutes. Guests can travel to the Garden of the Impossible from the main ferry port with a 10-minute taxi ride, 45-minute walk, or by electric bicycle.

Beaches

This will be the liveliest island in the area during summertime (May-Sept.). Favignana is the only one of the Aegadian Islands with a sand beach near the main harbor and can

be perfect for travelers of all ages. The swimming conditions in Favignana are often calm with clear waters.

Spiaggia Praia

Via Amendola; open 24 hours; free

A stone's throw from the ferry port, guests can get their first dip in Favignana at this free public beach with sandy shores. Bars and restaurants are located nearby and can be a great place to relax for the afternoon or get a drink before dinner at sunset.

Scogliera di Cala Rossa

Cala Rossa

This picturesque, rocky beach with clear turquoise water is located on the easternmost part of the north coast. The name of the beach comes from a violent battle in 241 BCE between the Romans and Carthaginians that took place right here on the shores and stained the waters of the sea with blood. Cala Rossa is surrounded by splendid tuff caves and cliffs. Nowadays, its transparent, crystal clear water and stone shore is celebrated as one of the most beautiful beaches in Italy. To reach Cala Rossa, continue north on Via Frascia to Strada del Cimitero. Make a right onto Contrada Torretta; at the end of the road it turns into a dirt path that leads down to the water in only another 10 minutes. The 2.7-mile (4.4-km) walk will take about one hour.

Lido Burrone

Costiera Mezzogiorno; tel. 349/8789528

This beach club with sandy shores is the only place with on-site amenities on the southern coast of the island, a 10-minute drive from the main harbor.

Scogliera Cala Azzurra

Strada Sterrata; tel. 328/9322431

This cove is located on the southeastern part of Favignana. It's the most popular bay for boats stopping in for the afternoon. The rocky shores of Cala Azzurra can be reached with a 10-minute drive from the main harbor, although most of its visitors will arrive by boat in summertime.

Shopping

Camparia Bottega

Via Armando Diaz, 18; tel. 0923/1987572; www. camparia.com/bottega; 10am-1pm and 5:30pm-10:30pm daily June, 10am-12:30pm and 6pm-11:30pm July-Sept.

This newly opened, female-owned boutique is sure to fill your suitcase with goodies to take home from Favignana. Filled with jewelry, clothing, housewares, woven baskets, ceramics, and books, the style oozing out of this shop will surprise you.

Food and Bars

Formica

Via Roma, 52; tel. 340/2126169; www.formicaosteria. com; open for dinner 7:30pm daily; €15-24

At Formica, Federica and Taka use their combined passion and respect for the sea by creating a range of blended dishes playing with Mediterranean and Asian flavors. Their daily menus follow the seasons and highlight local fishers, farmers, and natural winemakers.

Camparia Lounge

Via Armando Diaz, 26; tel. 320/4630936; www. camparia.com; breakfast and lunch 7:30am-4:30pm daily and aperitivo, dinner, and late-night drinks 7:30pm-2am daily July-Sept. only; cocktails €15, dishes from €18-23

This fully restored stone building originally used for tuna boat repair and fishing equipment storage in the 1870s has been transformed into a lounge restaurant open only in summertime. Outdoor tables overlook the water and the old tonnara tuna processing center.

Monique Concept Bar

Via Vittorio Emanuele, 22; tel. 0923/1781920; www. facebook.com/moniquebarfavignana; 7am-2pm and 6pm-3am daily

This is a lively spot for sharing a few drinks with friends at aperitivo time or meeting new

1: arriving in Favignana 2: Scogliera di Cala Rossa

people while traveling solo. The outdoor seating gets snagged up quickly since it's the perfect place for people-watching as boats pull into the port and the town begins to fill up. Stop by for the signature and classic cocktails, order a few small bites, and stay for the DJs and live music performances.

Bar Europa Gelateria

Piazza Europa, 16; tel. 0923/922477; 7am-1am daily in summer; €5

Make your way through the lineup of artisanal granita including flavors like lemon, almond milk, pear, banana, mulberry, prickly pear, pistachio, and jasmine. Sit down for a coffee break or try one of their gelati.

Accommodations

★ La Casa dell'Arancio

Via C. Colombo, 14; tel. 0923/1941541; www. lacasadellarancio.it; from €90

Just a five-minute walk from the harbor and ferry terminal in the town center of Favignana, La Casa dell'Arancio has rooms and suites available with amenities including Wi-Fi, air-conditioning, television, an outside courtyard space, breakfast, a communal terrace, and special assistance with transfers, bike rentals, and touring recommendations.

Elegantly placed North African furniture in the simply decorated rooms give the place a warm, welcoming feel.

Cave Bianche Hotel

Strada Comunale Fanfalo; tel. 0923/925451; www. cavebianchehotel.it; from €150

As the name suggests, it is in fact a hotel built within the cliffs of an open-air white stone cave. A four-star hotel in terms of its location and outdoor spaces, it has spartan-style bedrooms that are perfect for a beach holiday. Bed and breakfast only; half- or full-board meal options are available on request. Cave Bianche is located on the southern side of the island, close to Cala Azzura's rocky shores.

Getting There and Around

The best way to explore the Aegadian Islands, and Favignana in particular, is with a sailboat/catamaran, rented gommone, or by ferry.

From Trapani, there are multiple ferry and hydrofoil crossings per day to Favignana. All ferries depart from the port of Trapani (Viale Regina Elena). **Liberty Lines** (tel. 0923/873813; www.libertylines.it) offers a 30-minute aliscafo hydrofoil from Trapani to the **Favignana ferry terminal** on the northern coast of the island (€15).

seafood at Formica

From Marsala (Porto di Lylibeo, Lungomare Mediterraneo, 3), Liberty Lines offers 30-minute ferry crossings to Favignana (€13.30).

One-way ferry service with Liberty Lines also connects Favignana with Levanzo in just 10 minutes for €5.50. The ferry from Favignana to Marettimo takes 45 minutes (€10).

On the island, you can rent a scooter or bicycle with **Noleggio Isidoro** (Via Giuseppe Mazzini, 40; tel. 347/3233058; www.noleggio isidoro.it; 8am-7pm daily). Small cars, bicycles, e-bikes, scooters, and motorboats can be rented through **Grimaldi** (Lungomare Duilio, 14; tel. 339/1609239; www.noleggiogrimaldi.it; 8am-7pm daily) or **Noleggio Brezza Marina** (Via Molo S. Leonardo, 9; tel. 347/3004522; www.noleggioautofavignana.com).

Taxi transfers can be booked by phone through **Favignana Taxi Service** (Piazza Madrice, 73; tel. 338/8388800) and cost approximately €15 per ride to reach most beaches and accommodations from the main port.

MARETTIMO

Though not the smallest of the three main islands, Marettimo is the least developed, with hiking trails crisscrossing its mountainous and rocky landscape, and cats roaming free in search of a quick seaside snack. The ancient name of the island was Hierà Nèsos ("sacred island" in Greek).

Marettimo is the wildest, greenest, and most mountainous island of the Egadi archipelago. Its rich biodiversity stems from its ancient detachment from the mainland, with over 500 unique plant species and a considerable population of donkeys, horses, goats, and peregrine falcons. In the mid-19th century, the native Marettimari, originating from the Spaniards, emigrated to areas such as Portugal, Northern Africa, and Alaska to work in the salmon fishing industry.

The dolomite and limestone island has only 300 year-round residents and is supported these days by tourism, mostly during the summer period. It is a popular destination for boat tours from Trapani and Marsala, and is accessible mainly with ferry transfers from mainland Sicily. It is typically just a brief day trip from mainland Sicily, but charter boat tours will spend a few days here during their programs.

Orientation

Ferries arrive in the minuscule central harbor

Punta Troia Castle

at **Porto Scalo Nuovo** on the eastern side of Marettimo. All the bars, cafés, restaurants, and grocery shops are concentrated in this area and can be reached on foot. Punta Troia Castle is located on the northeastern tip of the island, 2.4 miles (3.9 km) north of the harbor. The rest of the island is not easily explored on foot. The coves and swimming spots around Marettimo are often visited only by boat, making a boat rental or tour almost necessary to make the best of a day here. Only residents are permitted to have cars on this island.

Sights

Punta Troia Castle (Castello di Punta Troia)

tel. 347/8216676; www.isoladimarettimo.com; 10:30am-6pm daily; €4

This hilltop watchtower, dating back to the Saracen period, sits at 380 feet (116 m) above sea level on the Punta Troia promontory of the Aegadian island of Marettimo. Around 1140, King Roger II transformed it into a real castle, then in the late 1700s it became a prison incarcerating 52 political prisoners within an old cistern referred to as "the pit" in 1793 before being abolished by King Ferdinand II in 1844. The castle can be reached on foot in about two hours from the village of Marettimo or by boat with a 10-minute walk up the hill. In July and August, it will be extremely hot, so bring water with you and wear sturdy shoes for hiking. The journey to get to the castle is in itself the core of this experience, and the castle is considered a main highlight on the island for the breathtaking panoramic views from the top.

Beaches

Spiaggetta dello Scalo Vecchio

Located in the island's main town and port, this is the first beach you'll spot when you arrive in Marettimo by ferry. It is a prime location for **snorkeling.**

La Praia dei Nacchi

tel. 368/3438107

For those looking for a more secluded and natural area than the beach at the port, the pebbled La Praia dei Nacchi at the southern tip of the island can be a better option, reached with a 25-minute walk or accessible by sea with a boat.

Hiking

Marettimo has a hot and dry climate, and hiking is best enjoyed in spring and autumn. However, the popular time of year is summer, when any treks should be initiated either early in the morning or later in the afternoon because of the intense heat. Make sure to pack lots of water and everything else you'll need for exploring the island on foot. Sturdy hiking shoes or sneakers are highly recommended.

Castello di Punta Troia Hike

Distance: *2.4 miles (3.9 km) one-way*
Time: *2 hours up and 90 minutes back to town*
Trailhead: *Porto Scalo Vecchio*

From the Scalo Vecchio port, proceed north along the coast on Via Campi, passing the heliport on your left side. After about 0.5 mile (0.8 km), turn left onto the walking path that begins at the foot of the mountain. At 2.1 miles (3.3 km), there is a trail that runs perpendicular across the route, where you'll have access to the sea on either side of the promontory at Scalo Maestro and Cala Maniuni. This is where you can descend for a swim; otherwise continue straight on for the last stretch of the hike, following switchback turns, all the way up to the Punta Troia Castle. For the most part, this trail is challenging, with little to no shade. During the summer, pay attention to high temperatures and plan for an early morning departure. Bring enough drinking water and wear sun protection and sturdy shoes.

Boat Tours

Marettimo Giro dell'Isola con Pippo

Via Umberto, 44; tel. 327/7688194; www. marettimoconpippo.com; 9:30am-4:30pm daily May-Sept.

Departing from the Molo di Scalo Vecchio port, locals offer boating excursions around Marettimo including private trips (€240 for up to 8 guests, €350 for 9-12 guests) and two daily island trips (€35 per person for 3.5 hours). The morning program departs at 10:30am, and guests for the afternoon tour embark at 3pm. Guests can refresh with stops for swimming, visit the grotto caves, and enjoy seafaring tales and history from the captain.

Food and Bars
La Cambusa
Via Giuseppe Garibaldi, 5; tel. 338/3178711; www. facebook.com/lacambusamarettimo; 9am-1pm and 5pm-10pm daily; €5-10
Stop into this deli for your cambusa (the groceries stocked up to bring aboard a boat), stay for an aperitivo drink with snacks, or enjoy a zero-frills sit-down dinner. The large deli counter is piled high with cured meats, cheeses, and prepared foods like stuffed tomatoes, meatballs, marinated sun-dried tomatoes and oil-preserved vegetables, and caponata. La Cambusa can make sandwiches or charcuterie platters or pack up some ready-to-eat foods to take away.

Il Pirata Ristorante
Via Scalo Vecchio, 27; tel. 0923/923027; www. ilpiratamarettimo.it; noon-2pm and 5pm-11pm daily; €25-50
Make sure to call ahead to book a table on the enclosed terrace of this waterfront restaurant. Marettimo is a small island and there are not many options for dining out, especially within walking distance of the port. It's a family-owned restaurant, now managed by Luana and Anna, the daughters of original owners Franco and Michelina Carriglio. Il Pirata is known for its zuppa di aragosta, a stewed tomato-based lobster broth served family-style in a big metal bowl with pieces of broken spaghetti and butterflied spiny lobster shells on the side.

Accommodations
Marettimo Residence
Via Telegrafo, 3; tel. 0923/923202; www. marettimoresidence.it; from €90
Only a five-minute walk from the ferry port, this four-star hotel offers simply appointed beach house stays for those looking to spend a few nights in Marettimo. It was built with natural materials with an aim to respect the environment, using solar panels, water purification for irrigating the gardens, and filtration for drinking water. This small holiday village of sorts includes 30 apartments and 10 suites. Small pets are allowed upon request, and staff can organize excursions such as donkey rides, snorkel or scuba diving lessons, and boat tours.

Getting There and Around
From Trapani, there are multiple ferry crossings per day for all three of the Aegadian Islands, departing from the port of Trapani (Viale Regina Elena). **Liberty Lines** (tel. 0923/873813; www.libertylines.it) offers a 1-hour 15-minute trip to **Porto Scalo Nuovo** in Marettimo (€18).

From Marsala (Porto di Lylibeo, Lungomare Mediterraneo, 3), Liberty Lines offers 30-minute ferry crossings to Favignana (€11.10); from there you can transfer to continue on to Marettimo. When first arriving in Favignana, the ferry to Marettimo takes 45 minutes (€10.50), or take a 30-minute trip from Levanzo to Marettimo for €9.80.

Once on the island, Marettimo is best explored on foot.

LEVANZO
Populated with only 450 people, the smallest Aegadian island, Levanzo (2 sq mi/5.2 sq km), like the others, is known for its clear waters and picturesque fishing village in the main port.

The island is characterized by pebble beaches, white limestone rocks, clean crystalline water, and the quaint fishing port filled with old wooden boats. The island of Levanzo is also known for the prehistoric cave paintings that were discovered at the Grotta del Genovese cave.

Orientation and Planning
Ferry boats arrive at the main harbor, Cala

Dogana, on the southern coast of Levanzo, and everything you'll need is concentrated in this area. Visitors cannot bring cars with them on the ferry, so you'll be getting around on foot. Levanzo has no private beach clubs or sandy swimming areas. Make sure to bring everything you need for a swim and pack water shoes for small children. You are on an island off an island: Remember that life moves slower and you'll ease right into Sicily's rhythm.

Sights
Grotta del Genovese
tel. 0923/924032; www.grottadelgenovese.it; open only for scheduled visits; tours from €10

Discovered completely by accident in 1949, the Grotta del Genovese ancient limestone cave sanctuary on the northwest coast of Levanzo features paintings and engravings dating back to the Paleolithic and Neolithic periods. Reservations to visit the grotto on a guided tour can be made through the website.

Beaches
On the sleepy fishing island of Levanzo, all the "beaches" you'll find are wild, rocky, and secluded areas, without amenities. They are also all open 24 hours and free to the public.

Cala Fredda's white pebble beach after Punta San Leonardo (10 minutes; 0.3 mi/0.5 km) and **Cala Minnola**'s flat rock shore and emerald waters after the Florio family houses (20 minutes; 0.9 mi/1.4 km) are the two swimming areas most easily reached on foot via a dirt road heading east from the harbor.

Cala Faraglione is on the southwestern coast, overlooking the iconic stone stacks and the island of Marettimo. This pebble beach is a beautiful spot for the golden hour and sunset. Reach it on foot (40 minutes; 0.9 mi/1.4 km) from the harbor, following along the pedestrian path to the northwest on Via Pietrevarate, then an unpaved trail down to the sea. Arriving by electric bike is recommended.

Cala Tramontana, below the limestone cliffs on the northwest part of the island, is much easier to reach by boat. Those who

enjoy a light hike can arrive on foot with a 90-minute (2.6 mi/4.2 km one-way) walk up the hill cutting straight across the island. The path is partially unpaved, unmarked, and without any streetlights. Begin by walking north above the harbor in the direction of the Capo Grosso lighthouse; after 1.7 miles (2.7 km), veer off to the left on an unpaved fork and start the descent to the water. If you get to an old iron gate, you've gone too far; turn back and take the turn where the path splits. This is the largest bay on Levanzo, and as the name suggests, it's the perfect spot to catch the sunset, although make sure you have time to safely walk back to town.

Food and Bars
Ristorante Bar Romano
Via Calvario, 5; tel. 0923/924001; 7:30am-11pm Wed., 8am-11:30pm Thurs.-Tues.; €12-25

The upstairs coffee bar and terrace is open throughout the day, and the restaurant is open for lunch and dinner service. Request a table on the terrace overlooking the water. Following its philosophy of serving locally caught seafood, a note on the bottom of the menu irreverently declares, "In the absence of fresh fish, fresh fish will be used." House specialties feature dishes such as the catch of the day grilled on lava stone, pasta with shrimp and pistachios, or smoked octopus with breadcrumbs and rosemary. Whole fish are brought to the table when ordering, to be selected based on size and priced out by their weight. Make sure to ask for the price per 100 grams or per kilo and the approximate weight of the fish to be sure of what your bill will end up being.

Panetteria La Chicca
Via Calvario, 23; tel. 393/0425562; www.panetteria-la-chicca.business.site; 8:30am-1:30pm and 6pm-8pm daily; €5

Stop by this bakery in the main town for savory snacks, sandwiches, and bread to take away for your beach lunch here on the island

1: Levanzo **2:** port of Levanzo

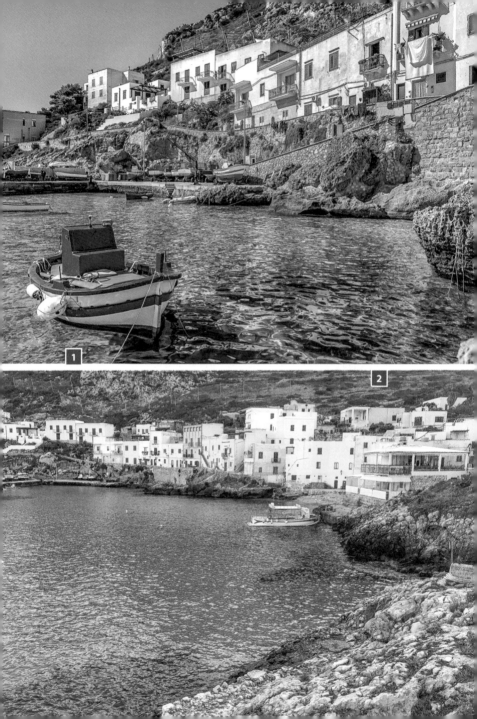

of Levanzo. Try their pane cunzatu made on a mufaletta bun, kabbucio-stuffed pizza baked in the wood-fired oven, arancini (fried rice balls), savory pastries, or traditional deli sandwiches. The staff is friendly and everything is affordable, even the aperitivo specials in the evening, where you can get a spritz cocktail for €3 and charcuterie plates for €5.

Accommodations
Dolcevita Egadi Eco Resort
Via Capo Grosso; tel. 347/5518961; www. dolcevitaegadiresort.com; from €160
Located just 1,640 feet (500 m) above the main harbor and they offer scheduled shuttle services at set times throughout the day. Of course, you can reach the resort on foot along a panoramic path from the main town. This small eco resort features ten simply appointed rooms and a palm tree-lined solarium with sun loungers, barbecue areas, outdoor pool with a view of the sea, hot tub, steam room and a spa/wellness center for massages. Rooms are equipped with a Wi-Fi service, safety deposit box, smoke alarm and fire extinguisher. The Dolcevita team can assist guests with planning hiking, snorkeling, or biking adventures.

Getting There and Around
From Trapani, there are multiple crossings per day for all three of the Aegadian Islands. All ferries depart from the port of Trapani (Viale Regina Elena). **Liberty Lines** (tel. 0923/873813; www.libertylines.it) offers a 25-minute transfer to the ferry terminal on the southern tip of Levanzo (€16).

From Marsala (Porto di Lylibeo, Lungomare Mediterraneo, 3), Liberty Lines offers 30-minute ferry crossings to Favignana (€13); from there you can transfer to continue on to Levanzo.

One-way ferry service with Liberty Lines connects Favignana with Levanzo in just 10 minutes for €5.50, or take a 30-minute trip from Marettimo to Levanzo for €9.80.

Once on the island, Levanzo is best explored on foot.

Pantelleria

Called the "black pearl of the Mediterranean," the volcanic island of Pantelleria, 90 miles (145 km) south of Trapani, is famous for its winemaking, cultivation of olives and capers, rocky beaches, and deep cobalt-blue waters. The entire island became a national park in 2019. The untouched swimming spots, natural hot springs, mountain trekking, fresh local seafood, and passito wine tastings will steal the heart of any adventurous traveler looking to explore the hidden islands off mainland Sicily. Easily accessible with a direct flight with DAT Airlines from Trapani, Palermo, Catania, and a few main cities within Italy, or by ferry service from Trapani, a trip to Pantelleria should last at least three days, but everything can be explored on a deeper level with a week-long stay.

Orientation
The small villages known as frazioni are spread out over the 31-square-mile (80-sq-km) island, which takes about an hour to circumnavigate by car along the perimeter road. Outside of the central town of Pantelleria, the other main areas to explore are Kamma, Gadir, and Scauri. Pantelleria's main town is the central hub for ferry arrivals/departures, shopping, pharmacies, banks, and post offices. Keep in mind that it is also the only place on the island to fill up your rental car or motorino with gas. Scauri on the southern coast has a small port where chartered boats can dock. In summertime, there are great options here for beach bars, gelato, and nightlife. Pantelleria's wineries and vineyards are speckled throughout the island, terraced into the mountains and along the coastline. Make

sure to reserve your accommodations, restaurants, car rentals, and boat tours ahead of time, especially in July and August when the island becomes more than three times as populated as usual.

SIGHTS
Arch of the Elephant
(Arco dell'Elefante)
Cala Levante; open 24 hours; free

The Arch of the Elephant is one of the most recognizable places on the island. The elephant-shaped rock formation seems to arch its trunk out for a dip into the sea.

Lago Specchio di Venere
Contrada Zinedi; open 24 hours; free

Lago Specchio di Venere, the iconic lake known as "Venus's Mirror," is a must-see stop on a trip to Pantelleria. Its thermal hot springs and the soothing mud from the bottom of the lake are said to have healing properties. Keep an eye out in May and September when flamingos pass through the lake on their migration paths. There are generally no services available at the Specchio di Venere lake; one or two trattorie are open only in summertime.

Vineyards

Pantelleria was known as a raisin-producing island before the seedless raisin arrived in Europe and crushed their business. Farmers have been growing vines here for centuries, now making high-quality wines particularly from the native zibibbo grapes, traditionally used to make passito (a dessert wine naturally sweetened with the addition of dried raisins). Top vineyards include:

- **Donnafugata Winery Farmhouse** (Contrada Khamma, 6; tel. 0923/915649; https://visit.donnafugata.it/en/wineries/pantelleria; 11am brunch, 5pm zibibbo wine tasting, 6:30pm wine and food tasting June-Sept.; tastings €24-50)
- **Marco De Bartoli** (Contrada Bukkuram, 9; tel. 0923/918344; www.marcodebartoli.com; by appointment only)

- **Cantina Basile** (Via S. Michele; tel. 0923/917205; www.cantinabasile.it; by appointment only)

BEACHES AND NATURAL POOLS

The best thing to do on Pantelleria is relax by the sea. However, there are no sand beaches on the island; water shoes are recommended for all of its rocky beaches. There are no amenities available at any of these swimming spots, and traveling with small children may be much more difficult than in other parts of Sicily. Visitors should bring along a beach towel and enough water and snacks for the day.

Balata dei Turchi
Località Balata dei Turchi; open 24 hours; free

At the southernmost tip of the island, you'll find one of the best swimming spots, Balata dei Turchi. Here, solidified lava creates a sloped, rocky ramp into the sea surrounded by stunning cliffs and clean, clear water.

Laghetto delle Ondine
Punta Spadillo; open 24 hours; free

Located a 20-minute walk from the parking site near the Punta Spadillo lighthouse on the north coast of the island, the emerald-colored Laghetto delle Ondine is a natural saltwater pool and another pleasant place to swim and sunbathe, especially on days when the sea is rough.

Cala Tramontana
Tracino, Khamma; open 24 hours; free

Cala Tramontana is a small cove on the eastern side of the island, not far from the Arco dell'Elefante, with a constructed sundeck that gives visitors a nice place to rest.

FOOD
Ristorante Altamarea
Via Scauri Porto, 5; tel. 0923/918115; www.facebook.com/altamareaclub; 8pm-11:30pm Tues.-Sun. Easter-mid-Oct.; entrées €12-20

Located in the port of Scauri on the southern coast of the island, Ristorante Altamarea is a

great option for a more upscale meal including antipasti, pastas, main course options, and desserts. **Kayà Kayà,** its summer "chiringuito" beach bar (open for lunch 12:30pm-3pm) is the summer hot spot.

Osteria Il Principe e il Pirata

Strada Punta Karace, Gadir; tel. 0923/691108; www. ilprincipeeilpirata.it; open for lunch and dinner June-Sept.; entrées €16-23

Osteria il Principe e il Pirata offers traditional Pantescan fare like couscous, the bacio pantesco dessert, and fresh seafood dishes using high-quality ingredients. It's a notable restaurant, included in the Slow Food guide in Italy.

Themà Restaurant & Lounge

Via Monastero, Scauri; tel. 0923/408120; www. sikeliapantelleria.com; open to the public for lunch noon-3pm, aperitifs on the roof, and dinners 7pm-11pm daily; reservations required

In the mood to splurge? Try an island dining experience like no other at Themà Restaurant & Lounge at the Sikelia Luxury Resort. Pantelleria was never known for its fine-dining options before, but this five-star resort took care of it. Beautifully plated and creatively designed dishes by chef Roberto Conti play with Arab-African flavors and top-notch ingredients.

Il Gelato di Ulisse

Via Scauri Basso; tel. 338/2456933; www.facebook. com/IlGelatoDiUlisse; 7am-midnight daily in summer

After a long day in the sun at the port of Scauri on the southwestern coast of the island, treat yourself to an artisanal gelato from Il Gelato di Ulisse. Test out the innovative flavors like chocolate with salted capers!

ACCOMMODATIONS

Couples, families, and groups of friends often lean toward renting their own private house during a vacation to Pantelleria. Look for dammusi rentals. These traditional stone houses of Arab origin are uniquely found only on this island.

Le Case Del Principe Pantelleria

Contrada Kattibuale, tel. 338/7484553; www. lecasedelprincipepantelleria.com; vacation home rentals Mar.-Oct.; from €630 per week

Le Case Del Principe Pantelleria is a group of seven simply appointed vacation homes, built in the 1970s by Prince Paolo Sallier de La Tour and his wife Costanza Tasca d'Almerita, who created a little oasis of peace and relaxation in the place they loved. Not far from the village/port of Pantelleria, they are among the very few places on the island to have direct access to the sea! Fully equipped houses each include a kitchen, private terrace, indoor/outdoor dining spaces, and everything you need for a relaxing, self-sufficient holiday. Their selection of guesthouses can accommodate up to two, four, or seven guests. Wellness, trekking, and wine-tasting retreats round out the season in spring/autumn and can be booked for groups who want to be together but with their own personal space.

Parco dei Sesi

Strada Perimetrale Ovest, 95, tel. 375/5660194; www. parcodeisesi.com; guest rooms/suites and the grande dammuso villa are available to rent for short stays year-round

Located on the west coast of the island, the charming guesthouse oasis at Parco dei Sesi is owned by a young, creative couple who chose to make their family summer house and artist studio their home. Margot and Massimiliano offer chic, airy rooms and meticulously designed suites. Guests can enjoy optional on-site meals and a gorgeous in-ground pool facing the sunset. In the off-season they also host artist residencies, retreats, and small weddings on their stunning property.

INFORMATION AND SERVICES

- **Visit Pantelleria:** www.visitpantelleria. com

1: Arch of the Elephant **2:** Cantina Basile passito wine

GETTING THERE
By Air

The most efficient way to travel to Pantelleria year-round is by flying.

Pantelleria Airport

Contrada Margana; tel. 0923/911172; www. aeroportodipantelleria.it; reduced airfare rates available for residents of Pantelleria

The Pantelleria Airport is located in the north-central part of the island, only 3.1 miles (5 km) from the town/harbor, and is quickly reachable from all surrounding areas. The main town, Pantelleria, is 2.2 miles (3.5 km) from the airport and can be reached with a quick seven-minute drive or €20 taxi ride. At the airport, travelers can rent a car or request taxi services.

Direct flights are available year-round with **Danish Air Transport** (www.dat.dk) from Palermo (45 minutes; €65), Trapani (40 minutes; €48), and Catania (1 hour 10 minutes; €68). **Alitalia** (www.alitalia.it) offers flights from Milano Linate and Roma Fiumicino only in summer (May-Sept.). **Volotea** (www.volotea.com) provides service from Venezia (1 hour 45 minutes; €45), Verona (1 hour 45 minutes; €50), Torino (1 hour 40 minutes; €265), and Milano Bergamo (1 hour 50 minutes; €267) airports May-September.

By Ferry

The **Liberty Lines** ferry departs from the port of Trapani (Liberty Lines ticket office, Via Ammiraglio Staiti, 29, Trapani; tel. 0923/873813; www.libertylines.it) and arrives at the main town of Pantelleria. Check the timetables for seasonal availability.

Recommended for travelers arriving in Pantelleria without their own car, the passenger-only **fast ferry** (once daily June 10-Sept. 30; departs Trapani at 1:40pm, arrives at Pantelleria at 3:50pm.; €43 per person, €15 fee to bring a bicycle), known as an aliscafo, takes only 2 hours 10 minutes from the port of Trapani to the island of Pantelleria.

There is also an overnight ferry available if you are bringing your own vehicle. The ferry terminal is located in the harbor of the main town of Pantelleria.

GETTING AROUND
By Car

A vehicle rental is practically mandatory for an enjoyable stay on the island of Pantelleria, and there are affordable options for car and scooter rentals right at the Pantelleria Airport arrivals gate. **Autonoleggio Policardo** (Pantelleria Airport, Contrada Margana; tel. 0923/912844; www.policardo.it; 7am-8pm Mon.-Fri., 6:30am-8pm Sat.-Sun.; car rentals €25-50 per day, scooters €20-50 per day with 2 helmets included) has automatic transmission vehicles, FIAT Panda or FIAT 600 models, midsize Grande Puntos, and minivans available.

Citroën Méhari Roadster Rental (Autonoleggio Brignone, Via G. Galilei, 4; tel. 347/1053892; www.autonoleggiobrignone.it; 9am-8pm daily; standard rate for Méhari rental: €280 per week, August high season rates: €400 per week, €70 per day) allows you to explore the island in style with a Citroën Méhari, a doorless, vintage utility vehicle, the perfect beach cruiser for your summer adventures. The Brignone car rental office is located near the port in the village of Pantelleria and is convenient for those arriving with the ferry boat.

By Taxi

At the airport, travelers can request taxi services from reputable companies such as **Battista Greco** (Pantelleria Taxi Driver, Pantelleria Airport, Contrada Margana; tel. 333/6590529).

Marsala

Current-day Marsala is a Baroque-style city of 83,000 inhabitants, with a strong nightlife, food, and wine culture. The fashionable Marsalesi know how to enjoy the slow life. The nearby beaches, sea salt flats, archaeological sites, Aegadian Islands, wineries, and marsala producers add the cherry on top to the charm of this small city and its long, illustrious history.

It was founded as Lilybaeum by the Carthaginians in 397-396 BCE, after the nearby island of Mozia was destroyed. Sicily's history of foreign domination continued through the centuries, from the Romans to the Byzantines, Arabs, Normans, Swabians, Anjou, and Aragonese. The town was named Marsala from Marsa Allah, "the port of Allah," by the Arabs.

Via XI Maggio and Via Garibaldi are the main streets of the old town. The historic center begins at the Porta Garibaldi city gate in Piazza Mercato. Facing the sea, the Norman gate, topped with a crowned eagle and rebuilt in 1685, is now dedicated to Giuseppe Garibaldi and his "thousand" men who in 1860 landed in Marsala to conquer the Kingdom of the Two Sicilies. Just steps through the Porta Garibaldi, Marsala's main outdoor food market, dozens of restaurants and bars, and the central Piazza della Repubblica with its principal church, the Chiesa Madre Parrocchiale di San Tommaso di Canterbury, await. On the coast, at the crook of Via Boeo, Marsala's cape marks the westernmost point of mainland Sicily at Capo Boeo. Known best for its wine production and world-renowned fortified marsala, this beautiful town has more to offer than only that.

SIGHTS
Chiesa Madre Parrocchiale di San Tommaso di Canterbury
Piazza della Repubblica; tel. 0923/716295; www. chiesamadremarsala.eu

Located in the central square, the main cathedral in Marsala is commonly referred to as the Chiesa Madre or simply as the Duomo, while locals call it Matrice in the local dialect. It was erected as a Norman cathedral around 1176, and was dedicated to the English saint, Thomas Becket. The lower part of its towering facade is traditional Baroque style, while the top portion and bell tower are in the Barochetto style of at least 100 years later. This unique blending of architectural styles follows a common thread throughout other parts of Sicily; here we see Norman-style interiors and a more elaborate Baroque style on the exterior.

Chiesa del Purgatorio
Via Sebastiano Cammareri Scurti, 24; 7:30am-noon and 4pm-7pm Mon.-Sat., 10am-noon and 4pm-7pm Sun.; free

This 18th-century Baroque-style church is one of the main highlights of the historic center of Marsala. Set in a quiet piazza with a central fountain, also 18th-century Baroque, this church was completed in 1710 and includes various frescoes inside. Even from the outside, the facade of this church is monumental.

Museo degli Arazzi Epoca Fiamminga
Via Giuseppe Garraffa, 57; tel. 0923/711327; www. museodegliarazzimarsala.com; 9am-1pm and 4:30pm-7:30pm Tues. and Thurs., 9am-1pm Wed. and Fri.-Sun.; €4 entrance fee

The Museum of Flemish-era Tapestries in Marsala showcases southern Italy's most valuable collection of Flemish tapestries from the late 16th century. Eight intricate wool and silk Flemish tapestries depict the conquest of Jerusalem by the Roman emperors Vespasian and Titus during the Jewish-Roman wars. They were donated in 1589 to the cathedral by the Italian Catholic archbishop of Messina and former archpriest of Marsala, Monsignor Antonio Lombardo, a Marsala native who some say received them as a gift from the queen of Spain.

Museo Archeologico Baglio Anselmi

Lungomare Boeo, 34; www.turismocomunemarsala. com/museo-archeologico-lilibeo.html; 9am-7:30pm daily, last entry at 7pm; €4

The Baglio Anselmi is now the seat of the Regional Archaeological Museum, but was previously used as a winemaking facility. The main highlights of the museum include the exhibition and conservation of two shipwrecks, one Punic and the other Roman, as well as a collection of amphorae and other archaeological finds dating back to the 2nd and 1st centuries BCE.

The Punic combat ship, built for about 68 rowers, dates back to the 3rd century, when it was used during the battle of the Egadi Islands in 241 BCE. It was discovered in 1971 near the Lagoon of the Stagnone of Marsala.

The well-preserved Roman cargo ship of Marausa is estimated from as early as the 3rd century CE. It was discovered in 1999 and recovered in 2008 only 492 feet (150 m) from the coast in the sea between the island of Levanzo and Trapani. At 89 feet long (27 m) and 30 feet wide (9 m), it is the largest wreck of the time ever pulled out from these waters. The ash wood frames and fir floorboards contained African amphorae, which contributes to clarify the importance of trade relations between Sicily and Africa in the late Roman era.

Mozia

Isola San Pantaleo; www.isoladimozia.it; €6 boat transfer

The ancient Phoenician colony of Mozia (also referred to as Motya) was built on a tiny island with shallow waters in the Stagnone Lagoon, just a stone's throw off the coast north of Marsala. It continues to be one of the most important archaeological sites in western Sicily. This powerful and prosperous settlement has foundations from as early as 800 BCE. During the Carthaginian period, it was one of the Phoenicians' most important

commercial colonies due to its proximity to North Africa. Mozia fell in 397 BCE to Dionysius I, the Greek tyrant of Syracuse, before being conquered by the Romans during the First Punic War. Basilian monks settled on the island and renamed it San Pantaleo during the Middle Ages, and in 1888 the island was rediscovered and purchased by Joseph Whitaker, a wealthy Sicilian-English ornithologist and archaeologist.

The small island (111 acres/45 ha) can be explored only on foot (30 minutes to cross the island; 1 hour to circumnavigate), with boat service connection from the mainland outside Marsala. Highlights of the island include the **Museo Giuseppe Whitaker** (tel. 347/6551666; www.museodimozia.it; 10am-2pm and 3pm-7pm daily; €9) archaeological museum and its marble statue of the Motya Charioteer made between 460 and 450 BCE, the **Necropoli** stone burial grounds dating back to the 7th-6th centuries BCE, the **Tophet** open-air cemetery/sanctuary, the **Cappiddazzu** and **Korthon** temples, ruins of the fortified walls and barracks, a house of mosaics made with black and white pebbles, and a small plot of private vineyards owned by the Whitaker Foundation and cared for by the Tasca d'Almerita winemaking family. Boat services depart from the **Imbarcadero Storico** every 30 minutes, and the 0.6-mile (1-km) trip takes around 12 minutes to arrive in Mozia. Driving from Marsala, it will take approximately 15 minutes by car to reach the ticket office at the dock for Mozia.

TOP EXPERIENCE

★ VINEYARD VISITS AND WINE TASTING

One of Italy's most specialized winemaking styles is having a resurgence. Chefs, sommeliers, and wine lovers are once again singing the praises of marsala, a fortified wine made here in the charming city of Marsala

1: Chiesa del Purgatorio **2:** Tophet cemetery on Mozia **3:** Cantine Florio di Marsala

on the west coast of Sicily since the 1770s. John Woodhouse, a British wine merchant, started out distributing other fortified wines like sherry, port, and madeira before arriving in Marsala. He found the location ideal for growing grapes and strategic for shipping wine, with its very hot and windy summers with mild and fairly dry winters, and he developed marsala as another high-alcohol beverage that could withstand long voyages by sea from Sicily to England.

Ranging from amber to toasted golden brown to ruby red in color, marsala's incredible range is its most unique characteristic. In different bottles you'll recognize notes of bitter almonds, burnt honey, vanilla, and spices, or the essence of dried figs, carobs, balsamic, or dried fruits. Although marsala is commonly paired with desserts or dark chocolates, it can also be served with aged cheeses and marmalade, fresh oysters, smoked fish, or Sicily's famous tuna roe bottarga.

Cantine Pellegrino

Via del Fante, 39; tel. 0923/719911; www. carlopellegrino.it; tastings available by reservation only Mon.-Sat.

The Pellegrino family is one of only three original 19th-century founders of the marsala trade still in existence, handing vineyards down from father to son for seven generations. Cantine Pellegrino is located in the northern part of the town of Marsala, and winery tours include a tasting of five marsala wines accompanied by five typical Sicilian dishes (2.5 hours; €50 per person, minimum 4 participants). Walk-in tastings are available at the **Ouverture** wine shop.

Cantine Florio di Marsala

Via Vincenzo Florio, 1; tel. 0923/781111; www.duca.it/ florio; by appointment only 9am-1pm and 3:30pm-6pm Mon.-Fri., 9:30am-1:30pm Sat.; tours from €15

Cantine Florio has been in continuous operation since 1862, owned by one of Sicily's most prominent families, famous in the world of winemaking, tuna fishing, and motor racing.

Besides its line of internationally recognized aged marsalas, Cantine Florio is also known as a quality producer of amaro liqueurs. The winery is located right in the town of Marsala, near the marina.

Marco De Bartoli

Contrada Fornara Samperi, 292; tel. 0923/962093; www.marcodebartoli.com; 9am-1pm and 3pm-6pm Mon.-Fri.

In 1978, Marco De Bartoli, an agronomist and racing car connoisseur, took over the 200-year-old Samperi estate and built a name for himself in the marsala winemaking world. Its soleras method uses mainly native grillo grapes to carefully mix small portions of older vintages with new vintages to create outstanding marsala wines. Vineyard visits and wine tastings can be organized by reservation. The Samperi estate is located 20 minutes southeast of the center of Marsala. Check their website to confirm driving directions, as this location is a bit difficult to find.

FOOD

Busiate

Via Sebastiano Cammareri Scurti, 20; tel. 334/5640801; www.busiate.com; noon-3pm Mon.-Sat.; €4-10

Ever needed pasta on the fly? Stop by Busiate for a taste of Sicily in a to-go cup. The first of its kind, it was founded here in Marsala by the folks who brought you Ciacco Putia. The name busiate is used to describe the traditional corkscrew-shaped pasta in the province of Trapani. At this fast, casual takeaway shop, you can pick the size of your fresh pasta portion and pair it with one of the sauces of the day. Eat it outside in the square or as you stroll through Marsala on foot.

★ Ciacco Putia Gourmet

Via Sebastiano Cammareri Scurti, 3, tel. 0923/711160; www.ciaccoputia.it; 11:30am-3pm and 6pm-11pm Mon-Sat; dishes from €6-12

Francesco Alagna and Anna Ruini are spearheading a revolution for top-quality food and wine in Marsala. They strive to promote the city with full meals paired with special marsala wines. At Ciacco, they say "The artichoke is the enemy of good wine, but the artichoke is the best friend of Vecchio Samperi," a 20-year-old signature wine from Marco De Bartoli made with the traditional solera method of adding new, fresher wines to barrels containing wines already aged. Learn more about marsala and taste Chef Francesco's local specialties in this welcoming bistro in the heart of the city center.

Salumeria Da Salvatore

Piazza Goffredo Mameli, 5; www.salumeria-salvatore.it; 8am-3pm and 6pm-midnight daily; under €15

Stop by this specialty foods deli at the Garibaldi city gate to get a sandwich or charcuterie platter, enjoy a bottle of wine, or pick up supplies for a day at the beach. The high-end display case is filled with traditional Sicilian cured meats, hard-to-find cheeses, cured tuna products, olives, and more. The friendly owners are always ready to help you source the best products and can vacuum seal items for travel.

Pellegrino Ouverture

Lungomare Battaglia delle Egadi, 10; tel. 0923/719970; www.carlopellegrino.it; 10am-7pm Mon.-Sat.; €15-65

Ouverture is the modern tasting room for Cantine Pellegrino's wine tourism offerings. Located just down the street from the winery on the coast of Marsala in front of the Salinella park, Pellegrino Ouverture is a tasting room, mini museum, wine shop, and showroom for its locally made wines and marsalas. One-to two-hour options can include a tasting of three or four wines with small snacks or a full lunch overlooking the Aegadian Islands.

Parrinello Pescheria e Cucina

Via Vincenzo Florio, 4; tel. 392/0844887; www. parrinellopescheriaecucina.it; 8:30am-2:30pm and 4:30-11:30pm Mon.-Sat., 8:30am-2:30pm and 7:30pm-11:30pm Sun.; €35 raw seafood platters, €12-25 main course dishes

Located on the coast of Marsala, less than a 10-minute drive south of the historic center, this mecca for Sicilian seafood is a must. Its famous raw crudo platters are packed with delicacies, from langoustines to red shrimp from Mazara del Vallo, with lightly dressed tuna tartare, shucked oysters, and fasolari brown callista clams. The ambience is warm, chic, and welcoming.

Le Lumie Ristorante

Contrada Fontanelle, 178/B; tel. 0923/995197; www. ristorantelelumie.com; 7:30pm-10pm daily; entrées from €16-25

Take a short drive outside the town center for dinner at Le Lumie. Since 2009, chef Emanuele Russo has focused his menus entirely on local Sicilian flavors and seasonal ingredients, many of which are sourced from gardens and farms producing only for this restaurant. The extensive wine list includes over 400 labels, with about 75 percent from Sicilian winemakers. This restaurant is only accessible by car or taxi. Self-driving guests can follow Via Trapani out of the city center to Contrada S. Giuseppe Tafalia and Contrada Fontanelle (20 minutes; 5.5 mi/8.8 km). Request a table outside for views of the Aegadian Islands and a picturesque Sicilian sunset.

ACCOMMODATIONS

Viacolvento

Via XIX Luglio, 46; tel. 388/4079295; www. viacolventomarsala.it; from €88

Rent a room or an apartment with your own kitchen at this four-star spot in the center of Marsala. Explore the town on foot or spend a few days with a rental car to travel the west coast of Sicily. Airport transfers from Trapani or Palermo can be organized upon request.

Hotel Carmine

Piazza del Carmine, 16; tel. 0923/711907; www. hotelcarmine.it; from €109

While on a wine-tasting tour of Marsala, guests can stay in this three-star hotel in the city center for a little rest and relaxation within walking distance of the town's top restaurants. Named for the nearby Convento del Carmine convent, the Hotel Carmine was fully renovated in 2015 within a historic 17th-century palace. Traditional hotel amenities include Wi-Fi connection, air-conditioning, television, minibar, and room service. The antique furniture, ceramic majolica tile flooring, modern comforts, and convenient location are a few of this charming hotel's perks.

Agriturismo Baglio Donna Franca

Contrada Florio, 1; tel. 0923/967240; www. donnafranca.it; from €115

This four-star resort is located on the vineyard-lined hills of Marsala's wine country, a 20-minute drive northeast of the city center along the SS115. In homage to Donna Franca Florio, a noblewoman and socialite of the Belle Époque, this 19th-century stone-walled baglio is bursting with old-world style. Thanks to the care of the current owners, the Ansaldi family, the estate includes a beautiful outdoor swimming pool, fifteen guest rooms for overnight stays, an in-house restaurant (12:30pm-2pm by reservation only, dinner service 7:30pm-10:30pm daily) featuring local, organic ingredients, and the opportunity to enjoy special activities such as cooking lessons or wine tastings.

Information and Services

- **We Love Marsala:** www.welovemarsala. com

GETTING THERE AND AROUND

Marsala can be reached by car from Trapani in 35 minutes along the SS115 state road. Guests driving from Agrigento can arrive in 2 hours, along the coastal road SS115. Marsala can also be reached by bus service with **Autoservizi Salemi** (www.autoservizisalemi.it; 2 hours 35 minutes; €10) from Palermo, dropping off at the Marsala bus station, or with **Autolinee Lumia** (www.autolineelumia.com; 2 hours 30 minutes; €11) from Agrigento, arriving in Piazza Caprera.

The main train station is located on Via Augusto Elia (a 17-minute walk to the town center at Porta Garibaldi), where **TrenItalia** (www.trenitalia.it; 38 minutes; €3) services connect with Trapani. Tickets can be purchased in advance online or from an automated kiosk at the station, and must be time-stamped before boarding the train.

The historic center of Marsala is easily explored on foot. The main marsala producers have facilities right in the center of town, while small artisan producers are located outside town and require a car to reach them, since bus services are not available for these excursions.

The Southwestern Coast

The southwestern side of Sicily is a great place to plan a road trip with your own rental car. Passing seemingly endless almond and olive groves, the landscapes change drastically as you travel along the southern coast of Sicily heading toward Agrigento and the World Wildlife Fund-protected beachfront at Torre Salsa. Make a point to drive along the strip of sea salt-producing flats on the road between Trapani and Marsala, where in spring and autumn you can even spot magnificent migrating pink flamingos. From the Greek ruins in Selinunte and the Valley of the Temples to Scala dei Turchi's terraced limestone beach, this is a region within Sicily chock-full of history and natural wonders.

MUSEUM OF THE DANCING SATYR
(Museo del Satiro Danzante)

Piazza Plebiscito, Mazara del Vallo; tel. 0923/933917; www.mazaraonline.it/satiro/museo_satiro_01.htm; 9am-7:15pm daily; €6 entrance fee

This small archaeological museum can be

found in the historic center of **Mazara del Vallo,** a strategic fishing port town founded by the Phoenicians on the west coast of Sicily, 40 minutes south of Marsala. The museum, inside the Church of Saint Egidio, has a small collection of amphorae vessels used to transport wine, and the main exhibition, the larger-than-life-size ancient Dionysian *Dancing Satyr* bronze Greek sculpture. Pulled up from the sea in two phases, only the leg was found first in 1997; the rest of the torso and head of the sculpture was discovered in the net of a local fishing boat, the *Captain Ciccio,* by Francesco Alagna in 1998. After an elaborate restoration, with similar techniques used on the two *Riace Bronzes* found in 1972 in Calabria, at the Instituto Centrale per il Restauro in Rome and a brief exhibition at the Louvre Museum in Paris, the *Dancing Satyr* found its home again here in Mazara del Vallo. Experts estimate that it dates back to the Hellenistic period, somewhere between the 3rd and 2nd centuries BCE, and could possibly be a piece made by the renowned sculptor Praxiteles. This impressive find is the highlight of a quick stop in Mazara del Vallo.

Getting There

From Trapani (1 hour; 31mi/50km), take the SS115 state road south following the Trapani-Marsala route, then turn right onto the SS118 toward Marsala/Mazara del Vallo/Petrosino and back onto the SS115 into the city center of Mazara del Vallo. From Marsala (30 minutes; 14mi/23km), take the SS115 state road to Via Marsala in Mazara del Vallo. From Palermo, the drive is 1.5 hours (81 mi/130 km), heading close to Castellammare del Golfo and Castelvetrano; from Agrigento, it's also a 1.5-hour drive (72 mi/116 km). Bus service from Palermo is also available through **Autoservizi Salemi** (www.autoservizisalemi.it; 2 hours; €9.20), from the bus terminal on Via Fazello to Via Casa Santa 71 in Mazara del Vallo, a 20-minute walk to the museum.

SELINUNTE ARCHAEOLOGICAL PARK
(Parco Archeologico di Selinunte)

Via Selinunte, Castelvetrano; tel. 0924/46277; www. selinunte.gov.it; 9am-7pm daily; €6 entrance fee

Located in the town of Castelvetrano, along the southwest coast of Sicily, Selinunte is one of the largest archaeological sites in Europe. The remnants of this Greek settlement, dating back to 628 BCE, sit on a plain high above the golden-sand coastline below. Left abandoned for over 2,500 years, Selinunte was originally

Selinunte Archaeological Park

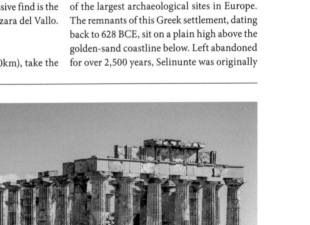

one of the most powerful cities in Magna Graecia, or the Greek colonies of southern Italy, once thought to have had as many as 30,000 inhabitants. Little else is known about Selinunte's history, besides evidence that the city ultimately fell to a powerful alliance between the nearby Segestans, Carthaginians, and Athenians.

The extensive ruins of Selinunte include several temples, the largest of which is known as Temple E, which will be one of the first things you see upon entering the park. Visitors can also explore the remains of a port; an acropolis, or public gathering space; several necropolises; and the skeleton of the city's streetscape, including what would have been residential and commercial buildings. The widespread archaeological park (657 acres/266 ha) is walkable, but golf-cart transportation can be organized upon request, and there's also a tiny tourist train that can take you on a set tour of the sites (€6). To do the park justice, devote 3-4 hours.

Getting There

From Trapani (1 hour; 56 mi/90 km), take the autostrada A29/E90 highway to Via Caduti di Nassirya in Castelvetrano and follow the SS115 state road to Selinunte. From Palermo, the drive is 1.5 hours (75 mi/121 km); from Agrigento, it's also a 1.5-hour drive (62 mi/97 km). Once you arrive in Castelvetrano, there are two entrances to the archaeological park: one in the village of Marinella di Selinunte on Selinunte Street, the other in the village of Triscina di Selinunte on Mediterraneo Avenue.

RISERVA NATURALE ORIENTATA TORRE SALSA

SP75 in Siciliana; tel. 0922/818220; www. wwftorresalsa.com; open 24 hours; free

The Torre Salsa Nature Reserve is a 4-mile (6.4-km) stretch of sandy beaches and 1,880 acres (760 ha) of limestone cliffs, juniper fields, wetlands, and rolling hills along the southern coast of Sicily near the town of Siciliana,

about 30 minutes west of the provincial capital of Agrigento. There is a beautiful orchid garden on the WWF property, just down a dirt road from the **visitor center.** Guided visits can be organized through the nature reserve's office on Monday, Wednesday, and Friday year-round. Guests visiting without taking a guided tour can enjoy walking/hiking or exploring the beaches on their own.

Food
Ristorante La Scogliera

Via San Pietro, 54, Siciliana Marina; tel. 0922/817532; www.facebook.com/lascoglierasiciliana; 7pm-11pm Mon., 11:30am-3:30pm and 7pm-11pm Tues.-Sun.; €35-50

Nestled between the Torre Salsa Nature Reserve and the city of Agrigento, this beachfront treasure features fresh seafood. La Scogliera is a family-run restaurant with indoor and outdoor dining areas overlooking the cliffs and marina of the small village of Siciliana. Treat yourself to a seaside feast of raw langoustines, oysters, and raw fish carpaccio; spiny lobster in tomato sauce; pasta with nero di seppia squid ink; or grilled mix plates of the catch of the day.

Getting There

To reach the beaches at Torre Salsa, from Agrigento take the SS115, exiting at Montallegro, then follow the signs for Riserva Torre Salsa on SP87. After about 2.1 miles (3.3 km), turn left and follow signs until you reach the Pantano entrance (45 minutes; 20 mi/33 km). From Marsala, head east toward Sciacca and continue on SS115, exiting for Montallegro - Torre Salsa. Follow the signs for the Riserva Torre Salsa along SP87 for about 2.1 miles (3.3 km), then turn left and follow the signs leading to the Pantano entrance (1 hour 40 minutes; 68mi/110km).

★ SCALA DEI TURCHI

SP68 in Realmonte; open 24 hours; free

Save time to visit the smooth, white-terraced marl stone cliffs of the Scala dei Turchi, one of Sicily's most seductive beach sites. Just outside the city of Agrigento, near the town of Porto Empedocle, in Realmonte, this bright clay and limestone rock formation appears out of nowhere, cascading like a whitewashed scala (staircase) sloping down to the sea. Pack a lunch and plenty of refreshments to spend the day lying out on the cool white stone, or visit in the off-season for a more tranquil sightseeing experience. Water shoes are recommended for small children. There are no amenities available right at the Scala dei Turchi, but can be found with a short walk down the beach toward **Punta Grande,** at places such as the Chiosco Lido snackbar or the Lounge Beach Club. Visitors should bring along a beach towel, sunscreen, and a hat or beach umbrella.

This breathtakingly wild beachfront can be difficult for travelers with mobility issues since an actual staircase connects the paid parking areas along the SP68 state road with the shore below. For those wanting to take a peek and snap a few photos without heading down to the sea, there is a scenic lookout point, **Belvedere Scala dei Turchi** (open 24 hours; free) located 0.5 mile (0.9 km) west of the Scala dei Turchi, also along the SP68 road.

To reach the Scala dei Turchi by car from Agrigento and the Valle dei Templi (20 minutes; 7.1 mi/11.5 km), follow SS115 west through Porto Empedocle, then toward Contrada Punta Grande/SP68 following signs for the Zona Lidi (beach club zone) and parking areas.

Coming from Palermo (2 hours; 90 mi/145 km), take the SS624 Palermo/Sciacca route south to SS115. Then head east toward Realmonte and follow the signs for Scala dei Turchi.

SPIAGGIA PORTO EMPEDOCLE

Via Lungomare Nettuno, 1-62, Porto Empedocle; open 24 hours; free

The 3.7-mile (6-km) stretch of soft sand shoreline to the west of the small fishing hamlet of Porto Empedocle connects the famous white stone shores of the Scala dei Turchi to the west and San Leone on the eastern side. It's a popular summer destination for families with small children as well as locals and tourists. The seafront offers clean, clear, emerald-green waters and restaurants, bars, beach clubs, and free public beach space. Porto Empedocle is also the hometown of author Andrea Camilleri, known for his *Inspector Montalbano* series. Tourism began to pick up after the fictitious town of Vigata in his series, modeled after Porto Empedocle, was featured in the television adaptation of his works.

Arrive by car from Agrigento and the Valle dei Templi in under 20 minutes along the SS115 state road, or from Scala dei Turchi beach in less than 10 minutes (3.7 mi/6 km) on SP68.

Agrigento and Valle dei Templi

Archaeology buffs should make a point of checking out this part of the southwestern coast of Sicily. Founded in 581 BCE as Akrágas, Agrigento was a prime center of commerce on the trade routes from Africa to Europe. The Valle dei Templi, outside the city of Agrigento, contains some of the best-preserved Greek ruins in the world. While it now has a population of around 60,000, it is estimated that during the 5th century BCE, there were anywhere from 200,000 to 800,000 citizens in this area. The province of Agrigento is also known for its agricultural production of almonds and olives.

Though the modern city is not one of Sicily's most beautiful towns, the golden limestone ruins of the Valle dei Templi should not be missed and are worth going out of your way to visit. All along Sicily's southern coast, travelers can enjoy an afternoon at the golden-sand beaches of Agrigento, perfect for a comfortable swim, especially with small children in tow.

SIGHTS

TOP EXPERIENCE

★ Valle dei Templi

Coastal state road SP4 in Agrigento; tel. 0922/1839996; www.parcovalledeitempli.it; 9am-7pm daily; adults €12, reduced rates €7, combined ticket to temples and Giardino della Kolymbetra €17, concessions €11, free first Sun. of the month

Sicily's most-visited historical attraction is the Valley of the Temples, which showcases well-preserved and restored Greek ruins that easily stand toe-to-toe with those in Greece. The massive Archaeological and Landscape Park of the Valley of the Temples is one of the largest archaeological sites in the world, extending for over 3,000 acres (1,214 ha), with forests of almond and olive groves, grapevines, myrtles, carob trees, and dwarf palms.

Known as Akrágas in ancient times, this splendid Greek colony competed with the cities of Segesta and Selinunte at its peak. The long archaeological park—walkable if you've got the stamina—is split into two sections, the eastern zone and the western zone, with car parks and ticket offices in the northeastern and southwestern corners. It's speckled with eight ancient temples dating from 510 to 430 BCE: the temples of Hera (known by the Romans as Juno), Concordia, Heracles, Zeus, Castor and Pollux, Hephaestos, Demeter, and Asclepius. The best-known temples are in the eastern zone, including the **Temple of Concordia.** Built approximately 2,500 years ago, it's the largest Greek ruin in Sicily and one of the best-preserved temples in the world. It's easily recognizable, with tall, fluted Doric columns and a rectangular shape that closely resembles the Parthenon in Athens. At the western end, save time to visit the Kolymbetra Gardens just down the street.

Plan to spend at least 2-3 hours on a walking tour of the temples. Audio guides are available in Italian, English, French, Spanish, German, and Chinese for €5, with a deposit of identification card or driver's license. Private certified guides are highly recommended to best enjoy your visit. **Michele Gallo** (tel. 360/397930) is one of the top guides recommended by the park. It's also possible to be shuttled around both of the archaeological park's zones on small electric **shuttles** that run from both ticket offices. Summer visits are extremely hot and can be overcrowded. February and March, while the almond trees are in bloom, are the most beautiful months to visit, but if you want to escape the crowds, you'll have the archaeological park all to yourself in autumn or winter.

1: the beautiful countryside around Agrigento 2: Giardino della Kolymbetra 3: the limestone terrace of Scala dei Turchi 4: the ruins at Valle dei Templi

July-mid-September, evening tours are offered through **Luci in Valle** (Lights in the Valley). Call ahead for reservations or book online (€10 plus the entrance fee, children under 12 free). The tour meets at the tree-lined area of the Temple of Juno.

Museo Archeologico

Contrada San Nicola, 12, Agrigento; tel. 0922/401565; www.coopculture.it; 9am-7:30pm Mon.-Sat., 9am-1:30pm Sun.; adults €8, reduced rates €4, joint ticket with Valle dei Templi €13.50

This archaeological museum, on the site of a former convent, features a collection of Phoenician, Greek, Etruscan, Carthaginian, and Roman artifacts, including sculptures from the surrounding area of the Valle dei Templi and Agrigento as well as Selinunte. Guided tours are available and should be booked in advance.

Giardino della Kolymbetra

Via Panoramica de Templi, Agrigento; tel. 335/1229042; www.fondoambiente.it/luoghi/giardino-della-kolymbethra; 10am-11pm daily; adults €17, European residents €11, students €11, 17 and under free

Combine your trip to the Valle dei Templi with a walk through the Kolymbetra Gardens, accompanied by their ancient aqueduct. This hidden paradise consists of centuries-old olive groves, citrus trees, and wild gardens, now overseen by FAI (Fondo Ambiente Italiano), a nonprofit organization that helps protect and preserve Italy's cultural heritage. Guided tours are available upon request.

East of Agrigento
Farm Cultural Park

Cortile Bentivegna, Sette Cortili, Favara; tel. 0922/34534; www.farmculturalpark.com; 10am-10pm Tues.-Thurs., 10am-midnight Fri.-Sun.; gallery €5

This cultural center and contemporary art gallery, open since 2010, is located in a series of courtyards within the historic center of Favara, 12 miles (19.3 km) east of Agrigento. Founders Andrea Bartoli and Florinda Saieva purchased the property in this abandoned town center and completely transformed the area to include a test kitchen, a garden cocktail bar, and artisan shops. It has been a fresh resurgence of creativity and energy for the town of Favara, with its art exhibitions, dynamic outdoor murals, street art, workshops, and educational events.

BEACHES
Spiaggia di San Leone

Via Nettuno and Viale delle Dune, San Leone; open 24 hours; free

Make a stop to have a swim along the long stretch of soft golden sand at San Leone. This is a top summertime destination for beachgoers visiting the area around Agrigento, including the nearby Scala dei Turchi and Valley of the Temples. The beach is located just 4 miles (6.4 km) south of Agrigento and was named after Pope Leone II of the Byzantine Papacy, who was originally from Sicily. Free beach access, intriguing dining destinations, sand dunes and natural vegetation, the 0.25 mile (0.4 km) Lungomare Falcone Borsellino tree-lined seafront walking path, and nightlife activity are among the handful of perks for adding this beach to your road trip along the southern coast.

TOURS
Essence of Sicily

tel. 0922/605810; www.essenceofsicily.com

The Agrigento-based agency Essence of Sicily organizes an authentic series of cultural, culinary, and sightseeing experiences. Single-day excursions can be set up to explore Agrigento's Valle dei Templi as well as Taormina, Catania, Ragusa, Syracuse, Palermo, and Trapani. Contact the company directly for pricing and reservations for a Sicilian family lunch, hands-on cooking lesson, winery visit, or guided Sicilian heritage tour.

FOOD
Agrigento
Aguglia Persa

Via Francesco Crispi, 34; tel. 0922/401337; www.agugliapersa.it; 7pm-11pm Wed.-Mon.; entrées €12-16

Aguglia Persa is a seafood-focused restaurant

located inside Villa Catalisano, a Liberty-style noble palace designed by Ernesto Basile (also known for his work on the Teatro Massimo opera house in Palermo). Here guests eat like locals, feasting on exceptional cuisine cooked either with modern techniques or over charcoal fires stoked with oak and cherry wood. Make sure to try chef Vincenzo Ravanà's house specialty, sarde beccafico-stuffed sardines breaded with panko and kataifi strands, served with pickled onions and candied orange. Beautifully plated dishes are served up at affordable prices, and meals can be enjoyed in the stunning courtyard or indoor dining room. Brothers Alessandro and Vincenzo, along with Vincenzo's wife Cristina Abbate, were the former owners of Salmoriglio, a celebrated but now closed restaurant in nearby Porto Empedocle.

Osteria Ex Panificio

Piazza Giuseppe Sinatra, 16, tel. 0922/595399; www.
osteriaexpanificio.it; 12:30pm-2:30pm and 7:30pm-
11pm daily; entrées €15-46
This renovated rustic osteria has been recognized with the Bib Gourmand award from the Michelin dining guide. Set in the historic city center of Agrigento, near Teatro Pirandello in a former World War I-era bread bakery, Osteria Ex Panificio features regional meat and seafood options from a rotating seasonal menu while paying homàge to its flour-dusted roots with unforgettable homemade bread and warm Sicilian hospitality.

Valle dei Templi
Il Re di Girgenti

Via Panoramica Valle dei Templi, 51, Agrigento; tel.
0922/401388; www.ilredigirgenti.it; 12:30pm-2:30pm
and 7:30pm-10:30pm Wed.-Mon.; antipasti €10,
entrées €12-18
Slip deeply into an Arabian dream at the stunning Il Re di Girgenti restaurant overlooking the Valle dei Templi in the heart of Agrigento. Taste your way through a menu of carefully thought-out and surprisingly affordable dishes, from grilled octopus with fava beans and carob dust to fresh ravioli with John Dory fish and sea urchin sauce. Pair your meal with regional wines, and enjoy sourdough breads baked daily in-house.

ACCOMMODATIONS
Valle dei Templi
★ **Villa Athena**

Via Passeggiata Archeologica, 33; tel. 0922/596288;
www.hotelvillaathena.it; from €120
This luxurious 18th-century villa hotel has an extraordinary view of the Temple of Concordia, and if you request a temple view, you'll be able to see it lit up at night from your window, balcony, or terrace. The prime location, beautifully manicured garden, Michelin-mentioned Terrazza degli Dei hotel restaurant, and Villa Athena Spa built around an ancient Greek cistern can be just what you need to relax after a long drive or full day of sightseeing.

Doric Boutique Hotel

Strada E.S.A. Mosé - San Biagio, 20; tel.
0922/1808509; www.doric.it; from €167
This 22-room boutique eco-hotel offers unique views overlooking the Temple of Juno in the Valle dei Templi. The resort also features an in-house restaurant, spa and wellness center, Jacuzzi, and infinity pool. The air-conditioned accommodations are minimally decorated with panoramic photo murals of the nearby Scala dei Turchi white stone beach, but the real pièce de résistance is the deluxe suites that even include their own private swimming pools and mini patios overlooking the property's vegetable and herb gardens.

GETTING THERE AND AROUND
Though Agrigento has a train station that connects to Palermo, the southwestern coast of Sicily is best explored with your own car. The beaches, archaeological sites, and top dining options are not very accessible with public transportation.

By Car

The drive from Palermo to Agrigento (2 hours 15 minutes; 80 mi/129 km) cuts south through the center of the island on a series of winding country roads. Plan for some extra time along these roads, especially in summertime when the surrounding area becomes extremely busy. From Trapani, the drive is 2 hours (110 mi/177 km). From Catania, it's also a 2-hour drive (100 mi/161 km). The coastal drive from Marsala to Agrigento (2 hours 10 minutes; 84 mi/135 km) passes by the Greek temples from the 7th century BCE in Selinunte and the charming town of Sciacca along the SS115 state road.

From the city center of Agrigento as well as the Agrigento train station, the Valle dei Templi can be reached with a 10-minute drive or taxi ride. The walk will take about one hour and is not recommended in the height of summer when it is extremely hot. Cars can be rented in the city center of Agrigento with a prior reservation from **Avis** (Via Empedocle, 95; tel. 0922/596154; www.avisautonoleggio.it; 8:30am-1pm and 3:30pm-7pm Mon.-Fri., 9am-1pm Sat.) or **Hertz** (Via Empedocle, 13; tel. 0922/403091; www.hertz.it; 9am-12:30pm and 4pm-6pm Mon.-Fri., 9am-noon Sat.).

By Train
Agrigento Centrale Station
Piazza Guglielmo Marconi

Train service to Agrigento is provided by **TrenItalia** (www.trenitalia.it). Tickets can be purchased in advance online or from an automated kiosk at the station, and must be time-stamped before boarding the train. Bathrooms are available on the train. Daily service runs every hour from **Palermo Centrale** (2 hours; €10 one-way). The train station in Agrigento is not located near the Valle dei Templi, and a short 10-minute taxi ride (€15) down the hill will be required. Agrigento is not easily reached with public transportation from Trapani or Marsala.

By Bus
Agrigento Stazione Autobus
Piazzale Fratelli Rosselli

SAIS Trasporti (tel. 091/6171141; https://saistrasporti.it) operates buses from **Catania Fontanarossa Airport** (2 hours 40 minutes; from €11) five times per day. It's also possible to travel from Palermo by bus with **Camilleri Argento & Lattuca** (tel. 0922/471886; www.camilleriargentoelattuca.it; 2 hours; from €9). Agrigento is not easily reached with public transportation from Trapani or Marsala.

The Aeolian Islands

Located between Sicily and the toe of mainland

Italy's boot, the seven volcanic islands of the Aeolian archipelago erupted from the sea off Sicily's northeastern coast some 700,000 years ago. Today, Stromboli, on its eponymous island, still erupts every 30 minutes on average all year round. Now the Isole Eolie, as they're called in Italian, are best known as a summer holiday destination, often visited on sailing excursions and multiday island-hopping adventures. They offer a unique mix of geological and archaeological cultural sights, fine-dining options, outdoor adventures, luxurious hotels, beautiful beaches, and hidden rock coves along with numerous natural attractions. Milazzo, where most visitors to the Aeolian Islands will catch the ferry, is a vibrant town with a stunning smooth pebble

Highlights

Look for ★ to find recommended sights, activities, dining, and lodging.

★ **Vineyard Visits and Malvasia Tastings:** Wine lovers can enjoy vineyard visits and tastings on Lipari and Salina to sample the local varietal, malvasia delle lipari, grown in this area since Greek times (pages 155 and 162).

★ **Sunset in Pollara:** From land or sea, the colorful sunset view overlooking Pollara on the northwest coast of Salina is one of the loveliest in the archipelago (page 160).

★ **Luxury Resorts on Salina:** Relax in the Aeolian Islands at one of Salina's top resorts, known for their in-house dining options, spa services, and breathtaking panoramas (page 166).

★ **Stromboli's Volcano Tours:** Continuously erupting like clockwork for the past 5,000 years, the active volcano on Stromboli can be visited with a guided excursion where guests can hike up to 1,300 feet (400 meters) above sea level (page 170).

★ **Gran Cratere della Fossa:** Straight up the mountain from Vulcano's harbor, a one-hour intermediate hike leads visitors up an unpaved path to the expansive outer ridge of the island's steaming volcanic crater for expansive 360-degree views (page 174).

beach, a long, green mountainous cape overlooking the Aeolian Islands, and a lively culinary scene and aperitivo culture, especially during the summer months.

ORIENTATION

Sicily's seven-island Aeolian archipelago is about 35 miles (56 km) off the northeastern coast. Milazzo, located on a finger of land jutting into the Tyrrhenian Sea along the northeast coast of mainland Sicily, is the main departure point to the islands, with hydrofoils operating year-round. June-early September, ferry services also connect Palermo with the Aeolian Islands. The islands are positioned in the Tyrrhenian Sea between the regions of Sicily and Calabria. Starting from west to east approaching from Palermo, the small islands of Alicudi, Filicudi, and Salina are in a line; Lipari is due south of Salina, with Vulcano just a bit farther south. Panarea and Stromboli branch off to the northeast of the other islands. Stromboli is the closest to the toe of the boot in mainland Italy and can be reached by ferry from Naples, while the first stop for those visiting from Sicily is Vulcano, located a mere 17 nautical miles (27 km) north of Milazzo.

PLANNING YOUR TIME

Lipari is the largest island and main transportation hub. **Salina** and **Stromboli** are great for day trips, while **Panarea** and **Vulcano** are often visited as part of a boat tour departing from the main ports on each island or a island-hopping holiday to try to explore as many of them as possible. **Alicudi** and **Filicudi** are the most rustic of the "seven sisters." With fewer amenities, these islands are often overlooked by travelers pressed for time.

The logistics of getting to the archipelago and their relaxed vibe mean that a day trip is not the best way to visit these islands; it takes at least five nights to get the full Aeolian experience—a mix of relaxing at resorts, visiting

multiple islands, eating delicious food, wine-tasting tours, long days at the seaside, and outdoor adventures. If planning to visit a single island, a two- or three-day trip will suffice for a quick introduction. The Aeolian Islands are extremely seasonal, and most resorts, restaurants, and hotels will close for a break during the off-season, remaining open only **April/May-September/October**. Make sure to plan ahead for your transportation, accommodations, and restaurant meals. Reservations are required in the high season (June-August) due to availability. They are also recommended during the shoulder season when many places may be closed. In winter, the ferry and hydrofoils are active to mainly service local people, so even if there is a ferry, it may not mean everything you plan to experience will be open and available.

For more information on planning your trip to the Aeolian Islands, **Loveolie** (www.loveolie.com) is the official tourism website, providing history, information, and recommendations for accommodations, dining, and excursions.

GETTING THERE

The only way to get to the Aeolian Islands is by boat. The archipelago's main hub is the largest island, Lipari, but it's also possible to get directly to most of the other islands from Sicily, or even from mainland Italy. There are two types of boats: slower **ferries,** which include the option to take along a motorino scooter or car; and faster **hydrofoils,** built for passenger service only.

In Sicily, the principal port of departure to the Aeolian Islands is **Milazzo,** on the island's northern coast. Take your car with you on the ferry (to Lipari, Vulcano, or Salina), or leave your car at one of many parking lots near the port, including **Garage del Porto** (Via Giorgio Rizzo, 82; tel. 348/2635179; www.garagedelportomilazzo.com). Parking costs around €12 per day.

Previous: Marina Lunga, Lipari; mineral deposits seen along the Gran Cratere hike; Tenuta di Castellaro winery on Lipari.

The Aeolian Islands

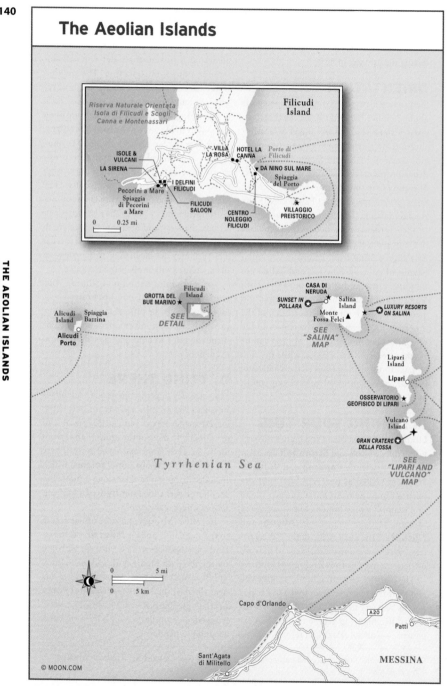

Filicudi Island

Riserva Naturale Orientata
Isola di Filicudi e Scogli
Canna e Montenassari

Porto di
Filicudi

ISOLE &
VULCANI
LA SIRENA

VILLA
LA ROSA
HOTEL LA
CANNA

DA NINO SUL MARE

Spiaggia
del Porto

Pecorini a Mare
Spiaggia
di Pecorini
a Mare

I DELFINI
FILICUDI

FILICUDI
SALOON

CENTRO
NOLEGGIO
FILICUDI

VILLAGGIO
PREISTORICO

0   0.25 mi

GROTTA DEL
BUE MARINO ★

Filicudi
Island

SEE
DETAIL

CASA DI
NERUDA

SUNSET IN
POLLARA ✪

Salina
Island

LUXURY RESORTS
ON SALINA

Monte
Fossa Felci ▲

SEE
"SALINA"
MAP

Alicudi
Island

Spiaggia
Bazzina

Alicudi
Porto

Lipari
Island

Lipari

OSSERVATORIO ★
GEOFISICO DI LIPARI

Vulcano
Island

GRAN CRATERE ✪
DELLA FOSSA

SEE
"LIPARI AND
VULCANO"
MAP

T y r r h e n i a n   S e a

0   5 mi

0   5 km

Capo d'Orlando

A20

Patti

Sant'Agata
di Militello

MESSINA

© MOON.COM

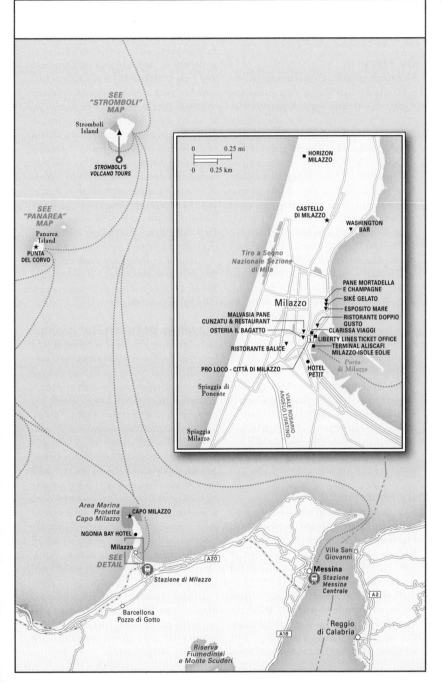

THE AEOLIAN ISLANDS

SEE "STROMBOLI" MAP

Stromboli Island

STROMBOLI'S VOLCANO TOURS

SEE "PANAREA" MAP

Panarea Island

PUNTA DEL CORVO

0   0.25 mi

0   0.25 km

HORIZON MILAZZO

CASTELLO DI MILAZZO

WASHINGTON BAR

Tiro a Segno Nazionale Sezione di Mila

PANE MORTADELLA E CHAMPAGNE

SIKÉ GELATO

Milazzo

ESPOSITO MARE

MALVASIA PANE CUNZATU & RESTAURANT

RISTORANTE DOPPIO GUSTO

OSTERIA IL BAGATTO

CLARISSA VIAGGI

LIBERTY LINES TICKET OFFICE

RISTORANTE BALICE

TERMINAL ALISCAFI MILAZZO-ISOLE EOLIE

PRO LOCO - CITTÀ DI MILAZZO

HOTEL PETIT

Porto di Milazzo

Spiaggia di Ponente

VIALE ROSARIO ANGELO LIVATINO

Spiaggia Milazzo

Area Marina Protetta Capo Milazzo

CAPO MILAZZO

NGONIA BAY HOTEL

Milazzo

SEE DETAIL

Stazione di Milazzo

A20

Villa San Giovanni

Messina

Stazione Messina Centrale

A2

Barcellona Pozzo di Gotto

Reggio di Calabria

A18

Riserva Fiumedinisi e Monte Scuderi

It's also possible to visit the Aeolian Islands from Palermo in Sicily and from Naples on mainland Italy.

By Ferry

Siremar (090/364601; www.siremar.it) connects the Aeolian Islands from Sicily and Campania with large traghetto ferry services.

Daily ferry services are available from Milazzo to the Aeolian Islands, with most of them connecting through Lipari. Prices range €10-18 for one-way service with an additional €53-85 surcharge for automobiles and €23-37 for motorbikes. Ferries depart to Alicudi (3 hours) and Filicudi (2 hours 15 minutes) twice per day, to Lipari (1 hour) 13 times, to Salina (1 hour 35 minutes) 11 times, to Vulcano (50 minutes) 10 times, and to Panarea (2 hours) or Stromboli (1 hour 10 minutes) 4 times per day. The Siremar ticket office is located in the ferry terminal at the **Port of Milazzo** (Via dei Mille, 23; tel. 090/9283415); tickets can be purchased in the ferry terminal office, but in the summer season it's always recommended to purchase your tickets in advance online.

Siremar ferry services to the Aeolian Islands are also available from Naples, though only on Tuesday and Friday, departing at 8pm. Prices for the approximately 15-hour journey start from around €40 each way, or from €120 with the surcharge for automobiles. Timetables and ticketing information can be found online at www.directferries.com.

By Hydrofoil

This is the most convenient way to reach the archipelago. **Liberty Lines** (formerly Ustica Lines; www.libertylines.it) serves all the islands with quick and efficient aliscafo hydrofoil ferries (for passengers only—no cars or motorbikes).

There are frequent crossings from Milazzo's **Terminal Aliscafi Milazzo-Isole Eolie** (Via Luigi Rizzo, Milazzo; tel. 340/9023731; 45 minutes-3 hours depending on the island; from €19) and Messina's **Molo**

d'imbarco Rizzo (Via Luigi Rizzo, Messina; tel. 347/0095781; 1.5-2.5 hours; from €30).

Hydrofoil services are available from Palermo's cruise terminal harbor (on the opposite side of the Via Francesco Crispi and SS113; tel. 091/324255; 2-5 hours; from €36) June-first week of September only, departing at 1:50pm. Service from Palermo is provided to Alicudi (daily; 1 hour 55 minutes), Filicudi (daily; 2 hours 30 minutes), Santa Marina Salina (6 times per week; 3 hours 20 minutes) and Rinella (6 times per week; 3 hours), both on Salina, Lipari (6 times per week; 3 hours 55 minutes), Vulcano (daily; 4 hours 10 minutes), Panarea (daily; 4 hours 40 minutes), and Stromboli (once per week; 5 hours 25 minutes). Timetables and ticketing information can be found online.

Note that crossings are more limited in the off-season, especially from Messina and Palermo, and ferries may be delayed or canceled by rough conditions.

Traveling Between the Islands

Frequent ferries (operated by **Siremar**) and hydrofoils (operated by **Liberty Lines**) connect all the islands year-round, though some islands are more connected than others; for example, Lipari, as the largest island, has connections to all six other Aeolian islands. Travel times and fares range from 25 minutes and €15 on a hydrofoil (from Alicudi to Filicudi) to 4 hours and €40 on a ferry (from Alicudi to Vulcano). Unless you're traveling with your own vehicle on a ferry, you're most likely to find yourself on a hydrofoil, which are generally quicker, cheaper, and more frequent than the ferries. There are Liberty Lines ticket offices on every island; visit their easy-to-navigate website (www.libertylines.it) for the complete set of timetables and fares.

It's also possible (though much more expensive) to travel by private sailboat or yacht; especially at the main ports in Lipari or Salina, you'll find boat tour companies right in the port to organize trips.

Chartering a Boat in the Aeolian Islands

Although public transportation via ferry is available, the most luxurious way to explore the Aeolian Islands is by boat. Full-day and weeklong experiences allow travelers to gain access to off-the-beaten-path swimming coves and secret island spots only visible by sea.

MOTONAVE GLENTOR

Piazza Santa Marina, 5, Santa Marina, Salina; tel. 331/7475167; www.salinapermare.it; from €75 per person

Travelers looking to plan a single-day trip can contact Motonave Glentor to set up private adventures or sign up for a group tour on its 65-foot (20-m) motorboat. Its information booth is located right in the ferry boat harbor of Santa Marina on the island of **Salina.** Day-trip excursions departing from Salina start at €75 per person with an additional fee of €15 per person for lunch on board featuring local recipes and fish-based pastas. The company also organizes sunset programs with aperitivo near the faraglioni rock formations in Pollara, or even a full-day 10-hour tour to see Stromboli's Sciara del Fuoco

sailing the Aeolian Islands

eruptions by night with swimming stops along the way in Panarea. Captain Angelo Zavone's team can also create custom tours for private groups with advance notice, depending on availability.

IL MARE A VELA

Via A. Paternostro, 48, Palermo; tel: 339/8138472; www.ilmareavela.it; €2,400-5,000 per week

When planning ahead for a more extended stay and full exploration of the Aeolian Islands, Il Mare a Vela offers weeklong sailboat trips in summertime (Sat.-Sat.). Guests will be responsible for the additional costs of a professional captain, bed sheets, end-of-the-week cleaning fee, gasoline, and groceries. Fun-loving captain Alessandro Minaudo's *Easy Way* is a 49-foot (15-m) Sun Odyssey performance sailboat with three cabins, three bathrooms, and indoor and outdoor dining areas. Occasionally, Il Mare a Vela will also offer weekend sailing trips in spring or autumn, or summertime cabin charters where guests can book one room instead of renting out the entire boat. Contact the team for additional details, reservation requests, and availability. It sets sail from Palermo only at the beginning of the season; charter programs can be organized from the port of Capo d'Orlando (40 mi/65 km west of Milazzo on mainland Sicily) or Lipari.

GETTING AROUND

Most of the islands are small enough to be explored on foot or by renting a bicycle or motor scooter. For short trips, taxis are usually available, especially in the towns. On the islands of Panarea and Stromboli, golf-cart taxi services are available. It's also possible to bring your own vehicle to Lipari, Vulcano, and Salina by ferry.

Itinerary Ideas

DAY ONE

Depart mainland Sicily to arrive in Lipari in the afternoon.

1 Check into your room at **Hotel Mea Lipari** and relax at the pool for the afternoon.

2 Enjoy a stroll through the town center and spend the evening at **Il Giardino di Lipari** enjoying an aperitivo and dinner in its hidden garden oasis.

DAY TWO

1 Head to the **Marina Lunga** and take a 30-minute ferry ride on a high-speed hydrofoil with Liberty Lines to the island of Salina.

2 With a reservation, meet your captain from **Salina Relax Boats** in the port of Santa Marina for a half-day boat trip around the island, with stops in Rinella and Pollara for refreshing dips in the crystalline sea.

3 A 15-minute taxi ride will take you to the northeastern tip of the island for a luxurious lunch at the **Capofaro Locanda & Malvasia** resort on the Tasca d'Almerita vineyard property.

4 Head back to the port near **Piazza Santa Marina** to catch the ferry back to Lipari.

5 Refresh back at your room in Hotel Mea before a bottle of wine and dinner at **Osteria San Bartolo** on the Via Francesco Crispi seafront.

DAY THREE

1 Eat a hearty breakfast at Hotel Mea before walking down to the **Marina Lunga** to board your one-hour morning ferry for a day-trip adventure to Filicudi.

2 Meet your guide, Flavia Grita from **Associazione Nesos,** for a three-hour outdoor trekking adventure through the natural landscapes of Filicudi on a hike from the port to Valdichiesa to the village of Zucco Grande in search of abandoned ruins overlooking the coast of Siccagni.

3 After your hike, treat yourselves to an authentic Aeolian lunch at **La Sirena** near the harbor before catching the one-hour ferry back to Lipari.

4 Make a reservation to spend the evening with a sunset vineyard visit and wine tasting at **Tenuta di Castellaro,** with round-trip shuttle service from the port.

5 If you're still hungry after a long day, stop by **Liparo Re Ristorante** for a late dinner in the town center.

6 **Bar Pasticceria D'Ambra** is open all night long for any last granita cravings before calling it a day.

Itinerary Ideas

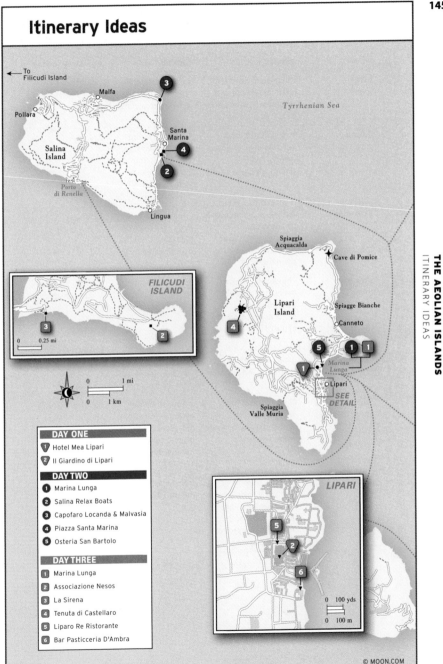

To Filicudi Island

Malfa

Pollara

Salina Island

Tyrrhenian Sea

Santa Marina

Porto di Renella

Lingua

FILICUDI ISLAND

0   0.25 mi

Spiaggia Acquacalda

Cave di Pomice

Lipari Island

Spiagge Bianche

Canneto

Marina Lunga

Lipari

SEE DETAIL

Spiaggia Valle Muria

0   1 mi
0   1 km

DAY ONE
1 Hotel Mea Lipari
2 Il Giardino di Lipari

DAY TWO
1 Marina Lunga
2 Salina Relax Boats
3 Capofaro Locanda & Malvasia
4 Piazza Santa Marina
5 Osteria San Bartolo

DAY THREE
1 Marina Lunga
2 Associazione Nesos
3 La Sirena
4 Tenuta di Castellaro
5 Liparo Re Ristorante
6 Bar Pasticceria D'Ambra

LIPARI

0   100 yds
0   100 m

© MOON.COM

Which Aeolian Island?

Island	Why Go	Getting There	How Long to Stay
Lipari (page 152)	White-sand beach and charming harbor with restaurants, shops, and bars accessible on foot	45-minute hydrofoil ferry from Milazzo, 10 minutes from Vulcano	2 nights
Salina (page 160)	Vineyard visits and wine tastings, exclusive resorts, and fine-dining options	1.5-hour hydrofoil ferry from Milazzo, 25 minutes from Lipari, 30 minutes from Panarea, 40 minutes from Filicudi	2 nights
Stromboli (page 167)	Active volcano erupting on cue every 20-30 minutes, black-sand beach, and quaint town center	1-hour 10-minute hydrofoil ferry from Milazzo, 30 minutes from Panarea	1 night
Vulcano (page 173)	The closest island to mainland Sicily, with a steaming volcanic crater at the summit of the island	40-minute hydrofoil ferry from Milazzo, 10 minutes from Lipari	Half-day trip from Milazzo or Lipari
Panarea (page 177)	The VIP island with great dining options, shopping, and nightlife	1-hour 20-minute hydrofoil ferry from Milazzo, 30 minutes from Salina	1 night
Filicudi (page 182)	Chic but still off the grid, with natural landscapes and beautiful swimming coves	2-hour 10-minute hydrofoil ferry from Milazzo, 25 minutes from Alicudi, 40 minutes from Salina	Half-day trip from Alicudi or Salina
Alicudi (page 187)	Completely off the beaten path with barely any amenities. This is the long-lost flower child island, beloved only by more-adventurous travelers	3-hour hydrofoil ferry from Milazzo, 25 minutes from Filicudi	Half-day trip from Filicudi or Salina

Milazzo

Many people just pass through Milazzo en route to the Aeolian Islands, but if you find yourself with time to kill here before your ferry, don't be too disappointed. There are great options for dining, gelato, or granita within walking distance of the ferry port. This seaside town is flanked by the sea on both sides of the promontory and overlooked by the dramatic cape and its Castello di Milazzo. Its population of 31,000, known as the Milazzese, like to refer to their town as the "Milan of the south." The pace of life here is slow: There's always time for an aperitivo with friends, and unlike in many other towns in Sicily, the locals truly enjoy dining out.

The seaside in Milazzo is also one of the most beautiful on the northern coast, with places to swim on both sides of town. With access to the shore along Via Panoramica on the east side and Via Tono/Via Spiaggia di Ponente on the west, the convenience of popping over to the shore for a swim in the middle of a city cannot be beat. From the panoramic overlook on the central cape, the Aeolian Islands seem just an arm's length away at Milazzo's most northern point. There are beach clubs speckled along the Spiaggia di Ponente on the west coast, and free public beach space as well. Here, guests can relax in the clean, clear water and leave sand-free after enjoying the day on the smooth, tiny pebbled shore. Free public outdoor showers are also available throughout the city, as a way to rinse off before leaving the beaches.

The train station in Milazzo is not located in the center of town, but a quick 10-minute taxi or bus ride will drop you right at the ferry port, with easy access to depart for the islands or explore the town on foot.

SIGHTS AND BEACHES
Castello di Milazzo
Salita Castello; tel. 090/9221291; www.comune.milazzo. me.it; 9am-1:30pm and 4:30pm-8:30pm daily May-Sept., 9am-6:30pm daily Oct.-Apr.; €5 entrance fee

Dating back to the Neolithic period around 4,000 BCE, the site of the Castello di Milazzo complex sits at the top of a hill overlooking the sea in the town center. This fortified area was an important military lookout during the Roman and Byzantine eras. Now, the surrounding areas feature a Norman castle with its Saracen tower and 16th-century Spanish walls, the main Duomo Antico cathedral, and a Benedictine convent. Another main highlight at the complex is the **MuMa Museo del Mare** (tel. 380/7641409; www.mumamilazzo. com; included in castle complex entrance fee), Milazzo's museum of the sea, which displays a giant 30-foot-long (9-m) skeleton of a sperm whale that was estimated to have weighed over 10 tons. The 1-mile (1.6-km) walk from the ferry port to the castle is uphill, so give yourself some additional time if you'll be visiting the castle on foot.

Capo Milazzo
Via Sant'Antonio, 3

Spend a few hours walking along the cape overlooking the Gulf of Milazzo. Leave your car at the public parking lot in front of the Il Faro café (Via Sant'Antonio, 3) and follow Via Sant'Antonio toward the trail, through lush vegetation and prickly pears, to head farther into the peninsula. There is also a tourist office where guests can pick up information about the area (**Info Point Area Marina Protetta;** at the crossroads with SP72). A main highlight of this area is the views of the Aeolian Islands and the **Piscina di Venere** ("pool of Venus"), an off-the-beaten-path destination for a swim in the shallow and natural swimming pool filled with water during high tide.

Spiaggia di Ponente
Via Spiaggia di Ponente, 124; open 24 hours; free

Enjoy some fun in the sun at Spiaggia di Ponente on the west coast of Milazzo. Just a

10-minute drive (€15 taxi ride) from the ferry port in central Milazzo, the smooth, minuscule pebbled beach is a comfortable change from the rocky shores found in the Aeolian Islands. Free public showers are available at the beach for rinsing off after a swim. Visitors can rent sunbeds/umbrellas and stop for a lunch break at **Horizon Milazzo** (Via Tono, 71; tel. 320/1919900; www.horizonmilazzo.it).

FOOD

Milazzo is a celebrated Sicilian food town. Part of the province of Messina, its cuisine is based mainly on seafood because of the city's long coastline, and features traditional Messinese dishes such as pidoni/pituni half-moon fried calzones; stoccafisso air-dried cod; pane cunzatu open-faced breads topped with ricotta infornata cheese, tomatoes, and salt-cured anchovies; pignolata chocolate- and lemon-covered fried dough; and semi-frozen Italian ice granita served with a fluffy brioche with its iconic tuppo button bun baked into the top. First- and second-course dishes focus on fish and seafood, while many restaurants also highlight raw dishes with Sicilian red shrimp or local capone, tuna, and swordfish. Many of Milazzo's top restaurants are located within walking distance of the ferry terminal.

Restaurants
Esposito Mare

Via Francesco Crispi, 67; tel. 090/9222012; noon-3pm and 7pm-11pm Thurs.-Tues.

Conveniently located on the southern end of the Marina Garibaldi seafront promenade and only a five-minute walk from the ferry boat terminal, Esposito Mare is a prime destination for fresh seafood in Milazzo. Expertly run by the top local restaurateur power couple, Chiara Surdo and Raffaele Esposito (of Osteria Il Bagatto, Pane Mortadella e Champagne, Pescestocco e Baccalareddu, and Picnic), service is seamless, and the food is to die for. Indoor and shaded outdoor seating is

1: waters off Capo Milazzo 2: Ngonia Bay Hotel 3: Milazzo

available, and the restaurant is open for lunch and dinner. Perfect for a meal before or after your transfer to the Aeolian Islands.

Osteria Il Bagatto

Via Massimiliano Regis, 11; tel. 090/9224212; https://osteria-il-bagatto.business.site; 8pm-1am Mon.-Sat.

If you're spending the night in Milazzo, this should be at the top of your list for dinner. Owner Chiara Surdo often sprinkles dishes onto the menu from her native region, Puglia. Not only an option but a destination for carnivores, the menu focuses on carpaccio, tartare, pastas, wild porcini or truffle-topped dishes, salumi antipasti starters, and juicy steaks that might be just what you're looking for after dining on only seafood for a few days in the islands. A great wine list and cozy atmosphere keeps diners at the table into the late hours. Reservations are recommended. One block away from the ferry port, Osteria Il Bagatto is a terrific option for those arriving in the evening from the Aeolian Islands with plans to spend the night in Milazzo. It even has guest rooms to rent at **Locanda del Bagatto** (Via Massimiliano Regis, 7; tel. 090/9224212), right upstairs, for those rolling out the door after a few bottles of wine.

Malvasia Pane Cunzatu & Restaurant

Via Massimiliano Regis, 18; tel. 331/4979643; www.ristorantemalvasiavulcano.it/menumilazzo; 6:30pm-midnight Tues.-Sun.; dishes €10-18

This sister restaurant to the beloved namesake spot on the island of Vulcano offers typical Milazzese specialties including shareable, hefty pane cunzatu ("seasoned bread") dishes piled high with a variety of toppings including tomatoes, ricotta infornata cheese or mozzarella, olives, capers, anchovies, raw red onion, and oil-cured tuna plus plenty of bottles of Sicilian malvasia wine or cocktails. Start off your meal with the bruschetta alla carrettiera, with rustic fresh tomato sauce and ricotta infornata cheese, and be sure to ask about their daily specials. Indoor and outdoor dining is available; reservations are recommended.

Malvasia is another great option for evening dining, just steps away from the ferry port.

Ristorante Doppio Gusto

Via Ammiraglio Luigi Rizzo, ½; tel. 090/9240045; www.ristorantedoppiogusto.it; 12:30pm-2:30pm and 7:30pm-11pm Tues.-Sun.; dishes €15-24

A two-minute walk from Milazzo's ferry terminal, Michelin guide-mentioned Ristorante Doppio Gusto is a local favorite for fresh pasta dishes, abundant seafood options, and original Sicilian-inspired creations. It's led by brothers, executive chef Matteo Maiorana and general manager Renato Maiorana, who pride themselves on serving up true flavors of Sicily with traditional dishes mixed with innovative pairings.

Ristorante Balìce

Via Ettore Celi, 15; tel. 090/7384720; www.baliceristo. com; 7:30pm-10:30pm daily; small plates €18-27, tasting menus €50-90

Treat yourself to a meal at the up-and-coming Ristorante Balìce. The young, talented chef/owner, Giacomo Caravello, spent his formative years cooking with Martina Caruso at Signum on the island of Salina before returning to his hometown to open this fine-dining restaurant. It offers pristine service and a contemporary menu with an open kitchen format. Chef Caravello is a rising star to keep your eye on as he strives for Michelin-star status. The dining room is flawlessly designed but still maintains the vibe of a fresh young restaurant. À la carte and tasting menus are available, and reservations are highly recommended since it is only open for dinner service.

Sweets

★ Washington Bar

Via Marina Garibaldi, 94; tel. 090/9249045; 7am-12:30am Tues.-Fri., 7am-2am Sat.-Sun.; €2.50 granita, €3 with a brioche included

Granita is a local specialty here in Milazzo and all over the province of Messina. Washington Bar is the all-time classic destination for a sweet treat along the Marina Garibaldi seafront promenade, open for almost 40 years.

Its brioche buns are baked in-house and are among the very best in town. There are indoor tables across the street in wintertime and outside in the garden overlooking the Marina Garibaldi seafront in summer. The extensive list of homemade granita flavors includes lemon, strawberry, coffee, pistachio, almond, chocolate, frutti di bosco berries, tangerine, peach, and watermelon served with or without whipped cream and a fluffy brioche on the side for dipping.

Siké Gelato

Marina Garibaldi, Via Francesco Crispi, 81; tel. 328/5770022; www.sikegelato.it; 1pm-midnight Tues.-Sat., 11:30am-midnight Sun.

This tiny family-owned gelateria is the sister outpost of a historic pastry shop from 1932, Gelateria D'Angelo in Monforte San Giorgio. Siké draws inspiration for its artisanal gelati from the high-quality flavors of Sicily, featuring carob, ricotta and candied orange, pistachio from Bronte, almond and chamomile, lemon flower with walnuts, olive oil with lemon zest, and black fig. On the more exotic side, it also makes gelato with passionfruit and rum, calendula flowers and jasmine, mango, feijoa fruit, white chocolate with finger limes, Calabrian bergamot, banana and cardamom, and an extensive range of different chocolates. Siké is also conveniently located just a five-minute walk from Milazzo's ferry terminal.

BARS

Pane Mortadella e Champagne

Via Francesco Crispi, 87; tel. 090/9223260; antipasti plates €5-15

Another important pit stop just steps away from the ferry terminal, this is the hot spot for those seeking a traditional aperitivo in Milazzo. Sip on a few drinks or a bottle of bubbly with a tasting of charcuterie platters and bruschette, or pop in during the day for specialty deli sandwiches to take away for a travel day to the Aeolian Islands. Outdoor dining and a few seats are available at the bar; reservations are recommended.

ACCOMMODATIONS

Hotel Petit

Via dei Mille, 37; tel. 090/9286784; www.petithotel.

it; from €75

This charming three-star hotel is five minutes on foot from the best restaurants in town and Milazzo's ferry terminal for easy transfers to the Aeolian Islands. The nine guest rooms are available for single, double, triple, and quadruple occupancy, spread out over two floors. Modern amenities such as 32-inch LED televisions, Wi-Fi, 24-hour concierge, a private parking garage, air-conditioning, and heating are available. Hotel Petit retains its simple Mediterranean charm with Sicilian details like traditional maioliche-tiled flooring made in Santo Stefano di Camastra, a bountiful breakfast spread, and a terrace facing the harbor.

Ngonia Bay Hotel

Piazza Angonia, 10; tel. 090/9281326; www.ngoniabay.

com; from €155

Located on the Spiaggia di Ponente west coast, a 10-minute (€15) taxi ride from the ferry terminal, Ngonia Bay is a stunning oasis, perfect for a romantic weekend getaway from the more touristed towns of Cefalù and Taormina or for a relaxing stay in Milazzo before taking off for the Aeolian Islands. Named for the Greek term used to describe this "corner" of the promontory, the hotel is on a property owned by the aristocratic D'Amico and Calapaj families of the Tonnara del Tono. Here you can enjoy the lush, shaded gardens, a private pool patio, and chef Dario Pandolfo's panoramic contemporary restaurant on the rooftop. Suites named for the Mediterranean winds are modernly designed with ample space, small terraces, rain showers, minibars, air-conditioning, and Wi-Fi service. The unique Provençal casetta (cottage) is tucked away in the garden with its own bedroom, kitchenette, and outdoor seating area with a picnic table. Situated right on the beachfront, just steps from the public free beach and lido beach clubs, this hotel will charm you immediately upon arrival.

INFORMATION AND SERVICES

Visitor Information

Pro Loco - Città di Milazzo

Via Ammiraglio Luigi Rizzo; tel. 345/8838132; www. prolocomilazzo.com; 9am-1pm and 4pm-7pm Mon.-Sat., 9am-1pm Sun.

Right in front of the ferry terminal in the town center of Milazzo, the Pro Loco tourism office kiosk is a great place to pick up information on the area.

Luggage Storage

Clarissa Viaggi (Via Ammiraglio Luigi Rizzo, 23; tel. 090/9240248; www.clarissa viaggi.com; 8am-1pm and 4pm-7:30pm Mon.-Sat., 8am-12:30pm Sun.) offers luggage storage near the port.

GETTING THERE AND AROUND

Milazzo can be reached by trains operated by **Trenitalia** (www.trenitalia.com) from Catania (3 hours; €11), Taormina (2 hours; €8.40), and Palermo (2 hours 30 minutes; €14). After arriving at the **Stazione di Milazzo** (Via degli Orti; www.trenitalia. com) train station on the outskirts of town, you'll need to take the bus (AST; www. aziendasicilianatrasporti.it; €1.50) or a 10-minute taxi (Mylae Taxi; tel. 327/5470875; www.mylaetaxigaragemilazzo.com; €5 per person) to reach the ferry terminal, the **Terminal Aliscafi Milazzo-Isole Eolie,** also known as the Molo Marullo, in the **Porto di Milazzo** (Liberty Lines ticket office: Via Ammiraglio Luigi Rizzo, 10; tel. 090/9146027), about 2.5 miles (4 km) away.

Another option is to drive: From Taormina, Milazzo is a 1-hour drive (53 mi/85 km); from Catania, a 1-hour 40-minute drive (81 mi/130 km); and from Palermo, a 2-hour 10-minute drive (120 mi/193 km).

Lipari

Lipari is the largest of the Aeolian Islands, covering an area of 14 square miles (36 square km). It's easily reached in one hour via hydrofoil from Milazzo, or in four hours on a ferry from Palermo in summertime. Most visitors to this central island hub arrive in the port and promptly take off on another ferry to another island—but they're missing out. Although there are a few options right in the harbor for a delightful granita, glass of wine, or quick shopping spree, the magic of Lipari is only truly discovered beyond the port.

The fairly hilly landscape has great views of the nearby island of Vulcano and Mount Etna on mainland Sicily; traversed by motorino scooter, rental car, or e-bike, you'll pass coastal vineyards, smooth pebbled beaches, and the pristine white cliffs, once quarries where 200 tonnes of pumice stone were extracted each year. Beyond the coast, Lipari slowly reveals more secrets, from fascinating museums on archaeology and volcanology to trekking and excursions through old volcanic craters. Enjoy fresh and simply prepared island food featuring seasonal vegetables, with native capers speckled throughout as many dishes as possible. Lipari's diverse range of wild, rocky coastlines and sand beaches and its central location in the archipelago offer enough for more than a day trip.

Orientation

Ferries to Lipari arrive in the main port, **Marina Lunga,** right in the central town (also named Lipari) on the southern side of the island. Though many restaurants, bars, cafés, shops, and accommodations are located in walking distance of Lipari town, there are amazing options for swimming, wine tasting, dining, and overnight stays scattered across the island. Taxis available near the port can be helpful for reaching your accommodation if you are planning to stay the night, or rent a scooter or car to venture out to the beaches near **Canneto** on the east coast and **Acquacalda** on the northern side. The hilly landscape and dramatic coastline are also great for trekking experiences, and the island is easy to navigate on its main perimeter roads, the **SP179** and **SP180.** Circumnavigating the island by car will take approximately one hour.

SIGHTS
Museo Archeologico Eoliano L. Bernabò Brea

Via Castello, 2, tel. 090/9880174; www.facebook.com/museoLipari; 9am-7:30pm daily; adults €6, ages 18-25 €3, first Sun. of month free

The Bernabò Brea Museum is located inside the angular 15th-century walls of the **Castle of Lipari,** about a 10-minute walk south of the port along the coast. During the construction of the castle, many important artifacts were uncovered, leading the builders of the time to realize they were digging into what was once the center of Neolithic life on the island. Many of these finds are now housed in the archaeological museum, made up of six pavilions showcasing prehistoric and classical objects collections from across the islands, and exhibits related to volcanology and paleontology. This regional museum is dedicated to its late director, Italian archaeologist and prehistoric expert Luigi Bernabò Brea, one of Italy's most famous archaeologists.

Belvedere Quattrocchi

SP179, 3, Quattropani; open 24 hours; free

Located 2.5 miles (4 km) west of the central town of Lipari, this scenic overlook along the SP179 is a great place to catch the sunset, admire the dramatic rock formations off the northwestern coastline, or spot the difficult-to-access Spiaggia Valle Muria beach cove below.

Lipari and Vulcano

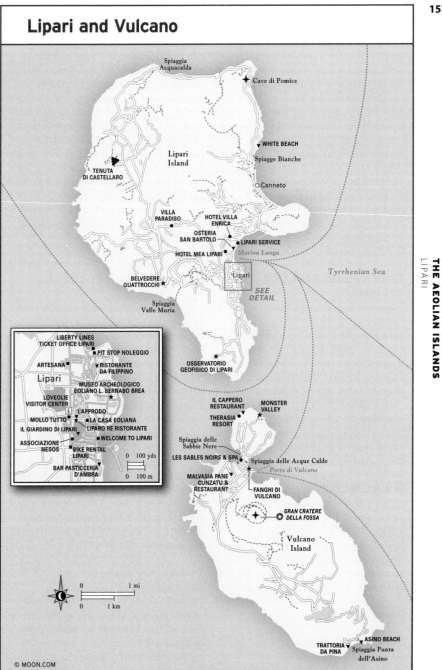

Spiaggia Acquacalda

Cave di Pomice

Lipari Island

WHITE BEACH

Spiagge Bianche

Canneto

TENUTA DI CASTELLARO

VILLA PARADISO

HOTEL VILLA ENRICA

OSTERIA SAN BARTOLO

LIPARI SERVICE

HOTEL MEA LIPARI

Marina Lunga

Tyrrhenian Sea

BELVEDERE QUATTROCCHI

Lipari

SEE DETAIL

Spiaggia Valle Muria

Lipari

LIBERTY LINES TICKET OFFICE LIPARI

PIT STOP NOLEGGIO

ARTESANA

RISTORANTE DA FILIPPINO

MUSEO ARCHEOLOGICO EOLIANO L. BERNABO BREA

LOVEOLIE VISITOR CENTER

L'APPRODO

MOLLO TUTTO

LA CASA EOLIANA

IL GIARDINO DI LIPARI

LIPARO RE RISTORANTE

ASSOCIAZIONE NESOS

WELCOME TO LIPARI

BIKE RENTAL LIPARI

BAR PASTICCERIA D'AMBRA

0   100 yds
0   100 m

OSSERVATORIO GEOFISICO DI LIPARI

IL CAPPERO RESTAURANT

MONSTER VALLEY

THERASIA RESORT

Spiaggia delle Sabbie Nere

LES SABLES NOIRS & SPA

Spiaggia delle Acque Calde

Porto di Vulcano

MALVASIA PANE CUNZATU & RESTAURANT

FANGHI DI VULCANO

GRAN CRATERE DELLA FOSSA

Vulcano Island

0   1 mi
0   1 km

TRATTORIA DA PINA

ASINO BEACH

Spiaggia Punta dell'Asino

© MOON.COM

Cave di Pomice

SP180, Porticello

The mystery of the crystal clear waters of Lipari is revealed when visitors take a look at the pumice quarries overlooking the sea in Punta Castagna on the northeastern coast of the island, which actually aid in filtering the seawater. This natural volcanic rock is light in weight due to the cooling process from eruptions dating back most recently to the 5th century CE. Up until 2007, Lipari's main industrial site employed thousands of locals and produced at least two hundred tons of pumice per year. Although the island's mining days are over and the area is now protected from further extraction, the remaining pumice cliffs in Lipari have left behind pure white landscapes and white-sand beaches.

Osservatorio Geofisico di Lipari

Contrada San Salvatore; tel. 090/9811650; www.ingv.it; open 24 hours; free

Located on the southwestern part of Lipari, this scenic overlook and public observatory is a popular spot for a bird's-eye view of the island of Vulcano. The observatory can be reached with a 10-minute drive or on foot with a 2-hour (3.5-mi/5.6-km round-trip) hike from the Chiesa S. Bartolomeo Extra Moenia church in the main town, through San Salvatore to the panoramic viewpoint overlooking the west coast of Lipari.

BEACHES

Lipari's shorelines are a mix of soft white sand, smooth black stones, and rustic swimming spots. For the rockier beaches, especially if you're traveling with children, consider bringing water shoes, and be sure to bring along everything you many need for your beach day, including sunscreen, swimwear, drinking water, and of course a few snacks or a picnic lunch.

Spiaggia Valle Muria

Pianogreca; open 24 hours; free

One of the closest beaches to Lipari town is also one of the island's hardest to access, but Spiaggia Valle Muria is worth the trek. It's a 25-minute walk down a steep, unpaved mountain path leading to this bare, rocky beach, where a local named Barni sometimes sells refreshments out of a cave-like hut. Otherwise, it is imperative to bring everything you will need for a beach day here, including extra drinking water, sunscreen, and maybe a beach umbrella. To get here, follow the SP179 to the panoramic Belvedere Quattrocchi viewpoint and then make a sharp right, following the sign for Pianogreca, a 10-minute drive. At the end of the road, leave your car or motorbike and begin the hike down to the sea. The only other way to get here is to hire a boat and anchor offshore.

Spiagge Bianche

Contrada Ghiozzo, Canneto; tel. 338/5239290; open 24 hours; free

Considered one of the most beautiful beaches on the island, with comfortable sandy shores, dramatic white pumice-stone cliffs, and warm turquoise waters, Spiagge Bianche is a busy spot in summertime, when it fills up with sunbathers, families, and endless rows of beach umbrellas. The **White Beach** lido club (www.whitebeachlipari.com; €25 for 1 umbrella and 2 beach beds) is a great option for beachgoers who want more amenities, and even hosts DJ sets and beach parties. Rentals can be reserved ahead of time through its website. Spiagge Bianche in Canneto can be reached by car from Lipari in 15 minutes along SP180 from Lipari town, or via public bus (Guglielmo Urso; tel. 090/9811026; www.ursobus.it; €2.30) from the main port.

Spiaggia Acquacalda

SP179, Acquacalda; open 24 hours; free

The smooth black Aeolian stone (known as cuti) beach of Acquacalda on the north coast of Lipari overlooks the nearby islands of Salina and Panarea, the perfect spot for catching the sunset. There are no public facilities here in Acquacalda, but the nearby

Naghet Cafè (Via Giuseppe Mazzini, 29/32; tel. 366/5951145; 10am-10pm daily) is a great place to stop for a coffee, cold beer, granita, snack, or bathroom break. Acquacalda is a 20-minute, 6-mile (9.7-km) drive from Lipari town on the SP180. Since the stone beach is black, it becomes very hot in summertime, so bring along a beach towel or blanket as well as water shoes to move around more easily.

★ VINEYARD VISITS AND WINE TASTING
Tenuta di Castellaro
Via Caolino; tel. 345/4342755; www.tenutadicastellaro. it; by reservation only; €35 per person

Located at 1,100 feet (335 m) above sea level, the Tenuta di Castellaro winery offers vineyard visits and tastings with an incredible sunset view. You'll be able to try three wines with food pairings from its underground stone wine cellar, the largest in the Aeolian Islands. Reservations are available through the website and can include optional round-trip shuttle service from the port. Tours run like clockwork, and the staff at Tenuta di Castellaro is very organized and professional. At the end of the visit, guests can purchase wine from its shop to take home. The winery

also has three minimalist-chic accommodations available on the property to rent (from €200 per night).

RECREATION
Guided Tours
Associazione Nesos
Corso Vittorio Emanuele II, 24; tel. 331/5660771; www. nesos.org; group tours from €15 per person, private guides €120-180 per day

Flavia Grita and her team at Nesos offer expert-led trekking excursions, hikes, nature walks, bird-watching, and foraging experiences on all the Aeolian Islands. On Lipari, you can join Flavia and her trusted donkey on nature walks through old volcanic craters, mountains, and vineyards. Nesos also offers guided hikes and cycling excursions for all levels, with stops for swimming and a picnic.

Boat Tours and Rentals
Welcome to Lipari
Piazza di Marina Corta; tel. 333/9253584; www. welcometolipari.it

Discover beautiful coves and caves on Welcome to Lipari's boat trip from Lipari to Vulcano. Departing at 10am from Marina Corta in Lipari, this eight-hour excursion takes guests around Lipari toward Vulcanello

Spiaggia Valle Muria

THE AEOLIAN ISLANDS
LIPARI

on the island of Vulcano, with several swimming stops. Highlights on the tour include Lipari's faraglioni, Grotta degli Angeli, Grotta del Cavallo and the Pool of Venus, Gelso, and the port of Levante before returning back to Lipari. The cost is €40 per person for group tours and €480 for a private boat for a maximum of 12 guests. Reservations must be booked one week in advance and can be done online with a partial deposit payment.

Lipari Service

Via Francesco Crispi; tel. 090/9886156; www. lipariservice.it; €70-160 per day for 8 guests

Since 1989, Lipari Service has offered motorboat rentals for 8-20 guests with seasonal rates and the option to hire a captain. They can also arrange sailing trips, yachts, or catamarans to make the most of your adventures in the Aeolian Islands.

SHOPPING
★ La Casa Eoliana

Via Giuseppe Garibaldi, 47; tel. 347/7227743; www. lacasaeoliana.it; 10am-2:30pm and 5:30pm-midnight daily

Francesca Parisi's small concept shop, or putia as it's called in Sicilian dialect, sells one of the most iconic gifts to take home after a trip to the Aeolian Islands—jewelry made with the cuore eoliano. This symbolic Aeolian heart is linked to the history and culture of the local people, invoking providence and generosity, as this thousand-year-old technique was featured as the heart-shaped wedge keystone ensuring stability at the top of a wood-burning stove. Inside this shop, the various rings, necklaces, and bracelets with the cuore eoliano are the key focus, although it also has a selection of coffe di paglia (decorated Sicilian shopping baskets), Moors head candlestick holders, scarfs, and pendants. La Casa Eoliana also ships directly via its online shop.

Mollo Tutto

Corso Vittorio Emanuele II, 83; tel. 090/9812491; www. mollotuttoshop.com; 9:30am-1am daily

Lipari is the headquarters of this casual nautical-themed brand, whose carefree island-life motto is "throw it all away." All the T-shirts, tote bags, sweatshirts, and backpacks here are created by fashion designer Natalie Rossi. The signature products are available among other traditional Aeolian souvenirs and ceramics in this shop.

Artesana

Corso Vittorio Emanuele; tel. 333/3880026; www. artesanaluisamendoza.com

Forget about the masses of souvenir shops on the main strip in Lipari and head straight to Artesana. Colombian-native and owner Luisa Mendoza has a keen eye for the best artisan treasures, from jewelry to bags, home goods, hand-painted wooden chili peppers, ceramic tile coasters, and Aeolian hearts along with specialty items like her favorite colorful woven acrylic Mochila Wayúu bags made by women in this northern Colombian indigenous tribe. Pick up your last-minute gifts from the Aeolian Islands at Artesana while supporting a small and creative female-owned business.

FOOD
Restaurants
Liparo Re Ristorante

Via F. Maurolico, 25; tel. 090/9488140; www.liparore. com; 7:30pm-midnight daily

There's something for everyone at Liparo Re. The multiple open kitchens focus on the restaurant dishes, a fish and meat grill, Mediterranean-style sushi, and pizza. Whole fish and high-end international steaks are priced per 100 grams. Tables are laid out in a hidden outdoor garden in the back, with citrus blooming all around and a towering banana tree in the center. It's owned by the local Aeolian Charme Collection hotel group, and friendly service and professionalism are part of its core philosophy.

★ Osteria San Bartolo

Via F. Crispi, 109; tel. 090/8961317; www. sanbartolovineriaedispensa.com

Husband-and-wife team Danilo Conti and Luisa Fernanda Mendoza opened Osteria

San Bartolo in summer 2020, serving up simple coastal dishes, innovative cocktails, and the best natural wine on the island, right on the Marina Lunga yacht harbor. Tucked away just a five-minute walk from the ferry port, in the opposite direction of the bustling town, Osteria San Bartolo is an ideal option for those staying overnight on boats in the harbor or visitors looking for an authentic local night in Lipari. Reservations are recommended in summertime.

Ristorante da Filippino

Piazza Giuseppe Mazzini; tel. 090/981100; www.filippino.it; 11:30am-3pm and 7pm-11pm daily; €30-50

Open for over 110 years, Ristorante da Filippino is a classic choice for traditional dining in Lipari. Located near the castle, this spacious, informal restaurant offers a large selection of local seafood dishes, authentic Sicilian cooking, and a beautiful open-air terrace. The restaurant is still managed by the Bernardi family, and it remains a reliable choice for classic Aeolian cuisine on the island.

Cafés and Light Bites

Bar Pasticceria D'Ambra

Via Salita San Giuseppe, 5; tel. 090/6019225; www.facebook.com/pasticceriadambra; open 24 hours; €5

Take an afternoon break at Pasticceria D'Ambra in Marina Corta near the port of Lipari. The D'Ambra brothers are always ready to welcome you with a refreshing Aperol spritz aperitivo, fresh fruit granita, traditional ricotta-filled Sicilian cannolo, or a few bomboloni fritti (fried donuts) in their small, family-run bar with outdoor seating overlooking the water.

BARS AND NIGHTLIFE

Il Giardino di Lipari

Via Nuova, Strittu Longu; tel. 339/3299029; www.ilgiardinodilipari.com; 6:30pm-2:30am daily in summer; cocktails €10-13, antipasti €8-15, mains €12-24

Enjoy chic hand-crafted cocktails, dinner, and live music in Luca Cutrufelli's tropical garden lounge, where you can lie back on a lawn chair under the lemon trees with a gin fizz or caper martini in hand. Il Giardino di Lipari also serves dinner, including dishes like amberjack tartare with nectarines and avocado, roasted peppers stuffed with couscous, pasta with sun-dried tomatoes and almonds, and various charcuterie platters and bruschette. It's located just a 10-minute walk from the port.

L'Approdo

Via F. Maurolico, 18; tel. 366/9435461; www.facebook.com/approdowinebar

Follow the live music down the street and head to L'Approdo for a late-night summertime festa in Lipari. This pub/cocktail/wine bar hosts musicians and DJs nightly in summer, right in the center of town. Within walking distance from the ferry port, it's a good stop for an aperitivo, or show up later in the evening when the music gets started and sometimes turns into a dance party in the streets.

ACCOMMODATIONS

Villa Paradiso

Contrada Cugna; tel. 339/1405583; www.villa-paradiso-sicily.com; from €50

Claudio Cafarella is a charming Messina native who owns this group of cozy hillside guesthouses. The property has a beautiful terrace where guests can meet up for aperitivo or dinners, but it's also a great place for solo travelers. The houses are all equipped with a small kitchenette, private terrace, and interiors decorated with vintage and recycled furnishings. Most of the bungalows are attached to one another, but there are also some more-private options. Villa Paradiso is located on the top of the mountain near the district of Pianoconte, easily reachable with a quick motorino ride from the port of Lipari. It is not recommended to stay here without any mode of transportation, and scooters can be rented directly through Villa Paradiso upon request.

Hotel Villa Enrica

Str. Serra - Pirrera, 11; tel. 090/9880826; www.hotelvillaenricalipari.com; from €80

Another property of the Aeolian Charme Collection hotel group and a Sicilian wedding destination, Villa Enrica is a romantic boutique hotel with an infinity pool overlooking the sea. Classic, Superior, and Junior suites are equipped with Wi-Fi service, satellite TV, room safe, minibar, hair dryer, and air-conditioning. June-September, set aside time to just relax by the pool and enjoy some drinks from the lounge bar just above the bay of Marina Lunga.

★ Hotel Mea Lipari

Via Paolo Borsellino e Giovanni Falcone; tel. 090/9812077; www.hotelmealipari.it; from €100

Aeolian Islands expert and luxury hotelier Sarah Tomasello waits to welcome you to Lipari at Hotel Mea. Take your cocktail poolside at one of the two swimming pools and enjoy the panoramic view of Lipari's Marina Lunga. All the rooms at this refined, four-star boutique hotel have their own private terrace. The professional staff can help guests organize dinners, excursions, and spa treatments, and can connect you with many of the local beach clubs on the island. Hotel Mea is easily reached on foot from Lipari's harbor.

INFORMATION AND SERVICES

- **Loveolie Visitor Center:** Via Vittorio Emanuele, 165; tel. 090/9812894; www.loveolie.com/en/salina
- **Hospital:** Ospedale Civile di Lipari; Via S. Anna; tel. 090/98851; www.asp.messina.it
- **Pharmacy:** Pharmacy Cincotta; Via Giuseppe Garibaldi, 60; tel. 090/9811472

GETTING THERE

The main port on Lipari is **Marina Lunga,** tucked into a natural harbor just off the island's main town of Lipari, where you'll find a **Liberty Lines** (tel. 090/9812448; www.libertylines.it) ticket office for hydrofoils to all the other Aeolian islands, as well as numerous options for private boat tours and rentals. Lipari is the main travel hub for the archipelago, with crossings from Milazzo approximately 15 times per day (about 1 hour; from €12).

GETTING AROUND

Perhaps the best way to get around Lipari is zipping between the mountain and the sea on a scooter or e-bike. Lipari can also be explored by car. Clearly marked taxi services are available for hire near the port (€15 for 2 people with luggage from the ferry port to Canneto). There are also bus routes run by **Guglielmo Urso** (tel. 090/9811026; www.ursobus.it; €2.30) linking Lipari town to the rest of the island's coast; check the bus information kiosk in town for schedules and fares.

- **Car and Motorino:** Pit Stop Noleggio; Via T. M. Amendola, 42; tel. 090/9880344; www.pitstopnoleggio.it; 8:30am-7pm daily
- **E-Bikes:** Bike Rental Lipari; Via Stradale Pianoconte, 5; tel. 368/7535590; www.bikerentalipari.com; €25-35 per day
- **Taxi:** Taxi Service Marina; tel. 339/4847085

1: Villa Paradiso 2: Hotel Mea Lipari

Salina

Nicknamed "Isola Verde," or Green Island, Salina is the Aeolian port of call for lovers of food, wine, and exceptional resorts. The name Salina refers to the sea salt that was produced from the lake in Lingua, but dating back to the 4th century BCE, the ancient Greek settlement on this island was known as Didyme, referring to the island's two mountain peaks, called the "twins." This 10-square-mile (27-sq-km) island is recognized on the UNESCO World Heritage Site list and has one of the archipelago's limited protected nature reserves, the **Riserva Naturale del Fossa delle Felci e dei Porri.** Salina is the greenest of the seven islands and home to over 400 varieties of plants including grapevines for wine-making, wild capers, and olive trees. It's also the land of malvasia wine, a fruity yet herbaceous golden grape that was anciently referred to as the "nectar of the Gods," first imported by the Greeks to the island of Salina around 588 BCE. This island is central enough for day trips to the other Aeolian islands, but its luxurious fine dining, wineries, and accommodations mean many of its guests never want to leave.

Orientation

The island of Salina covers 10 square miles (26 sq km), making it the second largest in the archipelago after Lipari. Unlike all the other Aeolian Islands, Salina does not belong to the comune of Lipari; however, it is also split into three districts: Santa Marina, Malfa, and Leni. **Santa Marina,** the main port of the island of Salina, with only 900 residents, can be explored on foot in less than half an hour and features a clean stone beach next to the harbor and several restaurants, cafés, and boat tour offices. It is the island's town center on the east coast and central port for ferries arriving in Salina. Here in Santa Marina, guests can pick up groceries, stop at the pharmacy, bank,

and browse through small artisan shops. On the southeastern coast of the island, **Lingua** is a small fishing village with pebbled beaches, a lighthouse, and the picturesque 18th-century Vallone Zappini bridge.

On the northern coast, **Malfa** is named for immigrants from Amalfi on the Italian mainland, who relocated here in the 17th century. It's known for the production of malvasia grapes and is home to most of the top hotels and resorts on the island, some of which have views of Stromboli and Panarea on the horizon. The island's lighthouse and Tasca d'Almerita family winery both get their name from the **Capo Faro** cape on the northeast corner.

Pollara, the location of the 1994 film *Il Postino,* is located on the northwestern side of the island. The picturesque town is a popular place to swim and watch the sunset. Crossing the island by car, from Santa Marina to Pollara, will take about 25 minutes.

Finally, **Leni** is the largest of the three, covering all the interior mountainous parts of the island along with **Rinella,** a coastal village on the southern shores and a secondary port for ferries arriving on Salina.

SIGHTS AND BEACHES
★ Pollara

Don't miss a stop in Pollara, made famous by the 1994 film *Il Postino,* which boasts one of the most beautiful coves in the archipelago. Its location on Salina's northwest coast makes it the best place to watch the **sunset** on the island. Overlooking the faraglione stone stacks, the view also encompasses the island of Filicudi in the distance. It is a picturesque place for a swim, often filled with boats visiting for the afternoon in front of the old fishing storages called "balate," carved from the stone cliffs with a steep staircase leading up from the water.

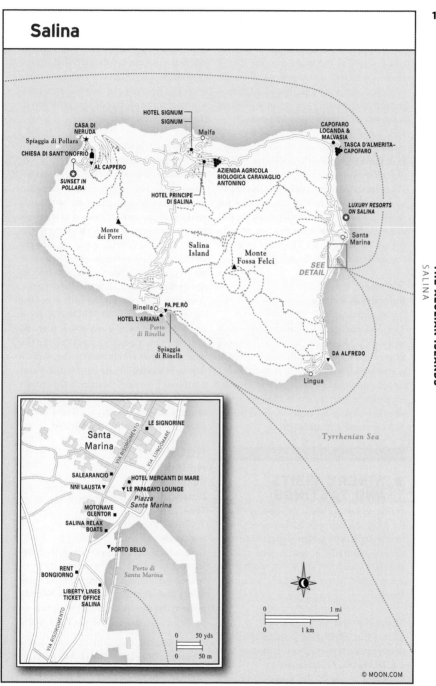

Salina

Spiaggia di Pollara

Via Massimo Troisi; open 24 hours; free

The amphitheater-shaped beach in Pollara, which served as the location of the film *Il Postino,* is located underneath a cliff on the northwest corner of Salina. From land, it's accessed by a steep staircase, which means Pollara is not accessible for travelers with mobility issues. Just off the shore, the 115-foot-high (35-m) faraglione volcanic rock formation emerges from the sea, said to be the remains of a volcanic crater submerged over 100,000 years ago. There are no amenities available at this beach, so plan to bring everything you will need for the day and stop off at a bar for a refreshment and bathroom break before heading down to the sea. Pollara is always a highlight on a boat trip and is much easier reached by sea.

Rinella
Spiaggia di Rinella

SP182; open 24 hours; free

The sand- and stone-lined free public beach of Rinella is located on the southern coast of Salina. This is the most well equipped beach on the island, with tabacchi shops, grocery stores, cafés, and a pizzeria, all within walking distance from the shore. This beach was also the backdrop for scenes in the 1949 film *Vulcano* starring Anna Magnani.

TOP EXPERIENCE

★ WINERY VISITS AND TASTINGS

Malfa, on Salina's northern coast, is known for the production of malvasia grapes. Greeks first brought these golden grapes to Salina in the 6th century BCE, and the wine that results is at once fruity and herby, which led to the moniker "nectar of the Gods" in ancient times.

Tasca d'Almerita - Capofaro

Via Faro, 3; tel. 090/9844330; www.tascadalmerita.it/ tenuta/capofaro; by reservation only at 10:30am, 3pm, and 5pm May-Oct.; €30-120 per person

Capofaro is one of the Tasca d'Almerita winemaking family's most picturesque estates, located on the edge of Salina near a mid-19th-century lighthouse. A tasting of its malvasia wines can be paired with light dishes from the resort restaurant (reservations required). Capofaro can be reached with a 10-minute drive or taxi ride along SP182 from the Santa Marina port.

Azienda Agricola Biologica Caravaglio Antonino

Via Provinciale, 33; tel. 339/8115953; www.caravaglio. it; by reservation only at 6pm Apr.-Oct.; €15 per person

Nino Caravaglio is an innovative and hardworking organic wine producer responsible for the very first dry malvasia wine in the Aeolian Islands, something that could be enjoyed throughout a meal instead of as a sweet after-dinner drink. Nino's vineyards span 30 different plots over 50 acres (20 ha) of land, a great place for a relaxing, no-frills wine tasting. Ninety-minute visits include a tasting of four wines along with a tour of the cellar and overview of winemaking practices and the personal stories of this winery. Caravaglio's winery is located 10 minutes (4 mi/6.4 km) northwest from Santa Marina in the district of Malfa. Reservations are mandatory, and sending them a friendly reminder before your arrival is highly recommended.

RECREATION
Hiking
Pollara Hike

Distance: *4.8 miles (7.7 km) round-trip*
Time: *2.5 hours*
Trailhead: *Chiesa di Sant'Onofrio, Piazza Sant'Onofrio*

Generally considered an easy route, the walking trail in Pollara, on the northeast side of Salina, leads nature lovers from the Church of Saint Onofrio through the **Casa di Neruda** house and surrounding scenery made famous by the film *Il Postino,* past the Pollo traffic

1: boating off the island of Salina 2: the winemaking estate of Tasca d'Almerita - Capofaro 3: dessert at Da Alfredo 4: seafood pasta

light, and on to the panoramic viewpoint on SP183 where you can spot the nearby Scoglio Faraglione stone formations.

Boat Rentals
Salina Relax Boats
Via Lungomare, Santa Marina Salina; tel. 345/2162308; www.salinarelaxboats.com; from €25 per person

With three kiosks on the island of Salina, the Salina Relax Boats company organizes daily group boat trips to all the Aeolian Islands, exclusive private boat excursions, boat and dinghy rentals with a skipper, island transfers, nautical charters, and mini cruises. The affordable pricing, professional English-speaking staff, and easy booking process make it a great choice.

Motonave Glentor
Piazza Santa Marina, 5, Santa Marina; tel. 331/7475167; www.salinapermare.it; from €75 per person

Have a blast and relax at sea with Glentor's motorboat excursions in Salina. Captain Angelo Zavone and his friendly crew offer three-hour trips departing from either Santa Marina, Malfa, Lingua, or Rinella. Guests will enjoy the spacious boat equipped with a sundeck, bathrooms, and optional catering services. Private and group experiences are available upon request and can be booked ahead via email or in person at the info booth in the Santa Marina harbor. Private tours of Salina or an evening trip to Stromboli can be organized with advance notice.

SHOPPING
Le Signorine
Via Risorgimento, 79, Santa Marina; tel. 366/1439888; www.lesignorine.it; open May-Sept.

This quaint costume jewelry shop, named "the young ladies," has been owned and operated since 2013 by two sisters, Rossana and Serena, in the same location where another pair of original founding sisters, Marietta and Concetta, once had their store in Santa Marina. In the shop you can find mostly costume jewelry along with a variety of ceramics, jewelry boxes, vases, tableware, and candles made by local artisans along with a small children's section. While only open during the tourism season, Le Signorine has an online shop where its products can be purchased anytime.

Salearancio
Via Risorgimento, 154, Santa Marina; tel. 090/9843433; www.salearancio.com; 9am-1:30pm and 4pm-8pm Mon.-Sat., 9am-1pm and 4:30pm-8pm Sun.

Salearancio is the top boutique clothing store in Santa Marina, where you'll find the most stylish island duds along with purses, sunglasses, and unique jewelry. Make sure to check out its home decor store, **Follie di Casa** (Via Risorgimento 140, tel. 090/9843494), just a few doors down, for ceramics, housewares, furniture, and antiques.

FOOD
Santa Marina
Nni Lausta
Via Risorgimento, 188; tel. 090/9843486; www. nnilausta.it; noon-3pm and 7pm-11pm daily; €9-14

Fresh local seafood plays a starring role in this inviting Mediterranean restaurant. Pull up a seat under the pergola in Nni Lausta's cozy patio garden and enjoy a delicious fish-centric meal at this casual beach tavern near the port of Santa Marina Salina.

Porto Bello
Via Lungomare, 2; tel. 090/9843125; www. portobellosalina.com; noon-3pm and 7:30pm-11pm Mon.-Fri., noon-2:45pm and 7:30pm-11pm Sat.-Sun.; €20-40

Located in the harbor of Santa Marina, Porto Bello is a top destination for dinner on the terrace. In summertime, it also has a lounge area for after-dinner drinks. Maybe you just missed the ferry and have a few hours to kill before the next one; turn around and you'll find one of the best places in town for a delicious seafood lunch overlooking the sea.

Lingua
Da Alfredo
Via Vittorio Alfieri, 11; tel. 090/9843075; www.
facebook.com/daalfredosalina; 9:30am-5:30pm daily
Apr.-Oct.; granita €3, pane cunzatu from €9-13
This casual café features some of the best granita on Salina, as well as huge pane cunzatu (open-faced sandwiches piled high with seasonal ingredients including tuna, olives, sun-dried tomatoes, mozzarella, arugula, and capers). This is a great place to catch some shade near the Lingua beachfront and take a break from the fierce Sicilian summer sun with a cold beer and light lunch or just a glass of granita. Reservations are recommended in July and August.

Malfa
★ Signum
Via Scalo, 15; tel. 090/9844222; www.hotelsignum.it/
en/signum-restaurant/the-kitchen; 12:30pm-3:30pm
and 7:30pm-10pm daily Easter-Oct.; tasting menus
€120-140 per person
Located in the Hotel Signum resort, celebrated island native chef Martina Caruso's exceptional restaurant has been awarded with one Michelin star, and it continues to be one of the top destinations for fine dining in the Aeolian Islands. Chef Caruso's cuisine is an extension of her heart and soul, featuring mesmerizing dishes like fried red mullet with ginger broth and black olives, breaded barbecued spatula (scabbard) fish with almonds and a leche de tigre ceviche sauce, and caper-infused desserts.

Pollara
Al Cappero
Via Marina, 8; tel. 345/7063256; €15-25
Call ahead to reserve a table outside for a sunset aperitivo overlooking the west coast in Pollara. The friendly staff serves up local specialties from Salina including caper farm snacks, Hauner wine, and cocktails.

Rinella
Pa.Pe.Rò
Strada Provinciale, 16; tel. 090/9809161; www.
instagram.com/pa.pe.ro; 8am-midnight daily; €8-24
If you find yourself on the southern coast of Salina in Rinella, stop by this family-owned locale for a meal or after-dinner drinks and live music. Pa.Pe.Rò is open all day for breakfast, lunch, aperitivo, and dinner, featuring dishes such as ricotta granita or gelato, pane cunzatu, stuffed eggplant, arancini, pastas, and fish entrées made with typical ingredients sourced from local producers. It has been in operation since 2006 and was named for the sibling owners—Paola, Peppe, and Rosanna.

BARS AND NIGHTLIFE
Santa Marina
★ Il Limoncino
Via Giuseppe Verdi, 6; tel. 333/1145775; www.instagram.
com/illimoncinosalina; 7pm-2am daily in summer; €6-10
For a good time in Salina, wander 10 minutes down the seafront path from the Santa Marina port and you'll arrive at a lemon. That's the little limoncino, Roberta's secret bright yellow kiosk bar that's shaped like a lemon and offers delicious cocktails and live music in summertime. There are no tables, just the stone wall to perch on. Her unique cocktails are concocted with prepped mixers made from fresh homegrown fruits like apricot puree, and the black mojito is a refreshing blend of rum, ground licorice powder, cane sugar, and mint served with a licorice candy straw. The vibe is as intoxicating as the beverages.

Le Papagayo Lounge
Piazza Santa Marina, 5; tel. 333/1410974; 6pm-3am
daily in summer; €12 cocktails
Options for nightlife in Santa Marina are slim, but there is often live music at Le Papagayo. This outdoor lounge is situated in the main piazza, only five minutes away from the harbor where the boats dock for the night and just down the street from the Mercanti di Mare hotel for those staying overnight in the main town of Salina.

ACCOMMODATIONS
Hotels
Hotel Mercanti di Mare
Piazza Santa Marina, 7, Santa Marina; tel.
090/9843536; www.hotelmercantidimare.it; from €100

Just steps from the main harbor in Santa Marina, this endearing three-star hotel is perfect for those looking for an easy place to rest on a short stay in Salina or while island-hopping in the area. The friendly staff provides a continental breakfast on the terrace in the mornings, and the rooms are simply appointed with terracotta-tiled floors, antique furniture, Wi-Fi, and televisions. Some of the higher-level rooms have their own terraces with hammocks, beach lounge chairs, and sea views overlooking the island of Lipari.

★ Luxury Resorts

Spend your time on Salina in one of its top luxury resorts to relax and experience the beauty of the island with access to top dining options, spa treatments, and concierge services for additional adventures.

Hotel L'Ariana

Via Rotabile, 11, Rinella; tel. 090/9809075; www. ilborgodirinella.com; from €125

This historic villa and boutique four-star hotel in Rinella was built between 1907 and 1909 as a private residence. Restorations took place in 2019 when it was purchased and redesigned, keeping with the classic Liberty style of the early 1900s. In 2020, Hotel L'Ariana became part of the UNA Hotels group as one of its UNA Esperienze listings, known for properties on mainland Italy and especially in Milan.

The name stems from a semi-submerged rock nearby that was featured in the Prince Alliata of Villafranca's series of underwater short films shot in the bay of Rinella. This prestigious location, with views of Mount Etna across the sea, has easy access down a private staircase to the water for a quick swim. The in-house restaurant and La Grotta lounge bar offer a stunning location for a meal or aperitivo. There are 15 spartan-style rooms including Standard double rooms with terraces facing the garden, Classic rooms accommodating a maximum of three guests with partial sea views, and Superior rooms

with sea-facing windows with the option to host up to five guests. The Deluxe suites for two or three guests have their own terraces with south-facing sea views of Lipari, Vulcano, and Filicudi. Set on the coast overlooking the aquamarine sea, Hotel L'Ariana is situated near Salina's secondary harbor and ferry port, within walking distance from restaurants, bars, and shops.

Hotel Principe di Salina

SP182, 3, Malfa; tel. 090/9844415; www. principedisalina.it; from €170

This four-star luxury accommodation nestled in the lush vegetation of the Isola Verde boasts a relaxing geothermal pool. Hotel Principe di Salina can organize cooking classes, private events, and personalized travel itineraries for your trip to Salina. The 12 rooms with private terraces and sea views are perfect for catching the sunrise or sunset overlooking the nearby islands of Stromboli and Panarea.

Hotel Signum

Via Scalo, 15, Malfa; tel. 090/9844222; www. hotelsignum.it; Easter-Oct.; from €200

Hidden away in the green paradise of Salina, this four-star boutique hotel offers an infinity pool overlooking the Gulf of Malfa, a library, a wellness center, a bar, and one of the very best restaurants on the island. The concierge service is at your disposal to organize mountain excursions, boat trips, and wine tastings. The port of Malfa and nearby Spiaggia dello Scario beach are accessible on foot.

Capofaro Locanda & Malvasia

Via Faro, 3, Capo Faro; tel. 090/9844330; www. tascadalmerita.it/tenuta/capofaro

The Tasca d'Almerita winemaking family's five-star resort is surrounded by 11 acres (4.5 ha) of vineyards overlooking the sea on the northeast coast of Salina. Views of the islands of Stromboli and Panarea in the distance, the high-end on-site restaurant and wine bar, tennis court, pool, spa services, and wellness programming provide all the perks needed for a welcoming, relaxing, and luxurious stay with top-notch service. Capofaro can be reached with a 10-minute drive or taxi ride along SP182 from the Santa Marina port or shuttle service provided by the resort. Stays in July and August require a minimum booking of three nights.

GETTING THERE

Ferries to Salina arrive at the **Porto di Santa Marina,** just off the island's main town on the western side of the island, as well as at **Porto di Rinella** on the south coast, both of which have a **Liberty Lines** (www.libertylines.it) ticket office (Santa Marina: tel. 090/9843003; Rinella: tel. 090/9809170). Though not as busy as Lipari, Salina's ports are well connected with the other Aeolian islands and the Sicilian mainland, with hydrofoils to Lipari (20 minutes, 6 sailings daily; €9), Milazzo (1.5 hours, 3 sailings daily; €23); and even Palermo (3.5 hours, 1 sailing daily; €51), though less frequently and in summer only. Santa Marina in Salina is connected by ferry to Lipari (25 minutes), Panarea (30 minutes), and Filicudi (40 minutes).

GETTING AROUND

You can explore the island of Salina on a scooter from **Rent Bongiorno** (Via Risorgimento, 222; tel. 090/9843409), located in the main port. It should be fairly easy to find taxis in the major comuni of Santa Marina and Malfa, or call **Taxi Salina di Daniela** (Via Risorgimento, 81, Santa Marina; tel. 333/6167491) to organize transfers in advance. While the other Aeolian islands offer more in terms of exploring on your own, Salina is the island where you treat yourself, and after getting to your accommodation, you may not need to move around much. Check with your hotel or resort to see if it can provide shuttle services or organize island transfers. Salina is also a great place to explore with a car or motorino.

The main ports of Salina are also connected by aliscafo hydrofoil service provided by **Liberty Lines** (www.libertylines. it; Santa Marina tel. 090/9843003; Rinella tel. 090/9809170). The ride from Santa Marina to Rinella (10 minutes; €7) can be a quick and easy option for those traveling without a car.

Stromboli

The nearly 5-square-mile (13-sq-km) Aeolian island of Stromboli is made up of one of only three remaining active volcanoes in all of Italy. The red neon lava sputting from the volcano is seen best in the evenings, but white-and-gray smoke puffs out of Stromboli all day long, following rhythmic eruptions that occur every 20-30 minutes, almost like clockwork.

The natural elements here have always dictated the pace, strength of the people, and landscape of this small island, nicknamed the "Lighthouse of the Mediterranean." After a devastating tsunami in 2002 and arson fires that swept through 617 acres (250 ha) of land in 2022 followed by terrible mudslides, the people of Stromboli pulled together to overcome and protect their island.

In 1950, Stromboli gained international fame when Italian director Roberto Rossellini's *Stromboli: Terre di Dio,* starring Swedish actress Ingrid Bergman, was filmed on the island. While filming, the cinematic buzz started when the news broke that Ingrid and Roberto began their famous and scandalous love affair here in Stromboli. The brick-red house on Via Vittorio Emanuele where they lived still remains and was converted into a cultural association in her name. There is also Bar Ingrid, nestled at the top of the hill in the main square, Piazza San Vincenzo, where many tourists stop for an aperitivo on the outdoor terrace or simply to take photos of the panoramic view overlooking the sea and the rock formation of Strombolicchio.

The active stratovolcano takes up most of the island with layers of hardened volcanic

Stromboli

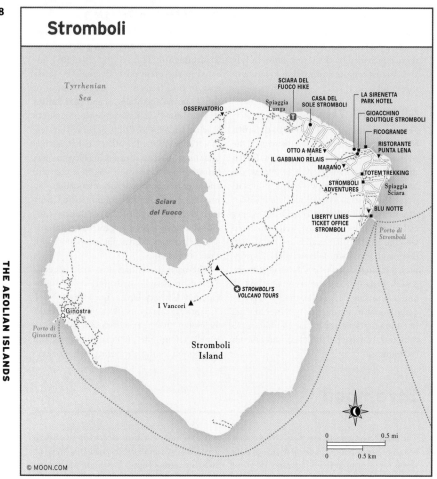

ash, rocks, and lava flows, except for two extremely small coastal villages: Stromboli, on the northeastern coast; and Ginostra to the southwest. Several companies offer nighttime excursions and boating adventures to view the nighttime eruptions.

Orientation

Most of the island is made up of its large volcanic mountain. The only towns located here are the main village of Stromboli on the northeast side and the tiny district of Ginostra on the southwest. Due to the volcano's active state, it is not safe to build anywhere other than these two small areas. Ferry services use the main port of Stromboli, and a few options for the hydrofoil will also stop in Ginostra.

SIGHTS
Stromboli

The island of Stromboli and its volcanic mountain are one and the same. Stromboli is visible on the horizon from the islands of Panarea and Salina. While you'll see it puffing smoke throughout the day, the bright

---

1: eruption on the Stromboli volcano 2: town of Stromboli 3: beach at Ficogrande

volcanic eruptions can be seen best only at nighttime from the water with a boat tour or from specific points on the island, such as the Osservatorio restaurant (along the Sciara del Fuoco hike) or the panoramic points at 951 or 1,312 feet (290 or 400 m) above sea level.

BEACHES
Ficogrande
Via Marina; open 24 hours; free

This black volcanic pebble coast is a better-serviced option for a beach on Stromboli, where you'll find restaurants, beach bar kiosks, and beach chair and umbrella rentals. Just past the Sciara beach, Ficogrande is located near the tourist port where ferries arrive, and slightly downhill from the town of Stromboli. Although there are no public restrooms at this beach, the cafés and bars along the main strip allow paying guests to use their facilities.

Spiaggia Lunga
Via Avv. Domenico Cincotta; open 24 hours; free

Following the perimeter road for 30 minutes on foot, from the port heading northwest, you'll find black-sand beaches speckled between private homes, hotels, and rocky shores. Spiaggia Lunga is a 0.6-mile-long (1 km) shoreline with free public beach areas. Stop by the **Capra Babba** (www.instagram.com/caprababbastromboli; open for breakfast, lunch, and sunset aperitivo) chiringuito beach shack for refreshments and evening cocktails.

Sciara
Via Marina; open 24 hours; free

Starting immediately at the main harbor and ferry port, the 0.6-mile (1-km) stretch of black-sand beach is a popular area for swimming when just popping on shore after arriving in Stromboli. The public beach space is lined with some fishing boats and is located just in front of the main road, Via Marina, where guests can stop in to bars and restaurants for convenient refreshments.

RECREATION
★ Volcano Tours

Hikes to the top of Stromboli are strictly regulated. Although it is possible to hike the volcano independently, hikers aren't permitted higher than 1,300 feet (400 m) up the 3,012-foot (918-m) volcano unguided. The hike is also enhanced with a professional guide, who can provide additional information and the added security that comes from knowing you won't be accidentally walking into a crater. The ascent takes around three hours, and most hikes begin in the late afternoon or early evening, so as to arrive at the crater when the regular eruptions glow neon red against the dark sky.

Stromboli Adventures
Via Roma, 17; tel. 339/5327277; www. stromboliadventures.it; 10am-7pm daily; from €30

Unforgettable experiences led by Stromboli Adventures' alpine guides take guests extremely close to Stromboli's active craters at night. Departing from Stromboli town center, the night trekking excursions can reach heights of over 2,950 feet (900 m) above sea level to view the projectile, firework-like glowing eruptions. Allow at least six hours for this moderate hike.

Trekkers should be in good health and used to walking as well as equipped with the proper recommended gear, including a mandatory helmet (provided), flexible non-slip shoes or trekking boots, long pants, headlamp, an extra T-shirt plus a windbreaker and sweatshirt or fleece, electric flashlight, 1.5-2 liters of water per person, and snacks. All equipment can be rented from **Totem Trekking** (Piazza di San Vincenzo, 4; tel. 090/9865752; www. totemtrekkingstromboli.com).

Hiking
Sciara del Fuoco Hike

Distance: *5 miles (8 km) round-trip*
Time: *3-4 hours round-trip*
Trailhead: *Near Spiaggia Lunga, in Piscità, approximately 1 mile (1.6 km) northwest of Stromboli town*

The hike to this popular viewpoint, with a stunning view of Stromboli's eruptions at night (if at a distance), is the highest hikers can go unguided. It's a switchbacking trail up the coast, with the **Osservatorio** restaurant (Via Mulattiera Salvatore Di Losa) about halfway up (more celebrated for its panoramic views than its food). Because of the loose volcanic soil and some steep sections, hikers should be well equipped with proper hiking shoes, water, and warm clothing, especially if hiking at night (in which case you'll also need a headlamp). All this gear and more can be bought and rented from Totem Trekking in Stromboli town center.

Boat Tours
Chez Peulo
Ficogrande; tel. 339/2109807; chezpeulo@gmail.com; 8:30am-1pm and 4:30pm-8pm daily; from €20 per person

The best way to admire the eruptions of Stromboli's volcano is at night, and even more so from a safe distance at sea. These night excursions take guests out to sea to view the puffs of smoke, ash, and red incandescent eruptions near the blackened Sciara del Fuoco volcanic cliff, without having to spend several hours trekking up the volcano on foot. Evening tours depart at 6:30pm and 8pm, including views of the eruptions and a stop for an aperitivo in Ginostra. Daytime tours depart at 10:30am and 3pm daily.

SHOPPING
Gioacchino Boutique Stromboli
Via Monsignor Antonino di Mattina, 28; tel. 090/986122; www.delfinaletizia.com; 9:30am-1:30pm and 5pm-9pm daily in summer

Young Neapolitan-native Delfina Letizia spends four months per year working side-by-side with her father, Gioacchino, in a small boutique that he's operated since 1973 just steps away from Ficogrande's black-sand beach. Her timeless coverups, bright dresses, and handbags celebrate Italian beach culture with a touch of bohemian vibes.

Totem Trekking
Piazza San Vincenzo, 4; tel. 090/9865752; www. totemtrekkingstromboli.com; 9:30am-1pm and 4pm-8pm daily

Gear up with everything you need for a trek up the volcano in the Stromboli town center at Totem Trekking. It sells equipment and offers rentals for items such as headlamps, hiking boots, binoculars, sleeping bags, walking sticks, and windbreakers. If it seems complicated to make it up to the mid-range elevations on your own, hiring a professional guide is highly recommended.

FOOD AND BARS
Ristorante Punta Lena
Via Marina, 8; tel. 090/986204; www. ristorantepuntalena.business.site; 12:15pm-2:30pm and 8pm-midnight Mon.-Tues. and Thurs., 8pm-midnight Wed., noon-2:30pm and 8pm-10:30pm Fri.; €25

When arriving from the port of Stromboli, Ristorante Punta Lena is located at the very beginning of the Ficogrande beach. This Michelin-recognized seafood restaurant with a beautiful terrace overlooking the sea serves dishes like octopus salad; marinated anchovies; gnocchi with olives, capers, and amberjack; and pasta with wild fennel and cured bottarga tuna roe.

Osservatorio
Via Salvatore di, Mulattiera Salvatore di Losa; tel. 090/9586991; www.facebook.com/ osservatoriostromboli; reservations mandatory

The Osservatorio is the highest panoramic restaurant, where guests have the chance to watch the volcano's eruptions while eating dinner. It is known for its pizza but also serves some simple salads, pastas, and fish entrées; however, you are mainly there for the location and the experience of dining on an active volcano. Make sure to reserve a table outside for the best views of the volcanic eruptions. Indoor dining space is also available for unpredicted rainfall. Reservations are mandatory, and shuttle service is (sometimes) provided and scheduled based on your reservation time. After dinner, make sure to get your name on the waiting list for shuttle service back down to the base of Stromboli. Adventurous guests can walk up or down the hill, but they will need sturdy shoes and flashlights.

Marano

Via Vittorio Emanuele; 8:30am-1pm and 5pm-8pm Mon.-Sat., 9am-1pm Sun.

Stop in this Italian deli and wine shop in the center of Stromboli for delicious sandwiches and snacks to pack for a hike or beach day.

Otto a Mare

Via Vittorio Emanuele; noon-2am daily Aug., 7pm-2am daily July and Sept.

Located in the town center of Stromboli and open only in summertime, this chic garden cocktail bar features creative house-made cocktails and small seasonal dishes enjoyed under Stromboli's volcano.

Blu Notte

Via Marina; tel. 348/4694646

A perfect stop for a welcome spritz when arriving in Stromboli, Blu Notte is a dive bar located between the port of Stromboli and the town's main beachfront strip that turns into one of the very few nightlife spots on the island in the evening, with crowds dancing barefoot and pouring onto the black-sand beach nearby. There are only a few stools at the bar, but fear not, the party continues right outside.

ACCOMMODATIONS

Casa del Sole Stromboli

Via Domenico Cincotta; tel. 090/986300; www. casadelsolestromboli.it; private rooms from €80 per night, shared options from €30 per person

Stromboli tends to be a bit more rustic than the neighboring posh islands of Salina or Panarea. Casa del Sole is an island hostel unlike anything you've ever seen before. The simply furnished rooms, communal kitchen and outdoor dining spaces, and rooftop terrace can be a great option for those who want

to enjoy the simplicity of Stromboli without the expense of staying in a boutique hotel. Casa del Sole is reachable with a 25-minute walk or quick golf-cart taxi ride from the port, located between the Ficogrande and Spiaggia Lunga beaches, just 15 minutes from the highly regarded Punta Lena restaurant. Adventurous beachgoers can reach the Grotta d'Eolo cove in just 2 minutes down an unmarked, rocky pathway.

Il Gabbiano Relais

Via Vito Nunziante; tel. 338/8049982; www. ilgabbianostromboli.it; from €150 per night

Il Gabbiano Relais is a hidden oasis with a private garden pool, just 66 feet (20 m) from the Ficogrande beach. Native "Strombolano" Vito Russo and his wife, Federica Masin, renovated this exclusive four-star hotel from the legendary Il Gabbiano nightclub where they first met. The eight apartments and suites feature sea views, private gardens, and terraces built in the traditional Aeolian style.

La Sirenetta Park Hotel

Via Monsignor di Mattina, 33; tel. 090/986025; www. lasirenetta.it; €90-300 per night with discounted rates for weeklong stays and honeymoons

This four-star hotel is centrally located along the main beachfront road in the town of Stromboli, perfect for exploring the island on foot and spending time on the black-sand beaches just outside your door. With room for up to 46 guests, this peaceful and luxurious hotel is a top destination for accommodations in Stromboli.

GETTING THERE

Stromboli has two ports: the **Porto di Stromboli** (Liberty Lines ticket office: tel. 090/986003), on the eastern coast, and the smaller **Porto di Ginostra** (tel. 331/5979914) to the west, mostly used as a destination for sunset aperitivo. One of the archipelago's main attractions, Stromboli is well connected to the other islands, as well as to Milazzo and even Palermo in summer.

Ferries from Milazzo depart for Stromboli

(1 hour 10 minutes-2 hours 55 minutes) at 6am, 7am, 8am, 9:40am, 1pm, 2:30pm, 3:45pm, and 4:30pm; or Ginostra (1 hour 25 minutes-2 hours 40 minutes) at 6am, 7am, 8am, 1pm, 3:45pm and 4:30pm. Ferries from Lipari depart for Stromboli (1 hour 10 minutes-1 hour 55 minutes) at 8:10am, 9:15am, 10:50am, 2:15pm, 3:40pm, 4:45pm and 6:05pm; or for Ginostra (55 minutes-1 hour 40 minutes) at 8:10am, 9:15am, 2:15pm, 4:45pm and 6:05pm. Ferries from Salina Santa Marina depart for Stromboli (1 hour 15 minutes) at 8:40am, 9:40am, 9:45am, 4:15pm, and 5:20pm; or for Ginostra (1 hour) at 8:40am, 9:40am, 2:40pm, and 5:20pm. Ferries from Panarea depart for Stromboli (40 minutes) at 9:10am, 10:20am, 10:25am, 12:05pm, 3:10pm, 4:50pm, 5:15pm and 6:40pm; or for Ginostra (25 minutes) at 9:10am, 10:25am, 3:10pm, 5:15pm and 6:40pm.

Be sure to check the timetables before planning your trip since schedules and pricing may change depending on the season and day of the week.

GETTING AROUND

Stromboli is small enough to explore on foot, though to travel between the towns of Stromboli and Ginostra, you'll need to take a boat or arrive in the port by ferry service, since there is no road connecting the two towns. Ferry service provided by **Liberty Lines** (www.libertylines.it; €7.80) from Stromboli to Ginostra takes about 10 minutes.

Island-style electric golf-cart taxi services are available when arriving in the port of Stromboli. **Taxi Alberto** (tel. 379/1440404; €10) is one of the more popular companies providing services to help guests get around the island and transport luggage.

Vulcano

The 8-square-mile (21-sq-km) island of Vulcano is the closest of the Aeolian Islands to mainland Sicily. Its main attraction is the still-active Gran Cratere della Fossa. Named after Vulcan, the Roman god of fire, who they believed built his blacksmith forge here, Vulcano islet has lent its name to all the volcanoes around the world. Nowadays, the island has approximately 950 inhabitants.

Vulcano is known as a complex stratovolcano with varying landscapes including lava flows, hardened ash, and the main crater, which still has hot, active fumarole vapors steaming from its moon-like canyon terrain, expelling sulfur, boric acid, and ammonium chloride into the air. Since as early as the 5th century BCE, records of its volcanic activities have continued until the most recent eruption over 130 years ago, which lasted from August 1888 to March 1890.

As of 2020, Vulcano's famously stinky mud baths have been closed off, restricting access to the hot springs and mud bathing areas,

known for their healing purposes. There are potential plans to build a complex of spas in its place. However, it remains closed for now. The local government and trained volcanologists have always kept a close eye on the volcanic activity of the area, and when there is any threat of strong fumaroles coming from the crater, restrictions are placed on hiking up to the caldera.

Orientation

Orient yourself on this pear-shaped island with Vulcanello on the northern tip above the isthmus with its surrounding beach destinations, the main crater and ancient mud baths centrally located, and Gelso and its elusive black-sand beach on the southern coast. Porto di Vulcano, the main port, is where the ferries arrive on the eastern shore. Vulcanello was originally its own island, formed by an eruption in 183 BCE, but through a series of additional eruptions it has been joined with the island of Vulcano since around 1550. Small harbors are available for private boats docking in Vulcano: the Marina di Vulcanello on the northeast, Porto di Ponente on the northwest, and Porto di Levante on the east, just north of the ferry port. Porto di Ponente is also the name of the largest village on the island, close to where the ferry boats arrive, where you'll find a handful of small bars, restaurants, and souvenir shops. Vulcano is one of the least-visited islands by tourists; although there are several hotels and resorts here, it is most often explored by boat on day trips from Lipari or as a stop on a longer tour of all the Aeolian Islands. Most businesses will close by September or October, so be sure to plan your travels to Vulcano accordingly.

SIGHTS
★ Gran Cratere della Fossa
(Riserva Naturale Isola Vulcano)
The Gran Cratere is a 1,600-foot-wide (488-m) volcanic crater located at 2,740 feet (835 m) above sea level in the central part of the island, accessible only by hiking. Gran Cratere can be explored on a self-guided hike, following signs for the crater from the port (Vulcano Porto) to state road SP178. It is advisable to do the route either early in the morning or at sunset (leaving enough time to return before it gets dark) because there is no shade. The crater's hot sulfur vents are still active, and you'll be able to see steam rising from the ground, although some guests have been turned off by the smell, which changes depending on the wind and weather. Visitors are highly advised not to stand too close to the fumaroles or breathe in the gasses that arise from the crater. The path is unpaved and consists of walking on dirt trails, between rocks, and at a constant incline. This hike is only recommended for active travelers without any mobility restrictions. The 3.5-mile (5.6-km) round-trip hike will take approximately 2.5 hours but can be shorter if you decide to reach the summit and then head back down without circumnavigating the crater from all sides.

Monster Valley
(Valle dei Mostri)
Vulcanello; open 24 hours; free
This natural amphitheater is located on the northeastern part of Vulcanello where volcanic lava flows cooled into what looks like a series of lions, bears, eagles, or even dinosaurs, from which the area gets its name. Monster Valley can be explored on foot with a half-hour walk from the ferry port along SP179.

BEACHES
Spiaggia delle Sabbie Nere
Via Porto Ponente, 2; open 24 hours; free
On the west coast of Vulcano, this perfect destination to watch the sunset over Ponente Bay is one of the most beautiful volcanic black-sand beaches in the Aeolian Islands. The soft sand and shallow waters make for a comfortable place to take small children. Free public beach space and the **La Baia Negra** beach club with a restaurant and umbrella rentals (€15) are both available here.

Spiaggia Punta dell'Asino
Strada Serra - Pirrera; open 24 hours; free
The main attraction on the small black-sand beach at Punta dell'Asino is the **Asino Beach** (Strada Serra - Pirrera, 11; tel. 324/9845382; www.asinobeach.it; beach chair rentals for €15-25) club, where guests can stop for lunch or spend the day relaxing on lounge chairs under shaded umbrellas. Its restaurant focuses on wood-fired pizzas; stuffed pizza dough schiacciate filled with tomatoes, anchovies, and cheese; and fruit granita and classic packaged Italian ice creams.

Spiaggia delle Acque Calde
SP179; open 24 hours; free
A prime destination for a swimming break in Vulcano is the fine black-sand beach at Acque Calde (meaning "hot waters"), which bubble up in whirlpools from the clear blue sea. Just north of the thermal mud baths, this area is also referred to as the Spiaggia delle Fumarole

1: Porto di Ponente on Vulcano 2: Vulcano crater

for the submarine emissions of sulfur gas coming up like clouds from the earth's crust. Water shoes are recommended for easier access getting in and out of the water. **Chiosco da Genny** is a small beach bar shack that sells refreshments, sandwiches, and salads at Acque Calde.

FOOD AND BARS

Trattoria da Pina

Strada Provinciale 179, Gelso; https://trattoriadapina. business.site; tel. 368/668555; 12:40pm-2:15pm and 8pm-9:15pm daily; €12-24

This small, home-style Aeolian restaurant is a popular stop for those traveling around the island by boat. Seating is available on the open terrace overlooking the sea at the southern tip of Vulcano. Reservations are recommended.

★ Malvasia Pane Cunzatu & Restaurant

Via degli Eucaliptus; tel. 346/6039439; www. ristorantemalvasiavulcano.it; 7:30pm-10:30pm daily; €14-24

This restaurant, open since 2015, is the one place you need to visit for a casual dinner on Vulcano when arriving in the main port village. It's also known for its outpost in the center of Milazzo, and owner Maurizio Pagano's famous dish is the pane cunzatu, a massive open-faced sandwich with typical Aeolian toppings such as piccadilly tomatoes, mozzarella, oil-preserved tuna fillets, olives, anchovies, raw red onion, and oregano. There is outdoor seating on the terrace and in the garden, where guests can enjoy dinner and a few glasses of the local malvasia Sicilian wine, known for its honeysuckle aromas and pear notes.

Il Cappero Restaurant

Therasia Resort, Vulcanello; tel. 090/9852555; www. ilcapperoristorante.it; 7pm-11pm daily; 8-12-course tasting menus €140-160 per person

Test out the gourmet cuisine of 35-year-old Palermitan executive chef Giuseppe Biuso at this Michelin-starred restaurant inside the Therasia Resort on the west coast of Vulcanello. Small yet exceptionally elegant plates highlight the flavors of the Aeolian Islands, transformed into mouthwatering, innovative fine-dining creations. Reservations are required and a €150 deposit must be made to secure your seating. Children ages 10 and over are permitted, and the dress code is casual/elegant, with long trousers for men.

ACCOMMODATIONS

Les Sables Noirs & Spa

Porto di Ponente; tel. 090/9850; www.lessablesnoirs. it; from €130

This four-star hotel, located near the black-sand beaches on the west coast of the main town, offers one of the best spas around (open noon-9pm daily). Its volcanic ritual includes an enzymatic exfoliation and body massage with notes of amber, myrrh, and heated amber oil for an unforgettable and relaxing sensory experience. The wellness center is equipped with a sauna, Turkish bath, Kneipp Path hydrotherapy machine, sensory showers, indoor and outdoor whirlpools, and relaxation areas. Entry to the spa is not allowed for children under 16 years of age. The 53 rooms and suites are simply decorated with Mediterranean beach charm, including options for gardens or terraces. All rooms are equipped with air-conditioning, Wi-Fi, and television. Make sure to stop by the pool for a few hours or head over to the lounge bar to try an Aeolian bloody Mary made with house-made caper and wild fennel-infused vodka, fresh tomato juice, caper salt, lemon, cucumber, and pepperoncino during a sunset aperitivo on the terrace.

★ Therasia Resort

Vulcanello; tel. 090/9852555; www.therasiaresort.it; from €328

Splurge a little bit and enjoy a pampered stay at this five-star resort in Vulcanello. Pick a room with a view, overlooking the sea, the other Aeolian islands, the faraglioni stone sea stacks, or the volcanic crater either with or without a private furnished terrace with lounge chairs and tables. Rooms and suites feature high-end amenities (satellite TV, air-conditioning, minibar, safe, and Wi-Fi connection) and Mediterranean decor (ceramics, lava stone fixtures, terracotta tiling). In-house dining options include Il Cappero, its Michelin-starred fine-dining restaurant; I Tenerumi, a vegetarian restaurant; the L'Arcipelago and I Grusoni restaurants; and the I Faraglioni and I Russuri outdoor bars. With private beach access, spa services, and candlelit couches on the terrace, this place could not get any more romantic.

GETTING THERE

Since Vulcano is the first stop in the Aeolian Islands when traveling from Milazzo, frequent hydrofoil fast ferries with **Liberty Lines** (www.libertylines.it; 50 minutes; €20) arrive at the **Porto di Vulcano,** near the island's main village on the east coast.

There are also ferries from Lipari to Vulcano for those already traveling through the islands, departing 20 times per day (10 minutes; €7).

For those traveling with a car, **Siremar** (Via dei Mille, 23; tel. 090/9283415; www.siremar.it) offers passage via traghetti ferries

from Milazzo (1 hour 40 minutes; €16 passenger ticket, vehicle fee depends on the make and model, small cars cost approximately €65).

In summertime (June-first week of Sept.), aliscafo fast ferries through Liberty Lines connect Palermo with Vulcano once per day at 1:50pm (4 hours 10 minutes; €53).

GETTING AROUND

While most travelers visiting Vulcano arrive either on boat excursions for a few hours or with the ferry from Milazzo before heading on to spend more time on the other islands, staying around the main port area and exploring on foot is manageable. There are **taxi services** (Taxi Vulcano Mr. Carmelo; tel. 370/3205728) available to make your way to other parts of the island, including Vulcanello in the north and Gelso in the south. Hotels and resorts may also provide shuttle services with prior notice. With your own vehicle, Vulcano can be discovered by car. A trip north from the harbor to Vulcanello will take less than 10 minutes, and the drive south to Gelso will take about 15 minutes, with both routes following the main road, SP179.

Panarea

Panarea is the smallest and the least elevated of the Aeolian islands, clocking in at only 1.3 square miles (3.4 sq km), with 280 year-round residents. It is known as a popular and fashionable Italian holiday destination, with a thriving nightlife in summertime (June-Sept.). Several isolotti (small outer islands and rock formations) also fall under the umbrella of Panarea, including **Basiluzzo,** a 0.4-square-mile (1-sq-km) island featured in the Italian film *L'Avventura* (1960) with Monica Vitti, which is sometimes referred to as the eighth Aeolian island and known in antiquity as Hycesia.

While not in fact a volcano, Panarea is the

largest subaerial component of the underwater volcanic complex between Lipari and Stromboli. It is also the oldest Aeolian island geologically speaking, emerging about half a million years ago. Settlements on the island date back to prehistoric times, as evidenced by the Bronze Age village on the Capo Milazzese promontory in the south of the island. During the Roman era, Panarea was used for strategic trade routes and as a military base. The western and northern parts are characterized by jagged cliffs and inaccessible coasts, but the south and eastern sides of the island are where the beaches, main village, and port are all located.

Panarea

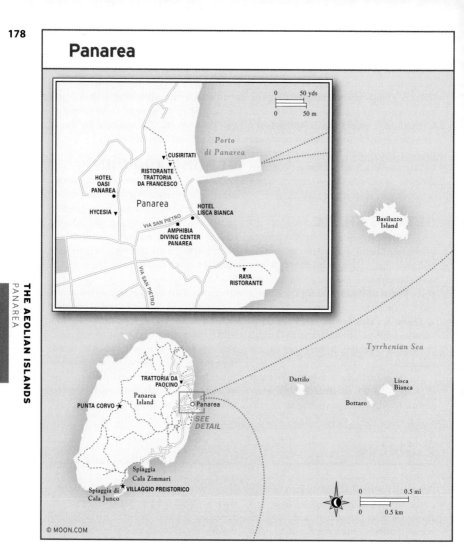

© MOON.COM

Orientation

While there are hiking trails and swimming holes located all around the island, the main town of Panarea is situated on the eastern side, where you'll find restaurants, hotels, shops, and the ferry dock.

SIGHTS
Villaggio Preistorico

Cala Junco; open 24 hours; free

This prehistoric Bronze Age village on Punta Milazzese dates back to the 14th century BCE and is reached by a one-hour walk from the main village, San Pietro, near the port. As it's accessed through the narrow isthmus Indiana Jones-style, visitors are recommended to wear closed-toed shoes and to be extremely careful while walking on the path since it does not have any railings. Here you will find the remaining foundations of 22 oval huts and the base of a rectangular structure that was most likely used as a place of worship. Many excavated objects including black ceramic pottery, millstones, and Mycenaean tools have been placed in the archaeological museum in Lipari. These discoveries prove that the settlement maintained close commercial relations with the Greek world.

Punta del Corvo

Riserva Naturale Orientata Isola di Panarea e Scogli Viciniori; open 24 hours; free

Hike up to the highest point on Panarea for a bird's-eye view of all six of the other Aeolian islands. The Punta del Corvo mountain peak is located in the nature reserve in the center of the island, accessible only on foot. Starting at the Chiesa di San Pietro in the main town, follow signs toward the Riserva Naturale Orientata Isola di Panarea and proceed in the direction of Punta del Corvo. Through 1.2 miles (1.8 km) of unpaved trails, stone paths, and cultivated land surrounded by vegetation, you will reach the peak at an elevation of 1,378 feet (420 m) above sea level. It will take about 1 hour and 30 minutes to reach the top. Keep an eye out for the *Silene hicesiae,* a rare purple flowering plant in the carnation family that is native to this area. Take in the awesome panoramic views before following the same trail back to town, then treat yourself to a well-deserved granita.

BEACHES

Although there are hidden swimming holes and hard-to-reach coves all around the island of Panarea, these two free public beaches are accessible on foot for those who arrive on the island without a sailboat, catamaran, or tour excursion. Both bays, Cala Zimmari and Cala Junco, are located on the southern coast, connected by a small isthmus, or lingua di terra ("tongue of land"), as it's called in Italian, with Cala Junco on the western side of the promontory and Cala Zimmari on the east.

Spiaggia Cala Zimmari

Via Drautto; open 24 hours; free

On the central part of the southern coast, at the foot of the promontory and east of Cala Junco, this dark golden, almost reddish sand beach is one of the most beautiful in Panarea. It can be reached by boat or on foot, either with a few minutes' walk via a trail off the end of Via Drautto or a 40-minute walk from the main town and ferry port. There are no amenities available here except for beach beds available to rent for shade; guests should

Villaggio Preistorico

prepare to pack everything they will need for the day. This destination will be full of people in summertime because of the comfort of the sand, and it is also popular for families traveling with small children.

Spiaggia di Cala Junco

open 24 hours; free

Stopping at the Cala Junco basalt stone beach for sunset is often the bucket list item to check off when visiting Panarea. Most guests travel here by boat for the turquoise, natural swimming pool waters, but it can also be reached with a 40-minute walk toward Punta del Torrione from the main town and ferry port, passing Cala Zimmari and Cala del Morto. A visit to the small amphitheater-shaped bay in Cala Junco can be paired with a stop at the nearby prehistoric village. When visiting on foot for sunset, make sure to leave enough time to return to the port safely afterwards. There are no amenities available; pack enough water and snacks for the day along with sunscreen/hats, water shoes, towels, and possibly a lightweight beach umbrella for shade. The beach is often crowded and the bay full of boats, and the terrain is not suitable for small children.

SHOPPING
Buganville

www.instagram.com/boutiquebuganville; €30-100

This chic boutique carries all the summer wear you didn't even know you were looking for, from stunning patterned sarongs to swimsuits, dresses, hats, woven bags, shoes, unique costume jewelry, and beachy tunics. It's located just up the hill from the port of Panarea. Pop in for a casual browse and try to not burn through your entire shopping budget.

RECREATION
Diving
Amphibia Diving Center Panarea

Via San Pietro; tel. 335/6138529; www.amphibia.it; 8am-7pm daily; from €60

This diving center, located in the main port of San Pietro, was the first on the island.

Four-hour snorkeling or intermediate-level diving excursions are available. Guests can discover the seafloor and wander among plants, shipwrecks, and underwater creatures as they are guided through this adventure. The center also offers multiple classes based on immersion and theory as well as a Bubblemaker program for children eight years and up.

Yoga
Yogarea

tel. 339/4530951; www.yogapanarea.com; group sessions from €15-35, private programming €70-100 per person

Ex-Milanese fashionista turned island goddess, Barbara Compostella is the founder and head teacher of Yogarea. Her roving studio organizes classes including sunset acro-yoga, candlelit yin yoga, hoopyogini hula hoop yoga classes, pranayama meditation, vipassana introspective practices, and vinyasa flow in various locations around the island. She also teaches aquatic programs including a sunrise SUP yoga on paddleboards or aqua yoga in the bay or pool. Private classes can be organized at your resort or apartment rental upon request.

FOOD AND BARS
Trattoria da Paolino

Via Iditella, 75; tel. 090/983008; open May-Oct.; €18-24

"View of Stromboli" catches your attention from the hand-written sign out front. Expect old-world hospitality without bells and whistles, and simple yet plentiful dishes in traditional Aeolian style. Indoor seating is available, but the outdoor tables on the terrace overlook the sea with views, as advertised, of the island of Stromboli on the horizon, sometimes puffing small smoke clouds above it while you dine.

★ Cusiritati

Via Comunale Mare, 70; tel. 090/983022; www. cusiritati.it; noon-2:30pm and 7:30pm-midnight daily; €30-60

An elegant outdoor dining experience

awaits just steps from the harbor in Panarea. Beautifully plated dishes and incredible service let you know that there is a feminine touch behind it. Cusiritati is a family-owned and female-run seafront restaurant, with Federica Sulfaro in the dining room, her sister Sabrina Sulfaro handling wine service, and their mother Marilena Merlino in the kitchen. Even the rest of the kitchen and dining room staff are predominantly female. Recipes are drawn from the influence of the family matriarch, Nonna Amelia, whose caper salad with vinegar is one of the top sellers on the menu.

Hycesia
Hycesia Hotel, Via San Pietro, 20; tel. 090/983041; www.hycesia.it; 8pm-midnight daily; €50-95

A fine-dining, Michelin-mentioned restaurant and award-winning wine cellar is just a five-minute walk from the harbor. Treat yourself to a high-end gourmet dinner at Hycesia on your visit to Panarea. Wine aficionados will enjoy selecting a top-notch bottle from the wine list that features over 1,000 different labels. The ambience is clean, relaxed, and coastal Mediterranean, while the food often leans toward Asian influences. Reservations are highly recommended.

Ristorante Trattoria Da Francesco
Hotel Francesco Panarea, Via San Pietro; tel. 090/983023; www.dafrancescopanarea.com

Since the late 1960s, this excellent seafood-focused trattoria has been featuring celebrated dishes like pasta with swordfish or tuna, eggplant parmigiana, caponata, pane cunzatu, fried squash blossoms, squid with malvasia wine sauce, and eggplant meatballs. Situated right in the harbor, it even offers high-end catered meals (Le Delizie di Nonna Pasqualina; tel. 090/983179), which might tempt those visiting Panarea on a sailboat or yacht. Reserve your table on the outdoor terrace overlooking the sea.

★ Raya Ristorante
Via Comunale Mare; tel. 090/983013; www.hotelraya.it; cocktails €20, mocktails €10

This hotel, restaurant, and nightclub is the epicenter of Panarea's summer nightlife. The terraced outdoor spaces offer sea views overlooking the harbor, where anyone who's anyone can stop in for sunset aperitivo, if they're willing to pay for the location, and take a few photos before leaving Panarea. Beautifully presented and well-mixed artisanal cocktails include unique ingredients such as malvasia wine, capers, jasmine, passion fruit, and chamomile. Music and DJ sets are organized throughout summertime, and the party goes well into the night. Dinner is served on the terrace and rooms are available, but mostly people come here for the ambience of the cocktail bar. Reservations are highly recommended.

ACCOMMODATIONS
Hotel Oasi Panarea
Via S. Pietro; tel. 090/983338; www.hoteloasipanarea.com; from €89

Head up the hill just six minutes on foot from the port and relax for the night at this charming four-star hotel paradise. Open since 2010, Hotel Oasi has various lush gardens with lounge chairs and cabanas, an outdoor swimming pool, and two in-house restaurants with open-air terraces and sea views. The outdoor spaces are the real treat. The rooms are extremely simple; however they are air-conditioned and include small private patios. Wi-Fi service is available throughout the property. Transfer service from the port, boat rentals, and helicopter excursions are available upon request.

★ Hotel Lisca Bianca
Via Lani, 1; tel. 090/983004; www.liscabianca.it; from €200

The whitewashed buildings with blue doors and windows make up the complex of this four-star hotel overlooking the sea, just 656 feet (200 m) from the ferry dock. The Mediterranean-style Classic or Junior suite rooms have views of either the garden or the sea, each one equipped with air-conditioning, though Wi-Fi service is only available on the terrace. Small pets are welcome. There is an on-site bistro bar that serves lunch and dinner as well as gelato and coffee throughout the day. The in-house lounge bar, Banacalii, is open sunset-2am. In July and August it hosts dance parties and DJs at night, bringing the nightlife of Panarea alive.

GETTING THERE

The **Porto di Panarea** (Via Comunale Mare; tel. 0565/912191) is situated on the eastern coast, overlooking the island of Stromboli and the minor island of Panarea. Aliscafo fast ferries serviced by **Liberty Lines** (tel. 090/9812448; www.libertylines.it) connect Panarea with direct routes from Santa Marina Salina (25 minutes; €10), Lipari (30 minutes; from €10) and Stromboli (25-40 minutes; from €11). Panarea can also be reached with an island-hopping fast ferry that departs from Milazzo (about 2 hours; from €22).

SNAV ferry services to Panarea are also available from **Naples Mergellina,** though only May-September, departing at 2:30pm and stopping at Stromboli on the way. Prices for the approximately five-hour journey start from around €50 each way. Timetables and ticketing information can be found online at www.directferries.com.

GETTING AROUND

In summertime there are restrictions on the number of cars arriving in Panarea, so for the most part transportation on the island is limited, primarily only **golf carts** that serve the island as taxi cabs. The small town and its whitewashed lanes can be explored on foot, as restaurants, bars, and shops are all reachable with a short walk, sometimes leading up the hill where guests have a great view of the harbor and Stromboli in the distance. Golf-cart taxis will be lined up in front of the port, ready to take you to your destination.

Filicudi

Filicudi has two main ports: Porto di Filicudi on the southern part of the east coast, where most ferries dock, and Pecorini a Mare, a popular nightlife spot on the southern shore where sailboats, yachts, and catamarans moor in the harbor. Monte Fossa Felci, which can be reached on a trekking excursion, is the highest peak on the island at 2,539 feet (77 m) above sea level. This tiny islet is one of the smallest of the Aeolian Islands, with only 200 year-round residents and a total area of 3.7 square miles (9.5 sq km). The remains of Filicudi's prehistoric village are situated at Capo Graziano in the southeast corner, a 15-minute walk south from the main ferry port. While Panarea is a bit more of a chic, VIP island, Filicudi is a sought-after holiday destination for those looking for a mixture of extravagance and nature, populated in summertime with mostly Italian visitors.

SIGHTS
Villaggio Preistorico

Località Capo Graziano; open 24 hours; free

Some say this Neolithic and Bronze Age period prehistoric village dates back to 3000 BCE, although it wasn't discovered until the 1950s. To arrive here within 15 minutes on foot, head south on Via Porto from the ferry terminal toward Via Filicudi Porto, turn right onto Località Le Punte e Piano del Porto, and follow trail signs to the left for Località Capo Graziano. Similar to the prehistoric village in Panarea, although much older, here you will find the foundation remains of 25 stone huts that were used until approximately 1430 BCE, based on the findings of ceramics excavated from the site.

Grotta del Bue Marino

Accessible only by sea, this water cave on the west coast of Filicudi is one of the island's most precious natural wonders and the largest cave in the Aeolian Islands. Once populated with monk seals (from which it takes its name), this iconic, gaping 98-foot-wide (30-m) cavern on the coastline has azure water that sparkles as the sunlight hits it during the day and reflects on the stone shore. It's a popular place to stop for a swim on a boat tour or drop the anchor down at sunset.

BEACHES

Spiaggia di Pecorini a Mare
Località Pecorini a Mare; open 24 hours; free
From the main ferry port, visitors can reach this beach on foot with a 45-minute walk (3.1 mi/5 km) or a 15-minute taxi ride. For those arriving in Filicudi here at Pecorini a Mare, the 2,790-foot-long (850-m) stretch of soft, round stone beachfront begins right below the village's main bars and restaurants. Water shoes are highly recommended. There are no amenities in the central part of this beach; however, there is a beach club, **Lido La Sirena** (Via Pecorini a Mare; tel. 348/3500272; www. pensionelasirena.it), and a small bar located on the western end of the beach, where guests can rent thatched umbrellas and lounge chairs. Keep in mind, this is the only beach club on the island.

Spiaggia del Porto
Via Porto; open 24 hours; free
The coast along the main ferry port on the east side of the island is another option for guests arriving by aliscafo from the other islands. Water shoes are also recommended for this stone beach, as well as lightweight beach umbrellas in addition to plenty of drinking water and snacks for the day.

RECREATION
Diving
I Delfini Filicudi
Via Pecorini a Mare; tel. 340/1484645; www. idelfinifilicudi.com; 8am-8pm daily
This diving school in Pecorini a Mare offers excursions to Filicudi's various underwater locations that will satisfy all divers,

from beginners to the most experienced. In addition to daily guided excursions, the company also rents diving equipment, snorkels, fins, and refill tanks. Popular diving destinations in Filicudi include Secca di Stimpaganto, Cassone, Grotta delle Ciprée, Scoglio della Fortuna, I Cunicoli, Scoglio Giafante, I Canaloni, and Grotta dei Gamberi. Local flora and fauna such as moray eels, sea sponges, colorful corals, sea bream, scorpion fish, groupers, yellow gorgonians, snappers, amberjacks, damselfish, and octopus can be spotted in many of these destinations.

Boat Rentals
I Delfini Filicudi
Via Pecorini a Mare; tel. 340/1484645; www. idelfinifilicudi.com; 8am-8pm daily
The same company with the diving school also offers boat rentals. There are different options available for day trips around Filicudi. The most popular is the traditional 19-foot (5.8-m) wooden gozzo, which is perfect for touring around small inlets and comes equipped with a swimming ladder, sun awning, and outboard motor and does not require a boating license. A 22-foot (6.7-m) gozzo will require a boating license and provides additional space and comfort for those who want to go farther, to the nearby islands of Alicudi or Salina. Rubber gommone dinghy motorboats are much faster and come in various sizes: a 16-foot (4.9-m) (no license required) or a 30-foot (9.1-m) boat with a more powerful engine.

SHOPPING
Isole & Vulcani
Località Pecorini a Mare, 1; tel. 328/9273631; www. isolevulcani.com; 10am-9pm daily in summer
Stop in this tiny boutique in the port of Pecorini a Mare for a new Italian-made swimsuit. Created by Daniela Fadda, Cristiano Fini, and Sara Goldschmied, "islands and volcanoes" offers standout contemporary designs for one-piece and bikini bathing suits for women, made from naturally dyed, organic jersey cotton.

FOOD AND BARS

Ristorante La Canna

Via Rosa, 43; Porto di Filicudi; tel. 336/926560; www.
lacannahotel.it/ristorante-filicudi; open for lunch and
dinner

Located in the La Canna Hotel near the main port, this restaurant owned by the Anastasi-Merlino family is open year-round, a wonderful perk for the smaller of the Aeolian Islands. The cuisine is traditional for the area, with seafood in abundance depending on what is caught daily. In summertime, it features fresh dishes including insalata caprese, grilled fish, and seafood-based pastas. In winter, a cozy fireplace adds to the relaxing atmosphere in the indoor tavern.

Da Nino Sul Mare

Via Porto; tel. 328/6559226; www.filicudieolie.it/
ristorante; open for breakfast, lunch, and dinner

This outdoor restaurant is more than conveniently located in the port of Filicudi, only a one-minute walk from where the ferry drops you off. The dining terrace overlooks the water in this casual locale, where visitors can try the local dishes including the catch-of-the-day specials and coastal Sicilian favorites. The menu changes depending on what's available, and it's a good place to enjoy home-cooked Aeolian-style cuisine without breaking the bank. Sandwiches, salads, arancini, and Palermitan-style sfincione focaccia pizzas are available at the bar for those heading to the beach or out to sea for the day. Granita and gelato are also always a good idea in a pinch.

La Sirena

Località Pecorini a Mare; tel. 090/9889997; www.
lasirenafilicudi.com

Just steps from the port of Pecorini a Mare, recognizable by the wide terrace and large handwritten sign, this seafront hotel restaurant is a great choice for those looking to taste the local specialties in Filicudi while dining al fresco. Also check out its small fish shack sister restaurant **Filicrudi** (www.instagram.

com/sushi_filicrudi), just around the corner, serving up Aeolian-style sushi and raw fish dishes June-September.

Filicudi Saloon

Località Pecorini a Mare; €2-8

The most common place to gather in summertime for drinks is in the small piazzetta square in Pecorini a Mare just in front of the Hotel Sirena building. Most drinks are taken in plastic to-go cups since all the nightlife exists outside on the beachfront. Stop by this historic small bar, known simply as "the saloon," for a glass of local malvasia wine, a cold beer, soft drink, simple mixed drinks, and a bag of potato chips just in time for sunset. New tables were added on a small seafront patio platform built during the summer of 2022, where guests can more comfortably sit at a table to relax over a few drinks on this mini pier.

ACCOMMODATIONS

Villa La Rosa

Via Rosa, 24, Porto di Filicudi; tel. 090/9889965; www.
villalarosa.itl; open May-mid-Sept.; from €85

This three-star villa is positioned less than 0.6 mile (1 km; 15 minutes on foot) from the Filicudi Porto and 2.5 miles (4 km; 10-minute drive) from Pecorini a Mare. Each of the spacious rooms is equipped with two or three beds, bathroom with shower, external thatched terrace, mini-fridge, air-conditioning, hair dryer, and security safe. Outside there are communal patio spaces, a peaceful garden, and a pool with beach lounge chairs. Villa La Rosa also offers half or full-board meals, room service, a restaurant conveniently located just across the street, as well as discounts on five-night stays. Staff can assist with scooter or car rentals for guests looking to explore a bit farther from the two port areas in the southern part of the island.

Hotel La Canna

Via Rosa, 43, Porto di Filicudi; tel. 336/926560; www.
lacannahotel.it

Open year-round, this 14-room three-star hotel located near the main port of Filicudi offers panoramic east-facing sea views of Salina and Lipari. Guests can easily arrive on foot when traveling by ferry service to Filicudi. Also owned by the Anastasi-Merlino family, on-site Ristorante La Canna offers hearty Aeolian cuisine at lunch or dinnertime. Free parking is available for those renting motorini scooters during their stay. The hotel also has a pool and solarium where guests can unwind and relax.

La Sirena

Località Pecorini a Mare; tel. 090/9889997; www. lasirenafilicudi.com

The one and only hotel in Pecorini a Mare is the simply decorated five-room La Sirena. Equipped with its own restaurant, sushi bar, and beach club, it has the market cornered in this tiny seafront village on the south coast of Filicudi. Single-, double-, and triple-occupancy rooms are available and include Wi-Fi service, air-conditioning, hair dryers, and breakfast. Upon request, staff can organize shuttle service from the Filicudi Porto, beach bed and umbrella rentals on its lido, and boat tours.

GETTING THERE

Ferry service and aliscafo hydrofoils arrive and depart in the **Porto di Filicudi** (Pontile di Aliscafi e di Traghetti) harbor, with frequent transfers through **Liberty Lines** (tel. 090/9812448; www.libertylines.it), especially in summertime.

From Milazzo (2 hours 30 minutes; €32),

the hydrofoil will first stop in Vulcano followed by Lipari, Santa Marina, and Rinella before arriving in Filicudi Porto. Service to Filicudi is available year-round from Rinella in Salina (25 minutes; €13) and Santa Marina Salina (40 minutes; €15), from Alicudi (25 minutes; €13), and from Lipari (1 hour 10 minutes; €19). In summer, June-first week of September, there is service available from Palermo, stopping first in Alicudi before arriving in Filicudi.

GETTING AROUND

There's no need for any mode of transportation here on Filicudi: Everything can be discovered on foot or by sea. In fact, only residents are permitted to have cars on this small island. Several local taxi drivers can provide a quick lift between the two ports: **Pietro & Francesca** (tel. 347/5171825), **Alessio Bonica** (tel. 340/1984307), or **Pino Randaggio** (tel. 340/1484653).

For those who want to explore Filicudi a bit deeper, it's possible to make plans ahead of time to discover the land and sea. Boating around the island is the best way to discover off-the-beaten-path destinations, hidden swimming spots, and the Grotta del Bue Marino cave. Motorino scooters can be rented from **Nino on Via Pecorini** (tel. 0368/7437104), and boat rentals are available through **Centro Noleggio Filicudi** (Via Porto; tel. 340/9579831; 9am-1pm and 2:30pm-8pm daily) in the main port.

Alicudi

The farthest-flung of the island chain, Alicudi is also the most rustic. There is no pharmacy or post office, barely any restaurants, and only a sprinkling of bed-and-breakfasts, some within walking distance from the port. All the buildings on the island are either located in the port or staggered up a steep hill; the islanders often refer to the location of their house based on how many steps it takes to get to it (anywhere up to 800). The fertile soil of this tiny, round island is covered in vegetation and cultivated with olives, grapes, prickly pear cacti, and capers.

The ancient name of the island was Ericusa, derived from the massive spread of heather, a plant that still characterizes the area today. Alicudi was formed roughly 150,000 years ago and has been scarcely populated since the 17th century. Recently, , Alicudi is populated with only 120 inhabitants, and the locals survive off fishing, agriculture, and tourism/hospitality in summertime.

Myths, folklore, and wonder have always surrounded this island, from stories of women growing wings and flying like witches through the air to stones falling from the sky, the ominous abandoned hamlet of Bazzina Alta, or the locals being poisoned by rye bread infected with a fungus that caused LSD-like hallucinations.

For those spending a few days on Alicudi, a boat rental is your best bet for exploring the island on your own. Circumnavigation will take about an hour to cruise around about 6 miles (9.7 km) of coastline. It is truly an island off another island, seemingly in the absolute middle of nowhere—a place for lovers of unspoiled nature and relaxation.

BEACHES

If you ask around looking for a beach club with lounge chairs under umbrellas and cocktails served to you on Alicudi, the locals might just laugh in your face or perhaps point you in the direction of a make-believe locale. The island of Alicudi is wild and natural with stone beaches open to the public—a perfect place for a late-night skinny dip.

Spiaggia di Alicudi Porto

Via Perciato; open 24 hours; free

This is the only beach accessible on foot from the ferry pier. The 2,300-foot-long (700-m) stone beachfront on both sides of the dock in the main town is the easiest option for taking a dip as soon as you arrive in Alicudi. Water shoes are recommended for small children; in fact, everyone will have a more comfortable swim with a pair.

Spiaggia Bazzina

Località Castello

Reachable only by boat, the stone beach on the northern part of the east coast is another destination for a swimming break during a boat trip around the island. This pebbled cove offers shallow, crystal clear blue water, ideal for snorkeling. There are no amenities available. Make sure to pack water and food on a day trip anywhere outside the main village in Alicudi.

RECREATION

Da Simone

tel. 334/5305872 or 327/9118007

Simone is the man you'll need to track down to rent a gommone motorboat in the port of Alicudi. He also offers boat tours of the island and tours to Filicudi, as well as rentals for day trips on your own.

FOOD AND BARS

The top dining experiences in Alicudi are the renowned "home restaurants" where guests are invited into a local cook's home to dine with them at a communal table. It's a great way to meet people, whether you are staying on the island for a few days or just passing through on a boat trip for the night. While not publicized much due to the fear of at some point being shut down for sanitation violations, they are not hard to find. All you need to do is ask around when you arrive and reserve a few places at the table for the most heartfelt home-cooked food in town. Family-style plates of polpette di pesce fish meatballs, totani fritti fried squid, pasta, and caponata just keep coming. Cash only, approximately €40 per person. Just ask for Silvio or Adriana.

L'Airone

Via Perciato, Alicudi Porto; tel. 389/1131593; €15-35
This will become your favorite bar after a few days on Alicudi—it's the only bar in fact. Start your day with a morning coffee/cappuccino and cornetto Italian croissant, stop by midday for a deep-fried arancini rice ball and an ice-cold granita, pop in for a bottle of water and a cold beer after a long day in the sun, stay for a plate of pasta or grilled fish for dinner and maybe another few beers later in the evening. What else is there to do? Just enjoy the pace and go with the flow of island life.

Alimentare

Via Perciato, Alicudi Porto; 9am-12:30pm and 3:30pm-7:30pm daily
The lone store in the port of Alicudi sells the bare necessities like staple grocery items including bottled water, pasta, coffee, beer, milk, and limited fresh fruits and vegetables. Fresh bread is even delivered on the ferry each day. Order some cold cuts or have the deli prepare a sandwich to take to the beach for the day, or pick up ingredients to prepare a meal if your holiday home has a kitchen.

ACCOMMODATIONS

★ Giardino dei Carrubi

Via XXIV Maggio; tel. 380/7836666; www.facebook.com/giardinocarrubi; from €98
Check out the Giardino dei Carrubi for an affordable overnight stay that doesn't require trekking all the way up the hill, only 365 steps up. Open May-September, this vacation home property can be reached with a 15-minute walk up the stone staircase of the main port. The communal open terrace space has views of the sea and the island of Filicudi in the distance, and is decked out with hammocks, a dining table, and shaded cushioned benches. Simply appointed, spartan-style guest rooms have panoramic sea views, Wi-Fi service, and a private bathroom with shower. Relax in the pure silence of Alicudi under the stars in your little slice of paradise.

Hotel Ericusa

Via Perciato; tel. 328/7495992; www.alicudihotel.it; from €160
"No frills" should be the slogan of this island; visitors come to Alicudi to relax, unplug, and slow down. All 21 guest rooms here have sea views, as the hotel complex spreads out along the coastline, just a five-minute walk from the ferry dock heading west on Via Lungomare Alicudi toward the southernmost tip of the island. Take a swim right out front and enjoy a complimentary beach umbrella. Open June 1-September 15. Rates can include half-board meals as well. The restaurant serves traditional hearty Aeolian dishes of grilled local fish, lobster, totani squid, salads, and pastas. At the bar, there's no shame in treating yourself to at least two granitas per day to refresh from the summer heat.

GETTING THERE

Alicudi is at the westernmost point and the first stop in the Aeolian Islands when traveling from Palermo. Hydrofoil fast ferries serviced by **Liberty Lines** (www.libertylines.it; 2 hours; from €36) connect with the **Alicudi Porto,** in the island's village on the southern coast, departing from Palermo twice per day at 1pm and 5:15pm.

There are also fast ferries from Milazzo to Alicudi (3 hours; €38), making stops on

Vulcano, Lipari, Santa Marina and Rinella on Salina, and Filicudi. For those already traveling through the islands, Alicudi is easily reached with Liberty Lines from Filicudi (25 minutes; €13), Santa Marina Salina (1 hour 10 minutes; €21), and Lipari (1 hour 40 minutes; €18).

No vehicles are permitted on Alicudi; traveling with your own car is not an option for this destination.

GETTING AROUND

Get ready to pound the pavement because getting around Alicudi only happens on foot. There are frightfully hardworking mules that are led up and down the mountain all day long, carrying merchandise to the houses above for about €20 per trip. To save these beautiful animals the hassle, try to pack lightly for Alicudi and plan to schlep your gear on your own.

Catania, Mount Etna, and Northeastern Sicily

Under the shadow of Mother Etna, on this com-pelling, action-packed coast of Sicily, you can enjoy luxurious resorts in Taormina, hike the volcano and taste wine grown on its slopes, and savor Catania's vibrant nightlife, all within an hour's drive. The history of the intricate black-rock city of Catania, the province's largest city and home to Sicily's biggest airport, is one of destruction and renewal. The Baroque city you see today was literally reborn from the ashes after repeated, devastating volcanic eruptions and earthquakes. Smaller and not as chaotic as Palermo, but more vivacious than timeless Syracuse to the south, Catania's spirited, youthful energy can be seen in its lively fish market and piazzas frequented by the city's large student population.

Highlights

Look for ★ to find recommended sights, activities, dining, and lodging.

★ **Piazza del Duomo:** Catania's main square is home to its Baroque cathedral and an elephant statue beloved by the city (page 196).

★ **Pescheria di Catania:** Sicily's top fish market, also known as A' Piscaria, is an exuberant, open-air culinary theater (page 201).

★ **Festa di Sant'Agata:** The multiday procession and religious festival attracts nearly one million people every February (page 205).

★ **Teatro Antico di Taormina:** This picturesque ancient Greek theater is nestled on the cliffs of Taormina overlooking the Ionian Sea (page 216).

★ **Climbing Mount Etna:** It's a rite of passage to summit Europe's highest volcano (page 225).

★ **Tasting Volcanic Wines:** The wines that come from the high-altitude, lava-stone-lined vineyards climbing Mount Etna are complex, mineral-rich, and utterly unique (page 228).

Catania, Mount Etna, and Northeastern Sicily

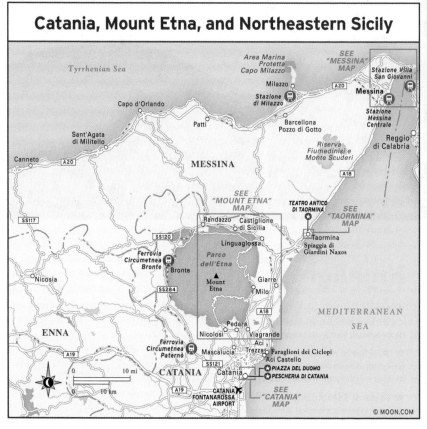

© MOON.COM

Just a short drive north, dramatically situated on cliffs overlooking the Ionian Sea, Taormina is the most-visited destination on Sicily's east coast, its ancient Greek heritage drawing tourists since the 19th century. The postcard-perfect scenery comes at a cost, as Taormina becomes very crowded in the high season. It's a place to splurge if you're looking for luxury and sea views, with a wide selection of lavish five-star hotels and award-winning fine-dining locales.

ORIENTATION

The northeastern coast is yet another Sicilian region that offers something for everyone, from archaeological sites to bustling cities, outdoor adventures, gorgeous beaches, and island excursions. The **A18** eastern highway connecting **Messina,** almost in Sicily's northernmost tip, to **Catania** makes coastal travel from the **Catania Fontanarossa Airport** to the cliffside town of **Taormina** extremely accessible. Traveling inland to **Mount Etna** to hike or sample wine can be a bit slower; the steep slopes of the 25-mile-wide (40-km) volcano require some time and patience to navigate; seasoned visitors often divide the area up into slopes and concentrate on one specific area. Also included within the province of Messina, the seven-island **Aeolian**

Previous: Teatro Antico di Taormina with Mount Etna in the distance; vineyards in the shadow of Mount Etna; climbing Mount Etna.

archipelago is about 35 miles (56 km) off Sicily's northern coast, accessible by ferry service from Milazzo, Messina, and Palermo.

PLANNING YOUR TIME

Flying into the Catania Fontanarossa Airport is the most efficient way to arrive on the eastern side of Sicily; traversing the rural roads of the island from the airport in Palermo takes at least 2-3 hours, depending on your destination. Though major cities like Catania and Taormina are connected by train, most travelers to this part of Sicily rent a car, the most convenient way to move from town to town and practically essential for visiting Mount Etna unless you're traveling with a tour.

This region deserves at least a five- to seven-day trip. **Catania** or **Taormina** is an ideal base from which you can take day trips to nearby attractions. Taormina can be visited in one day, although once you see the views, you'll want to stay much longer (if your budget allows). Catania offers cheaper accommodations and is worth a day or two of exploring, with some of the best nightlife on the island. **Messina** has always gotten the short end of the stick and is often used only as a stopover, but here you will also find great dining options, last-minute shopping, and nightlife.

The slopes of **Mount Etna** also require a few days in themselves, in order to pack in wine tastings (all of which must be reserved in advance), agriturismo farm stays, amazing restaurants, and some trekking or even skiing. Booking a **private driver** for wine-tasting trips is highly recommended, as driving after dark on the mountain roads should be avoided when possible; one of the best ways to hike to the summit is on a private tour. Be sure to bring good hiking boots and warm layers for any trip up Mount Etna, whose high elevation (11,000 ft/3,300 m) means cool temperatures are possible year-round and can even drop down to -12°C (10°F).

This region can be visited any time of year; **July** through **September** is generally busiest in any part of southern Italy, and prices increase drastically during this period. Harvest season in **September** and **October** means wineries will have plenty of work to do and tasting visits may be limited. To make the most of your trip, try quieter alternatives, like a springtime Mount Etna wine-tasting trip, skiing in March, seeing the ancient Greek theater of Taormina in the quiet of winter, or venturing to the Aeolian Islands from Messina in September.

Itinerary Ideas

THREE DAYS IN NORTHEASTERN SICILY

This three-day itinerary will give you a taste of northeastern Sicily, with a mix of fine dining and casual culinary experiences, winery visits, cultural sights, half-day guided tours, and unique, top-notch accommodations. Guided tours and accommodations must be reserved in advance, restaurant reservations are highly recommended, and calling ahead is a must if you want to visit any wineries.

Day One: Catania

1 Upon arrival in eastern Sicily at the Catania Fontanarossa Airport, transfer to the city center with a 10-minute drive or taxi ride or 25-minute train ride. Spend the morning watching the famous open-air culinary theater of the vibrant **Pescheria di Catania** fish market.

Itinerary Ideas

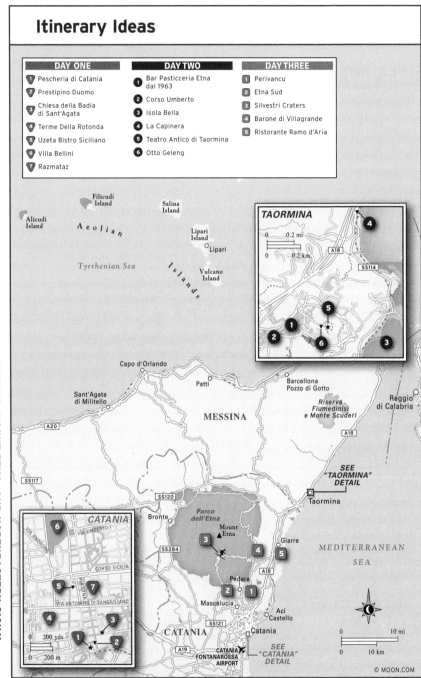

DAY ONE
1. Pescheria di Catania
2. Prestipino Duomo
3. Chiesa della Badia di Sant'Agata
4. Terme Della Rotonda
5. Uzeta Bistro Siciliano
6. Villa Bellini
7. Razmataz

DAY TWO
1. Bar Pasticceria Etna dal 1963
2. Corso Umberto
3. Isola Bella
4. La Capinera
5. Teatro Antico di Taormina
6. Otto Geleng

DAY THREE
1. Perivancu
2. Etna Sud
3. Silvestri Craters
4. Barone di Villagrande
5. Ristorante Ramo d'Aria

TAORMINA

0   0.2 mi
0   0.2 km

CATANIA

0   200 yds
0   200 m

Filicudi Island

Salina Island

Alicudi Island

Aeolian

Lipari Island
Lipari

Tyrrhenian Sea

Islands

Vulcano Island

Capo d'Orlando

Patti

Barcellona Pozzo di Gotto

Sant'Agata di Militello

Riserva Fiumedinisi e Monte Scuderi

Reggio di Calabria

MESSINA

SEE "TAORMINA" DETAIL

Taormina

Bronte

Parco dell'Etna

Mount Etna

Giarre

MEDITERRANEAN SEA

Pedara

Mascalucia

Aci Castello

CATANIA

Catania

CATANIA FONTANAROSSA AIRPORT

SEE "CATANIA" DETAIL

0   10 mi
0   10 km

© MOON.COM

2 Stroll through the Piazza del Duomo and step inside the richly decorated Cattedrale di Sant'Agata before stopping for an espresso and minna di vergine pastry at **Prestipino Duomo.**

3 Climb to the top of the **Chiesa della Badia di Sant'Agata** for a bird's-eye view of the city.

4 Tour some of Catania's ancient Roman sites, from the Teatro Romano to the nearby remains of thermal baths at **Terme Della Rotonda.**

5 Take a break with a light Sicilian lunch at **Uzeta Bistro Siciliano.**

6 You'll end up at the peaceful **Villa Bellini** park, where you can find a place to sit and snack on a baked good from nearby Pasticceria Savia.

7 Head back down Via Etnea toward Piazza del Duomo for a casual dinner and glass of wine at **Razmataz.**

Day Two: Taormina

1 Today, make a luxurious day trip (by train, private driver, or rental car) to the cliff-side city of Taormina. Start your morning with a traditional Sicilian breakfast at **Bar Pasticceria Etna dal 1963.**

2 Explore on your own to visit shops such as Majolica and Feliciotto in the historic center of Taormina, most of which are on or just off the main road of **Corso Umberto.**

3 Take the cable car to **Isola Bella,** a tiny island nature reserve floating in Taormina's bay.

4 Take a leisurely lunchtime break over a relaxing meal at Michelin-starred **La Capinera.**

5 In the afternoon, visit the **Teatro Antico di Taormina,** a well-preserved, ancient cliffside Greek theater built in the 3rd century BCE.

6 End your day with a sunset aperitivo on the picturesque terrace of another Michelin-starred restaurant, **Otto Geleng,** before the hour-long drive or train back to Catania.

Day Three: Mount Etna

1 After an early breakfast at your hotel, drive one hour north to Mount Etna, stopping at **Perivancu** en route to pick up picnic supplies for later.

2 Head to the **Etna Sud** cable car station, where you'll meet up with your guide from Go Etna for a half-day tour of Mount Etna's steaming craters, all the way up to the volcano's highest point.

3 After an adventurous morning, enjoy a picnic made up of locally grown ingredients overlooking the lunar landscapes of the nearby **Silvestri Craters.**

4 Head about 40 minutes east to the **Barone di Villagrande** winery for a pre-scheduled tour and wine tasting.

5 You've earned a quiet evening sipping volcanic wines during a special dinner at **Ristorante Ramo d'Aria,** another 20 minutes east, before heading back to Catania.

Catania

Founded by the Greeks as Katané in 729 BCE, Catania experienced much the same history of successive regimes as the rest of Sicily, from the Romans, to the Vandals, to the Byzantine Empire, to the Normans. Perhaps the most dramatic shaper of Catania's history is Mount Etna, a constant presence looming over the city's red rooftops.

Etna's largest recorded eruption occurred in 1669, followed by a devastating earthquake in 1693, which wiped out two-thirds of the population and nearly destroyed the entire city. This makes Catania's relationship with the volcano they call "Mamma Etna" conflicted: a symbol of destruction, but also of rebirth. The earthquake broke apart old lava flows in the surrounding area that were then used to rebuild the city and pave the streets of Catania with the distinctive black volcanic stone you see today. The repeated eruptions are also responsible for the city's wealth of Baroque architecture, the style in vogue when Catania was rebuilt in the early 18th century; Catania is included in the UNESCO World Heritage Sites known as the Late Baroque Towns of the Val di Noto.

A prosperous port since its founding, this unique black-rock city, the second largest in Sicily, is a university town with a vibrant nightlife and cultural scene rivaling that of Palermo. The Catanese are known for their open-mindedness and entrepreneurial spirit. With exceptional restaurants, street food, and bars, Catania is a top destination for travelers seeking an authentic Sicily.

Orientation

The center of Catania is its **Piazza del Duomo,** where you'll find the cathedral devoted to the city's patron saint, Sant'Agata. The vivacious morning fish market is located just off this main piazza. Most of the restaurants, hotels, and bars are located over the 0.6 mile (1 km) or so between the **Cattedrale di Sant'Agata** and **Villa Bellini** park to the north, along major avenue **Via Etnea.**

Catania is a busy commercial port, with most cruise ships and ferries docking at **Porto di Catania**'s Cruise Port, south of the city center. This means much of Catania's waterfront isn't exactly scenic, but it is convenient for people arriving by boat. Heading northeast up the coast on the **SS114** road, you'll pass the **Stazione Catania Centrale,** about 1 mile (1.6 km) from Piazza del Duomo, and after another 2 miles (3.2 km) or so, hit a more picturesque part of Catania's waterfront, lined by the **Lungomare Franco Battiato.**

SIGHTS
★ Piazza del Duomo

The history and legends of Catania are all condensed into its principal square, surrounded by historic palazzi housing lively cafés, all built in the city's trademark black lava stone. Most of the buildings visible today were built at the turn of the 18th century, after the earthquake that devastated much of the region, on the site of Roman baths dating to the 2nd century CE. This is the central meeting point of the city, where the massive Festa di Sant'Agata celebration takes place every February. The pièce de résistance, of course, is the cathedral dedicated to the patroness saint of Catania, Sant'Agata, dominating the cathedral's eastern side.

The piazza's principal entrance is from the south, through **Porta Uzeda,** a four-story-high Baroque portal built in the late 17th century. Cross the square north and you'll find yourself on Via Etnea, Catania's bustling main thoroughfare. Via Giuseppe Garibaldi, another main street, also crosses Piazza del Duomo from the west; walk about half a mile (1 km) down this street and you'll reach another major gate to the city, 18th-century, black-and-white-striped **Porta Garibaldi.**

There are a few other landmarks of note in

the square, the most eye-catching of which is definitely the basalt elephant statue, topped by an obelisk, perched on the 18th-century **Fontana dell'Elefante,** right in the center of the piazza. This bemused-looking pachyderm is said to date to Roman times and has become a symbol of Catania; locals look to it for good luck and protection from temperamental Mount Etna. The Catanese refer to the elephant as "u Liotru," a name said to derive from that of an 8th-century magician, Eliodoro, who is said to have rode the elephant through the city, mystifying the locals with his tricks. Near the entrance to Catania's outdoor fish market, southwest of Piazza del Duomo, the 19th-century marble waterfall **Fontana dell'Amenano** is named for the Amenano River, which flows underneath the city, toward the sea port.

Cattedrale di Sant'Agata

Piazza del Duomo; tel. 095/320044; www. cattedralecatania.it; 10:30am-noon and 4pm-5:30pm Mon.-Sat.; free

The Cattedrale di Sant'Agata, commonly referred to simply as **the Duomo,** was originally built in 1078, but has been destroyed and rebuilt several times after disastrous earthquakes and eruptions of Mount Etna. The current cathedral was built in Norman and Baroque styles using dark gray and black lava stones salvaged from imperial Roman structures, a typically Catanese architectural style that you'll see throughout the city. The distinctive, towering facade features a bell tower, granite Corinthian columns, and marble statues of Saint Agatha, Saint Euplius, and Saint Birillus, while the interior has a typical Latin cross layout, complete with an original 12th-century apse, medieval windows, several 17th-century paintings, and tombs including the final resting places of Catania's patroness herself, Saint Agatha, as well as favored son Vincenzo Bellini, best known for composing the opera *Norma.*

Consider a visit to the cathedral's **Museo Diocesano** (tel. 095/281635; www. museodiocesanocatania.com; 9am-2pm Mon.-Fri., 3pm-6pm Tues. and Thurs., 9am-1pm Sat.; €13 for access to the museum, Roman baths, and panoramic terraces) to view sacred treasures collected by the cathedral over the centuries, as well as the Terme Achilleane, the remarkably well-preserved 2nd-century Roman baths beneath the cathedral that were only discovered during excavations in the 18th century. You'll also get access to panoramic terraces on the cathedral's upper levels, which require stairs to reach and are not accessible to visitors with mobility issues.

The church is famous for housing an important silver reliquary of Saint Agatha, as well as the saint's relics, in one of its chapels, but they are not always open for public view. This makes the saint's appearance at the Festa di Sant'Agata all the more exciting.

Chiesa della Badia di Sant'Agata

Via Vittorio Emanuele II, 182; tel. 340/4238663; www. badiasantagata.wordpress.com; 9:30am-12:30pm Tues., 9:30am-12:30pm and 4:30pm-7:30pm Wed.-Sat., 9:30am-12:30pm and 7pm-8:30pm Sun.; €3

Located just around the corner from the Cattedrale di Sant'Agata, this Baroque church was built in the 1700s. Though its larger and more famous neighbor steals the spotlight, its solid white marble facade and octagonal dome are distinctive, and its interior boasts an impressive marble floor. But perhaps the most exceptional thing about this church is its rooftop (if you're willing to trek up several narrow staircases). From here, you'll see the Duomo from a different perspective, as well as the entire city center, much of the coast, and even Mount Etna. There is unfortunately no elevator to the rooftop, and the church itself is accessible only via a 12-step staircase.

Palazzo Biscari

Via Museo Biscari, 10; tel. 095/3287201; www. palazzobiscari.it; 9am-12:30pm and 5pm-6:30pm Mon.-Tues. and Thurs.-Fri., 9am-12:30pm Sat., 10:30am-12:30pm and 5pm-6:30pm Sun.; guided tours €5-10

Built for Prince Ignazio V in the 18th century,

Catania

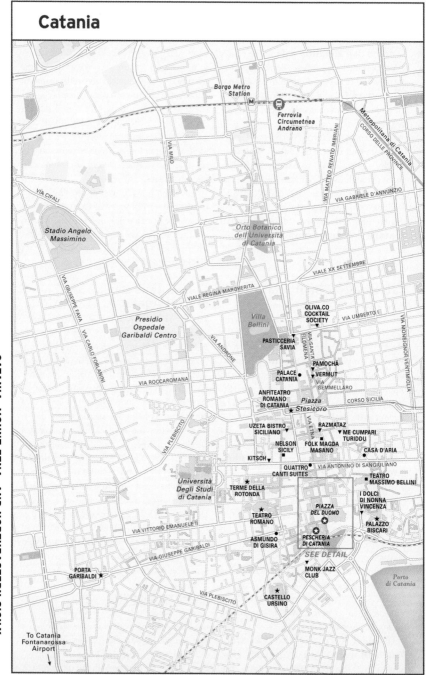

Borgo Metro Station

Ferrovia Circumetnea Andrano

Metropolitana di Catania

CORSO DELLE PROVINCE

VIA MATTEO RENATO IMBRIANI

VIA GABRIELE D'ANNUNZIO

VIA MILO

VIA CIFALI

Stadio Angelo Massimino

Orto Botanico dell'Università di Catania

VIALE XX SETTEMBRE

VIA GIUSEPPE FAVA

VIA CARLO FORLANINI

VIALE REGINA MARGHERITA

Presidio Ospedale Garibaldi Centro

Villa Bellini

OLIVA.CO COCKTAIL SOCIETY

VIA UMBERTO I

VIA MONSIGNOR VENTIMIGLIA

VIA SANTA EUPLEMENA

PASTICCERIA SAVIA

VIA ANDRONE

PAMOCHÀ

PALACE CATANIA

VERMUT

VIA GEMMELLARO

VIA ROCCAROMANA

ANFITEATRO ROMANO DI CATANIA

Piazza Stesicoro

CORSO SICILIA

VIA PLEBISCITO

UZETA BISTRO SICILIANO

RAZMATAZ

ME CUMPARI TURIDDU

VIA ETNA

NELSON SICILY

FOLK MAGDA MASANO

CASA D'ARIA

KITSCH

VIA ANTONINO DI SANGIULIANO

QUATTRO CANTI SUITES

TEATRO MASSIMO BELLINI

Università Degli Studi di Catania

TERME DELLA ROTONDA

PIAZZA DEL DUOMO

I DOLCI DI NONNA VINCENZA

PALAZZO BISCARI

TEATRO ROMANO

VIA VITTORIO EMANUELE II

ASMUNDO DI GISIRA

PESCHERIA DI CATANIA

SEE DETAIL

VIA GIUSEPPE GARIBALDI

MONK JAZZ CLUB

Porto di Catania

PORTA GARIBALDI

VIA PLEBISCITO

CASTELLO URSINO

To Catania Fontanarossa Airport

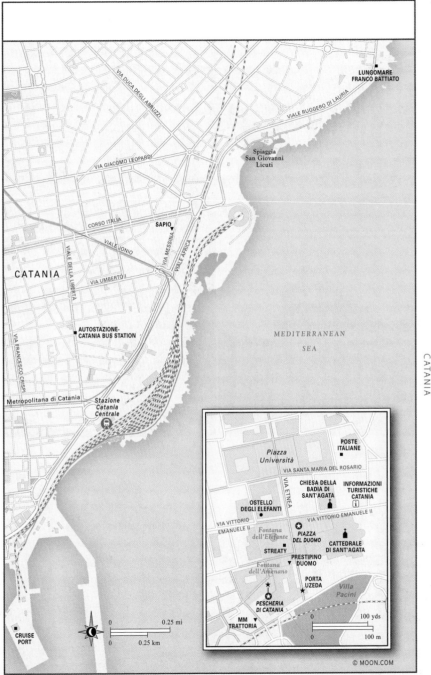

LUNGOMARE
FRANCO BATTIATO

VIA DUCA DEGLI ABRUZZI

VIALE RUGGERO DI LAURIA

VIA GIACOMO LEOPARDI

Spiaggia
San Giovanni
Licuti

CORSO ITALIA

SAPIO

VIA MESSINA

VIALE IONIO

CATANIA

VIALE DELLA LIBERTÀ

VIA UMBERTO I

VIA AFRICA

MEDITERRANEAN

SEA

AUTOSTAZIONE-
CATANIA BUS STATION

VIA FRANCESCO CRISPI

Metropolitana di Catania

Stazione
Catania
Centrale

CRUISE
PORT

0   0.25 mi

0   0.25 km

POSTE
ITALIANE

Piazza
Università

VIA SANTA MARIA DEL ROSARIO

VIA ETNEA

CHIESA DELLA
BADIA DI
SANT'AGATA

INFORMAZIONI
TURISTICHE
CATANIA

OSTELLO
DEGLI ELEFANTI

VIA VITTORIO
EMANUELE II

VIA VITTORIO EMANUELE II

Fontana
dell'Elefante

PIAZZA
DEL DUOMO

CATTEDRALE
DI SANT'AGATA

STREATY

PRESTIPINO
DUOMO

Fontana
dell'Amenano

PORTA
UZEDA

Villa
Pacini

PESCHERIA
DI CATANIA

MM
TRATTORIA

0   100 yds

0   100 m

© MOON.COM

this Baroque palace located behind the Cattedrale di Sant'Agata is one of the most distinctive palaces in Catania. You'll admire opulent salons, the mirrored, rococo-style "feast hall," the stucco-covered ballroom, and a wealth of precious frescoes covering the ceilings. Thirty-minute guided tours in Italian and English are available upon request.

★ Pescheria di Catania

Piazza Alonzo di Benedetto; 7am-2pm Mon.-Sat.; free

Most Italian cities have street markets lined with seasonal fruit and vegetable stands, but Catania's open-air seafood market, known as **A' Piscaria** in Sicilian, is truly unique. Located not far from the harbor, through an arched opening in the old city walls, the seafood—including tuna, swordfish, red mullet, shrimp, sardines, silver scabbardfish, and mackerel—is as fresh as it gets, sometimes still alive. Vendors spread their haul out on trays, stone work tables, and fishing buckets with the goal of selling everything out by lunchtime (which answers the question: Why isn't there any ice?).

Catania's fish market is not for the faint of heart: It's noisy, crowded, and sometimes bloody, but that's what makes it such an authentic spectacle, one that stimulates all your senses. This market is not generally as friendly as others you might find in Sicily, since fresh fish is not something most tourists are often compelled to purchase. The local fishers and vendors in the A' Piscaria market are there to work and sell to the local Catanese. As such, this rowdy open-air theater is best viewed from the street above, so you can avoid having to tiptoe around puddles of seawater and can respectfully stay out of the way of the fishers wheeling and dealing about that day's catch. If you don't have a gourmet kitchen at your disposal to cook the day's catch, you're in luck: The market is surrounded by seafood restaurants, and chances are if you order fish almost anywhere in Catania, this is where it came from.

1: Piazza del Duomo **2:** Cattedrale di Sant'Agata **3:** Pescheria di Catania **4:** Terme Della Rotonda

Piazza Università

Bordered by buildings belonging to the University of Catania and the main Via Etnea, this central town square in the heart of Catania's historic city center is the site of public events, outdoor dining, art exhibitions, and protests. Though no longer the modern center of the university, which moved a few kilometers away decades ago, this square is still a popular meeting point for students as well as a prime spot for watching the processions of the Festa di Sant'Agata in February. Notable features of the piazza include its four bronze candelabra streetlamps, added in 1957, each one symbolic of a protagonist from Catanese folklore.

Roman Sites
Teatro Romano

Via Vittorio Emanuele II, 266; tel. 095/7150508; 9am-5pm Mon.-Sat., 9am-1pm Sun.; €3-6, first Sun. of month free

Catania is host to several notable classical sites, including not one, but two, ancient places of entertainment. Smaller, but closer to Piazza del Duomo and with more regular opening hours, Catania's Teatro Romano is sometimes still referred to by locals as the "tiatru grecu," as archaeologists believe that this Roman theater expanded on a preexisting Greek one, during a period when Roman Catania was undergoing rapid expansion in the 2nd century CE. Built of sandstone and basalt, it was large enough to host up to 7,000 spectators in its heyday, but today it is partially covered by the encroaching residential neighborhood surrounding it. You'll only need about an hour to visit this theater, its nearby odeon (a classical indoor theater), and other associated structures, which may have served as snack stands for visitors back in the day.

Terme Della Rotonda

Via Rotonda; tel. 095/7150951; 9am-1pm Mon.-Sat.; €6

Just a five-minute walk from the nearby Roman Theater and Roman Amphitheatre, the domed Roman baths of Terme Della

Rotonda is one of the several thermal complexes and saunas that remain from the Roman era in Catania. Skillfully built between the 1st and 2nd centuries, the Terma Rotonda and its treasured medieval and Baroque frescoes survived the earthquake of 1693, and this structure was even used as a model for the Pantheon in Rome.

Anfiteatro Romano di Catania

Piazza Stesicoro; tel. 095/7472268; www.regione.sicilia. it; 9am-12:40pm and 3pm-5:40pm Tues.-Sat, 9am-1pm Sun.; free

Today, what's left of Catania's other 2nd-century theater, the Anfiteatro Romano, is just a small section of the original, once one of the largest in the Roman world and the largest in Sicily, designed to host up to 15,000 spectators. After the decline of the Roman empire and the amphitheater's abandonment, many of its stones were used in the construction of the Cattedrale di Sant'Agata. The site's opening hours tend to be unreliable, but there's still a good view from the Piazza Stesicoro if you find it closed to visitors.

Castello Ursino

Piazza Federico II di Svevia; tel. 095/345830; www. comune.catania.it/la-citta/culture/monumenti-e-siti-archeologici/musei/museo-civico-castello-ursino; 9am-7pm daily; adults €6, reduced rate €3, students €2

One-third mile (0.5 km) southwest of the pescheria, this imposing 13th-century castle with thick, 100-foot-high (30-m) stone walls has been used as the royal residence of the rulers of Sicily, from the Aragonese to the Spanish Viceroys, as well as the seat of the Sicilian parliament, and as a prison. When it was finally acquired and restored by the city of Catania in 1932, the castle transformed once again to showcase art collections, regional artifacts, temporary exhibitions, and civil union ceremonies. It's worthwhile to just walk around the classically square castle's solid lava-stone walls and round towers, in the middle of parklike Piazza Federico II di Svevia, which has plenty of benches where

you can sit and contemplate the impregnable-looking fortress. Inside, you'll find the exhibits of the **Museo Civico,** including a decent collection of Greek and Roman sculptures and mosaics, which require about an hour to visit.

SPORTS AND RECREATION
Parks
Villa Bellini

Viale Regina Margherita, 6; tel. 095/320761; 6am-10pm daily; free

In 1864, the public gardens of Villa Bellini, on the northern end of the city center, were adapted from the botanical mazes built by the Prince of Biscari and his noble Sicilian family. Named for the local Catanese composer and town hero, Vincenzo Bellini, the landscaped lawns, gazebos, and fountains of the property make up the oldest urban park in Catania, located along the main avenue of Via Etnea. It's a perfect place to rest your feet and snack on the arancini you just picked up across the street at Pasticceria Savia.

Orto Botanico dell'Università di Catania

Via Etnea, 397; tel. 095/7102767; www. attivitaortobotanico.unict.it; 9am-7pm Mon.-Fri., 9am-1pm Sat. Apr.-Sept., 9am-5pm Mon.-Fri., 9am-1pm Sat. Oct-Mar.

Just north of the Villa Bellini gardens, Catania's botanical gardens host a collection of 50 species of palms, over 2,000 varieties of succulents, and rare Sicilian trees. Built in 1858 by Francesco Tornabene, a prominent botanist of the time, this 4-acre (1.6 ha) garden is currently used as a natural escape and educational center for the city's residents. It hosts outdoor concerts in the spring and summer, along with other performances in its neoclassical, freestanding colonnade.

Beaches

Despite being a coastal city intimately connected to the sea (as the Pescheria di Catania attests), Catania can feel quite separated from its waterfront, especially around the historic center. The nearby port is very commercial and mostly inaccessible to casual visitors, separated from the old town by the coastal SS114 road and train tracks leading to Catania's central train station. That said, there are a few nearby beaches where locals indulge in that very Sicilian summer pastime of stretching out on the sand. Still, for some of the best beaches Sicily has to offer, you'll want to travel farther from the city, whether you're visiting the luxury resorts around Taormina or the more secluded beaches of the island's southeastern coast.

Spiaggia San Giovanni Licuti

Via S. Giovanni Li Cuti; open 24 hours; free

About 2.5 miles (4 km) northeast of Piazza del Duomo, this is a small, rocky, free beach with pristine water that gets deep quickly, making for good swimming. There is a patch of black sand, making it more comfortable to just throw down a towel, but access to the water is either via the rocks or a small, wooden platform.

Spiaggia San Giovanni Licuti is near the beginning of the **Lungomare Franco Battiato,** Catania's 1-mile-long (1.6-km) paved seaside walkway, lined with more rocky beaches and various seafront cafés, restaurants, and bars. A pleasant round-trip walk up and down the promenade takes less than 45 minutes. To get here, you can take Bus 935 (www.amt.ct.it; €1) toward Pezzano Est from Piazza Stesicoro and get off at Messina Picanello FS, about a 30-minute trip, or it's a 10-minute taxi ride (approximately €10).

Aci Trezza

Via Lungomare dei Ciclopi, Aci Trezza; open 24 hours; free

Farther north of the city center (about 7 mi/11.3 km), on the 7-mile long (11.3-km-long) stretch of coast known as the **Riviera dei Ciclopi,** is another Catanese beach destination, with the added bonus of being associated with Homer's *Odyssey*. Off the coast of the charming fishing village of Aci Trezza, the **Faraglioni dei Ciclopi** (Via Lungomare dei Ciclopi, 119, Aci Trezza) are an arresting set of craggy stone islets emerging from the Ionian Sea. The most common legend describes the faraglioni as stones that the blinded man-eating giant, the Cyclops Polyphemus, threw into the sea in a rage to attack Ulysses's ships as they were sailing away.

Like most of the beaches on this part of the coast, it's not a true beach per se, but a rocky coastline where you can either throw down a towel or pay to access one of the beach clubs with amenities like lounge chairs and waterfront restaurants. Try **Ghenea Beach Club** (Via Lungomare dei Ciclopi, beach club access €6 per person, sunbeds from €10).

The faraglioni rock formations are best observed at sunrise from the beach in Aci Trezza, or, for an up-close and personal experience, rent a stand-up paddleboard through **Acitrezza SUP** (Lungomare dei Ciclopi; www.facebook.com/acitrezzasup; 9am-7pm daily; €10 per hour), or take a boat tour with **Sailing Tour Ciclopi** (tel. 349/8908190; www.facebook.com/sailingtourciclopi). Getting here with a rental car is a fairly easy 30-minute drive north of Catania, with cheap, rarely full parking in lots and garages along the coast. Or take Bus 534 (www.amt.ct.it; tickets €1 valid for 90 minutes, available at local tabacchi, or purchase on board with cash) from Piazza Borsellino, just south of Piazza del Duomo, to Terminal Aci Trezza, a ride of just over an hour.

Cooking Classes and Food Tours

Cotumè

Piazza del Duomo meeting point; tel. 328/1495832; www.cotume.it; cooking lessons with minimum of 4 participants Mon.-Sat. year-round; from €110 per person

Discover the layered cuisine of Sicily with a seasonal cooking lesson in the heart of Catania. Four-hour cooking lesson experiences include a walk through the Pescheria

di Catania to gather ingredients, hands-on cooking instruction, and a communal lunch. Your instructor, Loredana Balsamello, is a friendly, energetic, and knowledgeable local expert who will provide a great introduction to the city of Catania and a cultural journey through the cuisine of the island.

Sweets of Catania Experience with Casa Mia Tours

tel. 346/8001746; www.casamiatours.com; 3-hour tours at 10am or 4pm Mon.-Sat. by appointment only; from €290 for 2 people (tastings included)

During the morning or afternoon passeggiata, Casa Mia Tours takes guests on an adventure tasting their way through the city's typical pastry specialties. Tastings on the Sweets of Catania Experience may include cannoli, minne di Sant'Agata (sponge cake with ricotta cream), crispy sweet croccante (brittle) made with honey and almonds or sesame, chiacchiere (fried dough with powdered sugar), cocoa and star anise-spiced cassatelle (sweet ravioli) from the town of Agira, and a rame di Napoli (chocolate almond bonbon) cookie. The tasting might finish off with gelato, Sicilian granita, or a glass of local wine.

Streaty

Piazza del Duomo; tel. 351/5133552; www.streaty.com/ city/street-food-tours-in-catania; group tours available morning and evening; from €54 per person (tastings included)

Let local experts lead the way on a street food tasting tour in Catania: Streaty mainly offers three-hour group walking tours but can arrange private tours upon request. Guests have the option to book the Friday or Saturday evening street food tour through the backroads of the city, or the morning program, which includes a visit to the fish market, on Tuesdays and Saturdays. These programs are unfortunately not suitable for guests with vegan or vegetarian dietary restrictions.

1: Faraglioni dei Ciclopi **2:** Cotumè cooking lesson

ENTERTAINMENT AND EVENTS
The Arts
Teatro Massimo Bellini

Via Giuseppe Perrotta, 12; tel. 095 /7306111; www. teatromassimobellini.it; box office 9am-12:30pm Mon., Wed., and Fri.; tickets €10-20

Named for Vincenzo Bellini, the early 19th-century Catanian-born opera composer, the Teatro Massimo Bellini is Catania's main theater. The Sicilian Baroque theater opened with a performance of Bellini's masterpiece opera, *Norma*, in 1890, and has been the driving force of Catania's cultural scene for over 130 years. The glamourous, plush, deep red interiors and arched arcades also boast a ceiling fresco by 19th-century artist Ernesto Bellandi, and four tiers of box suites. The 1,200-seat theater hosts operas, operettas, dance performances, and jazz concerts and is also home to Catania's symphonic and chamber orchestras.

Festivals and Events
★ Festa di Sant'Agata

Piazza del Duomo; www.festadisantagata.it; Feb. 5; free

Catania's annual festival to celebrate Sant'Agata attracts around one million people, making it one of the largest and most popular religious festivals in the world. Devotees dressed in white robes carry the statue through the city on their shoulders. While watching the grand procession of Sant'Agata's silver reliquary as it makes its way through the streets, you'll grasp the importance of the saint to the city. Although the saint is cherished all year round, the celebration is a reminder to pray and give thanks on the occasion of her silver statue's careful removal from her chapel inside the Duomo. The best places to view the procession are in the Piazza del Duomo and along Via Etnea. In addition to this procession through the streets, there are fireworks, concerts, general revelry and debauchery, and a parade of cannalori (candle-bearing carts carried by representatives of the medieval guilds of the city).

If traveling to the city of Catania during

Catania's Patron Saint

Sant'Agata, the beloved patron saint of Catania, is also the patron of breast cancer patients, rape victims, nurses, and bakers, and the people of Catania have long prayed to her to protect them from eruptions from Mount Etna, fires, and earthquakes. Even if you aren't able to see her silver reliquary in the **Cattedrale di Sant'Agata,** only reliably on display during February's **Festa di Sant'Agata,** representations of Sant'Agata here are hard to miss. This is not only because they seem to be everywhere you look, but because the martyr is often—jarringly—depicted carrying her own breasts on a platter.

This striking image is based on the brutal nature of the saint's martyrdom. It's said that in the year 251 CE, her breasts were cut off when she refused to marry a Roman prefect in order to preserve her chastity and devotion to God. This legend has even found its way into Catania's signature sweet, the **minne di Sant'Agata,** an almond marzipan and sponge cake shaped like a breast, filled with sweet ricotta cream and garnished with a candied cherry on top. You can try this suggestive (and delicious) treat at local bakeries like **Prestipino Duomo** (page 208) or **Pasticceria Savia** (page 208).

Festa di Sant'Agata

the first week of February, be prepared for crowds and higher rates, and make sure to reserve accommodations well in advance and to call ahead to set up reservations for restaurants and tours.

Ricci Weekender

Various venues around Catania; tel. 334/9197095; www. ricciweekender.com; first weekend of Sept.; ticketed events €40-50

Imagine a music festival that also has amazing food and wine, and you've got a good understanding of Ricci Weekender. This small annual festival by a team of entrepreneurs, chefs, and DJs features unique event locations including parks and former factories.

SHOPPING

Nelson Sicily

Via Crociferi, 50; tel. 095/8361634; www.nelsonsicily. com; 10am-2pm and 4pm-8pm daily

Nelson Sicily was founded in 2013 by Giovanni Previti. Today, it ships hard-to-find natural and organic Sicilian wines all over the world from their headquarters on Via Crociferi in Catania.

Folk Magda Masano

Via S. Michele, 17/19; tel. 392/2075505; www. magdamasano.it; 10am-1pm and 4:30pm-8pm Tues.-Sat.

Folk is a carefully curated contemporary design shop with a great selection of ceramics, artisan crafts, jewelry, handbags, home decor, and clothing, all made by small producers in Sicily.

FOOD

In this region, between the Ionian Sea and steep Mount Etna, the local cuisine is a healthy mix of fresh seafood and hearty meat dishes, sweet pastries made with almonds and ricotta cream, and precious bright green pistachios added into both sweet and savory recipes whenever possible. The pride and joy of Catania is of course **pasta alla Norma,** named for Vincenzo Bellini's famous opera and made with tomato sauce, fried eggplant, a sprig of fresh basil, and grated ricotta salata cheese on top.

Catania also has a vibrant street food culture, stemming from the need for quick, cheap food to feed the masses, further driven by the late-night dining needs of a dense student population. Try **cipollata,** thinly sliced pancetta wrapped around a long spring onion; **cipollina,** baked puff pastries filled with tomato, onion, mozzarella, and ham; or **scacciata,** savory pies made with fresh tuma sheep's milk cheese and anchovies. More daring foodies may want to try some of Catania's many meat-based street snacks, including **polpette di cavallo** (horse meatballs), **arrusti** (mixed grilled meats, including donkey steaks, veal, pork ribs, and lambchops), **sanguinaccio** (pork blood sausage), and **zuzzo** (a mysterious meat jelly). You'll find the best vendors along **Via Plebiscito,** or in **Piazza Stesicoro,** near the Roman amphitheater.

Fine Dining
Sapio
Via Messina, 235; tel. 095/0975016; www.
sapiorestaurant.it; 7:30pm-11pm Tues.-Sun.; tasting
menus €80-110 per person
Sapio is an exciting addition to the city's array of more casual eateries. At the age of 26, in 2019, chef Alessandro Ingiulla earned the city of Catania its very first Michelin star. The tasting menu at Sapio dazzles guests with innovative seasonal dishes such as red mullet stuffed with chickpea puree and calamari or the duck breast with fermented red turnip greens, hazelnuts, and yogurt.

Wine Bars
★ Razmataz
Via Montesano, 17/19; tel. 095/311893; www.
razmatazcatania.it; noon-2am Tues.-Sun.; dishes €5-12
Razmataz is a winemaker's wine bar. This popular foodie destination is often filled with wine producers from Mount Etna and features seasonal meat and fish dishes with a homemade feel. The heated outdoor space

and the cozy dining room are perfect for any time of year. Try the grilled sausages, lemon leaf-wrapped meatballs, or the off-menu specialty of gnocco fritto (fried dough puffs) and thinly sliced Sicilian mortadella for a perfect make-your-own sandwich platter paired with a bottle of wine from Etna.

Bistros
Uzeta Bistro Siciliano
Via Penninello, 41; tel. 095/2503374; www.uzeta.it;
7pm-2am Tues.-Sun.; €10-20
Stop by Uzeta for a typical Sicilian meal paired with great drinks and good company, with a menu of tapas-style bites and authentic regional specialties such as arancini, pasta with local donkey-meat ragù, and a baccalà (salt cod) dish with oranges and fennel.

Trattorie
Me Cumpari Turiddu
Piazza Turi Ferro, 36/38; tel. 095/7150142; www.
mecumparituriddu.it; 7pm-1am Mon.-Sat., noon-1am
Sun.; €10-20
Me Cumpari Turiddu is one of the most celebrated restaurants in Catania, where you'll feel like you've just walked into a friend's vintage dining room. For Sunday lunch and daily dinners, it serves simple, traditional Sicilian cuisine with a touch of elegance, stemming from the stories and old recipe book of the owners' nonna, as well as typical street food dishes from all over the island. They make it a point to highlight Slow Food-certified ingredients and pair them with an all-organic and natural wine list.

Mm Trattoria
Via Pardo, 34; tel. 095/348897; www.facebook.com/
mmtrattoria; noon-2:30pm and 8pm-11pm Mon.-Sat.;
€20
After a walk through the outdoor fish market, stop by Mm Trattoria for a seafood lunch. This small bistro with indoor seating offers local fish and seafood dishes, pastas, and regional dishes from the Catania area. Reservations are recommended.

Cafés and Light Bites
Prestipino Duomo

Piazza del Duomo, 1; tel. 095/320840; www.prestipinoduomo.com; 7am-midnight daily; €5

The perfect spot for people-watching, with a large outdoor seating area in the Piazza del Duomo, this newly renovated, historic coffee bar is a local staple for a quick espresso or leisurely aperitivo. Try the candied orange peels dipped in chocolate or the city's specialty dessert, minne di Sant'Agata, a miniature version of a Sicilian cassata sponge cake with almond marzipan, sweet ricotta cream, powdered sugar glaze, and a bright red candied cherry on top (symbolizing Saint Agatha's breasts).

I Dolci di Nonna Vincenza

Piazza S. Placido, 7; tel. 095/7151844; www.dolcinonnavincenza.it; 9am-7pm Mon.-Sat., 9:30am-2pm Sun.; €5

Originating in the 1930s in the village of Agira, this historic pastry shop has carried on the traditions of preparing sweet Sicilian confections such as buccellati, amaretti, nocatole, cannoli, gelo di caffe, and croccante. It's a great place to track down local specialties such as chocolate rame di Napoli cookies and rosoli sweet liqueurs. If you run out of time, you can stock up on products from an outpost shop inside the Catania airport.

Pasticceria Savia

Via Etnea, 300-304; tel. 095/322335; www.lnx.savia.it; 7:45am-9:30pm Tues.-Sun.; €5

Founded in 1897 by Angelo and Elisabetta Savia, Pasticceria Savia is the top destination in Catania to find a perfectly crispy fried arancino rice ball. This pastry shop, located across from the Villa Bellini park, offers traditional sweets such as cannoli, minne di Sant'Agata, fruit-shaped marzipan bites, sfince di San Giuseppe ricotta-filled cream puffs, and rum-soaked babà cakes. The busy bar is filled with sweet and savory treats for a one-stop-shop afternoon snack, and table service is available outside.

BARS AND NIGHTLIFE

Catania is home to a large student population and is filled with cocktail bars, pubs, and cafés, guaranteed to entertain visitors late into the night. Weather permitting, youthful, lively crowds spill out into the streets and town squares. The nightlife is concentrated around **Via Gemmellaro** and **Via Santa Filomena,** just one block east of the main avenue, Via Etnea. Most of the city center will

arancini at Pasticceria Savia

be crowded, and the evenings can be noisy, especially on the weekends.

Cocktail Bars
★ Oliva.Co Cocktail Society

Via delle Scale, 3; tel. 349/1732075; www.olivaco.it; 6pm-2:30am daily; €8

This Manhattan-style speakeasy cocktail bar is the only hot tip you need to find the best cocktail in town. The elite bartenders are real artists who can prepare traditional drinks or passionately interact with guests to discuss the gamut of the world of spirits and mixology. The drink list includes classic cocktails such as the negroni, Manhattan, penicillin, or an old-fashioned, as well as craft beers and specialties made with homemade infusions. The staff is friendly, the vibe is pure old-school New York, and the music can't be beat. Oliva.Co is located on a small backstreet just down the steps from Via Umberto I.

Vermut

Via Gemmellaro, 39; tel. 347/6001978; www.facebook. com/vermutcatania; 11am-2am daily; €10

Vermut is a cocktail bar that specializes in Sicilian wines, vermouths, amari, and digestivi. This is the hot spot for a night out on the town in Catania. On weekends, crowds from this small bar pour out into the street and it becomes the perfect place to meet up. When it gets busy, make sure to stop by the cash register to pay for your drink before heading to the bar to order. Indoor seating is available and small bites can be ordered to go along with your drinks.

Kitsch

Via Antonino Di Sangiuliano, 286; tel. 095/2865503; www.facebook.com/kitschbistrot; 6pm-2am Thurs.-Tues.; drinks €5-8

Kitsch is one of Catania's finest cocktail bars, nestled on the steep terraced street of Via Sangiuliano. You'll be able to burn off some calories just in time to sip a classic cocktail like a Sazerac or one of Antonio's special concoctions from its Carta Siciliana.

Wine Bar
Pamochã

Via Gemmellaro, 46; tel. 095/3788588; www.pamocha. it; 6pm-2am Wed.-Mon.; 4 small sandwiches €6-9, bruschette €5-9

The name Pamochã derives from the words "pane, mortadella, e champagne"—or bread, salami, and everyone's favorite bubbly wine. This bar serves bite-size gourmet sandwiches, bruschetta, raw seafood platters, European oysters, and caviar paired with champagne, wine, and cocktails.

Live Music
Monk Jazz Club

Via Scuto, 19; tel. 340 /1223606; www.facebook.com/ MonkClubCatania; hours vary; most events free with purchase of drinks

Notable Italian and international jazz performances are regularly hosted at Monk, and a schedule of events can be found on its Facebook page. Reservations are recommended and can be organized by phone or by emailing centroculturalemonk@gmail.com.

ACCOMMODATIONS
Under €100
Ostello degli Elefanti

Via Etnea, 28; tel. 095/2265691; www. ostellodeglielefanti.it; €20

Centrally located inside a historic 17th-century palazzo, this hostel is an economical option, with rooms ranging from shared mixed dorms for up to 10 guests, to small rooms for up to 4 guests, to private rooms with double or single beds. All bunkbeds are equipped with a reading light, and there's free Wi-Fi, 24-hour reception, laundry service (€4), free breakfast 8am-9:30am, and access to a rooftop terrace. The helpful LGBTQ-friendly staff can assist solo travelers with navigating the city, and this is a great place to meet new people if you're traveling solo. When the city explodes with visitors in February for the Sant'Agata festival and hotel prices skyrocket, the rooftop of this hostel just happens to be one of the best views in town to watch the procession coming down Via Etnea.

★ **Casa d'Aria**

Via Pietro Antonio Coppola, 14; tel. 335/7713186; www. casadaria.it; from €77

These creatively decorated, affordable apartments are around the corner from the Teatro Massimo Bellini in the historic center of Catania. Owner Daria Laurentini designed the eight stylish apartments to showcase traditional Sicilian artistry with a modern twist. Each unit includes a simple kitchenette for preparing coffee or small meals, and with room for 2-4 guests, they are a steal. The 312-square-foot (29-sq-m) penthouse apartment has an adjoining rooftop terrace and seasonal hot tub (call or email ahead for reservations). In 2020, the building was updated with a small private elevator to help guests get to the third floor.

€100-200

Palace Catania

Via Etnea, 218; tel. 095/2505111; www.gruppouna.it/ esperienze/palace-catania; €115

This four-star hotel is a great location for business conferences and special events. The 94 elegant bedrooms and suites are appointed with classic dark oak furniture, white linens, traditional majolica tiling, televisions, and air-conditioning. All private bedrooms and suites are equipped with Wi-Fi, minibars, and Culti bath products designed especially for the Gruppo Una hotel group. An Italian-style breakfast at the hotel includes savory and sweet options, egg dishes, coffee, tea, juices, and gluten-free products. Grab a drink at the Etnea Roof Bar for a spectacular view of the city.

★ **Quattro Canti Suites**

Via Antonino Di Sangiuliano, 293; tel. 095/312432; www.quattrocantisuites.com; €145

The elegant Quattro Canti Suites hotel is the perfect place to stay in the center of Catania's busy downtown. The four bright, modern guest rooms and suites are located on the ground floor of a former convent. Each suite is appointed with modern furnishings and a refined style, equipped with Wi-Fi service,

minibar, coffeemaker, and a tea kettle, guaranteed to provide a peaceful and welcoming stay.

Asmundo di Gisira

Via Gisira, 40; tel. 095/0978894; www. asmundodigisira.com; €190

This boutique hotel combines luxurious living and eccentric art. The 11 guest rooms are decked out with Italian furnishings from the 1930s and 1960s. Located in Piazza Giuseppe Mazzini, one of Catania's busiest squares, each of the six exceptional Art Rooms have its own unique theme, from the epic *Story of the Moors* to the legend of Colapesce, a Sicilian boy who loved swimming so much he turned into a half-man, half-fish. There are an additional five Neoclassical Rooms to choose from, each with its own private balcony. Asmundo di Gisira serves up a delicious organic breakfast that can be enjoyed on the outdoor terrace right in the historic center of the city.

INFORMATION AND SERVICES

Check out the **Visit Catania** (www. visitcatania.co) and **City Map Sicilia** (www. citymapsicilia.it/en/catania) websites for help finding accommodations, city sights, and dining recommendations.

- **Tourist information:** Informazioni Turistiche Catania; Via Vittorio Emanuele II, 172; tel. 095/7425573; www.comune. catania.it; 8am-7pm Mon.-Sat., 8:30am-1:30pm Sun.

- **Hospital:** Presidio Ospedale Garibaldi-Centro, Piazza Santa Maria di Gesù, 5; tel. 095/7591111; www.ao-garibaldi.catania.it/ presidio-osp-garibaldi; open 24 hours

- **Police:** Polizia di stato questura catania, Piazza Santa Nicoletta, 8; tel. 095/7367111; www.questure.poliziadistato.it/catania; 8am-6:30pm Mon.-Fri.

- **Post office:** Poste Italiane; Via Santa Maria del Rosario, 17; tel. 095/2502150; www.poste.it; 8:20am-7pm Mon.-Fri., 8:20am-12:30pm Sat.

- **Pharmacy:** Farmacia Caltabiano Dr. Mauro Marcello; Piazza Stesicoro, 36; tel. 095/327647; 8:30am-1pm and 4:30pm-8pm Mon.-Fri.

GETTING THERE

With Sicily's largest airport, Aeroporto di Catania Fontanarossa, located just south of the city, most travelers to Catania are likely to arrive by plane. That said, if you're planning a trip around the whole island of Sicily, the island's second-largest city is connected to its train, bus, and highway networks, but infrastructure here is still less efficient than it should be. Trains heading north up the Ionian coast, toward Taormina and beyond, tend to be relatively fast and cheap, while a bus might be a better bet for traveling through the south and interior, toward Palermo. For the ultimate in flexibility, consider renting your own car.

The easiest way to travel from Palermo to Catania is by driving, hiring a private driver, or by direct bus service. Train service will connect Palermo and Catania, but the bus is faster. Catania is easily reached from Taormina and Syracuse by following the A18/E45 coastal highway that runs from Messina south to Catania and connects to SS114 for those heading all the way down to Syracuse. Taormina is often a stop for major cruise lines such as Norwegian Cruise Lines, which dock in the cruise terminal near Via Vittorio Emanuelle II in the port of Messina, and smaller boats that arrive from Taormina (20 minutes) in the bay of Giardini Naxos.

Though the **Cruise Port** (Terminal Crociere Sporgente Centrale; tel. 095/7465114; www.cataniacruiseport.com) at **Porto di Catania** is a possible Mediterranean cruise stop, no cruises from Catania were in operation at the time of writing.

By Air
Aeroporto di Catania Fontanarossa
Via Fontanarossa; tel. 095/7239111; www.aeroporto. catania.it

Catania Fontanarossa Airport is Sicily's largest, with flights to and from over 70 destinations including **Rome** (1 hour 15 minutes; €65), **Naples** (1 hour; €60), and **Milan** (1 hour; €25), as well as many other European destinations outside Italy. This single-terminal airport is wheelchair accessible, with a coffee bar, one full-service restaurant, and a self-service cafeteria, as well as a tabacchi, newsstand, duty-free shop, and small kiosks selling souvenirs.

From the airport, travelers can get to Catania city by taxi, train service, or bus. **Taxis,** available at the taxi stand right outside the arrivals hall, will cost around €25 each way for the 10-minute, 2.6-mile (4.3-km) drive. To schedule an airport transport or other private driving services in advance, contact **Sunny Sicily** (www.sunnysicily.com). **Trenitalia** (tel. 668/475475; www.trenitalia.com) runs a train service from the airport to Stazione Catania Centrale at least twice an hour, which takes 10-30 minutes depending on the number of stops (€2-3). Finally, **AMT** (www.amt.ct.it; €4), which operates Catania's bus system, runs Alibus 457 from the airport to Catania Centrale every 25 minutes or so 5am-midnight, a 30-minute ride. There is also a 1-hour 25-minute bus service from Fontanarossa to Taormina provided by **Etna Trasporti** (tel. 095/532716; www. etnatrasporti.it; €6).

If you prefer your own wheels, **rental cars** can be picked up at the Catania airport from companies such as **Hertz** (tel. 095/341595; www.hertz.com), **Enterprise** (tel. 095/346893; www.enterpriserentacar.it), and other smaller providers. Note that though a car can be useful for the wider region of northeastern Sicily, driving and parking in Catania can be difficult.

By Train
Stazione Catania Centrale
Piazza Papa Giovanni XXIII, 2; www.rfi.it/it/stazioni/ catania-centrale.html

The main transit station in Catania is located 1 mile (1.6 km; a 20-minute walk) northeast of the Piazza del Duomo, along the SS114 coastal road. Regular, convenient train services to **Taormina-Giardini** (1 hour; €5), **Syracuse** (1 hour 30 minutes; €8), **Messina Centrale** (2 hours; €9), **Milazzo** (2 hours 45 minutes; €10), and **Palermo** (3 hours 40 minutes; €16.40) are provided by **Trenitalia** (www.trenitalia.com). It's also possible to travel by train from other cities in Italy, though with cheap domestic flights, this is only advisable for those with time to spare. Tickets can be purchased inside the station or online and must be time-stamped before boarding. Bathrooms are available on the train and in the main stations, and there are usually plenty of taxis outside the station waiting to take you to the city center, or take **Alibus L-EX** (www.amt.ct.it; tickets €1 valid for 90 minutes, available at local tabacchi, or purchase on board with cash) to Piazza del Duomo, a 10-minute ride.

It's also possible to reach the slopes of Mount Etna from Catania via the **Ferrovia Circumetnea** train (www.circumetnea.it), which stops at various points around the volcano on its crescent-shaped, 69-mile (111-km) route. It leaves from the **Borgo Metro Station** (Via Etnea, 668), about 1 mile (1.6 km) north of Villa Bellini.

By Bus
Autostazione - Catania Bus Station
Via Archimede and Viale della Libertà
The main bus station is located across the roundabout from the Catania Centrale train station, accessible via taxi, Alibus (www.amts.ct.it/alibus) shuttle, or a 20-minute walk from Piazza del Duomo. Ticket offices are a block away, along Via D'Amico. Routes across Sicily are operated by several companies, including **SAIS** (Via D'Amico, 181; tel. 095/536168; www.saisautolinee.it), connecting Catania to **Palermo** (2 hours 45 minutes; €14), and **Interbus** (tel. 0935/22460; www.etnatrasporti.it), connecting Catania to **Syracuse** (1 hour 10 minutes; €5-8) and **Taormina** (1 hour 10 minutes; €4-7). Tickets must be purchased online or from the ticket office before boarding.

By Car
Sicily's eastern coast, from Messina on the island's very northeastern tip, to Syracuse in the south, is easy to navigate thanks to the coastal **SS114/E45** road. From **Taormina,** the city of Catania is located due south (34 mi/55 km; 50 minutes); from **Syracuse,** take the E45 north and, after passing Catania Fontanarossa Airport, continue toward the city center (40 mi/64 km; 50 minutes). From **Palermo** (120 mi/193 km; 3 hours) you'll follow the **E90** coastal highway east toward Messina before eventually heading inland on the **A19.** Stay alert; construction and detours are common on these rural roads.

Once you've arrived in Catania, the city's compact city center, with frequent one-way roads, pedestrianized streets, and relatively busy traffic, makes driving a hassle. That said, it can be useful to have your own transport to make day trips to the surrounding areas, especially Mount Etna, more flexible. **Parking** on the street, with spots indicated by white and blue lines, is theoretically possible, but in practice open spots in the city center are hard to find and often limited to one hour. The paid parking lot at **Parcheggio Borsellino AMT** (Via Cardinale Dusmet) is one of the most convenient, located just behind the Porta Uzeda city gate that leads into Piazza del Duomo; expect to pay around €20 per day. Or, inquire with your accommodation about options for parking.

GETTING AROUND
By Bus and Metro
Though many of Catania's sites are located in the city center, it may be useful to take a bus, operated by **AMT** (tel. 095/7519111; www.amt.ct.it), to the airport, train, and bus stations, or to Spiaggia San Giovanni Licuti. Tickets cost €1 and are good for transfers for up to 90 minutes, or you can buy a €4 ticket for the day. They can be purchased on board (with cash) or at tabacchi, newstands, and kiosks throughout the city.

The city also currently has one Metro line, also operated by AMT, with plans to expand it. Though there is one centrally located station under Piazza Stesicoro, it mostly runs to the outskirts of the city from there and won't be of much use to tourists. The one exception is the **Catania Borgo** (Via Caronda, 352a; 095/541111) station, where you can board **Ferrovia Circumetnea** (www.circumetnea.it), which nearly circles the Mount Etna volcano. Tickets (€1 for 90 minutes) are good for both buses and the Metro system.

By Taxi

In case you find yourself wanting a taxi to your accommodation after a night out in Catania's vibrant bar scene, or to get to the beach or back to the train station or airport, there are taxi ranks outside the train station and on Piazza del Duomo, or call **Radio Taxi Catania** (tel. 095/330966). Rates are reasonable, about €25 to the airport and

generally less than €15 for rides around town.

By Car

Though a car or private driver (try **Sunny Sicily;** www.sunnysicily.com) is useful for the region surrounding Catania, it is not necessary for getting around the city center, which is compact and crowded enough to make driving and parking a nuisance.

On Foot

The historic city center of Catania is best explored on foot. Use the Piazza del Duomo as your starting point and you'll find many of the main city sights are located within a 15-minute walk. The website/app www.gpsmycity.com offers self-guided walking tours and itineraries with downloadable maps highlighting the palaces, churches, and monuments of the city.

Taormina

One of Sicily's top destinations, Taormina is a picturesque town perched on the dramatic outcrop of Monte Tauro, with some of the most beautiful sea views in all of Sicily. Founded by the Greeks in the 4th century BCE, who gave it its famous Greek theater, it was taken over by the Romans in the 3rd century CE, who quickly saw its potential as an elite retreat. Like much of Sicily, Taormina was conquered by the Byzantines, Arabs, and eventually the Spanish, all of whom left their mark on this small town's architecture. It's a perfect town to explore on foot before a late-afternoon aperitivo in the checkered-tiled central square, Piazza IX Aprile.

You certainly won't be alone in admiring Taormina's beauty. You can find praise for it in the poetry of Ovid, the diaries of Goethe, and the witticisms of Oscar Wilde, and the list of famous visitors to Taormina reads like a who's who of Hollywood and the literati.

Today, the impeccably preserved Teatro Antico is brought back to life in the summer months with concerts and performances. Then there's the beach: An aerial tram connects the town with the breathtaking coast below. Save time to explore Isola Bella, a tiny, landscaped island connected to Taormina by a thin strip of sand, with views of the immense, turquoise sea from every angle.

Taormina's famed picture-perfect scenery means it is home to several four- and five-star hotels, as well as Michelin-starred fine-dining locations. If luxury is what you want, this is the place to treat yourself. The city does become very crowded in summer, when the beautiful nearby beaches and the small streets of the town are packed with travelers. Beat the crowds and visit in autumn and winter when hotel prices drastically drop, and you'll be able to tour the town's medieval streets almost all by yourself.

Taormina

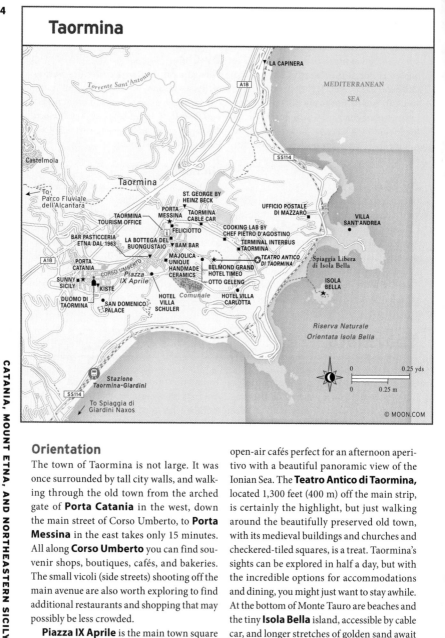

Orientation

The town of Taormina is not large. It was once surrounded by tall city walls, and walking through the old town from the arched gate of **Porta Catania** in the west, down the main street of Corso Umberto, to **Porta Messina** in the east takes only 15 minutes. All along **Corso Umberto** you can find souvenir shops, boutiques, cafés, and bakeries. The small vicoli (side streets) shooting off the main avenue are also worth exploring to find additional restaurants and shopping that may possibly be less crowded.

Piazza IX Aprile is the main town square in the center of Corso Umberto, filled with

open-air cafés perfect for an afternoon aperitivo with a beautiful panoramic view of the Ionian Sea. The **Teatro Antico di Taormina,** located 1,300 feet (400 m) off the main strip, is certainly the highlight, but just walking around the beautifully preserved old town, with its medieval buildings and churches and checkered-tiled squares, is a treat. Taormina's sights can be explored in half a day, but with the incredible options for accommodations and dining, you might just want to stay awhile. At the bottom of Monte Tauro are beaches and the tiny **Isola Bella** island, accessible by cable car, and longer stretches of golden sand await a short drive south of the city.

1: view of Taormina **2:** Teatro Antico di Taormina

SIGHTS
★ Teatro Antico di Taormina

Via del Teatro Greco, 1; tel. 0942/23220; www. parconaxostaormina.com; 9am-4pm daily Nov.-Feb., 9am-5pm Mar. and Oct., 9am-6:30pm Apr., 5pm-10pm May, 5pm-9:45pm June, 9am-7pm July-Aug., 9am-6pm Sept.; €10, reduced rates €5

The ancient Greek theater is by far the most important stop for any trip to Taormina. It was built in the 3rd century BCE by the Greeks using mostly red bricks, and they used it for musical and stage performances. It was later renovated by the Romans to host gladiator games, when it could hold up to 10,000 spectators.

Though there are many antique theaters in southern Italy, the Teatro Antico's size, excellent preservation, and spectacular location—literally carved out of the rock of Monte Tauro—make it unique. It's clear the natural surroundings were incorporated into the planning of this theater's stage, orchestra, and auditorium, which all dramatically overlook the Ionian Sea in one direction, with views of Mount Etna in the other. The iconic remains of the Corinthian columns were raised back up only in the 1860s, when Taormina was firmly situated as a destination on the European Grand Tour. Another unique feature of the Teatro Antico is that today it serves much the same function as it did thousands of years ago, making it very easy to take a seat in the auditorium and imagine the works of Aeschylus or Aristophanes being performed. These days, the theater is frequently used for theatrical performances during the summer months; visit www.aditusculture.com for a schedule of events.

Access to the theater comes with a map and audio guide that takes you through a prescribed route and gives context to ruins, such as the portico, where eventgoers would have purchased drinks and snacks during intermissions. It also includes entrance to the small Antiquarium museum, with objects found at the site.

Duomo di Taormina

Piazza Duomo, 1; tel. 0942/23123; www.comune. taormina.me.it; 8:30am-8pm daily; free

Taormina's principal Catholic church, also known by its full name, the **Basilica Cattedrale di San Nicolò di Bari,** dates to the 13th and 14th centuries. Parts of the cathedral are more recent, most notably its 17th-century doors, surrounded by elaborately carved columns decorated with the images of 22 saints. The building itself is a relatively modest, squat structure, made of stone imported from Syracuse, with an angular, medieval, almost fortress-like shape that has been admired by visitors as illustrious as Oscar Wilde, Johannes Brahms, Alexander Dumas, Guy de Maupassant, and Richard Wagner. The interior walls are whitewashed, with supporting columns of rose-colored marble, and there is a beautiful, gilded portrait of Christ behind the altar.

In front of the Duomo, the three-tiered marble **Fontana di Piazza Duomo** is topped by the symbol of Taormina, the half-human, half-horse crowned minotaur.

Villa Comunale

Via Bagnoli Croci; www.comune.taormina.me.it; 8am-6pm daily; free

Taormina's Villa Comunale is an urban oasis, filled with palm trees, magnolias, hibiscus, and several purely decorative Victorian garden buildings. It originally belonged to Lady Florence Trevelyan, the British noblewoman known best for purchasing the island of Isola Bella in 1890. It was constructed as a typical English garden, and she meticulously cared for the land and filled it with rare tropical plants that thrived in the Sicilian climate. Since 1992, the park has been in the care of the municipality of Taormina. Travelers visiting the ancient Greek theater should make a point to take the additional five-minute detour to Villa Comunale for some peace and quiet, away from the bustling streets of the historic city center.

Isola Bella

tel. 0942/620664; 9am-6pm Tues.-Sun.; €4

The tiny island of Isola Bella was originally gifted to the town of Taormina in 1806 by King Ferdinand I. In the late 1800s, it was acquired by Florence Trevelyan, a rich British noblewoman, who built lush tropical gardens and a private home there. In 2011, the island became the site of the Museo Naturalistico Regionale di Isolabella, a kind of natural museum managed by the World Wildlife Fund for Nature, which welcomes visitors who pay a daily entrance fee. Connected to the city of Taormina with a narrow, sandy strip of land, Isola Bella and the surrounding bay within the Ionian Sea have become the iconic image of this stunning coastal city. The island can be reached on foot after taking the three-minute cable car ride down from the town of Taormina.

BEACHES

Within the city of Taormina, beachgoers can enjoy the convenient free and public coastline down by the bay in view of Isola Bella, or head out of town to reach the sand beaches in **Giardini Naxos** to the south. Lidi, or beach clubs with amenities for paying guests like lounge chairs, umbrellas,

restrooms, and restaurants, are scattered along the coast.

Spiaggia Libera di Isola Bella

Mazzarò; open 24 hours; free

This lovely pebbled beach can be found in the neighborhood of Mazzarò, at the foot of Taormina, facing the bay in which Isola Bella is located. The picturesque islet, crystal-clear water, and spectacular location, nestled at the foot of Monte Tauro, make this a wonderful, if crowded, place to swim. In addition to the free beach, the **Lido Mendolia Beach Club** (Via Nazionale; tel. 0942/625258; www.mendoliahotel.com; 9am-6:30pm daily; 2 sun beds and an umbrella €40) is located nearby for those who want to relax with a few more amenities. From the city center of Taormina, this beach can be accessed by taking the **cable car** down to Mazzarò.

Spiaggia di Giardini Naxos

Via Naxos, Giardini Naxos

The beaches of Giardini Naxos, about 4 miles (6.4 km) south of Taormina, are considered among Sicily's best, not just for a relaxing day by the sea, but also for their well-known nightlife scene. With 2.5 miles (4 km) of mostly sandy beaches to choose from, you can

Spiaggia Libera di Isola Bella

throw down a towel in the free spiaggia libera, or splash out on a lido (likely cheaper than some of the beach clubs closer to Taormina). With a youthful crowd, this is the perfect place to catch a late-night beach party.

Though the 10-minute drive from Taormina might seem simple, in the summer months there's traffic and parking is difficult. Consider taking a taxi, which will cost approximately €20 one-way (taxi stations available at Taormina's train station and in Piazza Vittorio Emmanuele, off Corso Umberto). Interbus (www.interbusonline.com) also runs frequent buses between Taormina and Giardini-Naxos (10-20-minute ride, 2-4 times/hour; €2); buses leave Taormina from the Interbus terminal, not far from the Teatro Antico, and drop off near the Garden da Nino restaurant (Lungomare Tysandros, 74) in Giardini Naxos.

SPORTS AND RECREATION
Tours
Sunny Sicily
Salita Ciampoli, 3/A; tel. 338/5296915; www. sunnysicily.com

Sunny Sicily is an English-speaking private driver service based in Taormina and Syracuse that offers luxurious yet affordable airport transfers, half-day and full-day experiences, and cultural tourism options. The service can be especially useful for wine-tasting visits, multiday sightseeing itineraries, and transportation for groups and family trips.

Hiking
Parco Fluviale dell'Alcantara
Via Nazionale, 5, Motta Camastra; tel. 0942/985010; www.parcoalcantara.it; 9am-7pm daily; €1.50 entrance fee for guests using the stairs to reach the river; €8 at the private entrance with access to the elevator

Escape the crowds of Taormina with a refreshing trip to the Parco Fluviale dell'Alcantara, a protected 30-mile (48-km) natural area that's carved into dramatic gorges by runoff

from Mount Etna and the nearby Nebrodi Mountains. Impressive basalt columns and rock formations left over from volcanic eruptions add to the stunning natural landscape. Your first stop should be the **visitor center** (tel. 0942/989925) on Via dei Mulini in the tiny town of Francavilla di Sicilia, where you can learn about opportunities for river rafting, swimming, and hiking. Visitors can pay extra to access an elevator down to the river.

To arrive at the Parco Fluviale dell'Alcantara from Taormina, take Via Luigi Pirandello/SP10 on to Via Nazionale/SS114, continuing on to SS185 to Motta Camastra (12.8 mi/20.6 km; 35 minutes). A taxi will cost approximately €20 one-way.

Cooking Classes
Cooking Lab by Chef Pietro D'Agostino
Via Pirandello, 61; tel. 338/1588013; www. pietrodagostino.it/en/cooking-lab; 10am-1pm by reservation only; €120 plus taxes for group classes, €200 per person for private courses

Join a cooking class with one of Taormina's top chefs. Chef Pietro D'Agostino offers hands-on cooking programs for a minimum of eight participants on topics such as bread and pasta, innovative aperitivo, and personalized celebration menus. Adult programs, team building, and children's cooking classes can be organized in the Cooking Lab school kitchen in the city center of Taormina.

SHOPPING
Majolica - Unique Handmade Ceramics
Via Bagnoli Croci, 6; tel. 327/4075883; www. majolicataormina.com; 9:30am-8pm daily

Take a piece of Sicily home with you from this small ceramics shop filled with handmade plates, serving platters, olive oil bottles, vases, coffee sets, and home decor featuring traditional designs including prickly pears, florals, fish, Moor's heads, citrus, and more. Everything is produced right here in the shop by owner Maria and her sister Elvira.

Feliciotto

Corso Umberto, 5; tel. 0942/23280; www.feliciotto. com; 10am-10pm daily

This fresh and unique concept store stands out among the souvenir shop-lined streets of Taormina. The minimalistic shop is curated with cutting-edge Italian and international designer brands, niche streetwear lines, vinyl records, sunglasses, and sneakers. Feliciotto often hosts in-store events featuring art exhibitions, pop-up shops, and DJ sets.

La Bottega del Buongustaio

Via di Giovanni, 17; tel. 0942/625769; 9am-9pm daily

Since 1987, the Bottega del Buongustaio has been a staple in Taormina for all the best homemade preserves, wine and spirits, pastas, local honey, chocolates, marzipan fruit, and all kinds of typical Sicilian food products. This specialty food store has everything you'll want to take home with you after a trip to Sicily.

FOOD

Taormina is synonymous with luxury, from the accommodations to the food, so when budgeting for your trip to Sicily, save a little room for an extravagant meal in Taormina if you can. Reservations to most of the fine-dining restaurants below are essential.

Cafés and Light Bites

Bam Bar

Via di Giovanni, 45; tel. 0942/24355; 7am-11pm Tues.-Sun.; €3.50

Rosario Bambara's Bam Bar is the foremost stop for a quick coffee and a sweet treat in Taormina's historic center. His famous seasonal granitas include flavors such as Avola almond, pistachio, lemon, white fig, watermelon, and coffee. Order your granita with a fresh dollop of whipped cream and a fluffy brioche bun on the side for dipping.

Bar Pasticceria Etna dal 1963

Corso Umberto, 112; tel. 0942/24735; www. pasticceriaetna.com; 8am-midnight daily summer, 8am-9pm daily fall-spring; €5

This is the best old-school coffee shop in town. Bar Pasticceria Etna is a tiny store that has been serving up the best almond-based cookies, marzipan fruit, chocolate-dipped orange peels, and cannoli since 1963. Its dedication to Sicilian pastry traditions and friendly service has remained unchanged after all this time.

Fine Dining

Kisté

Via S. Maria de Greci, 2; tel. 333/3711606; www.kiste. it; 12:30pm-2:30pm and 7:30pm-10:30pm Tues.-Thurs. and Sat.-Sun., 12:30pm-2:30pm and 7:30pm-1am Fri.; tasting lunch menu €35, 5 courses €65, 8 courses €80, à la carte options €18-25

Kisté is a fairly new and approachable restaurant from chef Pietro D'Agostino, his partner Morena, and his two sisters. Located in the heart of the city center, inside the 15th-century Casa Cipolla, Kistè offers "easy gourmet" food for all, with the same high-quality ingredients and know-how you would expect from one of the city's best chefs.

La Capinera

Via Nazionale, 177; tel. 0942/626247; www. pietrodagostino.it/la-capinera; 12:30pm-2:30pm and 7:30pm-10:30pm Tues.-Sun. Sept.-June, 7pm-10:30pm Tues.-Sun. July, 7pm-10:30pm daily Aug.; 6-course seafood tasting menu €75, 9-course tasting menu €90, wine tastings €36-60, à la carte antipasti €23-37, main courses €27

Chef Pietro D'Agostino's one-star Michelin restaurant, La Capinera, is a romantic fine-dining destination on Taormina's Spisone beachfront. The natural blue and white interiors, solid oak handcrafted tables, and beautiful sea-facing terrace exude the same essence of history and magic that chef D'Agostino puts into each of his elegantly plated dishes.

Otto Geleng

Belmond Grand Hotel Timeo, Via Teatro Greco, 59; tel. 0942/6270200; www.belmond.com; 8pm-10pm Thurs.-Sat.; tasting menus for all guests at the table €150 per person, vegetarian menu €120 per person

This intimate fine-dining restaurant was named for the German artist who painted picturesque landscapes and was responsible for the boom in tourism here in Taormina during the late 1800s. Chef Roberto Toro's exclusive eight-table restaurant is located on the secluded Greek Theatre Terrace of the Belmond Grand Hotel Timeo, right in the heart of the historic city center. Chef Toro's meticulous dishes creatively reinterpret the flavors of Sicily in an atmosphere reminiscent of a dreamy, vintage Italian villa. Otto Geleng earned a coveted Michelin star just one year after opening. Reservations can be booked online or organized through the hotel's concierge. Dress code: elegant.

St. George by Heinz Beck

The Ashbee Hotel, Viale San Pancrazio, 46; tel. 0942/23537; www.theashbeehotel.it/st-george-restaurant; 7:30pm-10pm Wed.-Mon.; pasta dishes €35, main courses €45, 5-course tasting menu €130, 7-course tasting menu €160, wine pairings €40-90

Chef Heinz Beck's haute cuisine restaurant in Taormina quickly joined his impressive repertoire of Michelin-starred restaurants speckled throughout Italy. With 30-year-old chef Delfo Schiaffino commanding the kitchen, the St. George restaurant serves up a modern and revisited style of Sicilian cooking to the distinguished guests of the Ashbee Hotel and to nonguests.

ACCOMMODATIONS

Taormina is home to several notable high-end hotels with romantic accommodations, pools, and in-house dining options that will make you wish you never have to leave. In the height of summertime, July-September, hotels tend to fill up; reserving as early as possible is highly recommended to secure a coveted spot at one of these sought-after locales.

€100-200
Hotel Villa Schuler

Piazzetta Bastione, Via Roma, 16; tel. 0942/23841; www.hotelvillaschuler.com; from €168

Hotel Villa Schuler is a traditional Sicilian villa hotel that has been around since 1905. This charming and sophisticated four-star hotel is conveniently situated right in the historic center within a botanical park with awe-inspiring panoramic views. It's perfect for guests visiting Taormina without a car. Expect old-world hospitality from this charming third-generation, family-owned villa.

Over €300
Hotel Villa Carlotta

Via Pirandello, 81; tel. 0942/626058; www. hotelvillacarlottataormina.com; from €376

This independent four-star boutique hotel is more reasonable than other accommodations in Taormina. It features rooms, suites, and private villas with balconies or terraces, a rooftop restaurant, lush gardens, a pool, and extraordinary views of Mount Etna and the sea.

★ Belmond Grand Hotel Timeo

Via Teatro Greco, 59; tel. 0942/6270200; www. belmond.com; from €550

Since 1976, Belmond has been an iconic luxury hotel group with properties in the most exclusive locations around Italy and throughout the world. The Grand Hotel Timeo is situated right next to Taormina's ancient Teatro Greco, with priceless sweeping views of the Mount Etna volcano and the breathtaking Isola Bella in the Ionian Sea below. Apart from the stunning accommodations, the Literary Terrace & Bar of the Belmond Grand Hotel Timeo is one of the best places for an aperitivo al fresco, and the outdoor swimming pool, spa center, Timeo restaurant, and Michelin-starred Otto Geleng are not to be missed.

Villa Sant'Andrea

Via Nazionale, 137; tel. 0942/6271200; www.belmond. com; from €703

This sister hotel of the nearby Grand Timeo is also operated by the Belmond luxury hotel group. At Villa Sant'Andrea, guests can take advantage of the restaurant, spa, and private sun terraces, or just relax poolside. Follow the terraced tropical gardens down to Taormina's striking pebbled beach, in view of Isola Bella.

White Lotus

San Domenico Palace

The second season of *The White Lotus* television series, which premiered on HBO in the fall of 2022, was set in Sicily, and travel bookings to the island immediately skyrocketed. Although the characters of this comedy-drama series encountered more drama than the average visitor to Sicily will endure, the charm of this southern Italian island rightfully gained notoriety as a bucket-list trip option.

LOCALES

- Taormina's **San Domenico Palace** (Piazza S. Domenico de Guzman, 5; tel. 0942/613111; www.fourseasons.com/taormina), a five-star Four Seasons hotel, served as the branch of the *White Lotus* hotel chain at the center of the show. This historic property was a convent in the 14th century and opened as a resort in 1896. Prices for this resort have also increased with its visibility on the program, now ranging €2,200-5,000 per night for a room here in summertime. The show highlighted the resort's private infinity pool and lido deck, manicured Mediterranean gardens, and luxurious, spacious rooms and suites.

- The long, golden-sand beaches featured in the program's depiction of Taormina were actually shot on the shores of **Cefalù,** a 2.5-hour drive from where the fictional resort was depicted, seemingly just steps below the cliffs.

The concierge team can organize private sailing excursions upon request.

INFORMATION AND SERVICES

- **Visit Sicily:** www.visitsicily.info; strtaormina@regione.sicilia.it

- **Tourist information:** Taormina Tourism Office, Palazzo Corvaja, Piazza Santa Caterina; tel. 0942/23243; 8:30am-2pm and 3:30pm-6:30pm Mon.-Fri., 9am-1pm and 4pm-6:30pm Sat.-Sun. Dec.-Jan.

- **Post office:** Ufficio Postale di Mazzarò; Piazza della Funivia, 1, Mazzarò; tel. 0942/626193; www.poste.it; 8:20am-1:45pm Mon.-Fri., 8:20am-12:45pm Sat.

- **Pharmacy:** Farmacia British; Piazza IX Aprile, 1; tel. 0942/625866; 8:30am-2pm and 2:30pm-8:30pm Mon.-Sat., 9am-1pm and 4pm-8pm Sun.

- **Hospital:** St. Vincent Sirina; Contrada Sirina, Sirina; tel. 0942/5791

GETTING THERE
By Car

From Catania or the Catania Fontanarossa Airport, head north on the **E45** highway toward Taormina and Messina. The 41-mile (66-km) drive will take just over one hour. Most of the historic center of Taormina has been transformed into a pedestrian zone; ask staff at your accommodation what they recommend for parking. The main parking garage, **Parcheggio Lumbi** (follow signs for parking on approach to Taormina; €13.50 daily rate), is located outside the historic center but offers a free shuttle bus service into town.

By Train
Stazione Taormina-Giardini

Via Nazionale, 43, Villagonia; www.trenitalia.com
The closest train station for Taormina is shared between the city of Taormina and the beach town of Giardini Naxos to the south. Guests arriving with public transportation will need to take a 10-minute taxi ride up the hill to reach the city center (€15); there is a taxi stand outside the station. Taormina-Giardini can be reached by train service from **Trenitalia** (www.trenitalia.com) from **Messina Centrale** (1 hour; €5), **Catania Centrale** (40 minutes; €5,20), **Syracuse** (2 hours; €11), and **Milazzo** (1 hour 50 minutes; €8.40). Tickets can be purchased inside the station or online and must be time-stamped at the station before boarding.

By Bus
Terminal Interbus Taormina

Piazza Luigi Pirandello
Bus services to Taormina are provided by **Interbus** (tel. 0942/625301; www.interbus.it). Typical routes include **Catania Fontanarossa Airport** (1 hour 25 minutes; €8.20), **Catania** (1 hour 15 minutes; €5.10), and **Messina** (1 hour 45 minutes; €4.30). The Interbus terminal is more conveniently located than the train station, just behind the Teatro Antico di Taormina.

GETTING AROUND

The best way to explore the city of Taormina is on foot, along with the cable car from the main town down to Isola Bella. Avoid having a car in Taormina if at all possible, since the historic city center is mostly blocked off for pedestrian-only access.

By Cable Car
Taormina Cable Car (Funivia Mazzarò Taormina)

Via Luigi Pirandello, 3; tel. 0942/23906; www.gotaormina.com/en/taormina/cable_car.html; departs every 15 minutes 8:45am-8pm Mon., 7:45am-8pm Tues.-Sun.; one-way ticket €3, full-day €10
Taormina's gondola cable car provides service from the city down the hill to Isola Bella beach in only two minutes. The station in Taormina can be reached on a three-minute walk from the Porta Messina city gates.

By Taxi

If you need a taxi to Giardini Naxos, you'll find taxi ranks at Stazione Taormina-Giardini and in Piazza Vittorio Emmanuele, or call **Taxi Messina** (tel. 35/5861290; www.taximessina.com).

Mount Etna

Soaring to 10,990 feet (3,350 m), nearly two and a half times higher than Mount Vesuvius, Mount Etna is Europe's highest active volcano and one of the most active in the world. Its eruptions date back at least 3,500 years; the most devastating major eruption in recent history took place in 1992, lasted four months, and required local authorities to use dynamite to divert the intense lava flows. Called "Mongibeddu" in Sicilian and often referred to as "Mother Etna," the volcano's name stems from the Greek word "aitho," meaning "to burn." Mount Etna is inseparable from Sicily's folklore and myths; in Roman mythology, the god of fire, Vulcan, used Mount Etna as his metal workshop, and it was believed that sparks flew from the volcano whenever his wife Venus, the goddess of love and beauty, was unfaithful. Although Mount Etna still regularly belches smoke, occasionally dusts the city of Catania with ash, and has minor eruptions every few months, it is considered safe to visit, keeping in mind that trekking to the summit requires a guide.

The volcano is protected by 60,000-acre (24,000-ha) **Parco dell'Etna** (www.parcoetna.it), a landscape ranging from lush green valleys and citrus orchards to mountainous volcanic craters. With such a vast area to cover, it's wise to divvy up the mountain into slopes—south, east, and north. The microclimates of the different slopes and the mineral-rich, fertile soil lend themselves to abundant agricultural production and to growing some of the most interesting wine in Italy. Though the mountain may seem forbidding, there are actually many small villages at the volcano's base, living in its shadow, with quaint, rustic agriturismo farm stays and luxurious modern resorts built in old wine presses or with black lava stones from the area. Mount Etna is a pilgrimage for wine lovers and outdoor adventurers, and the farthest

south you're likely to ski within the boundaries of Europe.

Orientation

When planning a trip to Mount Etna, try to divide the volcano up into slopes. You may find that a winery you want to visit on the south slope and a hotel near Randazzo, on the north slope, might be too far apart.

The **south slope** is most accessible from Catania: A drive up to Viagrande, one of the main towns on this slope, takes only 25 minutes. This is the best place to start trekking experiences, especially to the volcano's summit, but also offers some great vineyard tours and wine tastings. At the **Rifugio Sapienza** resort in the comune of Nicolosi, the Funivia dell'Etna provides access to ski slopes November-March/April, a leg up to hikes, and tourist amenities including parking, bathrooms, tour guides, shops, bars, and snack stands for food and supplies. Note that it's impossible to access the summit of Mount Etna unless you're on a guided tour.

The **east slope** offers excellent dining, wine tasting, and overnight stays. Towns on the **north slope,** such as Randazzo and Linguaglossa, are slightly larger, while smaller Castiglione di Sicilia is considered one of the most beautiful villages in Sicily. The east and north slopes are most accessible from Taormina, with the closest town, Linguaglossa, a 35-minute drive away; from Catania, making your way to Randazzo will take about an hour. This area is notable for its wide selection of wineries, trattorias, and wine bars, but travelers who enjoy the great outdoors will love this lush green side of the volcano, too. The Piano Provenzana ski resort is located in Linguaglossa, with its own cable car and amenities, but as the higher elevations on this side of the volcano are covered in hardened lava from eruptions in the 1990s, it's considered less scenic and therefore less popular.

Mount Etna

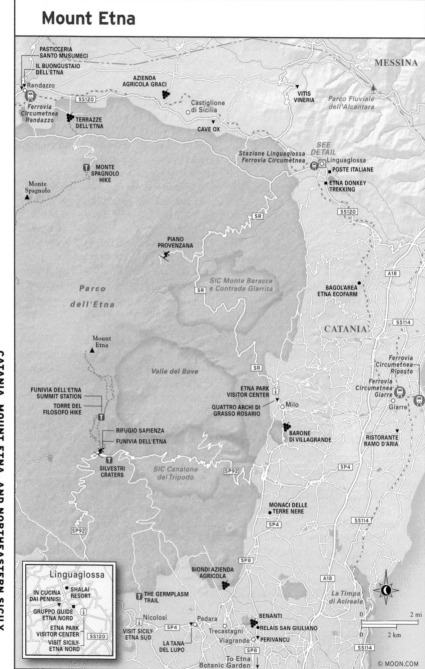

MESSINA

PASTICCERIA SANTO MUSUMECI
IL BUONGUSTAIO DELL'ETNA
Randazzo
SS120
AZIENDA AGRICOLA GRACI
Castiglione di Sicilia
CAVE OX
VITIS VINERIA
Parco Fluviale dell'Alcantara

Ferrovia Circumetnea Randazzo
TERRAZZE DELL'ETNA

Stazione Linguaglossa Ferrovia Circumetnea
SEE DETAIL
Linguaglossa
POSTE ITALIANE
ETNA DONKEY TREKKING

MONTE SPAGNOLO HIKE

Monte Spagnolo

SS120

PIANO PROVENZANA

SR

SIC Monte Baracca e Contrada Giarrita
SR

BAGOL'AREA ETNA ECOFARM

A18

SS114

CATANIA

Parco dell'Etna

Mount Etna

Valle del Bove

Ferrovia Circumetnea— Riposto

Ferrovia Circumetnea Giarre
Giarre

FUNIVIA DELL'ETNA SUMMIT STATION
TORRE DEL FILOSOFO HIKE

SR

ETNA PARK VISITOR CENTER
QUATTRO ARCHI DI GRASSO ROSARIO
Milo

RIFUGIO SAPIENZA
FUNIVIA DELL'ETNA

SILVESTRI CRATERS

SIC Canalone del Tripodo

SP92

BARONE DI VILLAGRANDE

RISTORANTE RAMO D'ARIA

SP4

MONACI DELLE TERRE NERE

SS114

SP92

SP4

SP8

BIONDI AZIENDA AGRICOLA

A18

La Timpa di Acireale

Linguaglossa

IN CUCINA DAI PENNISI
SHALAI RESORT
GRUPPO GUIDE ETNA NORD
ETNA PARK VISITOR CENTER
VISIT SICILY- ETNA NORD
SS120

THE GERMPLASM TRAIL

Nicolosi

VISIT SICILY- ETNA SUD
SP4
LA TANA DEL LUPO

Pedara
Trecastagni
Viagrande
SP8

BENANTI
RELAIS SAN GIULIANO
PERIVANCU

To Etna Botanic Garden

0   2 mi
0   2 km

SS114

© MOON.COM

Though the simplest way to get around Mount Etna is with a rental car, other great options include booking a tour or a private driver. There's also the **Ferrovia Circumetnea** (www.circumetnea.it) train route departing from Catania in the south and making a half-circle around the volcano, ending up at Riposto, some 20 miles (32 km) north of Catania. Though not the fastest way to travel, the train is scenic, and may make sense if you find it stops somewhere convenient to your Etna itinerary.

SIGHTS
Funivia dell'Etna

Stazione Partenza Piazzale Funivia Etna Sud, Nicolosi Nord; tel. 095/914141; www.funiviaetna.com; 9am-4pm daily; €30 round-trip

Even though it's expensive, you should think about taking the cable car up the Mount Etna volcano even if simply just for the 10-minute ride and the exceptional panoramic views, departing at the 6,305-foot (1,923-m) base and arriving at 8,215 feet (2,504 m). Cable cars depart continuously every few minutes all day long. At the top of the mountain there is a chalet bar, café, and gift shop where visitors can purchase refreshments and enjoy the panoramic views from Taormina to the Aeolian Islands on a clear day.

During the winter season (Dec.-Mar.), the Etna cable cars run daily for sightseeing or snowshoers, with the final departure at 4pm. For summer excursions, the final uphill departure is at 3:30pm. By telephone reservation only, the Funivia dell'Etna offers an additional Sunset Excursion on Monday, Tuesday, and Thursday, departing at 5:30pm. The shop at the cable car entrance has coat and shoe rentals available, which may be helpful when the top of the volcano remains covered in snow even in summertime.

TOP EXPERIENCE

★ HIKING

Parco dell'Etna is crisscrossed by dozens of hikes, from low-intensity walks to advanced treks. It's possible to do many of these hikes self-guided, but if you want to reach the summit of Mount Etna, you'll need to do so with a guide. This regulation was put in place in 2013—understandable when you consider the very real risk of hikers falling into an active volcano. Fortunately, there are plenty of options available, from old-fashioned hikes to night excursions and donkey treks, and if hiking isn't your priority, you can always just take the cable car up the slope to 8,200 feet (2,500 m) for a bucket-list view. Find additional trail maps and hiking information online at www.parcodelletna.it, www.myetnamap.it, and www.unescoparcoetna.it.

Mount Etna can be hiked year-round, keeping in mind that October-April there can be snow and low temperatures, while August will be extremely hot and crowded. Beat the heat by avoiding hikes during the middle of the day July-August. Any time of year, hikers on Mount Etna should wear layered clothing, a wind- and water-resistant jacket, and sturdy hiking boots, and bring plenty of water and snacks. For summer visits, pack sunscreen, insect repellent, a hat, and sunglasses. In winter, check the weather before traveling: You may want to pack insulated pants, a warm jacket, a hat, gloves, and lip balm to protect from the wind.

The volcano's hiking hub is **Rifugio Sapienza** (Piazzale Rifugio Sapienza, Nicolosi; tel. 095/915321; www.rifugiosapienza.com) on Etna's south slope, where you'll find parking (about €3.50 per day), trailheads, all manner of tour companies, hotels, restaurants, and other amenities. For a price, you can also hop on the panoramic **Funivia dell'Etna** cable car (Stazione Partenza Piazzale Funivia Etna Sud, Nicolosi Nord; tel. 095/914141; www.funiviaetna.com; 9am-4pm daily; €67 combined ticket with a walking guide at the top of the mountain or €30 for only the cable car ride). Though quite expensive, the 10-minute ride itself is breathtaking, and it helps you avoid a 1.5-hour, not terribly interesting walk from Rifugio Sapienza to the summit station.

Guided Treks

Hiring a private guide or joining a group tour is recommended for exploring Mount Etna to the fullest—and required to get to the 10,990-foot (3,350-m) summit. A knowledgeable guide will tell you all there is to know about the area's fascinating volcanic history.

Go Etna

tel. 366/3592490; www.go-etna.com/excursions/etna-summit-trekking; group rate €120 per person

This eight-hour moderate trekking experience begins at Rifugio Sapienza, where you will board the cable car before taking a 4WD vehicle up to the Valle del Bove crater to see the lava flow from the major eruptions in 1992 and 2001. You'll trek through ancient lava flows to the highest point possible on Mount Etna. Go Etna's group excursions are led by English-speaking guides and can be booked April-October. Private tours with hotel transportation can be arranged upon request.

Gruppo Guide Etna Nord

Piazza Attilio Castrogiovanni, 19, Linguaglossa; tel. 095/7774502; www.guidetnanord.com

The Gruppo Guide Etna Nord association offers a range of trekking for exploring the hidden natural treasures of Mount Etna. Its

5-6-hour private excursion leaves from Piano Provenzana on Etna's north slope, stopping at the craters and heading up to eruptive vents created in 1923, at 5,883 feet (1,793 m) above sea level. This easy-moderate trek requires a sturdy pair of boots, wind/rain-protectant clothing, and a hat. A more advanced full-day trek (7-8 hours) with snowshoes is offered in winter and springtime.

Funivia dell'Etna Guided Walk

Stazione Partenza Piazzale Funivia Etna Sud, Nicolosi Nord; tel. 095/914141; www.funiviaetna.com; 9am-4pm daily; €67 combined ticket with a walking guide at the top of the mountain, €30 cable car ride only

The Funivia dell'Etna offers the only certified excursion on the south slope, taking guests from the cable car's summit station and to the summit using off-road vehicles and some trekking. The entire round-trip journey, including the cable car, takes about two hours.

South Slope

Torre del Filosofo Hike

Distance: *4 miles (6.4 km) round-trip*
Time: *about 2 hours round-trip*
Trailhead: *Funivia dell'Etna Summit Station*
Information and Maps: *www.parcoetna.it*

This relatively moderate hike from the summit

---

hiking on Mount Etna

station of Funivia dell'Etna takes you about as close to the summit as you can get without a guide. Walking on the same makeshift road used by vehicles to get to the summit, which looms ominously to your left, you'll pass otherworldly craters created by eruptions in the early 2000s, some of them still steaming decades later. About halfway through, you'll reach the tower for which the hike is named, an observation tower constructed on the site of what was said to be the shelter built by the Greek philosopher Empedocles. Not much is left of the tower, which was built too close to the summit to last for long. The pinnacle of the hike is the impressively large Barbagallo Craters, which can be walked around in their entirety.

Note that it is possible to hike from Refugio Sapienza and avoid the €30 round-trip cable car ride. The path up the mountain, near where you board the cable car, is fairly obvious. To do this, add approximately three hours and 3 miles (4.8 km) to your round-trip hike.

Silvestri Craters

Distance: *0.6 mile (1 km) round-trip*
Time: *45 minutes round-trip*
Trailhead: *SP92, Nicolosi*
Information and Maps: *www.mapcarta.com*
Not far from Rifugio Sapienza, these two smaller craters at an elevation of about 2,300 feet (700 m) were formed by an eruption in 1892. They're a great option for travelers with kids, or those who don't have the time for the seven-hour guided hike to the top of Mount Etna and back. You'll enjoy 360-degree panoramic views from the top of the lunar landscape; the lower crater, just south of the SP92 road that winds up the volcano, can be traversed in about 30 minutes on a leisurely, slightly uphill 0.25-mile (0.4-km) walk. The upper crater, on the north side of the SP92, is reachable via a steeper climb; hikers can also continue to Monti Calcarazzi (add 20 minutes and 0.6 mi/1 km round-trip), a mountainous area created by an eruption in the 18th century.

The black surface, arid landscape, and lack of shade make this a very hot walk in the summer; start out early to beat the heat. It's not recommended to visit after dark.

The Germplasm Trail

Distance: *0.7 mile (1.1 km) round-trip*
Time: *1 hour round-trip*
Trailhead: *Via del Convento, 45, near the Monastero di San Nicolò L'Arena in Nicolosi*
Information and Maps: *www.parcoetna.it*
The Germplasm Trail is specially designed to stimulate all five of your senses, featuring plaques along the way to help you identify notable native plants. One of the easier routes on the volcano, this basic one-hour hike is wheelchair accessible and includes rest areas with benches, bathrooms at the entrance, and signage in Braille for visually impaired visitors.

North Slope
Monte Spagnolo Hike

Distance: *3.4 miles (5.5 km) each way*
Time: *2 hours 30 minutes round-trip*
Trailhead: *Pirao Etna Nord, 20-minute drive southeast of Randazzo*
Information and Maps: *www.parks.it or www.myetnamap.it*
On the northern slope, a 20-minute drive from Randazzo, this moderate trail with a 750-foot (230-m) elevation gain passes lava tunnels created in 1981, with beautiful views of the mountainous area north of Mount Etna. At the hike's highest elevation (4,700 ft/1,440 m), you'll find the Rifugio Monte Spagnolo, a picturesque stone hut for hikers spending the night on the mountain.

OTHER SPORTS AND RECREATION
Jeep and Donkey Tours
Etna Discovery

tel. 095/7807564; www.etnadiscovery.it/etna-jeep-tour-half-day-en; 4-hour programs at 9am and 3pm; €60 per person
This half-day tour of Mount Etna includes round-trip transportation from your hotel or meeting point. Your four-hour Jeep tour will be led by an expert tour guide. Off-roading

adventures include a tour of a lava tube and a walk around the crest of the craters.

Donkey Trekking

Piano Provenzana; tel. 349/3065136; www. etnadonkeytrekking.com; office 9am-8pm daily; 1-hour experiences from €25 per person

Take a ride through Mount Etna on these beautiful Ragusano-breed donkeys. Various 1-4-hour excursions are available year-round. Winter programs (Nov.-Apr.) include rides through snow-covered woods, vineyards, and olive groves.

Skiing

There are two locations for skiing on Mount Etna (www.etnasci.it), giving skiers the unique opportunity to hit the slopes in the middle of the Mediterranean. Day passes cost €15-35, and equipment can be rented at either Rifugio Sapienza or Piano Provenzana. Etna's high elevation means there can be snow year-round, with enough for skiing November-March, sometimes into April.

Rifugio Sapienza

Rifugio Sapienza-Montagnola, SP92, Nicolosi; tel. 095/915321; www.etnasci.it; 9am-3:30pm daily year-round; adult day pass €30

The slopes of Rifugio Sapienza, on the south slope of Mount Etna, stretch between 6,200 and 8,500 feet (1,900-2,600 m); five ski trails overlooking the Gulf of Catania and the smoking summit range from easy to intermediate. A six-seater cable car provides access to the slopes, and Etna Tourism Services offers ski and snowboard rentals (tel. 095/7807740).

Traveling for one hour by car from Catania, follow SP10 north to SP92 into Nicolosi until you spot signs for Etna Sud. The **Autolinea AST** bus service (tel. 095/7461096) also departs from Catania Centrale at 8:15am and returns at 4pm from the resort (€3).

Piano Provenzana

Via Provenzana, Piano Provenzana, Linguaglossa; tel. 095/643094; www.etnasci.it; 9am-4pm daily year-round; adult day pass €35, children's ticket €30

This resort is on the north slope of Mount Etna near the town of Linguaglossa at 5,900-7,500 feet (1,800-2,300 m), with amazing views of the Ionian Sea. There are 6.4 miles (10.3 km) of slopes available for skiing and snowboarding, though due to hardened lava on this side of the mountain from relatively recent eruptions, the runs at Piano Provenzana tend to be open less. Equipment rentals are offered by La Capannetta (tel. 328/9129666). From Taormina, it's a 30-mile (48-km) drive of just over an hour, though expect it to take longer on the twisty, sometimes snowy roads. From Linguaglossa, follow signs for Etna Nord - Piano Provenzana.

★ VINEYARD VISITS AND WINE TASTING

Mount Etna is home to over 150 wineries; with so many to choose from, the ones featured here are all exclusively local, rather than extensions of larger wineries. Reservations are required for all tastings in this area; walking into a winery for a tasting unscheduled is unusual. Keep in mind that September-November is harvest season, meaning smaller winemakers will have less time to receive visitors. It is not expected to purchase after a tasting, though wines are often available to buy or ship back home.

Wine Tours

Consider a private driver to take you to Etna's wineries, to avoid worrying about navigating mountain roads after your tasting.

★ Etna Wine School

www.etnawineschool.com; info@etnawineschool.com; half-day programs from €120 per person, full day €220

The half-day expert-led programs at the Etna Wine School include a visit to a single winery, while full-day programs include two wine estates and guided wine tastings. Founder Benjamin North Spencer is a U.S.-born writer and Wine & Spirits Education Trust-certified expert, and his book, *The New Wines of Mount Etna*, is a great resource for wine lovers visiting this area. Reservations must be made in advance; premium tastings, lunches, and transportation can be added for an extra fee.

Sunny Sicily Etna Wine Tour

Sunny Sicily, Piazza S. Antonio Abate, 7, Taormina; tel. 338/5296915; www.sunnysicily.com/tour/etna-wine-tour; 7-8-hour full-day experience; from €135 per person

Treat yourself to a full day of wine tasting with your own friendly, English-speaking luxury chauffeur. This experience includes door-to-door service to and from your hotel and a visit and tasting at two of Etna's top wineries.

South Slope
Benanti

Via Giuseppe Garibaldi, 361, Viagrande; tel. 095/7890928; www.benanti.it; daily visits by appointment only; Wine & Culture Experience €50 per person

The Benanti family is among the most respected wine producers on Etna, and the only one to have vineyards on all four of its slopes. Their vineyard in Viagrande is one of the most popular, well-organized, professional, and efficient on the mountain. Visitors can purchase wine on-site and take part in tours of the 19th-century estate, including the historic palmento wine press, 100-year-old nerello mascalese and nerello cappuccio vines, and wine tastings and food pairings inside a cozy country house.

Biondi Azienda Agricola

Via Ronzini, 55a, Trecastagni; tel. 347/5011310; www.ibiondi.com; by appointment only; €30 per person

Ciro and Stef Biondi took over these 17th-century vineyards in the comune of Trecastagni in 1999, and are now ranked among the leading natural wine producers on Mount Etna. Their high-quality wines focus on sustainability and respect for the territory. Guests can enjoy 90-minute tastings of 4-5 wines paired with local cheese, meats, and accompaniments, right in the middle of terraced vineyards. Biondi is one of the most accessible wineries on Mount Etna's southern slope, 30 minutes from Catania by car.

East Slope
Barone di Villagrande

Via del Bosco, 25, Milo; tel. 095/7082175; www.villagrande.it; by appointment only 11am-3:30pm and 6:30pm-10pm daily; tastings from €30 per person

Located at 2,300 feet (700 m) above sea level on the eastern side of the Mount Etna volcano, the Barone di Villagrande property has been owned by the Nicolosi Asmundo family since 1727. For the last 10 years, Marco and Barbara have been producing fine organic wines from the family vineyards overlooking Taormina. Their noble and historic 18th-century country manor also includes a Wine Resort, restaurant, and pool nestled between the vineyards, which host wine tastings, dinners, and overnight stays. It's one hour from Taormina and 35 minutes from Catania via the E45 coastal highway.

North Slope
Terrazze dell'Etna

Località Bocca d'Orzo, Randazzo; tel. 328/6175952; www.terrazzedelletna.it; Mon.-Sat. by appointment only; €20-35 per person

Since 2008, the Bevilacqua family has cultivated the land of the Contrada Bocca d'Orzo estate. Their 89 acres (36 ha) include terraced nerello cappuccio, nerello mascalese, carricante, chardonnay, pinot noir, and petite verdot vineyards, as well as chestnut forests and olive groves. Terrazze dell'Etna in Randazzo can be reached with a scenic, one-hour mountain drive from Taormina.

Azienda Agricola Graci

SP7, Contrada Arcuria, Passopisciaro; tel. 348/7016773; www.graci.eu; by appointment only; €45 per person for tasting of 5 wines

Alberto Aiello Graci has been making wine on his 5-acre (2-ha) family property since 2004. His high-density vineyards are planted at an altitude of 2,000-3,300 feet (600-1,000 m) above sea level and focus solely on indigenous grape varietals, set between towering lava stone walls. The certified organic wines are fermented using only wild yeasts. The Graci vineyards can be reached via a one-hour ride from Taormina, passing through the charming hilltop village of Castiglione di Sicilia.

FOOD

Due to Mount Etna's fertile volcanic soil, this part of the island offers exceptional produce, including foraged mountain greens, stone fruit, world-famous pistachios, wild mushrooms, flavorful extra virgin olive oil, local cheeses, and pork products and salami made from the black pigs that thrive in the mountainous landscape. As this is one of Sicily's most famous winemaking regions, high-quality local wines will be readily available in restaurants, grocery stores, and markets.

Rustic farm stays and restaurants are speckled throughout the mountainous region, and most winery visits will offer food pairing options or even a full lunch with advance notice, but most of the restaurants, bars, markets, pharmacies, and gas stations are clustered in the town centers. Always stock up on food or snacks (maybe even a picnic!) before embarking on an outdoor adventure.

South Slope
Perivancu

Via Vincenzo Bellini, 18, Viagrande; tel. 095/7894698; www.perivancu.it; 8:15am-1:30pm and 5pm-8:30pm Mon.-Tues. and Thurs.-Sat., 8:15am-2pm Wed. and Sun.; €10

Get a taste of Mount Etna and stock up on food to pack along with you on a hike or take home at the end of your trip. This small alimentari specialty food store and deli has been family-run since 1926 and features regional delicacies such as cured meats and cheeses, seasonal vegetables and fruit grown on the volcano, foraged mountain mushrooms, local honey, marmalades, and pesto, as well as a selection of wine and spirits from the area. Perivancu is located just 10 minutes south of the Benanti winery.

La Tana del Lupo

Corso Ara di Giove, 138, Pedara; tel. 095/7800303; www.ristorantelatanadelupo.it; 8pm-11pm Mon. and Wed.-Sat., 12:30pm-2:30pm and 8pm-11pm Sun.; €10-18

Only 25 minutes from the center of Catania in a small village between Nicolosi and Trecastagni, La Tana del Lupo is a casual tavern specializing in delicious meat dishes. The restaurant was completely renovated inside a traditional palmento winemaking press. Like any reputable restaurant on Mount Etna, its extensive wine cellar takes center stage.

East Slope
★ Ristorante Ramo d'Aria

Ramo d'Aria: Etna Country Hotel, Viale delle Provincie, 261, Giarre; tel. 334/6399145; www.ramodaria.it; 7:30pm-midnight with one rotating day closed per week; main courses €14-16

Nestled in a lush green lemon grove, this resort restaurant offers affordable contemporary dining on the eastern side of Mount Etna. Fresh seasonal dishes feature traditional Sicilian flavors of the land and sea using local artisanal ingredients such as pistachios, ancient wheat varieties, and local mountain cheeses, guaranteed to dazzle the palate of any food and wine lover.

Quattro Archi di Grasso Rosario

Via Francesco Crispi, 9, Milo; tel. 095/955566; www.4archi.it; 8pm-midnight Mon.-Tues. and Thurs.-Fri., 1pm-3:30pm and 7pm-midnight Sat.-Sun.; €15-25

At Quattro Archi, owner Saro Grasso and chef Lina Castorina proudly follow the philosophies of Slow Food. They work directly with small producers and select top-quality ingredients, always striving to provide good old-fashioned, down-home Sicilian cuisine and wood-fired pizza in their rustic osteria. Milo can be reached by car in 45 minutes from Taormina or Catania.

North Slope
Il Buongustaio dell'Etna

Via Umberto, 8, Randazzo; tel. 320/9760623; www.buongustaiodelletna.com; 9:30am-10pm Mon.-Fri., 9:30am-11:30pm Sat.-Sun.; meat and cheese platters €5-15

1: a tasty meal at Vitis Vineria **2:** vines at Terrazze dell'Etna

Treat yourself to one of this deli's epic meat and cheese charcuterie platters, piled high with salsiccia secca with wild fennel, pistachio salame, fresh provola, smoked scamorza, ricotta al forno, and a tasting of oil-preserved mushrooms, honey, and marmalades. Or, take one of its gourmet sandwiches along with you for a late-night snack once you get back to your hotel after a long day of wine tasting. Randazzo is accessible from Taormina in one hour, driving along the E45 highway to the SS1120.

Vitis Vineria

Via Tenente Tornatore, Castiglione di Sicilia; tel. 380/6304756; www.bottegavitis.com; noon-3pm and 7pm-11pm Thurs.-Tues.; antipasti €20, mains €14

A cozy night on the volcano is not complete without a few hours spent in a local wine bar. The selection of wines physically packed into every shelf, cantina, nook, and cranny of this tiny vineria, located in the picturesque mountainside town of Castiglione di Sicilia, is unparalleled. Test out seasonal specialties like wild mushroom soup, hefty hamburgers, and local cured meat and cheese platters. Castiglione di Sicilia is accessible by car from Taormina in 45 minutes via SS114 to SS185 and SP7.

Cave Ox

SS120, 78, Solicchiata; tel. 0942/986171; www.caveox.it; noon-3:30pm and 7pm-10:30pm Wed.-Fri., noon-3:30pm and 7pm-11pm Sat.-Mon.; €15-30

This is the local winemakers haunt on Etna. The simple osteria menu includes natural-leavened pizzas, pasta dishes, grilled meats, sausages, meatballs wrapped in lemon leaves, and slow-roasted lamb from the area. It's a great spot to join a tasting event or just settle in for a long night with a few too many bottles from Etna's best wine list, curated by owner Sandro di Bella. You'll spot its coral-colored exterior along the small road leading across the northern slope. Wine lovers will want to spend hours here, which can be ideal if you are staying nearby in Castiglione di Sicilia, Randazzo, or Linguaglossa.

★ In Cucina Dai Pennisi

Via Umberto I, 11, Linguaglossa; tel. 095/643160; www.daipennisi.it; 9am-11pm daily; €35

This hidden culinary treasure is located in the small mountain town of Linguaglossa. Saro and Lina Pennisi have partnered with the Shalai boutique hotel to revamp their historic family store into a butcher shop with its own contemporary bistro right in the middle of the cases of meat and sizzling grills. Dishes arrive at the table served on wooden boards, steakhouse-style. Guests arriving from Taormina can reach Linguaglossa by car in 30 minutes by following the E45 to SS120.

Pasticceria Santo Musumeci

Piazza Santa Maria, 5, Randazzo; tel. 095/921196; 8am-midnight Wed.-Mon.; €3 granita and gelati

Take a break from wine tasting and stop by the historic center of Randazzo to meet Giovanna Musumeci, one of the best artisanal gelato makers in Sicily. This small family bar with outside seating has a rotating menu selection that includes Sicilian almonds, local pistachios, hazelnuts, and citrus as well as gelato and granita made with seasonal fruit. At Santo Musumeci, they always use top-quality ingredients, traditional techniques, and a whole lot of love. Randazzo is accessible from Taormina in one hour, driving along the E45 highway to the SS1120. In winter hours are limited to 8am-9:30pm Saturday-Monday.

ACCOMMODATIONS

With choices ranging from eco-lodges to luxury accommodations and rustic farm stays, a night or two spent on Mount Etna will give guests the additional time needed for exploring the volcano and visiting wine producers without the need to drive back to Taormina or Catania. Resorts will often have their own in-house restaurant for a convenient and relaxing meal.

South Slope
Etna Botanic Garden

Via Trinità, 34, Mascalucia; tel. 337/955493; www.etnabotanicgarden.com; €70

Plan an escape to this garden oasis on the southern slope of Mount Etna. The rustic manor house sits on a 3-acre (1-ha) property filled with citrus orchards and botanical gardens. Choose from its two rooms or six apartments, enjoy a poolside break and the excellent organic breakfast, or cook for yourself in one of the kitchenette-equipped cottages.

Relais San Giuliano

Via Giuseppe Garibaldi, 280, Viagrande; tel. 095/9891671; www.relais-sangiuliano.it; classic rooms from €145, family suites €200-260

Add a little glam to your trip to Mount Etna. This 12-room dimora storica noble country home can host up to 31 people. The lush gardens, gorgeous swimming pool, sun terrace, spa, fitness center, and restaurant are especially equipped for couples and families. This is a perfect pick at the foot of Mount Etna, stylishly designed to provide a relaxed family atmosphere. Pets are welcome, too!

East Slope

★ Monaci delle Terre Nere

Via Monaci, Via Pietralunga, Zafferana Etnea; tel. 095/7083638; www.monacidelleterrenere.it; from €497

Monaci delle Terre Nere is the place where slow living and luxury meet. The 60-acre (25-ha) estate includes carefully renovated historic farmhouses, the main 18th-century manor house, and sustainably built villas and suites. Each space celebrates its original elements, such as exposed wood-beamed ceilings and lava-stone walls. Owner Guido Coffa considers himself a custodian of the land, and his passion for sustainability and respect for the natural surroundings shine through in every aspect of this magical paradise. The mountainside manor house can be reached by car in 35 minutes from Catania and 40 minutes from Taormina.

Bagol'Area Etna EcoFarm

Via Presa, Mascali; tel. 333/3050663; www.bagolarea. it; from €75

Spend your time on Mount Etna at a small natural winery and organic fruit farm. Cinzia and Diego's property was once the largest vineyard in the Etna region. The 150-acre (60-ha) area includes terraced vineyards, organic fruit groves, chestnut forests, and eco-friendly accommodations and guesthouses. Overnight rentals at Le Case del Bagolaro range from small one-bedroom sunlit studios to eco-lodges, "glamping" tents, and even a 270-square-foot (25-sq-m) vintage roulotte camper van. This is a great choice for groups

villa at Monaci delle Terre Nere

and families who are looking for ample space, fresh mountain air, panoramic views, and privacy. Located in the outskirts of the town of Mascali, Bagol'Area can be reached by car in 50 minutes from Catania and 40 minutes from Taormina.

North Slope
Shalai Resort

Via Guglielmo Marconi, 25, Linguaglossa; tel. 095/643128; www.shalai.it; €145

After a day of outdoor adventures, treat yourself to a little rest and relaxation. In Sicilian dialect, "Shalai" means "full of joy," and that's exactly what you'll experience in this elegant and contemporary resort. This 13-room boutique hotel is located in the historic center of Linguaglossa. Candle-lit spa treatments are available in the wellness center, and the resort restaurant is not to be missed. Linguaglossa can be reached by car in 35 minutes from Taormina or 50 minutes from Catania.

INFORMATION AND SERVICES

The online resource **My Etna Map** (www.myetnamap.it) and its printed maps were created in partnership with the Visit Sicily tourism board to help travelers discover the territory around Catania and the Mount Etna volcano. The guide includes seasonal itineraries, points of interest, and restaurant and hotel recommendations. Free printed maps can be found in many hotels, restaurants, cafés, and travel agency offices in the area.

There are many visitor centers throughout the Mount Etna area, including several run by Parco dell'Etna and a few others run by Visit Sicily.

- **Etna Park Visitor Centers:** www.parcoetna.it; Via A. Manzoni, 21, Fornazzo/Milo, tel. 338/2993077; and Piazza Annunziata, 5, Linguaglossa, tel. 095/643094
- **Visit Sicily - Etna Sud:** Via Martiri d'Ungheria, 36/38, Nicolosi; tel. 095/911505; www.visitsicily.info
- **Visit Sicily - Etna Nord:** Piazza Annunziata (corner of Via Marconi), Linguaglossa; tel. 095/643677; www.visitsicily.info

Other Services

- **Police:** Polizia Di Stato; Via Sottotenente Manchi, 6, Randazzo; tel. 095/921222; www.questure.poliziadistato.it
- **Hospital:** Azienda Sanitaria Provinciale Di Catania: Piazza Ospedale, 1, Randazzo; tel. 095/921056; open 24 hours
- You'll find **pharmacies** in major towns like Viagrande, Linguaglossa, and Randazzo.
- **Post office:** Poste Italiane, Viale Tommaso Fazello, 13, Linguaglossa; tel. 095/643663; www.poste.it; 8:30am-1:30pm Mon.-Fri., 8:30am-12:30pm Sat.

GETTING THERE AND AROUND

Though there is some public transportation to Mount Etna, including a slow (but scenic) train route, the best way to explore Mount Etna is with your own rental car. Most wineries and outdoor excursions will require you to arrive at a set meeting point somewhere on the mountain. Hiring a private driver is another good option, especially for vineyard visits.

By Car and Private Driver

The south and east slopes are easily reached by car from **Catania** (25 minutes) and **Taormina** (1 hour). The north slope is most accessible via a scenic, one-hour drive through the mountains from Taormina. The state roads and highways from Taormina and Catania are easy to navigate, but keep in mind that many roads in the Etna area are unmarked, unlit, and fairly dangerous for driving at night or during inclement weather. Allow more driving time than you think you need, and keep in mind that gas stations and restaurants are sparsely distributed around the perimeter of the volcano. When visiting wineries or country accommodations, double-check with your host for driving directions; often, they will even meet you at a central location so you can follow them to the destinations.

Though you may want to avoid driving on some of the tiny, narrow streets of mountainside towns, parking is for the most part easy and clearly signed, and rates are generally cheap or even free. **Refugio Sapienza** and the Funivia dell'Etna is a one-hour, 21-mile (34-km) drive from Catania and just over an hour (34 mi/55 km) from Taormina. Parking here costs €3.50 per day and is free after 5pm.

Private driver **Sunny Sicily** (Piazza S. Antonio Abate, 7, Taormina; tel. 338/5296915; www.sunnysicily.com) provides chauffeur services and organizes tours including vineyard visits on Mount Etna, with round-trip transportation from Taormina or Catania.

By Train
Ferrovia Circumetnea

Via Caronda, 352a, Catania; tel. 095/541111; www. circumetnea.it; approximately 6am-6pm daily; tickets range in price depending on distance, with discounted rates on round-trip services

This railway connects Catania with Riposto, traveling clockwise from the provincial capital city heading west along the south, west, north, and half of the east slope around Mount Etna for 69 miles (111 km). Unfortunately, it does not make a full round-trip loop back to Catania. Departing from the **Catania Borgo** (Via Caronda, 352a) Metro station, the journey from beginning to end of the line lasts about three hours (€8 one-way, €13 round-trip) and stops along the way in towns such as Randazzo and Linguaglossa before finally reaching **Stazione Riposto—Ferrovia Circumetnea.** It offers two special itineraries: the Il Treno dei Vini dell'Etna train and Wine Bus service, to discover Etna's best wineries; or the Treno su Due Ruote trip, which allows you to board the train with a bicycle and get off at the destination of your choice.

A short train ride with **Trenitalia** (www. trenitalia.com) can also be helpful to return to Catania without circling the volcano on the way back. Train service departs from the **Giarre-Riposto station** (Piazza Giuseppe Mazzini, 6, Giarre), which is about 0.9 mile (1.5 km) west of the Riposto Circumetnea station, for **Catania Centrale** (Piazza Papa Giovanni XXIII, 2, Catania) throughout the day (20-40 minutes; €3.40-8.50). This trip can also be taken in the opposite direction, taking the Trenitalia service to Giarre-Risposto and the Circumetnea scenic train on the way back to the Catania Borgo station.

Messina

Messina was founded by the Greeks in the 8th century BCE. The city was originally named Zancle, from the Greek word meaning "scythe," referring to the curved shape of the town's harbor, which in fact is the largest natural harbor in the Mediterranean. It was renamed Messene in the 5th century BCE before being taken over by Dionysius I of Siracusa, leading to the current name Messina. At first glance, the city of Messina doesn't seem so old at all. It was destroyed by a devastating earthquake in 1783 and another in 1908, which along with a powerful tsunami resulted in the death of 100,000 people and the nearly complete destruction of all of the city's ancient monuments, homes, and buildings.

The city was rebuilt between the 1920s and 1930s, calling in top architects from Italy to give the town a fresh new look and mix of architectural styles, along with many of the Liberty-style buildings of that period. Yet again, Messina incurred damages from the Allied invasion of Sicily and bombings in World War II in 1943. Many of the historic buildings seen today are replicas of the originals, either with limited original pieces reworked into the design or displayed for their preservation in the town's museums.

Messina

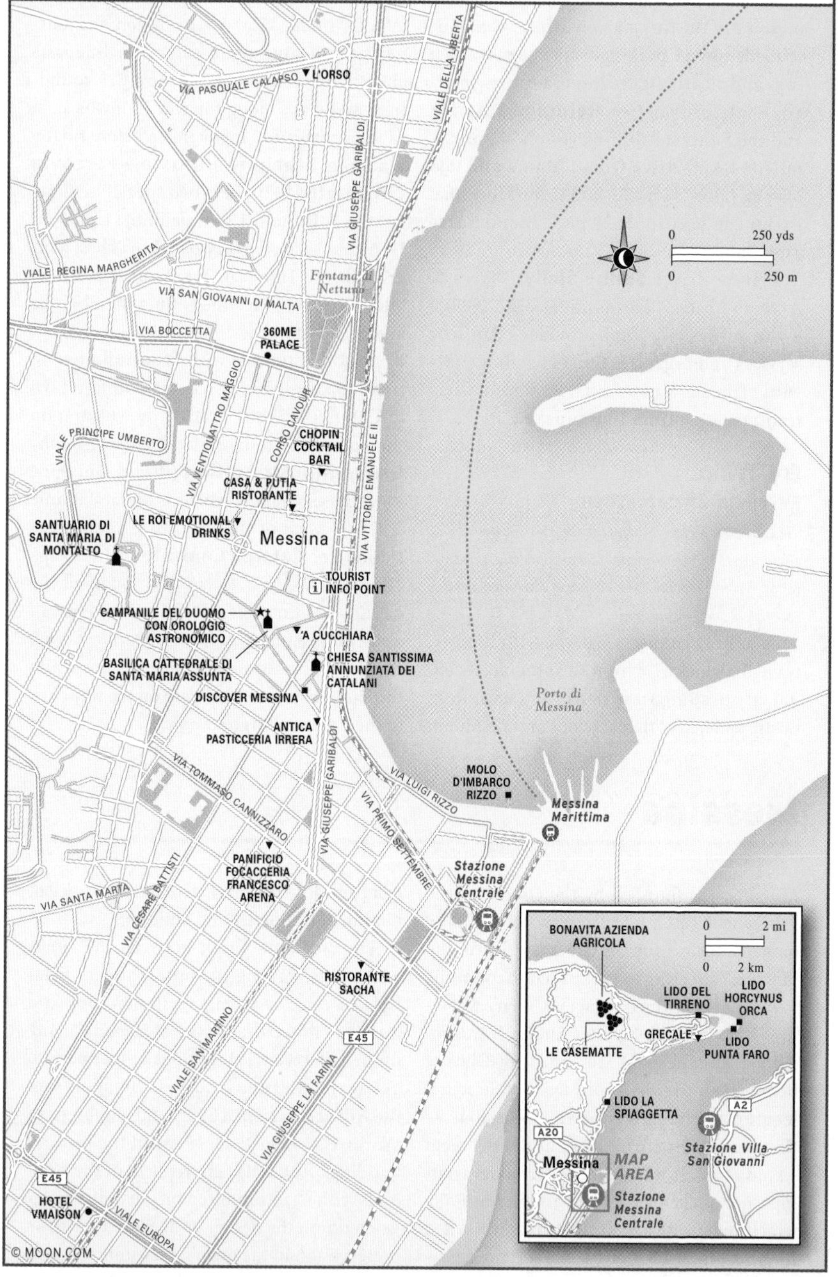
VIA PASQUALE CALAPSO
L'ORSO
VIALE DELLA LIBERTA
VIA GIUSEPPE GARIBALDI
VIALE REGINA MARGHERITA
Fontana di Nettuno
VIA SAN GIOVANNI DI MALTA
VIA BOCCETTA
360ME PALACE
VIA VENTIQUATTRO MAGGIO
CORSO CAVOUR
VIALE PRINCIPE UMBERTO
CHOPIN COCKTAIL BAR
CASA & PUTIA RISTORANTE
VIA VITTORIO EMANUELE II
LE ROI EMOTIONAL DRINKS
SANTUARIO DI SANTA MARIA DI MONTALTO
Messina
TOURIST INFO POINT
CAMPANILE DEL DUOMO CON OROLOGIO ASTRONOMICO
'A CUCCHIARA
BASILICA CATTEDRALE DI SANTA MARIA ASSUNTA
CHIESA SANTISSIMA ANNUNZIATA DEI CATALANI
DISCOVER MESSINA
ANTICA PASTICCERIA IRRERA
Porto di Messina
VIA TOMMASO CANNIZZARO
VIA LUIGI RIZZO
MOLO D'IMBARCO RIZZO
VIA PRIMO SETTEMBRE
Messina Marittima
PANIFICIO FOCACCERIA FRANCESCO ARENA
VIA SANTA MARTA
VIA CESARE BATTISTI
Stazione Messina Centrale
RISTORANTE SACHA
VIALE SAN MARTINO
E45
VIA GIUSEPPE LA FARINA
HOTEL VMAISON
VIALE EUROPA
© MOON.COM
0 250 yds
0 250 m
BONAVITA AZIENDA AGRICOLA
0 2 mi
0 2 km
LIDO DEL TIRRENO
LIDO HORCYNUS ORCA
GRECALE
LIDO PUNTA FARO
LE CASEMATTE
LIDO LA SPIAGGETTA
A2
A20
Stazione Villa San Giovanni
Messina
MAP AREA
Stazione Messina Centrale

Messina is the third-largest city in Sicily, with a population of more than 219,000 inhabitants. The city is also a busy hub for college students studying at the University of Messina, the world's first Jesuit college and one of the oldest universities in Italy. Its importance was based mainly on its strategic location at the northeastern tip of the island, which nearly connects with the mainland province of Calabria, agricultural abundance, and trade connections. The locals are a proud bunch, celebrating the roots of many of Sicily's food and wine specialties. The province of Messina includes three DOC (denominazione di origine controllata), designated winemaking classifications based on their location, including Mamertino in Milazzo and Malvasia delle Lipari in the Aeolian Islands. The intense ruby-red Faro DOC wines are the only ones grown within the city limits of Messina, made mostly from nerello mascalese, nerello cappuccio, and nocera grapes. These vineyards are cultivated in the countryside north of the city center, between the hills and the sea.

Orientation

Messina is located on the northernmost tip of the east side of the island, at the point where the slim Strait of Messina nearly connects Sicily with mainland Italy at Calabria, only 2 miles (3.2 km) away. The modern city center, the ferry terminal, and the main harbor can be found on the east coast of Sicily, 31 miles (50 km) north of Taormina and 59 miles (95 km) north of Catania.

Messina is often used as an arrival or departure point for ferries, hydrofoils, and cruise ships connecting the city with southern Italy or the Aeolian Islands.

After the devastating earthquake of 1908, the city was rebuilt with a grid layout and wide avenues, making it easy to get around.

Northeast of the city center, on the Punta del Faro promontory, there are two lakes—Lago Grande in Ganzirri and Lago Piccolo in Torre Faro—historically used for farming mussels, which are featured abundantly in traditional dishes in Messina. The seaside town of Ganzirri is located on the southern coast of the promontory, while Torre Faro is the easternmost area; both are destinations in summer months for their popular beachfront or lakefront restaurants.

SIGHTS

Campanile del Duomo Con Orologio Astronomico

Basilica Cattedrale di Santa Maria Assunta, Piazza Duomo; tel. 090/675175; www.messinarte.it

If you do one single thing in Messina, it should be making a point to visit the Duomo at exactly noon to see the magnificent astronomical clock in action. The 200-foot-high (60-m) tower of the Cathedral of Messina was transformed into the largest and most complex mechanical astronomical clock in the world in 1933. Once per day, the clock moves and plays music for approximately 12 minutes. Bystanders gather in a crowd in the front of the church square to admire the clock's movements while Franz Schubert's "Ave Maria" plays over the loudspeaker.

Levers and gears generate the movement of bronze statues representing the story of the city, including the city's heroines, Dina and Clarenza, who strike the bells before the rooster crows and a crowned lion (the symbol of the province of Messina) roars. A carousel represents the ages of life from a child to a young man, then to a warrior and an elderly man. A silhouette of the Sanctuary of the Madonna di Montalto appears on its hilltop and a dove flies over it. Depending on the time of year, one of four biblical scenes will be depicted, including either the shepherds bowing before baby Jesus, Joseph, and Mary; the Three Kings visiting Jesus held by Mary; soldiers keeping watch over the tomb; or the twelve apostles surrounding the Virgin Mary. On the side of the bell tower, the clock marks the current day on a calendar and shows the evening's phase of the moon on a large half-gold, half-black rotating sphere. The planets orbit around the sun at the dial's center and move through the signs of the Zodiac. The bell tower can also be visited via a staircase where guests can view the inside of this mechanical masterpiece (10am-1pm; €4).

Basilica Cattedrale di Santa Maria Assunta

Piazza Duomo, 29; tel. 090/774895; www.messinarte.it

The Roman Catholic cathedral of Messina is not only the principal church of the city but home to the world's largest astronomical clock in its bell tower, which animates daily at noon. Although originally built by the Normans in 1197, it was damaged and finally destroyed by the 1783 and 1908 earthquakes, leaving only the perimeter walls still standing. The inside was fully reconstructed following the original Norman design. Reproductions of the artwork and statues on display were also created, while the tombs of the archbishops and limited mosaics were salvaged. The cathedral's organ is the second-largest polyphonic organ in Italy, built in 1948. Within the small ticketed museum inside the cathedral, the golden manta (mantle) of the Madonna della Lettera is among the "treasures" you can find on display. Outside, the bell tower and clock can be found to the left of the church entrance, while on the right side, the building features unique Catalan Gothic elements.

Chiesa Santissima Annunzia dei Catalani

Via G. Garibaldi, 111; tel. 090/6684111; www. discovermessina.it; 8:30am-10:30am; free

This Catholic church is one of the very few structures in Messina that is situated below ground level due to the fact that the city was nearly destroyed by the earthquake of 1908 and subsequently rebuilt entirely. Built on the ruins of a classical temple dedicated to Neptune, the structure dates back to the 12th century and features Arab, Byzantine, and Roman architecture styles. Mass is held on the first Sunday of each month.

Fontana di Nettuno

Via G. Garibaldi; open 24 hours; free

Located just north of Messina's harbor in the

Piazza Unità d'Italia square, the Fountain of Neptune was originally placed in front of what is known today as Via Vittorio Emanuele II, but was moved after the earthquake. It was commissioned by Messina's Senate and built in 1557 by Giovanni Angelo Montorsoli, a Florentine sculptor and pupil of Michelangelo Buonarroti. The fountain depicts the legend of the mythological monsters of Messina—Scylla and Charybdis—along with Neptune, the god of the sea.

Santuario di Santa Maria di Montalto

Via Dina e Clarenza, 16; tel. 090/774816; donations are appreciated

Like many of the main landmarks in Messina, the 13th-century Catholic church and Sanctuary of the Madonna di Montalto was rebuilt after the earthquake. Nestled on the top of the Caperrina hill overlooking the port of Messina, it was founded in 1294 during the Vespers War. From the outside, there are panoramic views of the city and the Strait of Messina. Inside the church, constructed in 1928, there is a 14th-century wooden panel, a silver manta (mantle), a 15th-century wooden crucifix, and two marble 18th-century holy water fonts. A small museum room is hidden behind a door to the left of the altar and preserves important items including the rock crystal case containing a strand of hair the locals believe belonged to the Madonna della Lettera.

BEACH CLUBS

Stone beaches and private clubs can be found on the northern part of the city in the districts of Pace, Paradiso, and Sant'Agata, located between the city center of Messina and the Punta del Faro promontory. On the promontory, the southern side has stone beaches facing the Ionian Sea, while the northern coast facing the Tyrennian Sea in Mortelle has sandy shores. Beach clubs in these areas, along with the nearby bars and restaurants, are open only in summertime. At the very tip of the Punta del Faro promontory, where the lighthouse

Myths of Messina

The strategic position of Messina has many connections to the sea and has been known to be related to the cult of Poseidon, one of the Twelve Olympians and Greek god of the sea, also known as Neptune in Roman mythology. Sea creatures are present in many of the fountains and monuments all around the city. Two famous mythological tales are associated with Messina.

Fontana di Nettuno

COLAPESCE

Messina is home of one of Sicily's most famous legends in which a boy nicknamed "Colapesce" swam down into the underworld to confirm the triangle-shaped island of Sicily was being held up by three columns, one of which had been damaged by fire. Since Colapesce was an expert diver, the king, Federico II, sent him down to hold up the island of Sicily in place of the third column, which was located below Messina. This is where he stayed—and, it is said, continues to stay—for an eternity to keep the island afloat. Colapesce is the theme in one of the Art Rooms at Catania's **Asmundo di Gisira** boutique hotel (page 210).

SCYLLA AND CHARYBDIS

Another legend that gives mystery to the town is the tale of Scylla and Charybdis, two ravenous sea monsters, one on the current-day coast of Sicily and the other in Calabria, who swallowed up ships and invoked dangerous currents in the Straits of Messina. The **Fontana di Nettuno** depicts this legend with Scylla and Charybdis chained between Neptune (page 238).

and the pylon are located, is where the two seas meet at the Strait of Messina. Strong currents can be present here, and swimming should only be done in the daytime with extreme caution.

Lido La Spiaggetta

Via Consolare Pompea; tel. 328/6887554; www. lidolaspiaggetta.it; beach bed/umbrella rentals about €16

Here at La Spiaggetta, just a 15-minute drive from the port of Messina, all services visitors might need for a beach day are provided, including parking, bathrooms with showers, changing cabins, and rentals for small boats, pedal boats, windsurfing, and canoes, along with an in-house restaurant and bar. Beach tennis, aerobics, and windsurfing classes are offered through La Spiaggetta in the summer season. Keeping with the retro vibe of the disco beaches of the 1990s, the open-air Lounge Bar is a popular spot for summer nightlife in Messina.

Lido Punta Faro

Via Fortino, Torre Faro; tel. 393/3306374; www. facebook.com/mashalaiamare; 8am-2am daily

Located at the very point of the Strait of Messina where the Ionian and Tyrennean Seas meet, the Punta Faro beach club has one of the very few restaurants in the small village that remains open all year long (with limited hours in winter). In summertime, beach beds and umbrellas are available to rent, and this is a popular destination for beachgoers who want to take a dip overlooking the coast of Calabria, near the lighthouse and pylon of Torre Faro.

Lido Horcynus Orca

Via Fortino, Torre Faro; tel. 393/9771876; www. horcynusorcalido.it; 9am-8pm daily; beach bed rentals starting at €14

On the north shore of the promontory, a 30-minute drive from the center of Messina, yellow and blue beach umbrellas dot the sandy Tyrennean coast at the Lido Horcynus Orca, where guests can rent lounge chairs for the morning (9am-1:30pm), afternoon (2pm-7pm), or the full day. A playground area is also available for small children. Breakfast, snacks, lunch, aperitivo, and dinner are available from the bar. There is often live music in the evenings in summertime, and this becomes a chic place to stay after the sun sets.

Lido del Tirreno

Contrada Mortelle, SS113 Km 12, Mortelle; tel. 090/321001; www.lidodeltirreno.it; 9am-7pm daily; rentals from €15

The Lido del Tirreno beach club offers on-site facilities including changing cabins, hot showers, sunbed and bright red beach umbrella rentals, restaurant and bar options, a beach volleyball court, and a playground set for children. Suitable for guests of all ages, this classic bathing establishment on the north coast of Messina has been around since 1956. On-duty lifeguards and the golden-sand shores add to the comforts of a day trip for families with children.

WINERIES

Bonavita Azienda Agricola

Contrada Corso, Faro Superiore; tel. 347/1754683; www.bonavitafaro.com; tastings from €20 per person

Carefully farmed on the steep hill overlooking the Strait of Messina, the vineyards of Giovanni Scarfone are cultivated on 6.2 acres (2.5 ha) of clay and calcareous land surrounded by orchards. The vineyard is located at between 820 and 984 feet (250-300 m) above sea level, and some of their nerello mascalese, nerello cappuccio, and nocera vines are up to 80 years old. Bonavita approaches winemaking with a respect for its territory, vinifying

only two wines: a red and a rosè made from only indigenous grapes.

Le Casematte

Contrada Corso, Faro Superiore; tel. 090/6409427; www.lecasematte.it; tastings from €15 per person

Founded in 2008 by Gianfranco Sabbatino and ex-footballer Andrea Barzagli, Le Casematte strives to bring the Faro DOC district back into the spotlight of Sicilian winemaking. Located on 27 acres (11 ha) of land at 1,640 feet (500 m) above sea level in the hilly Faro Superiore village of Messina, Le Casematte organically produces nerello mascalese, nerello cappuccio, nocera, and nero d'avola varieties needed for the Faro DOC regulations, along with a small percentage of grillo and carricante grapevines with northern exposure facing the Tyrennean Sea. Oenologist Carlo Ferrini oversees the vinification and aging in its cellar. Visitors with prior reservations can be hosted for wine tastings in the panoramic showroom.

TOURS

Discover Messina

Via I Settembre, 110; tel. 090/2135672; www. discovermessina.com; 9am-1pm and 3pm-6pm Mon.-Fri.; 2-hour walking tours starting at €25 per person

Popular with cruise ship guests docking in Messina for the day, local tour company Discover Messina offers informative walking tours of the city as well as full-day organized trips to nearby Taormina, Savoca, Mount Etna, and the Aeolian Islands. The friendly, English-speaking guides are extremely knowledgeable and excited to share with you their special part of northeastern Sicily.

FOOD

L'Orso

Via Pasquale Calapso, 12; tel. 090/9573101; www. orsomessina.com; 7pm-11:30pm Tues.-Fri., 7pm-midnight Sat.-Sun.; pizzas €8-15

This award-winning pizzeria is located on the northern part of the city center near the Neptune Fountain. It has been open since 2014 inside a renovated theater space that became the first pub in Messina in the 1990s. L'Orso was awarded the "tre spicchi" title by Gambero Rosso in 2021 and has always focused on the best-quality raw ingredients, local-grown flours, and 100 percent Sicilian ingredients including traditional favorites such as Slow Food Presidium siccagno tomatoes and cured meats from the Nebrodi mountains. It has also been listed on the Italian "50 Top Pizza" list, one of the very few pizzerias in Sicily to be mentioned.

Casa & Putia Ristorante

Via S. Camillo, 14; tel. 090/2402887; www. casaeputiaristorante.it; noon-3pm Sun.-Mon., noon-3pm and 7pm-midnight Tues.-Sat.; dishes €16-22

Enjoy elevated home-style Sicilian cooking at this casual bistro and shop with indoor and outdoor seating in the heart of Messina's historic center. Treat yourself to dishes like the polpo a terra with roasted octopus tentacles, buffalo milk stracciatella cheese, and crispy tumminia bread, or the land and sea combination of red shrimp from Mazara del Vallo with cured lard from the black pigs of the Nebrodi mountains and a drizzle of Sicilian asphodel honey. Its small putia (Sicilian dialect for shop) has a range of sun-dried, unprocessed sea salts from Trapani, tomato conserves, caper marmellata, and wines or after-dinner liquors available for sale. This is a great stop for a taste of Sicily at the table or for something to take back home with you.

Grecale

Via Canalone, 124, Torre Faro; tel. 090/6402915; www. grecalemessina.com; noon-2:30pm and 7pm-11:30pm Tues.-Sun.; dishes €16-24

Grecale's indoor/outdoor restaurant and cocktail bar overlook the Strait of Messina in the Torre Faro seaside village on the Peloro cape in the most extreme northern tip of Sicily. Embracing Slow Food values, chef Andrea Giannetti focuses on seasonal dishes using local seafood and high-quality ingredients. The exceptional wine list includes organic and biodynamic producers. Keep in mind it also has a sister restaurant, **Kajiki** (Via

XXVII Luglio, 112; tel. 090/6402915; www. kajikimessina.com; 7pm-11:30pm Tues.-Fri., 12:30pm-2:30pm and 7pm-midnight Sat.-Sun.), focused on Japanese cuisine in the historic center of Messina.

★ 'A Cucchiara

Strada S. Giacomo, 19; tel. 090/711023; www.facebook. com/acucchiaramessina; 12:30pm-3pm and 8pm-11pm Mon.-Fri., 8pm-11pm Sat.; tasting menu €70

Just around the corner from Messina's Duomo, chef/owner Peppe Giamboi has the hottest spot in town if you're looking for high-quality food in a relaxing and cozy setting. Built in one of Messina's few historic palazzi, the restaurant has about 60 seats, including inside and outside dining, with an open kitchen concept to keep an eye on the action. Dining at 'A Cucchiara is an experience for locals and tourists alike. The staff is friendly and knowledgeable, the dishes are carefully thought out, and there's an impressive wine program. Guests can taste their way through a chef's menu or order à la carte to enjoy the seasonal specialties and traditional Sicilian flavors without any of the fuss of a fancy restaurant. 'A Cucchiara can also accommodate guests with special diets and food allergies. Reservations are highly recommended.

★ Ristorante Sacha

Via Nicola Fabrizi, 15; tel. 090/2939982; www. sacharestaurant.it; 12:30pm-3pm and 7:30pm-11pm Sat.-Thurs.; tasting menus €65-130, à la carte dishes €16-25, reservations required

Splurge a little bit in this Michelin guide-mentioned upscale restaurant. The bright yet somewhat sterile dining room automatically gives the first impression that this is not your usual locale. After interning in Spain, France, Milan, and Rome, Ristorante Sacha's young chef, Francesco Castorina, returned to his hometown of Messina to serve up revisited Mediterranean cuisine with a Sicilian spin. The prime spot is the chef's table in the kitchen, which can accommodate private reservations of up to four guests.

Cafés and Light Bites
★ Antica Pasticceria Irrera

Via G. Garibaldi, 79; tel. 090/3505384; www.irrera.it;
7:30am-2pm Sun.-Mon., 7:30am-8:30pm Tues.-Sat.

In a province that claims the distinction of the top granita, head over to Irrera for the best you can find in the city center. Granita is a semi-frozen Sicilian dessert made with sugar, water, and flavorings (traditionally almond, coffee, or lemon), which differs from gelato or sorbet by the lack of additional dairy and the amount of air whipped into it. Handed down from generation to generation, the Antica Pasticceria Irrera has been open since 1910. It remains a highly respected family bakery that sells Sicilian sweets including cassata cakes, cannoli, Messinese pignolata, nougats, marzipan fruit, cookies, and granita served with fluffy brioche buns. Specialty products are also made for the Christmas (pannettone speckled with candied orange peel and Calabrian citron) and Easter (marzipan lambs stuffed with chocolate-hazelnut filling and Colomba cake) holidays.

Panificio Focacceria Francesco Arena

Via T. Cannizzaro, 137; tel. 090/9218792; www.
masinoarena.it; 7am-10pm Mon.-Sat.

Following in his father's footsteps, third-generation baker and local Messinese Francesco Arena brings a fresh outlook to bread in the heart of Messina's city center, focusing on native Sicilian flours and natural yeasts. Open since 2002, Arena's bakery has been awarded with several notable prizes, including winning the title of Best Baker in Sicily and the "three loaves" ranking from Gambero Rosso. He is dedicated to the craft of preparing high-quality breads and focaccias that are naturally leavened and made with flour stone-milled from ancient grains, including maiorca, perciasacchi, russello, and timilia. Inside this bakery, customers can pick up a variety of freshly baked loaves, focaccia, grissini breadsticks, crackers, cookies, and additional savory or sweet snacks.

BARS AND NIGHTLIFE
Chopin Cocktail Bar

Via Pozzo Leone, 17; tel. 090/344336; www.facebook.
com/chopincocktail; 6pm-2am Tues.-Sun.; drinks €7-15

Scout out a great place to stop for a cocktail in the historic center of town, just around the corner from the Teatro Vittorio Emanuele theater. The interiors are decked out with vintage furniture and a grand piano-shaped display lined with bottles hanging over the bar. Live music and DJ sets are organized on the weekends.

Le Roi Emotional Drinks

Galleria Vittorio Emanuele III, 18; tel. 348/4990791;
www.leroiemotionaldrinks.it; 6pm-1:30am Sun.-Thurs.,
6pm-2:30am Fri.-Sat.; cocktails €10, mocktails €7

Voted one of the Best 100 Cocktail Bars in Italy, Le Roi Emotional Drinks is a top cocktail bar in Messina where guests can enjoy traditional Italian mixed drinks such as a spritz or negroni as well as micheladas, tiki drinks, and original concoctions. While most shops inside the Galleria Vittorio Emanuele have been turned into laser tag, escape rooms, or fast-food joints, Le Roi is the one-stop shop for the city's best cocktail. Tables can be reserved online to make sure your spot is secured.

ACCOMMODATIONS
★ Hotel Vmaison

Viale Europa, 59; tel. 090/2938901; www.vmaison.it;
from €114

This four-star boutique hotel in Messina, just a 20-minute walk from the port, is the second location by VMaison, owned by Veronica Zimbaro, in the Brera neighborhood of Milan. It's not only an eclectic-design hotel with stylishly furnished though small rooms and suites, but it also has a rooftop terrace bar on the top floor for breakfast or aperitivo drinks. The interior of this turn-of-the-19th-century building was designed by the VMaison team, and all the decor is available for sale from their catalog. Each guest room comes equipped with air-conditioning, television, Wi-Fi, bathrobes, a security safe, mini-bar, tea and coffee, plus an electric kettle.

Crossing to Sicily: The Train on a Ferry

With cheap nonstop flights to Palermo and Catania from cities like Naples and Rome, taking the train is certainly not the most effective way to travel between Sicily and mainland Italy. But those who opt for a train are in for a unique (if not very speedy) experience. Despite the multi-decade-long ongoing discussion of building a bridge to connect Calabria and the island, this is not expected to happen anytime soon, so trains between the two are loaded onto a ferry.

For more than 50 years, **Caronte & Tourist** (https://carontetourist.it) has operated ferries across the Strait of Messina for up to five million passengers per year. Southern Italy's somewhat unreliable infrastructure is certainly tested by the process of dividing up the train into segments and loading them onto the ferry, meaning delays are common. However, being on a train on top of a ferry is a one-of-a-kind experience. Although the ferry ride itself is quite short (20 minutes), passengers are allowed to exit the train and enjoy the crossing from the ferry deck. Traditionally, the journey is commemorated with an arancino (fried rice ball), and the ones sold from the ferry concession stand for €2.50 are quite delicious, and were featured on Stanley Tucci's CNN program, *Finding Italy*, in 2021.

Ferries arrive and depart from **Stazione Villa San Giovanni** (Viale Italia; tel. 090/364601) in Villa San Giovanni in Calabria, and from **Porto di Messina** (Via Vittorio Emanuele II, 27; tel. 090/6013209; www.porto.messina.it) in Sicily. The train then continues toward the **Stazione Messina Centrale** (Piazza della Repubblica). Ferries leave every 40 minutes during the day (5:20am-11:20pm) and every 1 hour 20 minutes at night (1:40am-4:40am).

Buses between Calabria and Sicily are also boarded on ferries, and Caronte & Tourist provides passenger and car ferry service, too. Below is a breakdown for travelers who prefer to avoid flying and have some time on their hands.

- **Train:** Trains run by Trenitalia (tel. 668/475475; www.trenitalia.com) connect Naples to Palermo (9 hours 25 minutes; from €35) and Catania (8 hours; from €30). From Rome, trains to Palermo take about 12 hours.

- **Bus:** Flixbus (tel. 123/99123; www.flixbus.com; from €29) provides bus service from Naples to Catania (9 hours 15 minutes) and from Rome to Catania (11 hours).

- **Car and passenger:** The passenger ferry costs €2.50 per person one-way, while most vehicles will cost €39 one-way (fare includes up to five passengers).

360Me Palace

Viale Boccetta, 42; tel. 335/6666386; www.360mepalace.it; from €117

The 360Me Palace "aparthotel" and guest house residence is located in a recently renovated historic building, just 15 minutes on foot from the port. The contemporary rooms and suites were designed by local architect Clara Stella Vicari Aversa. They offer single and double rooms as well as suites that also include a full kitchen setup. Every room is equipped with its own balcony along with the necessary amenities including Wi-Fi service, television, air-conditioning, mini-bar and coffee machine, hair dryer, bath products and a security safe. They have 24-hour reception service and can accommodate luggage storage or laundry services upon request. One of their Deluxe Suites even has a hydromassage Jacuzzi. With easy access to the ferry port, train station, and local sights, this is an easy option for those looking to stay a night in Messina before heading off to their next destination in Sicily.

INFORMATION AND SERVICES

- **Tourist Info Point:** Via Consolato del Mare, 23; www.comune.messina.it; 9am-5pm daily

GETTING THERE
By Train
Messina Centrale
Piazza della Repubblica

The main transit station is Messina Centrale, located in Piazza della Repubblica. It is serviced by **TrenItalia** (www.trenitalia.it) and includes popular routes connecting Messina by train with **Milazzo** (35 minutes; €4.60), **Taormina-Giardini** (1 hour 11 minutes; €5.20), **Catania Fontanarossa Airport** (1 hour 50 minutes; €9.20), **Catania Centrale** (2 hours; €9.20), and **Palermo Centrale** (2 hours 50 minutes; €15.50). Tickets can be purchased in advance online or from an automated kiosk or ticket window at the station and must be time-stamped before boarding the train.

Messina Marittima
Porto di Messina

Messina Marittima is the secondary train station for the city, connected also by **TrenItalia** (www.trenitalia.it). Trains departing for Calabria will depart from this station, which can be reached with a six-minute walk from Messina Centrale.

By Ferry
The **Messina Marittima** train station is located directly next to the **ferry terminal.** Although ferries and hydrofoils are also available from Milazzo, Messina connects to Sicily's **Aeolian Islands** with service through **Liberty Lines** (Via Luigi Rizzo; tel. 090/364044; www.libertylines. it; 5:30am-8:15pm Mon.-Fri., 6am-5pm Sat.-Sun.).

By Bus
Departing from the main square in front of the train station, bus services provided by **SAIS Autolinee** (Piazza della Repubblica, 12; www.saisautolinee.it; tel. 090/771914) offer connections to **Palermo** (2 hour 50 minutes; €14), **Catania** (1 hour 35 minutes; €8.40), and the **Catania Fontanarossa Airport** (1 hour 50 minutes; €8.40).

GETTING AROUND
The city center of Messina can easily be explored on foot. The train station and ferry/cruise terminal are located right in the heart of the centro storico, with many restaurants, bars, hotels, and city sights in the surrounding areas. Messina also has its own **tram system** (www.atmmessinaspa.it; tickets €1.50, day pass €4) for quickly making your way along the coastline of the city.

Syracuse and Southeastern Sicily

The southeastern corner of Sicily is a unique blend of luxurious Baroque architecture, ancient archaeological sites, windswept sand beaches, and top-notch food and wine.

Take a glimpse into Sicily's Greek history in Syracuse, or Siracusa in Italian, the region's largest city, whose Neapolis Archaeological Park is filled with remnants of its long, complicated past. The capital of the Greek colony Magna Grecia, which covered all of Sicily and southern Italy, Syracuse was once the Mediterranean's most powerful city, even defeating Athens in battle in 413. Described by the Roman scholar Cicero as "the greatest Greek city and the most beautiful of them all," Syracuse is not to be missed. Feel free to mix history with indulgence: The streets of Ortigia, a neighborhood on a small island

Highlights

Look for ★ to find recommended sights, activities, dining, and lodging.

© MOON.COM

★ **Parco Archeologico della Neapolis:** Syracuse's archaeological park is home to countless ancient Greek treasures, including the limestone Quarry of Paradise and the Ear of Dionysius cliffside grotto (page 251).

★ **Island of Ortigia:** The tiny, 0.6-square-mile (1.5-sq-km) island of Ortigia is the oldest part of the city of Syracuse, packed with restaurants, shops, historic monuments, and lovely places to swim (page 257).

★ **Noto's Baroque Architecture:** Among a wealth of Spanish-influenced Baroque towns in this part of Sicily, Noto stands out (page 273).

★ **Wine Tasting in Ragusa:** Learn about the top winemaking families, grape varietals, and Sicily's only DOCG-classified wine with a tasting trip through the fertile vineyards in the province of Ragusa (page 284).

★ **Villa Romana del Casale:** The precious remains of a luxurious Roman villa more than merit a half-day trip to inland Sicily (page 286).

★ **Chocolate in Modica:** While under Spanish rule, Modica adopted a specialized cold-processing Aztec technique to grind cacao beans, and you can really taste the difference (page 292).

south of Syracuse, are lined with shops, restaurants, cocktail bars, and specialty food markets guaranteed to keep you occupied for at least a few days.

Outside the city, discover the Spanish-influenced towns of Modica, Noto, and Ragusa, UNESCO World Heritage Sites rebuilt in the 18th-century Baroque style following a devastating earthquake in 1693. These small towns are living pieces of art with their limestone churches and palaces, and they also host some of Sicily's top restaurants. In Modica, pop into as many chocolate shops as possible to experience the crisp, gritty, delicious crunch of the town's famous cold-processed chocolate. And a few hours' drive inland, the isolated 4th-century Villa Romana del Casale and its one-of-a-kind collection of mosaics are certainly worth a trip.

The food and wine scene here is exceptional, from crudo plates of fresh seafood to rare local cheeses and small artisanal vineyards. Make a reservation for a winery visit, hands-on cooking lesson, extra virgin olive oil tasting, or cycling trip. Almost every city and town offers a seemingly endless bounty of its own regional specialties.

ORIENTATION

The southeastern part of Sicily is broken into two main provinces, **Syracuse** and **Ragusa.** In Syracuse, besides its wonderful eponymous city, the largest in the region, you'll find the Baroque town of **Noto,** picturesque small villages, and great **beaches.** The province of Ragusa also includes its eponymous town, as well as the chocolate capital of **Modica** and hillside **wineries.**

In the inland town of Piazza Armerina, northwest of Ragusa, the **Villa Romana**

del Casale is technically in the province of Catania, and a 1.5-hour drive from that city as well as its airport. But the villa makes for a great day trip from Syracuse, Ragusa, and even Agrigento in western Sicily as well. To the south, the town of **Caltagirone** is known for its ceramics.

PLANNING YOUR TIME

The city of **Syracuse** can be explored in a weekend, but the surrounding provinces of Syracuse and **Ragusa** require at least three days. Syracuse is a great choice for visitors to eastern Sicily who want to beat the crowds of Taormina and Noto. You'll likely need a **rental car** or to hire a **private driver** in this part of Sicily. There is sparse access to public transportation, even if each town is fairly compact and walkable once you get there. The main highway in the eastern part of Sicily is the **A19.**

The nearest airport is **Catania Fontanarossa Airport,** only an hour's drive north of Syracuse. Pick up your rental car and drive south; Syracuse, particularly the neighborhood of **Ortigia,** is a great place to base yourself for a few days, taking day trips to the surrounding towns, wineries, and beaches. Syracuse and Ragusa are definitely busiest in **July-August,** but they're equally enjoyable in the **low season,** especially September-October, when the weather is still just warm enough to take a swim and eat al fresco. In general, accommodations, tours, and cooking lessons here should be reserved in advance; most restaurants welcome walk-ins, but calling a day before to book a table may help you avoid disappointment, especially in summertime or around December 13, when all of Syracuse celebrates the festival of their patron saint, **Santa Lucia.**

Syracuse and Southeastern Sicily

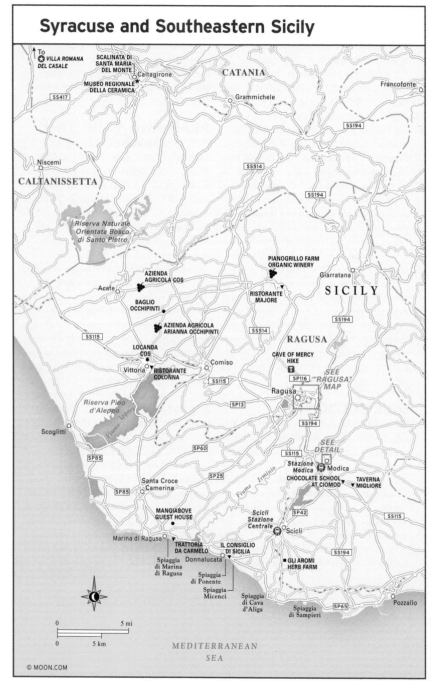

To
VILLA ROMANA
DEL CASALE

SCALINATA DI
SANTA MARIA
DEL MONTE
Caltagirone

MUSEO REGIONALE
DELLA CERAMICA

CATANIA

Francofonte

SS417

Grammichele

SS194

Niscemi

CALTANISSETTA

SS514

SS194

Riserva Naturale
Orientata Bosco
di Santo Pietro

PIANOGRILLO FARM
ORGANIC WINERY

AZIENDA
AGRICOLA COS

Giarratana

Acate

RISTORANTE
MAJORE

SICILY

BAGLIO
OCCHIPINTI

AZIENDA AGRICOLA
ARIANNA OCCHIPINTI

SS194

SS514

SS115

RAGUSA

LOCANDA
COS

Comiso

CAVE OF MERCY
HIKE

Vittoria

RISTORANTE
COLONNA

SS115

SEE
"RAGUSA"
MAP

SP116

Ragusa

Riserva Pino
d'Aleppo

SP13

SS194

Scoglitti

SP60

SEE
DETAIL

SP85

SS115

Stazione
Modica

Modica

SP25

CHOCOLATE SCHOOL
AT CIOMOD

TAVERNA
MIGLIORE

Santa Croce
Camerina

SP85

Fiume Irminio

MANGIABOVE
GUEST HOUSE

Scicli
Stazione
Centrale

SP42

SS115

Scicli

Marina di Ragusa

TRATTORIA
DA CARMELO

IL CONSIGLIO
DI SICILIA

Spiaggia
di Marina
di Ragusa

Donnalucata

GLI AROMI
HERB FARM

SS194

Spiaggia
di Ponente

Spiaggia
Micenci

Spiaggia
di Cava
d'Aliga

Spiaggia
di Sampieri

SP65

Pozzallo

0   5 mi

0   5 km

MEDITERRANEAN
SEA

© MOON.COM

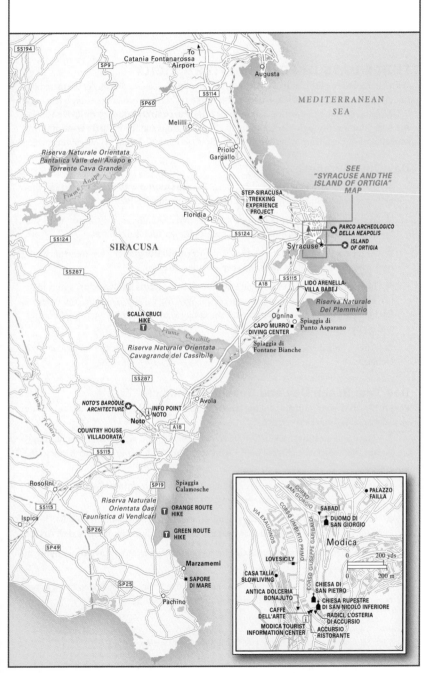

SS194

To Catania Fontanarossa Airport

SP9

Augusta

SP114

SP60

Melilli

MEDITERRANEAN SEA

Priolo Gargallo

Riserva Naturale Orientata Pantalica Valle dell'Anapo e Torrente Cava Grande

Fiume Anapo

STEP-SIRACUSA TREKKING EXPERIENCE PROJECT

Floridia

SS124

SS124

SEE "SYRACUSE AND THE ISLAND OF ORTIGIA" MAP

SIRACUSA

Syracuse

PARCO ARCHEOLOGICO DELLA NEAPOLIS

ISLAND OF ORTIGIA

SS287

A18

SS115

LIDO ARENELLA-VILLA BABEJ

SS287

SCALA CRUCI HIKE

Fiume Cassibile

Ognina

CAPO MURRO DIVING CENTER

Spiaggia di Punto Asparano

Riserva Naturale Del Plemmirio

Riserva Naturale Orientata Cavagrande del Cassibile

Spiaggia di Fontane Bianche

SS287

Avola

Fiume Tellaro

NOTO'S BAROQUE ARCHITECTURE

INFO POINT NOTO

Noto

A18

COUNTRY HOUSE VILLADORATA

SS115

Rosolini

SP19

Spiaggia Calamosche

SS115

Riserva Naturale Orientata Oasi Faunistica di Vendicari

ORANGE ROUTE HIKE

Ispica

GREEN ROUTE HIKE

SP26

SP49

Marzamemi

SP25

SAPORE DI MARE

Pachino

Modica inset

CORSO SAN GIORGIO

VIA EXAUDINOS

CORSO UMBERTO PRIMO

CORSO GIUSEPPE GARIBALDI

PALAZZO FAILLA

SABADÌ

DUOMO DI SAN GIORGIO

Modica

0   200 yds

0   200 m

LOVESICILY

CASA TALIA SLOWLIVING

ANTICA DOLCERIA BONAJUTO

CAFFÈ DELL'ARTE

MODICA TOURIST INFORMATION CENTER

CHIESA DI SAN PIETRO

CHIESA RUPESTRE DI SAN NICOLÒ INFERIORE

RADICI, L'OSTERIA DI ACCURSIO

ACCURSIO RISTORANTE

Itinerary Ideas

THREE DAYS IN SOUTHEASTERN SICILY

With a home base on the island of **Ortigia,** off **Syracuse,** you can reach many of the incredible surrounding cities like **Modica, Noto,** and **Ragusa** in less than two hours. Take a trip back to Greek and Roman times with a walking tour of the **Parco Archeologico della Neapolis,** and taste your way through Modica's famous chocolate shops and the **Vittoria winemaking region** with enough time in between for shopping, swimming, and nights out on the town.

Day One: Syracuse

1 Start your day on the island of Ortigia in **Piazza Duomo** with a cappuccino and cornetto before popping into the main cathedral, the Duomo di Siracusa.

2 Walk 10 minutes, past the 6th-century Tempio di Apollo on Via Cavour, until you reach the **Mercato di Siracusa,** where you can browse for local goodies.

3 At the northern end of the market, stop by **Fratelli Burgio** for a leisurely lunch featuring impeccable Sicilian meat and cheese platters (taglieri).

4 In the afternoon, visit the ancient **Parco Archeologico della Neapolis,** a 10-minute taxi ride or 30-minute walk north into central Syracuse via Corso Gelone. You'll need a few hours to explore all the stunning sites, including a Greek theater, Roman amphitheater, and mysterious grotto.

5 After a long day of sightseeing, grab some pizza at **Piano B,** across the bridge from Ortigia.

Day Two: Beach Day and Cooking in Modica

Be sure to reserve your intimate cooking class with **LoveSicily** in Modica in advance to ensure an unforgettable dinner experience.

1 Start your morning back in Ortigia's outdoor market and pick up some famous sandwiches and homemade cheeses from **Caseificio Borderi** to bring along with you to the seaside.

2 Relax for a few hours on the local public beach, the **Spiaggia di Cala Rossa.** Enjoy a refreshing swim and, when you get hungry, a picnic lunch.

3 Afterward, grab your rental car and take the one-hour drive southwest on E45 to explore the Baroque town of Modica and sample its famous chocolate at **Caffè dell'Arte.**

4 Meet chef Katia from **LoveSicily** for a cooking lesson and dinner at her home in Modica.

5 In the evening, drive back to Ortigia and, if you're feeling up for it, stop in for a craft beer or custom cocktail at **BOATS,** in view of the Tempio di Apollo.

Previous: Scicli; courtyard at Villa Romana del Casale; Orecchio di Dionisio.

Day Three: Ragusa

Be sure to reserve your visit to the **Arianna Occhipinti** winery, and a cooking class at sister property **Baglio Occhipinti,** in advance.

1 After breakfast at your hotel, take a 1-hour 45-minute drive west on SS194 into the province of Ragusa for a morning with the island's most fascinating young female winemaker at **Azienda Agricola Arianna Occhipinti.**

2 After the wine tour at Arianna's, drive 5 minutes north on SP68 to her sister's country home at **Baglio Occhipinti.** Fausta Occhipinti will welcome your group for a private, homemade Sicilian lunch with organic products grown on the property.

3 On the way back to Syracuse, stop by the Baroque town of Noto, a 90-minute drive on SS115, for a tasting of Sicily's best desserts from chef Corrado Assenza at **Caffè Sicilia.**

4 Finish up the road trip with a 30-minute drive north on E45 back to Ortigia. Treat yourself to a fine-dining meal at the historic **Ristorante Don Camillo.**

5 On your last night, enjoy a nightcap at Sicily's best natural wine bar, **Enoteca Solaria.** Take a final peek at the city's stunning Duomo cathedral lit up at nighttime, just around the corner.

Syracuse

Syracuse was founded by the ancient Greek Corinthians in 734 BCE, and its architecture, enticing atmosphere, and incredible food and wine all ooze with history. Though today Syracuse runs at a much slower pace than the other Sicilian metropolises of Palermo and Catania, in its heyday it was the biggest city in the Greek Empire, as evidenced by the wealth of well-preserved Greek theaters, stone quarries, and ancient caves in Parco Archeologico della Neapolis. A few millennia later, the locals are friendly and welcoming, large open piazzas are filled with light, and bright limestone monuments immediately capture the hearts of visitors.

The golden, atmospheric heart of Syracuse, the island of **Ortigia,** is southeast of the main city, just over a narrow channel across the Santa Lucia. Known as the old city, or città vecchia, Ortigia has it all, from ancient ruins to luxurious palaces, treasured jewels of Renaissance art, and a vibrant shopping and dining district, all within an area of only 0.2 square mile (0.5 sq km). The romantic views along the coastline and the sunlit piazzas make it a perfect home base while visiting the southeastern corner of Sicily.

SIGHTS
Central Syracuse
★ **Parco Archeologico della Neapolis**

Via del Teatro Greco; tel. 0931/66206; www. aditusculture.com/biglietti; 9am-7pm daily; adults €10, reduced rates €5, first Sun. of the month free, joint ticket with Museo Archeologico Regionale €13.50, limited free parking available

Located in the northern part of the city center, Syracuse's Neapolis Archaeological Park is home to the most diverse collection of Greek ruins in Sicily, attesting to the city's importance to the Greek, and later the Roman, world. This 86-acre (35-ha) area boasts Greek and Roman theaters as well as various structures and sites related to everyday life for the ancients, built between the 5th century BCE and 3rd century CE. Each element on its own is worth a trip, but to take in most of the

Itinerary Ideas

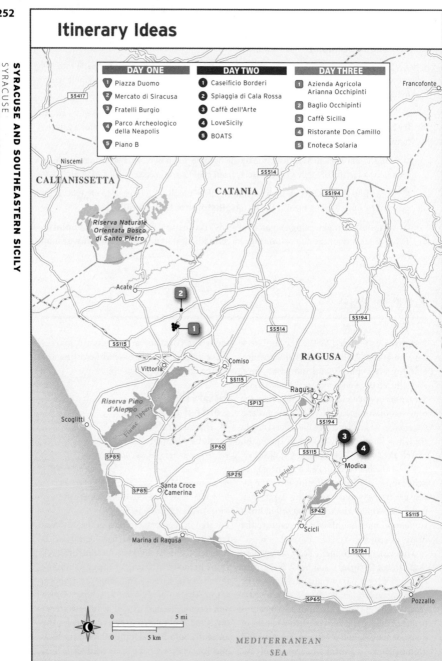

DAY ONE
1. Piazza Duomo
2. Mercato di Siracusa
3. Fratelli Burgio
4. Parco Archeologico della Neapolis
5. Piano B

DAY TWO
1. Caseificio Borderi
2. Spiaggia di Cala Rossa
3. Caffè dell'Arte
4. LoveSicily
5. BOATS

DAY THREE
1. Azienda Agricola Arianna Occhipinti
2. Baglio Occhipinti
3. Caffè Sicilia
4. Ristorante Don Camillo
5. Enoteca Solaria

Francofonte

SS417

Niscemi

CALTANISSETTA

CATANIA

SS514

SS194

Riserva Naturale
Orientata Bosco
di Santo Pietro

Acate

SS194

SS514

SS115

Comiso

RAGUSA

Vittoria

SS115

Ragusa

Riserva Pino
d'Aleppo

SP13

SS194

Scoglitti

SP60

SS115

SP85

SP25

Modica

Santa Croce
Camerina

SP85

Fiume Irminio

SP42

SS115

Scicli

Marina di Ragusa

SS194

SP65

Pozzallo

0   5 mi
0   5 km

MEDITERRANEAN
SEA

© MOON.COM

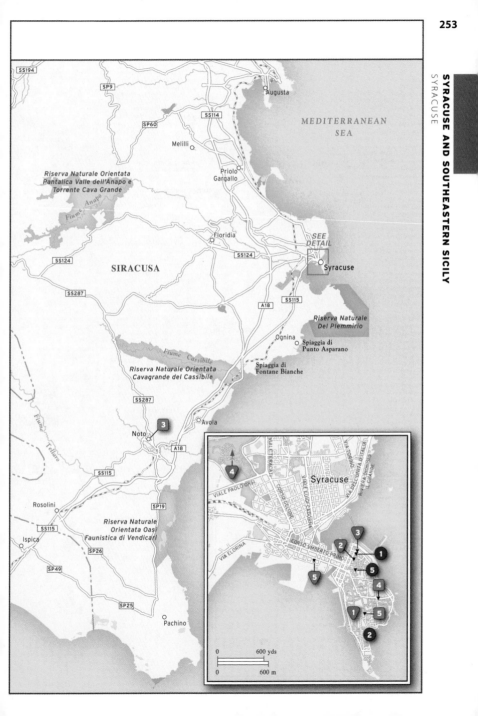

SS194

SP9

SP60

SS114

Augusta

MEDITERRANEAN
SEA

Melilli

Priolo
Gargallo

Riserva Naturale Orientata
Pantalica Valle dell'Anapo e
Torrente Cava Grande

Fiume Anapo

Floridia

SS124

SS124

SIRACUSA

SEE
DETAIL

Syracuse

SS287

A18

SS115

Riserva Naturale
Del Plemmirio

Fiume Cassibile

Ognina

Spiaggia di
Punto Asparano

Riserva Naturale Orientata
Cavagrande del Cassibile

Spiaggia di
Fontane Bianche

SS287

Avola

3

Noto

A18

Fiume Tellaro

SS115

Rosolini

SP19

SS115

Riserva Naturale
Orientata Oasi
Faunistica di Vendicari

Ispica

SP26

SP49

SP25

Pachino

VIALE PAOLO ORSI

VIALE TERACATI

CORSO GELONE

Syracuse

VIA TISIA

CORSO TIMOLEONTE

VIA ARCHIMEDE

RIVIERA DIONISIO IL GRANDE

4

CORSO UMBERTO PRIMO

VIA ELORINA

3

2

1

5

5

4

1

5

2

0   600 yds

0   600 m

Syracuse and the Island of Ortigia

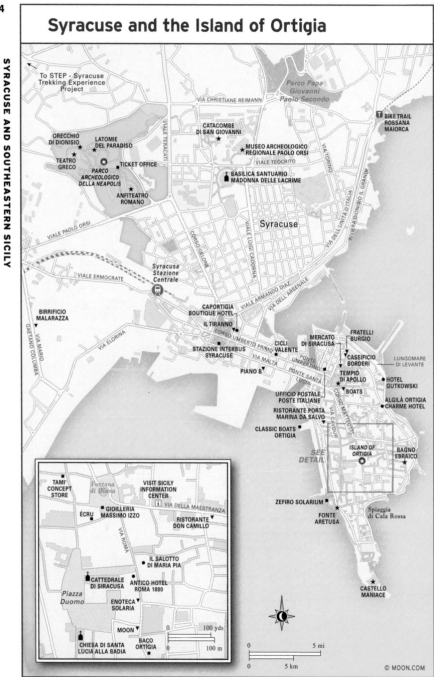

To STEP - Syracuse Trekking Experience Project

VIA CHRISTIANE REIMANN

Parco Papa Giovanni Paolo Secondo

T BIKE TRAIL ROSSANA MAIORCA

CATACOMBE DI SAN GIOVANNI

ORECCHIO DI DIONISIO
LATOMIE DEL PARADISO

MUSEO ARCHEOLOGICO REGIONALE PAOLO ORSI

VIALE TEOCRITO

TEATRO GRECO

TICKET OFFICE

PARCO ARCHEOLOGICO DELLA NEAPOLIS

BASILICA SANTUARIO MADONNA DELLE LACRIME

VIALE TERACATI

VIA TORINO

VIA DELL'UNITÀ D'ITALIA

RIVIERA DIONISIO IL GRANDE

ANFITEATRO ROMANO

Syracuse

VIALE LUIGI CADORNA

VIALE PAOLO ORSI

CORSO GELONE

VIALE ERMOCRATE

Syracusa Stazione Centrale

VIA MARIO GAETANO COLUMBA

BIRRIFICIO MALARAZZA

VIA ELORINA

CAPORTIGIA BOUTIQUE HOTEL

IL TIRANNO

VIALE ARMANDO DIAZ

VIA DELL'ARSENALE

CORSO UMBERTO PRIMO

CICLI VALENTE

MERCATO DI SIRACUSA

FRATELLI BURGIO

STAZIONE INTERBUS SYRACUSE

VIA MALTA

FONTE UMBERTINO

CASEIFICIO BORDERI

LUNGOMARE DI LEVANTE

PIANO B

PONTE SANTA LUCIA

TEMPIO DI APOLLO

HOTEL GUTKOWSKI

BOATS

UFFICIO POSTALE POSTE ITALIANE

CORSO MATTEOTTI

ALGILÀ ORTIGIA CHARME HOTEL

RISTORANTE PORTA MARINA DA SALVO

VIA CAVOUR

CLASSIC BOATS ORTIGIA

SEE DETAIL

ISLAND OF ORTIGIA

BAGNO EBRAICO

ZEFIRO SOLARIUM

FONTE ARETUSA

Spiaggia di Cala Rossa

CASTELLO MANIACE

Detail inset

TAMI' CONCEPT STORE

Fontana di Diana

VISIT SICILY INFORMATION CENTER

VIA DELLA MAESTRANZA

ÉCRU
GIOILLERIA MASSIMO IZZO

RISTORANTE DON CAMILLO

VIA ROMA

IL SALOTTO DI MARIA PIA

CATTEDRALE DI SIRACUSA

ANTICO HOTEL ROMA 1880

Piazza Duomo

ENOTECA SOLARIA

MOON

BACO ORTIGIA

0   100 yds

0   100 m

CHIESA DI SANTA LUCIA ALLA BADIA

0   5 mi

0   5 km

© MOON.COM

archaeological park, you'll need at least three hours. The **ticket office** can be found near the corner of Via Cavallari and Viale Augusto; you'll also find a café on-site.

The first site you'll see after leaving the ticket office is the 3rd-century **Anfiteatro Romano,** used for horse races and brutal gladiator competitions, and flooded for mock navy battles. Continuing north, the massive **Teatro Greco,** dating back to the 5th century BCE, presents a stark contrast to the later Roman structure. Enlarged and rebuilt by Hieron II, the Greek tyrant king of Sicily, in the 3rd century BCE, it was built to host more peaceful events, such as public meetings and early Greek plays by classic dramatists like Aeschylus, Epicharmus, and Phormis. May-July, they still offer Greek tragedy performances in the same place they could have been seen more than 2,000 years ago (tickets from €30); visit www.indafondazione.org for the schedule and more details.

Nearby, the **Orecchio di Dionisio** (Ear of Dionysius) is a 213-foot-long (65-m), 75-foot-high (23-m) grotto sliced into the cliffside, so named by the Italian painter Michelangelo Merisi da Caravaggio for its exceptional natural acoustics. Finally, you'll see the **Latomie del Paradiso** (Quarry of Paradise), where limestone was excavated to construct the metropolis you see around you today. On a grim note, the quarries were also used to hold more than 7,000 prisoners from the war between Syracuse and Athens. Today, the white stone landscape is overgrown with vegetation, fragrant Mediterranean plants, and citrus trees.

Basilica Santuario Madonna delle Lacrime

Via del Santuario, 33; tel. 0931/21446; 7am-1pm and 3pm-8pm daily; free

The massive, more than 300-foot-high (100-m) white spire of this modern sanctuary is hard to miss, one of the most striking buildings in Syracuse's skyline. About a block east of the Parco Archeologico della Neapolis, the conical stone structure is a relatively recent addition to the cityscape, built in the 1960s.

Museo Archeologico Regionale Paolo Orsi

Viale Teocrito, 66; tel. 0931/489511; www.aditusculture.com/biglietti; 9am-2pm Sun., 9am-7pm Tues.-Sat.; €8, joint ticket with Parco Archeologico della Neapolis €13.50

Browse through prehistoric, Hellenistic, and Roman artifacts in one of Europe's top archaeological museums. Inaugurated in 1988, this prestigious museum was named after Paolo Orsi, the Italian archaeologist and researcher who laid the groundwork for excavations, from the prehistoric through Byzantine eras, in southeastern Sicily. This thoroughly modern museum is a great supplement to the Parco Archeologico della Neapolis. Look for the famous Landolina Venus, a graceful (now headless) sculpture of the Greek goddess.

Catacombe di San Giovanni

Largo San Marciano, 3; tel. 0931/1561472; 9:30am-12:30pm and 2:30pm-5:30pm daily

Carved at the site of the city's ancient limestone aqueducts, this sacred burial ground with its labyrinth of underground tunnels has been used as a funeral chapel to ensure the transition of Syracuse's dead on to their eternal life for centuries. San Giovanni's Basilica and Crypt of San Marciano were built in the 6th century by the Byzantines and restored by the Normans in the 12th century. Beneath the 17th-century Basilica di San Giovanni, the church and its catacombs are only accessible on guided tours (30-40 minutes), which can be booked from the ticket office. The catacombs also feature ancient inscriptions related to the oldest nativity scene in the world as well as the first reference to Santa Lucia, the patron saint of Syracuse.

★ Island of Ortigia

Nestled in the Ionian Sea southeast of central Syracuse, the island of Ortigia is the oldest part of the city. Its sun-kissed principal square, **Piazza Duomo,** is home to Syracuse's main cathedral, the **Duomo di Siracusa.** Its main shop-lined avenue, **Corso Matteotti,** and the peripheral road that surrounds it, **Lungomare di Levante Elio Vittorini,** are lined with ancient ruins. Catch a sunrise from the waterfront, where you'll find **Fonte Aretusa** (a mythical freshwater spring), **Castello Maniace,** and the small public beach.

The island is accessible by car or on foot via the side-by-side **Ponte Santa Lucia** and **Ponte Umbertino** bridges, and you'll see a **bronze statue** as you're crossing the channel that separates the island from the rest of the city. Syracuse is the hometown of the Greek mathematician and physicist Archimedes, to whom the statue is dedicated.

Tempio di Apollo

Largo XXV Luglio; tel. 0931/1756232; open 24 hours; free

The inscriptions on the 6th-century BCE ruins of this Doric temple dedicate it to Apollo, the Greek god of archery, music, and dance, although there are records stating it was actually dedicated to his twin sister Artemis. It's possible to see the layers of Syracuse's history here: starting with ancient Greece, the temple was later transformed into a Byzantine church, then into an Arab mosque, and finally back into a church by the Normans.

Fontana di Diana

Piazza Archimede; open 24 hours; free

Built in 1907, this sculpture by Giulio Moschetti and his sculptor son Mario was commissioned by the city of Syracuse and dedicated to Diana, the Roman and Greek goddess of hunting. It features her with her dog, the river god Alpheus, four Tritons riding sea horses, and sea serpents in the waves.

Cattedrale di Siracusa

Piazza Duomo, 5; tel. 0931/65328; 9am-5:30pm daily; €2

With a history spanning over 2,500 years, the Cathedral of Syracuse (also called the Chiesa Cattedrale della Natività di Maria Santissima, or just *il Duomo*), is the main landmark in the oldest part of this magnificent city, as well as Syracuse's main cathedral. Built on the location of the ancient Greek temple of Athena, dating back to the 5th century BCE, it was transformed into a basilica by the Byzantines, into a mosque by North African Muslims, and changed back into a basilica by the French Normans. The earthquake of 1693 damaged the basilica and its facade; the stunning one you see today, featuring the Virgin Mary, Saint Peter, and Saint Paul, was rebuilt in the Baroque style. Uniquely, the original Doric columns of the Greek temple were preserved into the design of the cathedral's interior, where the massive, weathered structures evoke a sense of hushed awe.

Chiesa di Santa Lucia alla Badia

Via Pompeo Picherali, 4; tel. 0931/65328; 11am-4pm Tues.-Sun.; free

The main attraction of the Chiesa di Santa Lucia is *The Burial of Saint Lucy,* an oil painting by Italian Renaissance master Caravaggio. Depicting mourners and gravediggers surrounding the city's patroness just after she was killed for refusing to marry a Roman soldier, it was commissioned for the church in 1608 and is rumored to have been miraculously completed in only a month. The domed limestone church itself dates back to the middle of the 15th century and also contains two wooden crucifixes from the 14th century, Baroque doorways, frescoes, and 18th-century painted tiles. Note that the painting is often moved out of the church to be used in special exhibitions.

1: Cattedrale di Siracusa 2: Fontana di Diana in Ortigia 3: Latomie del Paradiso in Parco Archeologico della Neapolis

Try the online chat service at Secret Siracusa (www.secretsiracusa.it) to help find out where this magnificent painting is currently located.

Fonte Aretusa

Largo Aretusa; open 24 hours; free

The Fonte Aretusa is important to a Greek myth in which Arethusa, a nymph, inadvertently bathed in a stream, not knowing it was the river god Alpheus. Discovering this, she fled, Alpheus pursuing her until the goddess Artemis transformed Arethusa into this fountain to save her from the river god. Today, this beautiful natural fountain on the southwestern coast of Ortigia is one of the very few places in Europe where papyrus grows in abundance.

Bagno Ebraico/Mikveh

Via G.B. Alagona, 52; tel. 0931/21467; 10am-10pm daily; €5

This ancient mikveh, or traditional Jewish bath, was only discovered in 1989, when renovating the palace above it. It could be the oldest Jewish ritual bath in Europe, dating back to the 7th century. The three pools, located 59 feet (18 m) underground, contained pure spring water used by the Jewish community for religious purification rituals. The Jewish population here was once the most important, oldest, and richest in all of Sicily. Although the city of Syracuse no longer has a synagogue, there is still a Jewish Quarter, or Giudecca, located in southeastern Ortigia, between Via della Meastranza and Via Larga.

Castello Maniace

Via Castello Maniace, 51; tel. 0931/4508211; www. comune.siracusa.it; 11am-6:45pm daily; €4

The dramatic location of Ortigia's golden limestone, 13th-century castle made it a great place to defend the island and the city of Syracuse as a whole, and today it's the perfect place to stroll the substantial ramparts, with views of the sea. Inside is a small municipal

1: Castello Maniace 2: papyrus growing in Fonte Aretusa

museum that educates visitors on the castle's Norman-era history.

SPORTS AND RECREATION

Though you can find some lovely walks and beaches in the city of Syracuse itself, the surrounding area is filled with panoramic views and some of the region's most beautiful unspoiled nature, including the **Cavagrande** and **Vendicari Nature Reserves,** a one-hour drive southwest and 40-minute drive south, respectively, of Syracuse.

Tours

Agave Travel Creative

www.agavetravelcreative.com; info@ agavetravelcreative.com

Agave Travel Creative pairs you with an English-speaking guide for an incredible itinerary deeply rooted in cuisine and culture. Founder Marcello Baglioni curates unforgettable experiences in southeastern Sicily, from private guided visits to archaeological sites to almond orchards, olive groves, and forgotten villages. You may have an art historian, archaeologist, or cultural guide at your side to help you discover hidden gems, whether you are looking for a sunset sail around the island of Ortigia, an in-depth pizza-making lesson, or a private wine or olive oil tasting. Multiday itineraries can be completely customized to your special requests to unlock all of Sicily's secrets.

Classic Boats Ortigia

Molo Zanagora; tel. 320/3089694; www. classicboatsortigia.com; from €500

Captain Salvatore Signorelli offers private 4-5-hour sailing trips in the waters of Siracusa for up to five guests, departing from the Marina Yachting Club in Ortigia at 11am and 5pm. The *Fiesta* is a classic 30-foot (9-m) Tahiti Ketch wooden monohull sailboat that was built in 1922. On this unique experience, guests relax on the gorgeous and romantic boat as they sail around Siracusa while enjoying a couple of stops for swimming and a light aperitif. Reservations should be made well in advance, especially in summertime. During the warmer months, Classic Boats offers only the sunset evening program because of heat and wind conditions.

STEP - Syracuse Trekking Experience Project

Traversa Sinerchia, 20; tel. 335/8086973; www.step-syracusetrekking.it; 2 or more guests can join a group tour for €65 per person

STEP highlights the natural aspects of southeastern Sicily with outdoor adventure programs, including a seven-hour hiking trip to see the waterfalls in the Cavagrande Nature Reserve (including lunch and a break for swimming), or a four-hour visit to the bird sanctuary and old tuna factory at the Vendicari Nature Reserve.

Hiking and Cycling
Cicli Valente

Corso Umberto, 38; tel. 0931/60618

Mountain, e-bikes, and city bicycles can be rented from Cicli Valente, near the Ponte Umbertino bridge. Rentals come equipped with a lock and repair kit for €10 per day; helmets can be rented for an additional €3 per day. Discounted rates are available if renting the bicycles for longer than one week.

Bike Trail Rossana Maiorca

Cycling Distance: *9 miles (14.5 km) round-trip*
Cycling Time: *About 2 hours round-trip including stops*
Trailhead: *Monumento ai Caduti war memorial, Piazza Cappuccini, 5*
Information and Maps: *Pacer mobile app and www.mypacer.com/routes*

Cyclists and runners will love this off-the-beaten-path coastal excursion, named for the daughter of Sicilian champion free diver Enzo Maiorca. The Rossana Maiorca bike path was built on the abandoned railway stretch that once connected the industrial area of Targia with the city. Although the bike path is fairly short, fascinating views along the way are worth a stop or two. The trail begins at the

Monumento ai Caduti war memorial, about 1 mile (1.6 km) northeast of Ponte Santa Lucia, and leads past Greek quarries, World War II bunkers, fascinating rock formations, the ruins of the rail station, and a tonnara tuna factory. Bring a swimsuit: Off the main path, side roads lead down steep rocky paths to secret coastal swimming spots. The gravel paths are suitable for runners and any type of bicycle.

Beaches

Syracuse and the surrounding region boast many sandy beaches, in contrast to the rocky ones often found in the rest of Sicily. In Syracuse proper, most of the beaches are located around the island of Ortigia.

Spiaggia di Cala Rossa

Lungomare d'Ortigia; open 24 hours; free

A highlight of Ortigia's clean and clear coastline is the public beach located on the eastern side of the island, convenient for a quick dip on warm days, which occur throughout most of the year. The sandy beach is speckled with small stones, shells, sea glass, and pieces of colorful ceramic tiles, so water shoes are absolutely mandatory for small children. It can be reached by a short staircase leading down from Ortigia's main peripheral road, Lungomare di Levante Elio Vittorini.

Zefiro Solarium

Largo Aretusa, 2/10; www.zefirosolarium.com; tel. 345/6072755; from €40-50 for 2 sunbeds and umbrella

For those who want a little more comfort during their time on the seaside, the Zefiro beach club, on the western side of Ortigia, offers private access to the crystal blue sea below. The cool, fresh waters of the nearby spring mix with the seawater in this area to provide a refreshing and unique swim between the cool and warm currents. This lido deck is one of the only remaining private beach clubs left on the island where you can lie on a beach bed

---

1: Bike Trail Rossana Maiorca 2: Zefiro Solarium
3: Lungomare di Levante

Beaches Beyond Ortigia

beach in Arenella

Although Ortigia has its own wonderful beaches just a few meters from its bustling streets and fascinating monuments, sometimes you want a more peaceful and secluded place to take a dip. From the Plemmirio Nature Reserve down to the coastal hamlet villages of Arenella, Ognina, and Fontane Bianche, the coast here offers a range of places to swim, sun, and relax, all within half an hour from the heart of Syracuse.

RISERVA NATURALE DEL PLEMMIRIO
Via del Corindone, 31; tel. 0931/449310; www.plemmirio.eu; open 24 hours

underneath an umbrella and be served drinks or food. Enjoy the perks of the bar and restaurant services before the sun sets and it turns into more of a club atmosphere. Zefiro also has freshwater showers, bathrooms, and some shaded lounge areas. Reservations are recommended, especially in August.

Cooking Classes
Casa Mia Tours
tel. 346/8001746; www.casamiatours.com; by reservation only; group lessons €150 per person, private lessons €189 per person
To delve deep into the local culture, there's nothing quite like cooking in someone's home. This Sicilian cooking adventure starts in Ortigia's historic outdoor food market. With your host, you'll pick up ingredients for the lesson and create the menu while browsing. Guests are then welcomed into the elegant warmth of their host's home overlooking the Ortigia harbor. The experience includes a coffee or welcome aperitivo, a hands-on cooking lesson, and lunch paired with local bread, olive oil, and Sicilian wine. Contact Casa Mia for information and availability. Five-hour cooking lessons and lunch experiences in Ortigia can be organized for 2-6 people and should be booked at least one month in advance, especially in May-September.

A 20-minute, 9-mile (14.5-km) drive south of Syracuse on SS115 and SP58, the protected Plemmirio Nature Reserve was the dreamy location of country villas for Syracuse's wealthy in the 19th and 20th centuries. In addition to 4 miles (6.4 km) of stone quarry-lined coastline, Plemmirio is known for its excellent diving: You might spot shrimp, octopuses, parrot fish, amberjack, red scorpion fish, and even dolphins. Visit the **Capo Murro Diving Center** (Porticciolo di Ognina, Via Capo Ognina; tel. 331/324030; www.capomurrodivingcenter.it; 8:30am-8:30pm daily; from €40) for guided diving excursions.

LIDO ARENELLA - VILLA BABEJ

Traversa Renella, Arenella; tel. 0931/715025
At Arenella, a 20-minute drive from Syracuse (7 mi/11.3 km on the SS1115), umbrellas and sun beds (€12) can be rented from the lido (9am-7pm daily), and there are also free sandy and rocky beaches a few meters south of the beach club. This wide, fine-grained sand beach is also equipped with slides for guests with mobility restrictions as well as stationed lifeguards.

SPIAGGIA DI PUNTO ASPARANO

Traversa Capo Ognina, Ognina; tel. 0931/464657; www.syracuseturismo.net; open 24 hours; free
A bit farther south (25 minutes, 9 mi/14.5 km on the SS115), try this rocky beach with crystal-clear water for a more tranquil beach day.

SPIAGGIA DI FONTANE BIANCHE

Viale dei Lidi; open 24 hours; free
Farthest south (30 minutes, 10.5 mi/17 km on the SS115), this is the best-equipped beach on Syracuse's coastline. Sun beds and umbrellas can be rented (€20-40), and beachgoers also have access to restaurants, bars, bathrooms, and boat rentals. The white sand and calm, clean, warm, turquoise water are great for families.

FESTIVALS AND EVENTS

Ortigia Sound System Music Festival

Via Castello Maniace, 51; www.ortigiasoundsystem.com; late July; full-night pass €75
At the end of July, Ortigia transforms itself into a huge dance party; this international electronic music festival combines contemporary performances with Mediterranean tradition. Ticketed boat parties (€33), late-night DJ sets (starting at €10 per person), and large concerts are organized in various locations around the island, with the main stage at the **Castello Maniace.**

Festival of Santa Lucia (Festa di Santa Lucia)

Piazza Duomo, 5; www.siciliainfesta.com; Dec. 13-20; free
This celebration for Syracuse's patroness, Santa Lucia, takes place annually in December. Santa Lucia is a symbol of light, rebirth, and devotion to the people of Syracuse. The holy martyr was tortured and killed because she refused to marry a Roman soldier in the year 304. Her legend began on December 12 in the 17th century, when the island was suffering from famine and a ship filled with wheat mysteriously arrived at the port in the middle of the night. Desperate citizens

boarded the ship and took the grains home to be cooked immediately, without even grinding them first. The Syracusans credited Santa Lucia for saving them from starvation, since the boat arrived on her birthday. The symbolic sweet wheatberry dish cuccia is still eaten to this day in her honor.

The main celebration occurs on December 13, when the 16th-century silver statue of Santa Lucia is paraded through the streets upon the shoulders of men wearing green berets. Keep in mind when traveling to Syracuse in December that the city will be buzzing with festivities, and all reservations should be made well in advance. Apart from the main celebrations on December 13, the festival week includes additional events such as special church services and concerts.

SHOPPING
Island of Ortigia
Gioilleria Massimo Izzo
Piazza Archimede, 25; tel. 0931/22301; www.massimoizzo.com; 4pm-8pm Mon., 9am-1pm and 4pm-8pm Tues.-Sat.

Take a peek into the magical underwater world of Massimo Izzo's flagship jewelry boutique. His creative designs, inspired by Greek myths and marine creatures as well as Sicily's Baroque heritage, have been featured in publications such as *Vogue* and *Marie Claire*. Each piece of Massimo's original jewelry is made right here in Syracuse.

Écru
Via Consiglio Reginale, 30; www.instagram.com/ecru_ortigia; tel. 351/5239941; 10:30am-2pm and 4:30pm-8pm daily

Écru has stunning, unique vintage clothing for women along with costume jewelry and a limited selection of shoes. The selection of designer-brand articles and custom, one-of-a-kind, tailor-made pieces is unmatched. This is truly a place where you can find something special to wear on your trip or to take back home with you.

Baco Ortigia
Via Roma, 101/103; tel. 366/1766111; www.baco-ortigia.it; 10am-5pm Mon.-Tues. and Thurs.-Sat.

Milanese transplants from the Scuola Orafa Ambrosiana goldsmithing school, Simona and Marco offer a selection of creative jewelry made with silver, bronze, and precious natural stones in their shop in the heart of Ortigia. Their rings, bracelets, necklaces, and earrings are created in-house with inspiration taken from the island and the Ionian Sea. Inside their workshop and storefront, guests can peruse the items available and see how they are made.

TAMI' Concept Store
Via Cavour, 13; tel. 0931/465926; www.tamishop.com; 4pm-8:30pm Mon., 10am-1:30pm and 4pm-8:30pm Tues.-Sat., 11am-1:30pm and 4pm-8:30pm Sun.

This concept store is a great spot to find a gift before leaving Ortigia. It's filled with cookbooks, clothing, tote bags, kitchen gadgets, stylish office accessories, and a line of children's products. TAMI' also carries a selection of natural wine and beer.

FOOD
Central Syracuse
★ Piano B
Via Cairoli, 18; tel. 0931/66851; www.pianobsyracuse.com; 7pm-midnight Tues.-Sun.; pizzas €10-18

Eat at Piano B for artisanal pizzas made with top-level seasonal ingredients at affordable prices, located just three blocks north of the island of Ortigia. Friedrich Schmuck's pizzas are inspired by the flavors and techniques of his childhood split between Rome, the Dolomites, and Ortigia. Since opening in 2011, he has expanded the menu, now offering options like naturally leavened and gluten-free dough. Piano B was recognized by *Gambero Rosso* as among the top pizzerias of Italy and the Pizza of the Year in 2020. *Cronache di Gusto* named Piano B the Best Pizzeria in Sicily in 2018.

Il Tiranno

Caportigia Boutique Hotel, Viale Montedoro, 78; www.
iltiranno.it; 7:30pm-11pm daily, Sun. lunch Oct.-May;
mains €18-32

The fine-dining restaurant located inside the Caportigia Boutique Hotel offers à la carte options and innovative tasting menus from young chef Valentina Galli. His philosophy is based on technique, creativity, and the selection of the best ingredients.

Island of Ortigia

Mercato di Siracusa

Via Trento, 21; 8am-1pm Mon.-Sat.

The best way to introduce yourself to a new city is a quick trip through the local outdoor food market. Learn how the Syracuseni eat! The outdoor market in Ortigia is lively and approachable, with fresh, local seafood not found elsewhere, like spatola, costardelle, and sea urchin. Friendly vendors smile and sing as they announce their wares and welcome tourists to their shops. Small stands sell Sicilian spices, herbs, nuts, and dried fruit, and the local tomatoes are among the best on the island; take home as many sun-dried ones as you can carry, along with a packet of wild fennel seeds and some salt-cured capers. At the end of the market, specialty food shops showcase local cheeses, like primo sale, pecorino, ragusano, ricotta, and mozzarella.

Caseificio Borderi

Via Emmanuele de Benedictis, 6; tel. 329/9852500;
www.facebook.com/CaseificioBorderi; 7am-3:30pm
Mon.-Sat.; sandwiches €10

You know those big sandwiches that everyone has been talking about? This is where you get them. While walking through Ortigia's outdoor market, look for the people waiting in line, jump in, and enjoy an abundance of small samples while watching Signor Andrea Borderi work his magic. He creates jam-packed, customizable deli sandwiches filled with sliced mozzarella, arugula, potatoes and crushed garlic, olives, lemon zest, sun-dried tomatoes, chili peppers, and everything else you can dream of. Plan on sharing—the sandwiches are truly huge—and save room for the fresh mozzarella di bufala and Sicilian primo sale cheese with pistachios. This friendly family has been serving the best sandwiches in town since 1930.

Fratelli Burgio

Piazza Cesare Battisti, 4; tel. 0931/60069; www.
fratelliburgio.com; 7:30am-3pm daily; mains €7-12

This third-generation Italian deli is situated at the end of the Ortigia outdoor food market. Stop by for a casual lunch or pick up some goodies from the exceptional selection of hard-to-find Sicilian meats and cheeses in the salumeria. Fratelli Burgio prepares its own line of specialty food products in small glass jars that are easy to travel with. Treat yourself to a few of the top sellers, like caponata, sweet and sour onions, pickled chili peppers, wild fennel pâté, and peperonella spicy chile paste.

MOON

Via Roma, 112; tel. 334/2571002; www.moonortigia.
com; 7pm-11:30pm Wed.-Mon.; €8-15

"Move Ortigia Out of Normality" is a vegan restaurant and bar in the heart of Ortigia. Its fresh and seasonal menu is alluring even for non-vegans. The apple caponata and smoked eggplant ravioli offer their own twists on Sicilian classics while still sticking to high-quality, farm-to-table values. MOON often hosts live DJ sets and parties throughout the summer.

Ristorante Porta Marina da Salvo

Via dei Candelai, 35; tel. 0931/22553; www.
ristoranteportamarina.it; noon-2:30pm and 7:30pm-
10:30pm Tues.-Sun.; €15-22

Cozy up in this simple but chic restaurant for some of Ortigia's best seafood dishes. The vaulted stone ceilings dating back to the 1400s, elegantly plated dishes, and professional front-of-house service give the place a luxurious feel while keeping prices affordable. Chef Salvo Di Mauro and his son Giancarlo tell their family stories through their dishes. Enjoy lunch or dinner in this inviting dining

space, right in the heart of Ortigia's historic center.

Ristorante Don Camillo

Via delle Maestranze, 96; tel. 0931/67133; www.ristorantedoncamillo.it; 12:30pm-2:30pm and 8pm-10pm daily; tasting menu €60

Founded in 1985 by Camillo and Giovanni Guarneri, Don Camilo has continued to be the mecca of old-school dining in Ortigia. The dining room was constructed from the remains of a religious building that collapsed during the earthquake of 1693. This is a great spot for a classic Sicilian meal with outstanding formal and friendly service.

BARS AND NIGHTLIFE
Central Syracuse
Birrificio Malarazza

Via Gaetano Mario Columba, 49; tel. 340/6545668; www.birramalarazza.it; 8pm-midnight Fri.-Sat.

This spot has been serving artisanal beer made with Sicilian ingredients since 2014. Pull up a barstool in the tap room to taste craft beers like its blonde ale, session IPA, saison, amber ale, or rye. Pair your beers with one of the classic house-made sandwiches for a low-key night out in Syracuse.

Island of Ortigia
★ Enoteca Solaria

Via Roma, 86; tel. 0931/463007; www.enotecasolaria.com; 11am-2:30pm and 6pm-midnight Tues.-Sat.

Elisa Merlo and her husband Gianfilippo Russo run the top natural wine bar in Sicily, open since 1987. Enjoy hard-to-find natural Sicilian wines by the glass or the bottle from Vini Scirto, SRC, Cantina Giardino, Eduardo Torres Acosta, Etnella, and Frank Cornelissen. The curated wine list also includes international wines and top-level, classic Italian bottles like Barolo, Brunello di Montalcino, and Sassicaia. Bruschetta topped with caponata, wild fennel pâté, or cured anchovies and

1: fresh artichokes from Mercato di Siracusa 2: cheese from Caseificio Borderi 3: vegan ravioli at MOON

charcuterie boards with Sicilian salami and cheese pair perfectly with a bottle—or two or three. You'll never want to leave this place.

BOATS

Via dell'Apollonion, 5; tel. 339/1110294; www.facebook.com/boatsortigia; 7pm-1am Sun., 6pm-1am Tues.-Thurs., 6pm-2am Fri.-Sat.

"Based On A True Story" is one of a very few truly amazing cocktail bars in Sicily. The cozy speakeasy-style bar welcomes locals and tourists for live music, specialty drinks, and a friendly inclusive atmosphere, just across from the Tempio di Apollo. Owners Giulio Messina and Simone Di Stefano work closely with bar consultant Mattia Cilia to offer the best mixed drinks in town, along with artisanal beers, natural wines, and a menu of small bites. Signature drinks change with the seasons, from the Sterling Silver Irish coffee in winter to the Medusa's Skin, a riff on a classic Manhattan. Incredible nonalcoholic options are offered year-round.

ACCOMMODATIONS
Central Syracuse
Caportigia Boutique Hotel

Viale Montedoro, 76; tel. 0931/580576; www.hotelcaportigia.com; rooms and suites from €89

This luxurious five-star hotel is conveniently located just across the bridge from the island of Ortigia. Business travelers, tourists, and families will find everything they need, including high-speed Wi-Fi and rooms accessible for people with disabilities. The comfortable rooms are tastefully decorated with Italian ceramics, artisanal wooden furniture, and contemporary textiles. The hotel concierge can organize breakfasts, aperitivo and dinners, wine-tasting events, bicycle rentals, and information for touring the city.

Island of Ortigia
Il Salotto di Maria Pia

Via Roma, 45; tel. 339/4354520; www.ilsalottodimariapia.it; €105

This cozy home away from home is located in an early-20th-century palace. There's friendly service, quirky vintage decor, and a morning breakfast served in a beautiful basket filled with pastries and fresh fruit at your doorstep. The Maria Pia and Paola suites have double beds and views of the cathedral, while the Suite bedroom is equipped with a double bed and its own private terrace.

Antico Hotel Roma 1880

Via Roma, 66; tel. 0931/465630; www.algila.it; €138
The Antica Hotel Roma was founded in 1880, right between the cathedral and the Archbishop's Palace in the heart of Ortigia. Just steps away from the Piazza Duomo, this perfectly central hotel is a great find. The stairwell of the hotel showcases the remains of part of the Doric Temple of Minerva, and simply furnished hotel rooms are available for 1-4 guests, all with their own balconies. The Garden Suite and Spa has a built-in sauna and overlooks the hotel's internal courtyard garden.

Algilà Ortigia Charme Hotel

Via Vittorio Veneto, 93; tel. 0931/465186; www.algila. it; €188
Algilà Ortigia Charme Hotel was built on the street where all the 14th-century nobles of Syracuse once lived. Set in a historic building restored by architect Manuel Giliberti, it's designed with traditional Sicilian decor, antique furniture, and bright ceramics. Rooms and family suites are available for 2-7 guests. Classic, Superior, and Deluxe rooms and suites offer guests a city or sea view. The Deluxe Spa option includes access to a private sun terrace equipped with a hydro-massage hot tub overlooking the sea.

★ Hotel Gutkowski

Lungomare di Levante Elio Vittorini, 18; tel. 0931/465830; www.guthotel.it; from €220
The bright and airy rooms of this boutique hotel are a perfect home base for a short holiday in Ortigia. The Hotel Gutkowski consists of two fully renovated, 19th-century, pastel periwinkle palazzi. The

cozy, eclectic hotel rooms and two-person apartments can include upgrades with terraces and sea-facing views overlooking the coastal promenade on the east side of the island. The modern **Bistro Gutkowskino** is open 7pm-midnight Monday-Saturday and moves up to the rooftop for outdoor dining in summertime.

INFORMATION AND SERVICES

Syracuse is a very well-serviced city, with an easy-to-find array of pharmacies, post offices, healthcare services, and tourist information centers. In addition to the main Visit Sicily information center, **Visit Ortigia** (www. visitortigia.it) and **Secret Siracusa** (www. secretsiracusa.it) offer information on sightseeing, restaurant and hotel recommendations, and transportation.

- **Visit Sicily Information Center:** Via Maestranza, 33; tel. 0931/464255; www. visitsicily.info; 8:30am-1:30pm Mon.-Tues. and Thurs.-Fri., 8:30am-1:30pm and 2:45pm-5:45pm Wed.

- **Post Office:** Ufficio Postale Poste Italiane, Via Trieste, 3, Ortigia; tel. 0931/796051; www.poste.it; 9am-1pm and 3:30pm-6:30pm Mon.-Fri.

- **Pharmacy:** Farmacia Lo Bello, Viale Regina Margherita, 16; tel. 0931/65001; www.farmacialobello.com; 8:30am-1pm and 4pm-8pm Mon.-Fri., 9am-1pm Sat.

- **Hospital:** Ospedale Umberto I, Via Giuseppe Testaferrata, 1, Syracuse; tel. 800/013009; www.asp.sr.it; open 24 hours

- **Police Station:** Commissariato di Syracuse Ortigia, Via Vittorio Veneto, 154; tel. 0931/481411; www.poliziadistato.it; open 24 hours

GETTING THERE

The best way to get here is to fly into the Catania Fontanarossa Airport and then travel south by train, bus, or rental car.

By Air
Catania Fontanarossa Airport
(Aeroporto di Catania Fontanarossa)

Via Fontanarossa, Catania; tel. 095/7239111; www. aeroporto.catania.it

The airport in Catania is located 45 minutes north of Syracuse. This single-terminal airport is wheelchair accessible, with a coffee bar, one full-service restaurant, and a self-service cafeteria located in the terminal, as well as a tabacchi, newsstand, duty-free shop, and small kiosks selling souvenirs. Long-term, short-stay, and handicap parking spaces are available on-site.

Catania Fontanarossa Airport is one of the main airports in Sicily, with flights arriving and departing from over 70 destinations including **Roma Fiumicino** (1 hour 15 minutes; €65), **Naples** (www.volotea.com; 1 hour; €60), **Bari** (1 hour; €20) and many other European destinations outside Italy.

Syracuse can be reached by car from the Catania airport by following the A19 highway south to E45 and SS114, a 41-mile (66-km) trip. **Rental cars** can be picked up at the Catania airport from Hertz (tel. 095/341595; www.hertz.com), Enterprise (tel. 095/346893; www.enterpriserentacar.it), and other small rental providers. **Taxis** (tel. 328/8434403) will cost around €80 each way. For airport transports and other private driving services, contact **Sunny Sicily** (www.sunnysicily.com); luxury transfers to Syracuse cost around €125. **Interbus** also provides transportation from the Catania airport to the city of Syracuse (www.interbus.it; 1 hour 15 minutes; €6.50).

By Train
Siracusa Stazione Centrale

Piazzale della Stazione Centrale, 21; tel. 0931/69650; www.rfi.it/it/stazioni/Syracuse.html

The main transit station in Syracuse is located off Via Francesco Crispi, 0.9 mile (1.5 km) north of the bridge connecting Syracuse and Ortigia, a straight ride or walk along Via Corso Umberto I. Convenient train services from **Catania Centrale** (1 hour 20 minutes; €8.40), **Modica** (1 hour 45 minutes; €9.20),

and **Ragusa** (2 hours; €10) are provided by **Trenitalia** (www.trenitalia.com); to reach Syracuse from Palermo, you'll first need to travel to Catania (4 hours 40 minutes; from €19) and then board a train to Syracuse from there. Tickets can be purchased online or in the station, and must be time-stamped at the station before boarding. Bathrooms are available on the trains and in the main stations.

By Bus
Stazione Interbus Syracuse

Piazzale del Stazione, 11; tel. 0931/66710; www.interbus. it

Interbus provides frequent service from **Catania airport** (1 hour 15 minutes; €6.50), **Catania bus station** (1 hour 25 minutes; €6.50), **Noto** (1 hour; €4), **Palermo Centrale** (3 hours 15 minutes; €14), and **Taormina** (1 hour 15 minutes; €6.50). The main stops in Syracuse include Corso Umberto, 196 (near the Syracuse train station), Via Paolo Orsi (near the Neapolis Archaeological Park), or the main Interbus station.

By Car

From **Catania Fontanarossa Airport** (50 minutes; 40 mi/64 km), take the A19 highway, following E45 and SS114 toward Floridia/SS124. From **Catania** (45 minutes; 40 mi/64 km), take the A18 highway, following RA15 Tangenziale di Catania and continue on to the NSA339 Catania-Syracuse highway. Continue along the SS114 Orientale Sicula toward Syracuse. From **Palermo** (3 hours; 164 mi/265 km), the main A19 highway from Palermo-Catania cuts diagonally through the island. When you reach the RA15 Tangenziale di Catania, continue along NSA339 from Catania-Syracuse until you reach the SS114 state road to Syracuse. There is often construction on the highway, so give yourself extra time if crossing the island by car.

Once you have arrived in Syracuse, **Parking Talete** (Lungomare di Levante Elio Vittorini; open 24 hours) is a convenient open-air parking garage in Ortigia. A camera at the parking gate automatically registers your license plate as you enter the garage. Before departing, enter your license plate number into the self-serve kiosk machine and pay per hour or approximately €10 per day, depending on your stay. In the off-season, parking here is often free.

Otherwise, keep an eye out for clearly marked blue parking spots, which can be paid for by the hour at nearby kiosks (€1.50 per hour). White parking spaces are free, but make sure to check all nearby signs closely before leaving your car. Do not park in a yellow marked spot since these are generally restricted to residents only.

GETTING AROUND

The best way to enjoy Syracuse, especially Ortigia, is **on foot.** The farthest you may find yourself walking from Ortigia, where most of the restaurants and accommodations are concentrated, is about 30 minutes to the Parco Archeologico della Neapolis.

Taxis can be hailed at Piazza Pancali in front of the Tempio di Apollo or arranged by your hotel. There is a fleet of minibuses operated by **Sd'A Trasporti** (www.siracusadamare.it; single ride ticket €1), but most tourists don't find much need for it. Driving around the city is not recommended; the old city has very narrow streets, and the parking situation is difficult.

Sunny Sicily (tel. 338/5296915; www.sunnysicily.com) is an English-speaking private driver service based in Syracuse, with luxury Mercedes-Benz E, S, and V-class vehicles. The founder, Paolo Gallo, and his team of expert local drivers provide much more than just chauffeur services; their passion and knowledge of the island is unparalleled. Airport transfers, half-day and full-day transports perfect for wine tasting, or multiday sightseeing itineraries all around Sicily can be easily arranged through its website.

Around Syracuse

Outside its namesake historic city, the province of Syracuse offers so much more. Heading south, you'll discover beautiful countryside villages, wild nature reserves, and exceptional sandy beaches. A tour through southeastern Sicily is not complete without a visit to the late Sicilian Baroque town of Noto to enjoy almond pastries and the series of noble palaces and monumental treasures, but save time to enjoy a meal in the small fishing hamlet of Marzamemi. Travelers interested in outdoor adventures can opt to spend full-day excursions hiking, swimming, and bird-watching in the Vendicari or Cavagrande Nature Reserves. Following the coastline, these untouched natural escapes offer a chance to breathe in fresh Sicilian mountain air.

RISERVA NATURALE ORIENTATA CAVAGRANDE DEL CASSIBILE

Take a break from eating and drinking your way through Sicily with a half-day adventure to the majestic Cavagrande Nature Reserve (Contrada Monzello di Pietre SN, Avola; tel. 393/1818900; www.cavagrandedelcassibile.com; recommended to visit before 5:30pm; free), about an hour south of Syracuse. Formed by the Cassibile River, this secluded valley, with 6,700 acres (2,700 ha) of protected land, is filled with rushing streams, wild flora and fauna, and hiking paths around the Laghetti di Avola lakes. Visit the reserve for a hike, picnic break, or swim.

1: natural pool in Cavagrande Nature Reserve
2: tuna factory remnants at Vendicari Nature Reserve

Hiking
Scala Cruci Hike

Distance: *2.5 miles (4 km) round-trip*

Time: *1 hour*

Trailhead: *In front of the Cava Grande Ra Za Gina pizzeria, near the Laghetti di Cavagrande parking lot*

This challenging hike includes switchbacks with a 948-foot (289-m) altitude gain. After following along the Cassibile River, the trail leads to the largest of Cavagrande's lakes, Laghetti Principali, to finish up at the Cavagrande waterfalls. Bring water shoes and a swimsuit along for swimming, and wear appropriate hiking shoes and long pants, if possible, to protect yourself from any brush along the trail.

Getting There and Around

From **Syracuse** (45 minutes; 25 mi/40 km), take Viale Ermocrate onto SS124. Follow signs for Noto to SS287. Turn left toward Avola onto SP4 and follow this road to the nature reserve. From **Noto** (35 minutes; 12 mi/19.3 km), take SS115 to the Circonvallazione di Avola and follow the signs for Avola. Drive along SP4 for about 15 minutes to arrive at the nature reserve. A seven-hour full-day hiking excursion or a four-hour swimming trip to the Cavagrande Nature Reserve can be organized through **STEP - Syracuse Trekking** (tel. 335/8086973; www.step-syracusetrekking.it).

RISERVA NATURALE ORIENTATA OASI FAUNISTICA DI VENDICARI

The stunning Vendicari Nature Reserve (Contrada Vendicari, Noto; tel. 0931/468879; www.riserva-vendicari.it; 8am-7pm daily; free) stretches for 5 miles (8 km) over 1,420 acres (575 ha) of untouched beaches, wetlands, and the remains of salt pans and the Tonnara Bafuto factory, where tuna and mackerel were caught after mating, before they could return to the open sea. Enjoy the diverse flora and fauna of this beautiful natural area, from saltwater succulents, prickly juniper, and wild orchids to ducks, geese, swans, turtles, foxes, hedgehogs, and porcupines.

Hiking
Orange Route

Distance: *2.7 miles (4.4 km) one-way*

Time: *45 minutes one-way*

Trailhead: *Main entrance of Vendicari*

This moderately difficult hike passes by Vendicari Beach, the tonnara tuna factory, and several bird-watching observation cabanas, to finish at Calamosche Beach. Toward the end of the hike there is a series of steps to climb down that might be difficult for people with mobility issues.

Green Route

Distance: *3 miles (4.8 km) one-way*

Time: *45 minutes-1 hour one-way*

Trailhead: *Cittadella dei Maccari*

This moderately difficult hike passes by the remains of a 6th-century Byzantine village known as the Cittadella dei Maccari to the south of the park before ending up at the Tonnara di Bafuto.

Beaches

From north to south, the sand beaches along the coast of the Vendicari Nature Reserve are Spiaggia Eloro, Marianelli, Calamosche, Vendicari, and San Lorenzo.

Spiaggia Calamosche
northern end of the nature reserve along the Ionian Sea

Make sure to visit the exotic sandy Calamosche Beach, positioned in a small bay among the migratory homes of thousands of visitors including flamingos (in spring and autumn) and sea turtles (in May). The nature reserve is a tranquil oasis, and careful attention should be given to not disturb the area's incredible wildlife while observing. In 2005, the Legambiente Blue Guide named Calamosche the most beautiful beach in Italy.

Getting There and Around

The extensive area of the Vendicari Nature

☆ Baroque Noto Walking Tour

This tour of Noto's Baroque buildings demonstrates the wealth and opulence of this city's layered past.

- Starting on the eastern side of the town, begin your walking tour of Noto at King Ferdinand I's golden limestone **royal gate** (Porto Ferdinandea o Reale, 9, Largo Porta Nazionale; open 24 hours; free).

- Heading two blocks west on the main avenue, Corso Vittorio Emanuele, you will reach the grand staircase of the **Chiesa di San Francesco d'Assisi** (Corso Vittorio Emanuele, 142; free). This church was built in the 1700s and includes a Franciscan monastery and rococo-style stuccoes.

- Crossing back over the Corso Vittorio Emanuele, the next stop is the **Palazzo Ducezio** municipal hall (Corso Vittorio Emanuele; 10am-1:30pm and 3pm-6pm daily; €2). The palace was designed by Noto native architect Vincenzo Sinatra and features the oval-shaped Sala dei Specchi (Hall of Mirrors), neoclassical frescoes, and a panoramic rooftop terrace.

Palazzo Ducezio

- Turn right on Via Papa Giovanni XXIII toward Noto's main Roman Catholic **cathedral,** named for Saint Nicholas, in Piazza del Municipio. Pass the tourists sitting on the steps as you make your way up to admire the extravagant Baroque and neoclassical facade including a bell tower, clock, Corinthian columns, statues of saints, and the green doors at the main entrance.

- Just around the back corner of the cathedral is **Palazzo Nicolaci di Villadorata,** located on the corner of Via Corrado Nicolaci and Via Cavour (10am-7pm Mon.-Sat., 10am-1pm and 2:30-6pm Sun.; €4). Built as a private home in 1737, the recognizably Baroque facade features curved wrought-iron balconies adorned with sculptures of sea creatures, winged horses, half-eagle hippogriffs, and sphinxes. The €4 entrance fee grants visitors access to a select few of the 90 rooms of this palace.

- Continue following Via Cavour west and take a left on Via Giovanni Bovio to reach the **Chiesa di San Domenico** (5am-10pm daily; free) in Piazza XVI Maggio. This Roman Catholic church and monastery is a quintessential example of 18th-century Sicilian Baroque design. The marble altars, stuccoed domes, and Doric and Ionic columns of the facade are complemented by the lush sculpted landscaping in the piazza.

Reserve runs down along the coast of the province of Syracuse, with four entrances equipped with parking lots along the SP51 at Vendicari, Calamosche, Eloro, and Cittadella.

From **Syracuse** (40 minutes; 26 mi/42 km), take the E45 highway from Viale Ermocrate and SS124, heading south toward Noto. Take the exit for Noto/Polizia Stradale and continue on SP59, SP19, and Contrada Vendicari to reach the nature reserve.

TOP EXPERIENCE

NOTO

Come for the Sicilian Baroque architecture, stay for the sweet almond treats. Less than an hour south of Syracuse, nestled at the foot of the Iblean Mountains, the town of Noto is surrounded by hills covered with olive, almond, and citrus groves and dense wild evergreen shrubs. The southern coast of Sicily is its main almond producing region, which means here in Noto you'll find almonds that actually taste like almonds! Don't leave Noto without tasting almond gelato, almond granita, cassata cakes, or almond milk drinks.

The historic center of Noto has been the location for many productions including *L'avventura* (1960) starring Monica Vitti, *Malèna* (2000) directed by Giuseppe Tornatore and starring Monica Bellucci, and season two of *The White Lotus* (2022) television series, and was the set for commercial shoots for Dolce & Gabbana.

This area has always been affected by strong seismic activity. The new city of Noto was rebuilt following the major earthquake of 1693 that completely destroyed the area now known as Noto Antica. Today, Noto is considered the Capital of Baroque, recognized as a UNESCO World Heritage Site in 2002. Just off Corso Vittorio Emanuele, the main avenue of the centro storico, the narrow streets are filled with typical Baroque architecture, from the churches to the golden limestone palaces. Many buildings are lavishly decorated, with gargoyles and wrought-iron-trimmed balconies. Noto is a must-see on a trip to southeastern Sicily and can be enjoyed even with a half-day visit.

Sights
Cattedrale di Noto
Piazza del Municipio; www.diocesinoto.it; 9am-8pm daily; free

The pleasingly symmetrical, impressive limestone Cattedrale di Noto, with its column-lined facade and golden central dome, is a more staid example of Sicilian Baroque construction. Among many of the buildings to be rebuilt after the devastating earthquake of 1693, it is commonly referred to as the Chiesa Madre or Duomo, signifying that it is the most important church in the town. It is reached by a wide, grand staircase and is relatively simple and unornamented, with a timeless, monumental design. Inside, the timeless simplicity continues, with white walls adorned by golden carvings and frescoes. The cathedral

is dedicated to San Nicolò, a Christian saint from Greek times.

Palazzo Castelluccio
Via Camillo Benso Conte di Cavour, 10; tel. 0931/838881; www.palazzocastelluccio.it; open to guided visits 11am-7pm Wed.-Sun. Nov.-Mar., 11am-7pm daily Apr.-Oct.; general admission €12, guided visits €25, children under 12 free

Built in 1782 for the Marquis Corrado di Lorenzo del Castelluccio, the palace stands out among a plethora of Baroque-style buildings in Noto. You'll find a neoclassical theme, late 18th-century frescoes, and intricate flooring throughout the 54,000-square-foot (5,000-sq-m) palace—making it one of the largest noble residences in the area. The palace has only been open to the public since 2018. One-hour guided tours of this private historical monument include access to the palace living rooms on the main floor. Reservations are recommended.

Festivals and Events
Infiorata Flower Festival
Via Corrado Nicolaci, 1; www.facebook.com/Infiorata; third Sun. of May

The Infiorata Flower Festival and the Baroque historical parade in Noto is an annual celebration of spring. Since 1980, natural mosaics have been laid out on the town's main avenue every May to create a handmade tapestry of tiny, colorful flower petals.

Food
★ Caffè Sicilia
Corso Vittorio Emanuele, 125; tel. 0931/835013; www.caffesicilia.it; 8am-9pm Tues.-Sun. winter and spring, 8am-11pm summer and fall, closed Nov. and Jan. 8-Mar. 15; cannolo €3, cassatina €4, gelato €5

Although there are several amazing pastry shops in Noto, the most famous is Caffè Sicilia, chef Corrado Assenza'a fourth-generation gourmet pastry shop, featured in an episode of Netflix's *Chef's Table*. Located

---

1: Cattedrale di Noto **2:** can't-miss desserts from Caffè Sicilia

across from the Cattedrale di Noto, Caffè Sicilia has been making handmade artisanal desserts for over a century. Celebrated around the world, Assenza has become an iconic figure in modern-day Sicilian cuisine, a passionate, curious pastry chef who continues to make torrone nougat candies, granita with fluffy brioche buns, crisp ricotta cream-filled cannoli, small cassatine marzipan cakes, and other Sicilian sweets the same way his ancestors did. His respect for the local farmers and their products, such as almonds, honey, and pistachios, is unparalleled.

Ristorante Crocifisso

Via Principe Umberto, 48; tel. 0931/571151; www. ristorantecrocifisso.it; 12:30pm-2:30pm and 8pm-11pm Thurs.-Tues.; entrées €14-22, 8-course tasting menu €60 without wine pairings

This is a sleek and modern fine-dining restaurant. Chef Marco Baglieri's carefully crafted dishes are an homage to the food and wine of the region, highlighting exceptional ingredients like ancient Sicilian grains, piacentino ennese and caprino girgentano specialty Sicilian cheeses, local meat, seafood, and plant-based dishes.

Ristorante Manna

Via Rocco Pirri, 19; tel. 0931/836051; www.mannanoto. it; 12:30pm-2:30pm and 7:30pm-10:30pm Wed.-Mon.; €40-60

Roberta Assolari, Manuela Alberti, and chef Gioacchino Brambilla have created a smart and modern bistro within a newly restored classic Sicilian Baroque-style shell. The restaurant has a casual and tastefully designed chic feel to it.

Accommodations
San Carlo Suites

Corso Vittorio Emanuele, 127; tel. 347/6620548; www. sancarlosuites.com; from €188

This seven-room bed-and-breakfast is located on Noto's main avenue, directly above the famous Caffè Sicilia. Tasteful five-star rooms are decorated with modern furniture and original majolica tile flooring. The reception team can help plan guided tours, excursions, and wine tastings.

Country House Villadorata

Contrada Portelle; tel. 392/2022910; www. countryhousevilladorata.it; seasonal prices from €339

Built in a renovated 18th-century farmhouse with its own palmento mill, this four-star farmhouse hotel is made up of three guest rooms, a suite, a filtered freshwater outdoor pool, and dining. The 50-acre (20-ha) property includes a working organic farm producing olives, almonds, citrus, and biodynamic wine.

Information and Services

- **Info Point Noto:** Corso Vittorio Emanuele, 135; tel. 339/4816218; www. infopointnoto.it; 10am-6pm daily

Getting There and Around

After arriving in Noto, the quaint city is best explored **on foot.** The best Baroque churches, palaces, restaurants, shops, and cafés are all located on or near the main avenue, **Corso Vittorio Emanuele.**

From the **Catania Fontanarossa Airport,** it's a drive of just over an hour (57 mi/92 km). From **Syracuse,** the drive takes less than half an hour (24 mi/39 km). From **Modica,** the drive takes 45 minutes (22 mi/35 km). Visitors can park in the Parcheggio Centrale (Via Camillo Benso Conte di Cavour; tel. 349/0845075; www. parcheggionoto.it), a 4-minute walk from the Noto Cathedral.

Noto Train Station

Piazza Stazione, 5

Noto is also accessible by train and bus. **Azienda Siciliana Trasporti** (www. aziendasicilianatrasporti.it) runs about four buses a day from Syracuse, a journey of about an hour (from €3); the train, operated by **Trenitalia** (www.trenitalia.com; from €2), takes around 35 minutes. From Modica, the train takes about an hour (from €5.60). The station is a 15-minute walk south of the city center.

MARZAMEMI

The present-day hamlet of Marzamemi has a population of less than 370 inhabitants, who mainly survive on seasonal tourism. The draw of visiting this small village is the history of the local tonnara tuna fishery and the picturesque main town square, **Piazza Regina Margherita.** Located in the province of Siracusa on the Ionian Sea coastline, one hour south of the city of Siracusa and 30 minutes south of Noto, it can be a nice place to stop for an outdoor lunch or a leisurely stroll while exploring the southern tip of Sicily and its nearby coastal nature reserves.

The origins of the town's name are debatable but it derives from the Arabic meaning of the "harbor/bay of the turtledoves," referring to the birds that migrated through annually in springtime. The main characteristics of this quaint village include the tuna fishery, the prince's palace, the church of San Francesco di Paola, and approximately 50 houses situated around the central Regina Margherita piazza built by the Calascibetta barons to be used for sailors and fishers of the area. In ancient times Marzamemi also had many warehouses, used for storing wine barrels and sea salt produced in the nearby flats in Morghella and Marzamemi to be exported to northern Italy and other parts of Europe.

Marzamemi's history has changed drastically, from a 10th-century Arab village through the growth of its prosperous fishing industry and eventual decline, to a modern-day tourism destination. It can be an option for a half-day trip from Noto, Siracusa, or Modica, but is not advised to use as your home base. When visiting Marzamemi during the high season, particularly May-August, reservations are highly recommended for dining, especially in the restaurants positioned on the main square and overlooking the sea.

Sights
Tonnara di Marzamemi

Piazza Regina Margherita, 1; tel. 336/925590; www. tonnaradimarzamemi.it

The Tonnara di Marzamemi, the local tuna fishery, dates back to the year 1,000 during the Arab domination in Sicily. In 1642, it was sold during the Spanish period to the local Nicolaci di Villadorata noble family from Noto, who built new homes and expanded the factory, which remained actively in use until the 1940s before finally closing permanently in 1969. During the 18th century, it was known as one of the most important tuna fisheries in Sicily, where enormous tuna were brought in after being caught in the local waters, slaughtered and processed, then preserved in a canning factory for export. Although the tonnara is sporadically open for visitation, it is mostly used nowadays for special events, weddings, performances, and exhibitions, which makes it inaccessible when rented out for private use.

Tours
Sapore di Mare

Contrada Porto Fossa; tel. 324/9559572; www. escursioniinbarcamarzamemi.com

Skip dining in the crowded town square restaurants and head out on an adventure with a young fisherman/captain, Felice Barbarino, for a boating excursion and onboard meal in the turquoise waters of Marzamemi. Spend your day swimming, relaxing, and enjoying some typical fish-based Sicilian cuisine on a private or group trip. Options include a four-hour half-day excursion departing at 9am or 3pm, a full day with either lunch (9am-3pm) or dinner (4pm-10pm), a sunset aperitivo (7:30pm-9:30pm), or an evening party boat (8pm-midnight). Contact Sapore di Mare ahead of time and plan to spend a fun day in Marzamemi in style.

Uncovered Sicily

Via Valdossola, 8, Ragusa; tel. 388/8726610; www. uncoveredsicily.com; 3-hour program starting at €215

The half-day Fishing Villages of Marzamemi and Portopalo tour with Uncovered Sicily grants travelers access to a privately led afternoon visiting two coastal villages known for their historic tuna fisheries. Having a specialist by your side enhances the experience because of the deep knowledge they add to the visit.

Food
Cortile Arabo

Piazza Villadorata Marzamemi; www.cortilearabo.it; 7:30pm-10:30pm Mon.-Tues., 12:30pm-2:30pm and 7:30pm-10:30pm Wed.-Sun.; antipasti €14, mains €15-20, tasting menus €75-85 plus €35 for wine pairings

This chic and charming osteria di mare is nestled inside a typical central sandstone courtyard with three entrances, as required by traditional Islamic urban design. Fabulous dishes feature flavors of the sea like oysters, sea urchins, raw anemones, red shrimp, sardines, cured anchovies, swordfish, and smoked needlefish. Every dish intricately celebrates the flavors of the island with raw preparations directly from the sea, low-temperature cooking techniques, and wood ovens burning local carob and olive branches.

Taverna La Cialoma

Piazza Regina Margherita, 23; tel. 0931/841772; www.tavernalacialoma.it; 1pm-3pm and 7:30pm-11pm daily; antipasti €16, pasta dishes €15, mains €20

La Cialoma may be the most "Instagrammable" of all open-air Sicilian courtyards. The vintage tableware, teal wooden chairs, and hand-sewn, colorful textiles are simply iconic. The dishes at Lina Campisi's family-run restaurant highlight the local tradition of tuna fishing, featuring bottarga, salted anchovies, handmade pastas, and vegetables grown nearby in Pachino. Signora Lina's daughter Chiara Fronterrè and her husband Totò run the kitchen, while the youngest son Davide manages the front of house and the 400-label wine program. Request a table in its additional sea-view dining area.

Ristorante Donna Nina

Piazza Regina Margherita; tel. 327/6881222; www.facebook.com/DonnaNinaMarzamemi; 7pm-11:30pm daily

Donna Nina is the smaller sister-restaurant of Lina Campisi's famed Taverna La Cialoma, located just around the corner in the main picturesque piazza of the hamlet. Inside the upscale osteria, Donna Nina has a permanent photographic exhibition on display, dedicated to the inhabitants of the village of Marzamemi. Chef Corrado Dipietro's elegant menu at Donna Nina focuses on meat and fish entrées along with first-course pasta dishes,

Taverna La Cialoma

following the tradition of homestyle Sicilian cuisine. It also offers a small selection of wines and craft beers to pair with your meal. With only 30 seats, reservations are highly recommended.

Getting There and Around

Most visitors reach Marzamemi by car or motorino, on a tour, or with a private driver. The old town can be discovered on foot in an hour or so, mainly because of its limited number of attractions. Those looking to explore the beaches of the area will want to have their own mode of transportation. There is a small train station in Marzamemi; however, the connections are not extremely helpful for guests coming from the bigger nearby towns.

From the Vendicari Nature Reserve, head south for 25 minutes (9 mi/14.5 km) on SP19

toward Marzamemi. From Noto, the drive will take less than 30 minutes (14 mi/22.5 km) following SS115 and SP35 to SP108 on toward SP19. From Siracusa, a 45-minute (32.5 mi/52 km) drive on the state road SS124 to the A18/E45 highway toward Noto and then SP19 will lead to Marzamemi. From Modica, drive 26 miles (42 km) southeast along SP70 to SP32 and SP34, SP27, SS115, and SP26 toward Pachino and on to SP85 for a total of 50 minutes to reach Marzamemi. From Ragusa, take the 1-hour 10-minute drive (35.5 mi/57 km) southeast along SS194 to SS115 and back on SS194 to SS115 again, then SP49, SP22, and SP26 to SP85 for Marzamemi.

There is no direct route with public transportation to arrive in Marzamemi. A 45-minute taxi from Siracusa will cost approximately €100 each way; a 25-minute taxi from Noto will cost around €65.

Ragusa

Located just west of Syracuse, the province of Ragusa is home to several extraordinary Baroque cities, all built after the devastating earthquake that destroyed much of the region in 1693. The city of Ragusa and its historic district of Ragusa Ibla belong to the Late Baroque Towns of the Val di Noto UNESCO World Heritage Site, preserving Sicilian Baroque architecture and a deep-rooted food and wine culture.

Ragusa Ibla is the oldest district of the historic center of the capital city. Located in the eastern part of town on a hilltop 1,300 feet (400 m) above sea level, it is the perfect place to enjoy panoramic views of Ragusa's rural countryside. Its Duomo di San Giorgio is a textbook example of the splendid Sicilian Baroque style of architecture from the 17th and 18th centuries.

The province of Ragusa has one of the best food and wine scenes in all of Sicily, from wineries to Michelin-starred restaurants. And the coastline of Ragusa is perfect for a summer

holiday away from the crowds of other, more popular Sicilian beaches.

SIGHTS

Central squares in Ragusa include the **Piazza della Repubblica** and **Piazza Duomo,** located only a 10-minute walk away from each other. From Piazza Duomo where the Baroque Duomo di San Giorgio is located, **Corso XXV Aprile** runs east toward the Giardino Ibleo, a manicured public garden.

Duomo di San Giorgio

Salita Duomo, 13; Ragusa Ibla; tel. 0932/220085; www. duomosangiorgioragusa.it; 10am-1pm and 3:30pm-7pm Fri.; 10am-1pm and 3:30pm-7:30pm Sat.-Thurs.; free

The Church of Saint George is the Chiesa Madre or principal duomo church in the heart of Ragusa and one of the best expressions of the Sicilian Baroque style of architecture, with an extravagant, wedding cake-like facade ornamented by curlicues and stained glass. The single tower features both a bell

Ragusa

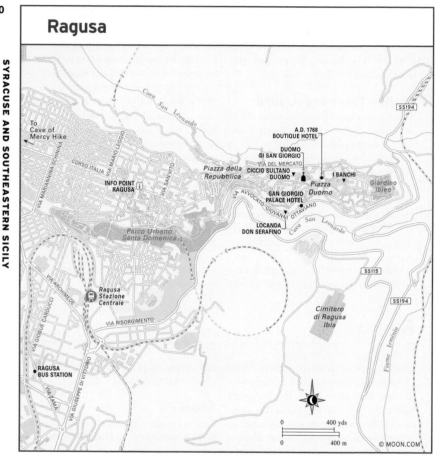

and a clock. Inside, the extravagance continues with gilded decor and a life-size statue of Saint George on a rearing horse. The Festa di San Giorgio is celebrated every year here during the last weekend of May or first weekend of June. Explore the religious relics of the city at the **Museo San Giorgio** (Salita Duomo, 15; 9:30am-12:30pm and 3:30pm-6pm daily, Sat.-Sun. only Nov.-Apr.) right next door.

Giardino Ibleo

Piazza Giovan Battista Hodierna, Ragusa Ibla; tel. 0932/652374; 10am-10pm Mon.-Fri., 10am-1am Sat.-Sun.

This city park was originally built as the gardens for the town's main villa. With a stunning panoramic view of the surrounding mountains, the manicured park includes three main churches, archaeological excavations, and a monument dedicated to fallen war heroes. Wander through the paths of this 3.7-acre (1.5-ha) park, where the lawns are filled with laurel bushes, oleander, and bougainvillea and the main Avenue of the Palms is lined with 50 date palms and pink blossoming judas trees.

1: Giardino Ibleo 2: Casa Mia Tours cheesemaking experience

HIKING

Cave of Mercy Hike
(Cava della Misericordia)

Distance: *4 miles (6.4 km)*

Time: *4-hour full loop trail*

Trailhead: *Between Ragusa and Giarratana along SP116*

Information and Maps: *www. circuitodellecaveiblee.it/en/cava-della-misericordia-2*

Eight miles (12.9 km) north of Ragusa, take a quiet afternoon walk through the lush valleys and grasslands of the Cava della Misericordia. This gorge and its limestone quarries are located along the tributary of the Irminio River within the Valley of Misericordia in the Hyblaean Mountains. **Uncovered Sicily** (tel. 338/8726610; www.uncoveredsicily.com; 4-hour excursions for €180 per group) organizes guided tours.

TOURS

Casa Mia Tours

tel. 346/8001746; www.casamiatours.com; from €300 for 2 people including tastings, transportation not included

Visit a small, family-run farm for a morning cheesemaking experience with Casa Mia Tours in the province of Ragusa, where Frisona cows graze freely. Trace the entire journey of the milk from the stables all the way to the creamery, where cheeses, such as provola, caciocavallo, tuma, and ricotta, are made right before your eyes. At the end of the demonstration, guests enjoy a cheese tasting along with other local specialties like bread, olive oil, and cured meats. Contact Casa Mia Tours to reserve this program.

FOOD

Start your day in Ragusa with a piece of **perpetua cake,** a cornetto, or a homemade brioche bun and a cup of granita made from local pizzuta almonds. For lunch, look for a slice of **scacce ragusane** (stuffed Sicilian flatbread) layered with tomato, eggplant, and **caciocavallo** cheese.

I Banchi

Via Orfanotrofio, 39, Ragusa Ibla; tel. 0932/655000; www.ibanchiragusa.it; breakfast 8am-12:30pm, lunch 12:30pm-3pm, aperitivo 3pm-7:30pm, dinner 7:30pm-midnight daily; pizzas €10, mains €10-16, family-style tasting menus €20-50, cocktails €8

A celebration of house-made bread, wine, and exceptional Sicilian olive oil is led by chef Peppe Cannistrà, a protégé of Ragusa's top Michelin-starred chef, Ciccio Sultano. This smart-casual restaurant's kitchen features the best of Sicilian baked goods, seasonal meat and fish dishes, chef's tasting menus, artisanal cocktails, oysters, and charcuterie platters served throughout the day.

★ Ciccio Sultano Duomo

Via Capitano Bocchieri, 31, Ragusa Ibla; tel. 0932/651265; www.cicciosultano.it/en/restaurant; tasting menus €90-160, wine pairings €28-50, à la carte dishes €30-39, cover charge €12 per person included with minimum order of 2 courses

Celebrated and world-renowned as the best chef in Sicily, Ciccio Sultano's love for his homeland, respect for small artisan producers, and exceptional interpretation of classic Sicilian flavors shine through in his innovative and perfectly plated dishes. This stylish, two-Michelin-starred fine-dining restaurant is located just steps from the Duomo di San Giorgio in the heart of Ragusa Ibla. His elegant dishes are a poetic journey through Sicily. It's absolutely worth a trip to Ragusa just to eat here.

Locanda Don Serafino

Via Avvocato G. Ottaviano 13, Ragusa Ibla; tel. 0932/248778; www.locandadonserafino.it; tasting menus €70-165, 3-course lunch menu €55, à la carte dishes €30-40

The imaginative menu in chef Vincenzo Candiano's Locanda Don Serafino was awarded one Michelin star in 2020. The restaurant is built in the caves of the converted warehouse of the Chiesa dei Miracoli in the historic center of Ragusa Ibla. With over 1,700 different labels, its wine cellar is one of the best in all of Sicily.

ACCOMMODATIONS
★ San Giorgio Palace Hotel
Via Avvocato Giovanni Ottaviano; tel. 0932/686983;
www.sangiorgiopalacehotel.it; from €65
This four-star hotel was built in a renovated 18th-century building just an eight-minute walk from the Duomo di San Giorgio. The 108-foot-long (33-m) stone tunnel entrance leads guests up to the reception with a private elevator, and the panoramic views of the Vallata di Santa Domenica from the San Giorgio Palace Hotel are unparalleled. The newly restored rooms are modestly decorated for a comfortable stay right in the heart of Ragusa Ibla.

A.D. 1768 Boutique Hotel
Via Conte Cabrera, 6; tel. 0932/663133;
www.1768iblahotel.it; from €110
This contemporary Baroque, four-star boutique hotel features eight rooms and two suites, located in the noble Palazzo Arezzo di Donnafugata, overlooking Piazza Duomo in Ragusa Ibla. La Carretteria, the hotel's ancient carriage house stables, are now open to the public and can be used by guests of the hotel for a place to enjoy a buffet breakfast or a break during the day.

INFORMATION AND SERVICES
The website **Scale del Gusto** (www. scaledelgusto.it) features special events in Ragusa and Ragusa Ibla including tastings, workshops, guided tours, demonstrations, masterclasses, outdoor dinners, and artistic exhibitions.

- **Info Point Ragusa:** Via Giacomo Matteotti, 79, Ragusa; tel. 0932/1911883; www.infopointragusa.it; 9:30am-7:30pm Mon.-Fri., 9:30am-6pm Sat., 9:30am-1:30pm Sun.

GETTING THERE AND AROUND
Most will likely arrive in Ragusa by **car,** but it is also possible to get here by **train and bus.** Once you arrive, park your car and check out the city **on foot.**

By Car
From **Syracuse,** Ragusa is a 1-hour 30-minute drive southwest (50 mi/81 km); from **Catania Fontanarossa Airport,** it's also 1 hour 30 minutes, a 65-mile (105-km) drive. From **Modica,** Ragusa is only 25 minutes away (10.5 mi/16.9 km).

By Train
Ragusa Stazione Centrale
Piazza Gramisci, 1; www.rfi.it/it/stazioni/ragusa.html
The main transit station in Ragusa is located within walking distance of the historic town center. Convenient train services from **Modica** (25 minutes; €2.20), **Noto** (1 hour 30 minutes; €7.50), and **Syracuse** (2 hours 20 minutes; €10) are provided by **Trenitalia** (www.trenitalia.com), and tickets can be purchased online or from the 24-hour automated machines in the station.

By Bus
Ragusa Bus Station
Via Zama, 53; tel. 331/6877678
Ragusa can be reached by **Interbus** (tel. 0931/66710; www.interbus.it) from **Catania airport** (1 hour 40 minutes; €9) or the **Catania bus station** (1 hour 50 minutes; €9). Timetables and fares from Ragusa to **Modica** (25 minutes), **Noto** (1 hour 50 minutes), and **Syracuse** (2 hours 45 minutes) are posted on the Azienda Siciliana Trasporti (AST; www.aziendasicilianatrasporti.it) website. A walk from the main bus station in Ragusa to the center of Ragusa Ibla will take about 45 minutes.

The **AST** city bus runs from the main bus station to the Giardino Ibleo in Ragusa Ibla (tickets €1.20 valid for 90 minutes).

Around Ragusa

This part of the island is frequented by travelers seeking out culture, architecture, Sicilian culinary specialties, incredible wines, and a coastline of golden-sand beaches. However, this area is best explored with a car or private driver. Train and bus services are limited yet available, but in order to visit wineries in and around Vittoria, countryside hotels and farmstays, or a beach destination outside the town centers, a car may end up being a necessity.

There is an enormous amount to explore in southeastern Sicily, including the smaller towns speckled through the provinces of Ragusa and Siracusa. Several stops can be scheduled into day trips while basing yourself for a few days in a larger town like Ragusa, Noto, or Siracusa, where there are more options for restaurants, hotels, bars, and shops. In this area around Ragusa, the must-see destination is the hillside Baroque town of Modica, but it's worth keeping Marina di Ragusa and Scicli on your radar if there is time for extended travel in this corner of the island.

★ VITTORIA WINE REGION

Treat yourself to an afternoon of wine tasting in the hills of Chiaramonte Gulfi and Vittoria in the province of Ragusa. This is mainly red wine country, although the winemakers in this area will produce additional lesser-known labels with white grapes. Vittoria is the home of the Cerasuolo di Vittoria wines, the only DOCG certified wines in all of Sicily. Their perfect blend of indigenous **frappato** and **nero d'avola** grapes creates a balanced cherry-red-colored wine with hints of black currant, pepper, and tobacco.

Visits to all vineyards in the area are by appointment only and should be scheduled with as much advance notice as possible.

Vineyard Visits and Wine Tasting
Azienda Agricola Arianna Occhipinti
SP68 Km 3, 3, Vittoria; tel. 0932/1865519; www. agricolaocchipinti.it
Arianna Occhipinti is an unassuming and fierce leader in the natural winemaking

Pianogrillo Farm Organic Winery

world. She started studying winemaking at 16 years old with her family at the COS winery in Vittoria. Always focusing on naturally produced wines in her home region of Ragusa, she grew from a single-hectare property to become a spearhead in a new generation of Sicilian winemaking. Her goal is to make high-quality wines from her frappato, nero d'avola, moscato, and albanello vines. A visit to the Azienda Agricola Arianna Occhipinti winery in the Contrada Bombolieri will include a walk through the vineyards, an overview of production activities, and a tasting accompanied by local cheese, olives, and extra virgin olive oil from the property.

Azienda Agricola COS

SP3, Km 14, 300, Vittoria; tel. 0932/876145; www. cosvittoria.it

Giusto Occhipinti and the whole team at COS winery in Vittoria are passionate people who love their land and strive to make wines with a true expression of the terroir of southeastern Sicily. They started with experimenting on family vineyards in the 1980s and have grown to be one of the most reputable Sicilian wine producers. Their Cerasuolo di Vittoria blend of native frappato and nero d'avola grapes is one of the best examples of this DOCG wine. Winery visits and tastings explore COS's natural values and ancient techniques of winemaking with barrels and clay amphorae.

Pianogrillo Farm Organic Winery

Contrada Pianogrillo, 8, Chiaramonte Gulfi; tel. 338/8193102; www.pianogrillo.it

The hilltop town of Chiaramonte Gulfi is located in Ragusa's DOC Vittoria winemaking region in southeastern Sicily. One of the highlights of this area is Pianogrillo's beautiful contrada filled with 170 acres (70 ha) of olive trees, most of which are 800-900 years old. The farm also has its own small agricultural museum and ancient wine cellar. The owner, baron Lorenzo Piccone Pianogrillo, is a true Renaissance man—a kind, multitalented, passionate artist and farmer. At his family farm, visits can be organized for a winery tour that includes a tasting of wines and homemade products like his exceptional tonda iblea extra virgin olive oil and local cheeses. And if you're lucky, he'll bring out some house-made nero ibleo salami to try.

Food

Ristorante Colonna

Via C. Alberto, 115, Vittoria; tel. 0932/1915825; www. ristorantecolonna.it; 1pm-2:30pm and 8pm-11:30pm Mon. and Wed.-Sat.; dishes from €17-33

Celebrated local restaurateur Angelo Di Stefano came back to Vittoria after working for several years in northern Italy to open up Ristorante Colonna in 2021. This small twenty-two-seat restaurant run by his family offers high-quality dishes inspired by the bounty of the region, at more affordable rates than a fine-dining meal in the nearby bigger towns of Sicily's southeast. You'll spot Angelo's smiling face in the dining room while his wife, chef Maria Concetta Di Stefano, runs the kitchen. The menu features both fish and meat dishes, and since you are in Vittoria, the wine list is, of course, exceptional.

Ristorante Majore

Via Martiri Ungheresi, 12, Chiaramonte Gulfi; tel. 0932/928019; www.majore.it; 9am-4pm and 6pm-11pm Tues.-Sat., 9am-4pm and 7pm-11pm Sun.; €25-35

Ristorante Majore is a tried-and-true, old-school classic in terms of Sicilian trattorias. Dating back to 1896, its vision has focused on highlighting dishes using the best pork products from the region. Pair your visit to a local winery with lunch here for your fill of local delicacies like antipasti salami platters, risotto, ravioli, porcini and truffle pastas, as well as pork chops, steaks, gelatins, baked meatloaf, stuffed ribs, and grilled sausages. Hearty dishes, a casual rustic setting, and the fourth-generation owners all aid in creating this restaurant's authentic old-world Sicilian charm.

Accommodations

Baglio Occhipinti

Contrada Fossa di Lupo, Vittoria; tel. 349/3944359; www.bagliocchipinti.com; from €176

This luxury farmhouse resort is an authentic family country house dating back to 1860, in the beautiful Sicilian countryside, located right down the street from sister Arianna Occhipinti's famed natural winery. Fausta Occhipinti's manor house is composed of five living rooms, 12 bedrooms with en suite bathrooms, and a large, fully equipped kitchen. The main living room is in the restored palmento antique wine press and has floor-to-ceiling windows facing the courtyard and an enormous old fireplace. The kitchen is original, with a wood-burning oven and a large stone sink. The bedrooms are spacious and luxuriously furnished in a vintage style, all equipped with en suite bathrooms decorated with old, traditional ceramics. All rooms are equipped with heating and air-conditioning. Guests are treated to a healthy organic breakfast spread every morning.

Cooking classes are available upon request; dishes may include scaccia ragusana (a folded local pizza), arancini, fresh pasta, and Sicilian cannoli. You'll be welcomed with a glass of wine, a walk through the garden to collect vegetables, and a six-course meal to follow.

Locanda COS

Azienda Agricola COS, SP3, Km 14, 300; tel. 0932/876145; www.cosvittoria.it; from €300

Locanda COS is a true wine-lovers hideaway. This historic 18th-century home in the heart of Vittoria is surrounded by vineyards, a garden, a maze, and a swimming pool and has a great view of the sunset. There are six suites and two large rooms around the main tower. Three of the suites have large private terraces overlooking the family vineyards. Meals are not included in the booking. The accommodations have built-in heating, air-conditioning, and Wi-Fi.

Getting There and Around

The best way to reach Vittoria and the town's wineries is by self-driving. Keep in mind, all winery visits and tastings will have to be reserved in advance. Otherwise, a taxi from Ragusa will take approximately 40 minutes and cost about €45. Vittoria is located 40 minutes west of Ragusa (15.3 mi/24.6 km); the state road SP52 will lead to SS115 and take you directly into the very small town. Follow directions from the wineries to reach your precise destination.

★ VILLA ROMANA DEL CASALE

SP90, Piazza Armerina; tel. 0935/687667; www.villaromanadelcasale.it; 9am-10pm daily; €10, free Mar. 8 for International Women's Day

Despite being relatively remote, this luxurious, sprawling Roman villa near the town of Piazza Armerina in the central province of Enna is one of the island's most-visited tourist destinations. Built in the 4th century CE as a private hunting-lodge-cum-grand-estate for an unknown Roman aristocrat, Villa Romana del Casale was named a UNESCO World Heritage Site in 1997. It's especially famous for its intricate mosaics, considered some of the finest and best preserved of their kind in the world.

Over an estimated 150 years of occupation, the villa was expanded multiple times, each time getting larger and grander, until the complex measured some 38,000 square feet (3,500 sq m). It was thought to be damaged by the Vandals in the 4th century CE, and was more or less abandoned after the destruction of the nearby town of Piazza Armerina by the Normans in the 11th century, followed by a landslide that had the silver lining of protecting Villa Romana del Casale from the elements over the centuries. Archaeological excavations began in the 1800s and miraculously revealed this one-of-a-kind, luxurious Roman estate.

The magnificent archaeological findings and collection of mosaics here were discovered during excavations by archaeologist Gino Vinicio Gentili, in the 1950s. It has been estimated that during the 5th and 6th centuries CE, the structures of the villa were renovated for defensive purposes, fortifying the original design by thickening the outer walls and closing in the aqueduct in the bathhouse rooms. During the 5th century, it became a sort of fortified city with the addition of a small group of houses known by the name of Casale, from which the villa's name derives.

Sights

Today, guests are welcome to visit the site with an entrance ticket or guided tour and follow a marked path throughout the villa to see Sicily's best collection of mosaics, featuring colorful designs including people, lions, antelopes, horses, wild boars, and deer, all highly decorated with laurel wreaths. You can explore thermal baths, the living areas for the unknown owners and their guests (including a throne room), and a lovely courtyard. The indoor site is now almost entirely covered with wooden planks along a one-way path leading guests through the site, to preserve the precious collection of mosaics. With so much to see, and so many interpretive signs to read, allow 2-3 hours to visit this site.

Entrance

Visitors start their walking tour by following the path through the villa's entrance and vestibule. Here, you'll see a three-bay honorary arch, decorated with two pairs of fountains inserted into the pillars. The significant mosaic in this area portrays two elegantly dressed figures with laurel crowns.

Thermal Baths

Through the first vestibule, you'll find the ancient thermal baths where the pavement is decorated with animal heads wearing laurel crowns and frescoed walls depict armed figures carrying shields. On the north side, the bath complex has a private entrance and what was probably used as a gymnasium with a chariot rider being pulled by horses. In the

frigidarium, there is also a large octagonal-shaped hall with mosaics of marine elements including cherubs on a boat surrounded by fish.

The Corridor of the "Great Hunt"

One of the villa's main features is the antechamber of the basilica known as the corridor of La Caccia, the "great hunt." Here there is a geographical map of the Roman Empire along with lions and wild beasts, mythological griffons, and armed horsemen.

Room of the Gymnasts

The Room of the Gymnasts features nine female athletes exercising in costumes resembling modern-day bikinis, as well as depictions of hunting expeditions and the mythical adventures of Hercules and Odysseus. The athletes have become the most recognizable element of the Villa Romana del Casale.

Private Apartments

In the west wing of the villa leading toward the basilica, the private apartments feature mosaics representing children in chariots being pulled by birds as well as small children hunting, mimicking the adults represented in the other rooms. A round mosaic known as the Lover's Embrace is thought to represent Cupid and Psyche, located in one of the bedroom alcoves.

The Basilica

After walking through the "great hunt" and up few stairs, the basilica is located between two of the apartments, which are decorated with elaborate mosaics made with precious marbles, coming from all over the Mediterranean, that cover both the floors and the walls. This room was used for significant ceremonies and contains a wooden throne where court was held.

Tours

You can hire one of a number of qualified guides at the entrance to the villa (tours from €60), or organize a full-day trip from Catania, Modica, Noto, Ragusa, Siracusa, or Taormina, which includes the ceramics capital, Caltagirone, with your own private driver via **Sunny Sicily** (tel. 338/5296915; www.sunnysicily.com; from €65 per person).

Information and Services

Even the standard entrance tickets should be reserved in advance. Bookings can be made on the villa's website or by email. For guided visits, the contact list for recommended guides who speak several languages is available on the website and will need to also be booked in advance. There is plenty of outdoor, unshaded parking available behind the villa. Here you'll also find bathroom facilities, a snack bar, and a souvenir shop beside the parking lot.

Getting There
By Car

The best way to reach the Villa Romana del Casale is by car; public transportation is not convenient for this excursion. Villa Romana del Casale can be reached on a half-day excursion from **Syracuse** (2 hours; 90 mi/145 km), **Catania** (90 minutes; 60 mi/97 km), **Ragusa** (90 minutes; 60 mi/97 km), or **Agrigento** (90 minutes; 60 mi/97 km).

From Catania, the scenic drive will take about 1 hour 30 minutes, traveling west along SS417 to SS125 and SS177 toward Piazza Armerina. The 1-hour 45-minute drive northwest from Ragusa and Modica will also pass through the ceramic city of Caltagirone via SS115 to SS514 and SS683, continuing on to Piazza Armerina by following SS124 to SS117. From Agrigento, the 1-hour 25-minute drive northeast along SS640 to SP42 and SP15 will pass through Sicily's "entroterra" countryside.

MODICA

Like many towns in the region, the two areas that make up Modica (Modica Alta and the valley of Modica Bassa) were rebuilt in Sicily's famous Baroque architectural style after the infamous 17th-century earthquake. During these years, Sicily was under Spanish rule,

and you can taste a remnant of the Spanish colonies of South and Central America here, which adopted the specialized Aztec cold-pressing technique of grinding cacao beans to make chocolate without melting the sugar crystals. Spend a day stopping in and out of Modica's famous chocolate shops and laboratories while discovering the hidden backstreets of the town, built into a steep slope. The city is characterized by terraced houses and stunning Baroque churches clinging to the sides of the hills. A short walk down the town's high street, Corso Umberto I, will lead you past architectural gems, shops, and restaurants. You may want to wander up the staircases of the smaller alleyways to find your perfect bird's-eye view of the opposite side of the town.

Sights
Duomo di San Giorgio

Corso S. Giorgio, Modica Alta; tel. 0932/941279; 8am-12:30pm and 3:30pm-7pm daily; free

This 18th-century Baroque cathedral is the principal duomo of Modica. As at many of the important monuments in southeastern Sicily, the reconstruction of the cathedral took place following the devastating series of earthquakes in the Val di Noto in 1542, 1613, and 1693. It was renovated by the same Syracusan architect, Rosario Gagliardi, who created the San Giorgio duomo in Ragusa. Look for the *Eventi del Vangelo e della vita di San Giorgio* painting by Girolamo Alibrandi, known as the Raphael of Sicily; the temple dedicated to Saint George; a marble statue of the Madonna della Neve; and a magnificent white-and-gold pipe organ. Plan your visit to the duomo at noon to witness the cathedral's floor sundial.

Chiesa di San Pietro

Corso Umberto I, 159A; tel. 0932/941074; 9am-12:45pm and 3:30pm-7:15pm Mon.-Sat.

The 18th-century Baroque church of Saint Peter is located front and center on the main avenue in Modica Bassa. Dedicated to the patron saint, this church features statues of the

12 apostles, three main naves with Corinthian columns, and a large central staircase starting on Corso Umberto I. Take a break from chocolate tastings and peek into this church to see the marble *Madonna di Trapani* and the wooden *San Pietro e il Paralitico* by Palermitan sculptor Benedetto Civiletti.

Chiesa Rupestre di San Nicolò Inferiore

Via Clemente Grimaldi, 691, Modica Bassa; tel. 0932/752897; 10am-1pm and 4pm-7pm daily; €2 entrance fee

Hidden away on a backstreet in Modica Bassa, the small church of San Nicolò Inferiore showcases one of the most significant collections of rock art in southeastern Sicily, with roots dating back to the Middle Ages. It was only discovered in 1987, then only used as a private storage garage. The church itself is carved from the rocks, and excavations uncovered a series of tombs, late medieval Byzantine frescoes, and late Norman and Swabian artwork.

Cooking Classes
★ LoveSicily

Via Ritiro, 7; www.lovesicily.com; 10am lunch programs, 5pm evening classes

While visiting Modica, spend a few hours with Katia Amore to discover the world of Sicilian cooking in her private home overlooking the San Giorgio Cathedral. Options for classes include pasta-making, cooking with Modica's famous chocolate, and traditional Sicilian cooking using local ingredients. All classes can be taught in English or Italian and begin with a short introduction to Sicilian culinary history and traditions. The experience lasts about three hours, including a welcome coffee or aperitivo, a hands-on cooking lesson, and a meal paired with wine. Lessons can be booked year-round depending on availability, for a minimum of two people.

Entertainment and Events
Festa di San Giorgio

Historic center of Modica; weekend following Apr. 23

Visit during the patron saint festival of San Giorgio, when a festive procession follows the saint through the streets of Modica Alta and on to Modica Bassa. Spectators enjoy a triumphant firework show and a grand procession. The impressive highlight of this joyful event are the men known as "Sangiorgiari" who carry the symbolic saint at a fast pace to simulate the gallop of his horse.

interior of Chiesa di San Pietro

Ceramics of Caltagirone

Scalinata di Santa Maria del Monte

Caltagirone, technically in the province of Catania but equidistant from Catania and Ragusa, is known as Sicily's city of ceramics. Its name derives from the Arabic words qal'at-al-jarar, the "castle of jars," or similarly qal'at al Ghiran, meaning "rock of the vases." The town's ceramic techniques date back to the introduction of the potter's wheel to Sicily, brought by the Greeks during the 8th century BCE. Add the influence of Arab glazing techniques, and you get the ceramics that are still commonly produced here today.

TRADITIONAL SICILIAN CERAMICS AND THE LEGEND OF THE MOOR'S HEAD VASE

The most common traditional ceramic you'll see in Caltagirone comes from a rather brutal, and very typically Sicilian, story. The head-shaped vase known as the Moor's head, or teste de moro,

Food

Radici, L'Osteria di Accursio

Via Clemente Grimaldi, 55; tel. 331/2369404; www. accursioradici.it; 12:30pm-2:30pm and 7:30pm- 10:30pm Mon., Wed., and Fri.-Sat., 7:30pm-10:30pm Sun., Tues., and Thurs.; entrées €12-15, desserts €6

A casual offshoot from Modica's top chef and restaurateur, at Radici chef Accursio Craparo experiments with dishes drawing on home cooking and Sicilian street food while always honoring local farmers and fishers. He dissects and reinterprets the flavors, aromas, and essences of traditional dishes like caponata, sfincione, panzerotto, and granita in an osteria setting.

Taverna Migliore

Via Modica Ispica, 95; tel. 0932/948669; www. tavernamigliore.it; 12:45pm-2:30pm and 7:45pm- 10:45pm Tues.-Sat., 12:45pm-2:30pm Sun.; mains €14-24

Taverna Migliore focuses on innovative dishes originating from quintessential home cooking. Chefs Lorenzo Ruta and Giorgetta Abbate take their guests on a sensorial journey in this restored natural stone country house surrounded by vegetable gardens. Seasonal menus feature playful dishes like a stuffed pasta with marinated squid. The 50-seat restaurant serves creative fare at an affordable price point.

originates in an 11th-century legend in which a beautiful young girl fell in love with a handsome Moorish man from her balcony. When she discovered that her lover was already married, with a family back home, she cut off his head and filled it with basil sprouts to be left out on her balcony as a sign of his infidelity. Many ceramics shops throughout Sicily feature a pair of vases representing these young lovers.

For a ceramic sight in Caltagirone that's much less gory, visit the **Scalinata di Santa Maria del Monte,** a ceramic tile-lined 142-step staircase in the center of town.

WHERE TO BUY CERAMICS

Caltagirone is completely filled with ceramic shops, most of which have a showroom in the center of town and a larger workshop on the outskirts of town. A few of the most notable include **Giacomo Alessi** (Corso Principe Amedeo di Savoia, 9; tel. 0933/221967; www.giacomoalessi. com), **Ceramiche Nicolo Morales** (Corso Principe Amedeo di Savoia, 28; tel. 393/9714113; www.ceramicmorales.com; 10am-1pm and 3pm-7pm daily), and **Crita Ceramiche** (Via Sfere, 17; tel. 340/5124624; www.critaceramiche.com; 9am-7pm Mon.-Sat.). If you can't make it to Caltagirone or prefer to shop from home, unique hand-crafted ceramics from **Maremoro** are available to purchase online (www.ceramichemaremoro.com).

LEARN MORE

While in Caltigirone, visit the **Museo Regionale della Ceramica** (Via Giardini Pubblici; tel. 0933/58418; 9am-6:30pm daily) for a great introduction to the city and the history of ceramic production in this area, with a small but interesting collection from the 17th to 18th centuries.

GETTING THERE

From Catania, drive along SS192 and SS416 to SS180, exiting at the Caltagirone Sud turnoff and following SS417 to SP196 on to Via Sfere and Via Roma to arrive in the Piazza del Municipio in Caltagirone. From Ragusa and Modica, take a one-hour drive northwest on the SS514 to SS683 to Via Noto in Caltagirone.

When arriving in Caltagirone, leave your car parked along Via Roma and walk toward the Scalinata di Santa Maria del Monte staircase. For additional information about visiting Caltagirone, contact the **Caltagirone Visit Sicily Tourism Office** (Via Volta Libertini, 4; tel. 0933/53809).

Accursio Ristorante

Via Clemente Grimaldi, 41; tel. 0932/941689; www. accursioristorante.it; 12:30pm-2pm and 7:30pm-10:30pm Tues.-Sat., 7:30pm-10:30pm Sun.; 4-course tasting menus €90, 8 courses €130 per person

Since 2016, Accursio Ristorante has offered Michelin-level fine dining in the heart of Modica. Chef/restaurateur Accursio Craparo is known as "the chef of two Sicilies," regarding his experience traversing the island from Sciacca to Modica. The dishes at Accursio are inventive, modern, and clean, always showcasing the quality of ingredients and the romanticism of his deep connection to many sides of this island. As Accursio is a great connoisseur of sparkling wines, you'll find an exceptional selection of bubbly on his wine list.

Accommodations
Palazzo Failla

Via Blandini, 5; tel. 0932/941059; www.palazzofailla. it; from €107

Spend the night in a 10-room, 18th-century aristocratic palace on the town's quieter side in Modica Alta. The rooms are furnished with original ceramic-tiled floors, antique vases, framed portraits, and Persian rugs. Guests are treated to a seasonal breakfast spread of cheeses, cakes, and freshly baked bread. Hotelier Giorgio Failla and Palermitan chef

☆ Modica's Chocolate and the Legacy of Spanish Rule

Antica Dolceria Bonajuto

For more than 200 years, from 1554 to 1860, Sicily was ruled by the kings of Spain. In addition to cultural, architectural, and culinary influences, Spanish rule meant products such as cocoa beans, corn, peppers, and tomatoes were introduced to the region. In Modica, the history of chocolate making dates back to the 18th century, when letters regarding Spanish trade routes were discovered by a local noble family. These documents contained a recipe revealing the secrets of Aztec chocolate-making.

Using simple tools, chocolate makers began experimenting and creating their own method. What makes Modica's chocolate so unique is the way they crush the sugar, grind the cocoa beans by hand, and combine the two ingredients at less than 104°F (40°C), without melting the cocoa butter. This process, inspired by the Aztecs, helps preserve all the beneficial nutritional and aromatic properties of the beans. The grainy consistency and crisp sugar crystals speckled through each bite make Modica chocolate immediately identifiable. These typical characteristics and the complex Aztec process have been awarded with IGP (Indicazione Geografica Protetta) recognition. The streets of Modica are lined with chocolate shops, including some historic producers that have been working with ancient techniques since the 1800s.

Francesco Mineo invite guests into the hotel's restaurant, Locanda del Colonnello, to experience creative and seasonal Sicilian dishes like saffron-infused sardine linguine and smoked pork belly from the nearby Hyblaean Mountains.

Casa Talía Slowliving
Via Exaudinos, 1/9; tel. 0932/752075; www.casatalia. it; from €140

This charming bed-and-breakfast has 11 rooms, all including a panoramic view of the Baroque town. Owners Marco Giunta and Viviana Haddad are architects from Milan. Every inch of the rooms, guesthouses, secret gardens, and terraces were renovated and upcycled to create something fresh, dreamy, and Mediterranean with a vintage feel. Their Buendia guesthouse is a duplex for five guests carved out of the stone walls. The Mandorlo

ANTICA DOLCERIA BONAJUTO

Corso Umberto I, 159; tel. 0932/941225; www.bonajuto.it; 9am-midnight daily; chocolate bars from €2.90-5, chocolate lab group tours and tastings €8 per person by reservation only

Antica Dolceria Bonajuto is world renowned for 150 years of chocolate production, making it the oldest chocolate factory in Sicily. In the heart of Modica's centro storico, six generations of family history are preserved in this tiny sweets shop, in the same location where Francesco Bonajuto opened the doors in 1880. It's now under the loving care of Pierpaolo Ruta, and in addition to the immense menu of artisanal chocolate bars are local specialties like cannoli, hot chocolate, panatigghi chocolate meat pies, and honey-poached orange peels called aranciata.

SABADÌ

Corso San Giorgio, 105; tel. 0932/1912327; www.sabadi.it; 9:30am-7:30pm daily; 50g chocolate bars €4

Simone Sabaini moved from northern Italy's Veneto region to Modica in 2008 with the hopes of creating a high-quality organic chocolate in a city filled with multigenerational historic chocolate shops. Sabaini uses four types of natural sugar cane, highly rated Ecuadorian cacao, and Slow Food Presidium-certified specialty ingredients like mandarin oranges from Ciaculli, white pepper from Sarawak, and fleur de sel from Trapani. He is taking the international market by storm with an incredible product, packaged with style. His chocolate shop, Sabadì, is near the cathedral.

CAFFÈ DELL'ARTE

Corso Umberto I, 114; tel. 0932/943257; www.caffedellarte.it; 7am-1pm and 3:30pm-9pm Mon.-Sat., 7am-1pm and 4:30pm-midnight Sun.; 100g bars €1.50

For nearly 60 years, Ignazio Iacono, along with his wife Gina and their children, have had their family chocolate shop right in a prime location at the center of Corso Umberto I in Modica. Their chocolates are produced following the ancient Modican traditions.

CHOCOLATE SCHOOL AT CIOMOD

Casa Ciomod, Via Nazionale Modica Ispica; tel. 0932/455412; www.ciomod.com; €25 per person

Just outside town, Innocenzo Pluchino welcomes you into his farmhouse test kitchen for an immersion in the world of artisanal chocolate-making. His passion and dedication to the craft shines through in every product: The attention to detail with cocoa sourcing, innovative packaging, creative branding, and especially the high-quality ingredients all go hand in hand with the level of care that Innocenzo brings to this project. In Chocolate School, guests learn all about the history of Modica's chocolate, the origins and the production of cocoa, and the nutritional value, and can create a bar of chocolate to take home with them. Contact Casa Ciomod for reservations, pricing, and availability.

and DolceVita guesthouses even have their own pools. Their "slow living" philosophy savors the moment and allows guests to slip into another world, away from their daily routines and atmospheres.

Information and Services

- **Modica Tourist Information Center:** Corso Umberto I, 1431; tel. 346/6558227; www.comune.modica.gov.it/site/ufficio-turistico; 9am-1pm and 3pm-7pm Mon.-Sat.

Getting There and Around

Modica is located 35 minutes from **Noto** (21 mi/34 km), 1 hour from **Syracuse** (45 mi/72 km), and 15 minutes from **Ragusa** (10 mi/16.1 km), making it a convenient stop on a road trip through the southeastern corner

Inspector Montalbano

Scicli and its coastal hamlets have been used for the fictitious town of "Vigata," inspired by the stories of Andrea Camilleri in his Inspector Montalbano book series and featured in the coinciding film and television programs. Camilleri wrote the first Montalbano book in 1994 at the age of 70 and went on to create over 100 stories, of which only about 30 were translated into English. The Inspector Montalbano television series premiered in Italy in 1999 but gained popularity when it was televised in Australia and the UK. In 2012, *The Young Montalbano* spinoff caught the attention of a new audience, many of whom then became intrigued by the books and had the urge to visit the places noted in the stories.

Sunny Sicily (Piazza S. Antonio Abate, 7, Taormina; tel. 338/5296915; www.sunnysicily.com; 6-8-hour full-day experience; from €82 per person), based in Taormina, offers a tour with this mystery series as its theme. The In Search of Inspector Montalbano tour retraces the footsteps of the series' title character through the picturesque backdrops of these mystery stories in Scicli, Noto, Modica, and Ragusa Ibla.

of Sicily. Once arrived in Modica, it's easy to get around **on foot. Uncovered Sicily** (tel. 338/8726610; www.uncoveredsicily.com; 4-hour excursions €180/group) runs guided walking tours.

The bus, operated by **Azienda Siciliana Trasporti** (www.aziendasicilianatrasporti.it), takes 2 hours 40 minutes from Syracuse (from €7) and 40 minutes from Ragusa (from €2).

Modica Train Station

From Ragusa, train service with **Trenitalia** takes 24 minutes (www.trenitalia.com; €2); from Noto, it's a 1-hour train ride (€6.20); and from Syracuse, it's 1 hour 50 minutes (€9.20). It's a bit of a hike up to Modica's city center, a 25-minute walk (1 mi/1.6 km), but taxis are usually at the ready for the 6-minute drive.

SCICLI

The late Baroque town of Scicli in southeastern Sicily shares the recognition of being a UNESCO World Heritage Site along with the towns of the Val di Noto, including Caltagirone, Militello Val di Catania, Catania, Modica, Noto, Palazzolo Acreide, and Ragusa. It sits in a gorge, 20 minutes southwest of Modica and just north of the sandy beaches of Donnalucata and Sampieri. It's a town of 27,000 inhabitants, known for agriculture and specifically its greenhouses,

used for the production of fruits and vegetables to be exported all over Italy. Scicli is worth a visit when extensively exploring the southeastern corner of Sicily and can be much less crowded than its neighboring towns of Modica, Ragusa, or Noto. Italian novelist Elio Vittorini wrote about Scicli, calling it "perhaps the most beautiful city of the world."

Sights
Baroque Architecture

Take a walk along **Via Francesco Mormina Penna** to see one of Sicily's most beautiful avenues and a clear example of late Baroque period architecture. Sicilian Baroque architecture evolved in the 17th and 18th centuries, and can be easily recognized by its over-the-top, lavish, and decorative design with distinctive flourishes and curves. There is nothing discreet about it; this was a rich period and the style reflects that.

Gli Aromi Herb Farm

Contrada Santa Rosalia, Scicli; tel. 342/0616781; www. gliaromi.it; 7am-noon and 2pm-6pm Mon.-Fri., 7am-noon Sat. Apr.-Oct., 7am-noon and 2pm-5pm Mon.-Fri., 8am-noon Sat. Nov.-Mar., farm visits 8am-noon

Located 20 minutes (6 mi/9.7 km) south of Modica, Enrico Russino's herb farm is one of the most precious gardens in all of Sicily. You may feel like you are driving into the middle of nowhere, but it will be worth it. Upon arrival, you'll be amazed by this family-run plant nursery. The farm produces over 200 varieties of native Sicilian and tropical plants including colorful sage, thyme, lavender, rosemary, chamomile, passion fruit, and geraniums.

The **Emotional Olfactory Journey** (6pm; €30 per person) is a multisensory tour of the property through smell, sight, touch, and taste. The group weaves their way through ornamental, aromatic, and medicinal plants including unique fields of pineapple sage, lemon thyme, stevia, orange geranium, and bergamot mint with Enrico's wealth of knowledge and undeniably passionate guidance, before ending the experience with a light aperitivo.

Festivals and Events

Scicli is a town known for its many festivals celebrated throughout the year, including the **Carnaluvaru ra Stratanova** at the end of February; the medieval festival for **La Cavalcata di San Giuseppe** on March 19; extensive celebrations during Holy Week and the **Il Gioia,** the procession of Uomo Vivo on Easter Day; and the patron saint festival on the last Saturday of May for the **Festa delle Milizie.** August sees many festivals, with the cultural and theatrical celebration of the **Basole Di Luce** in early August; the **Infiorata** flower festival also taking place each August; and **Sagra delle Teste di Turco** at the end of August, which features a local dessert made of an enormous beignet cream puff filled with sweet ricotta cream and dusted with powdered sugar. During **Christmastime,** several nativity scenes are on display throughout the town for **La Via dei Presepi.**

Food
Ùmmara
Via Aleardi, 9; tel. 0932/841329; www.ummara.it
Revered for its natural wine selection, Ùmmara has been a staple in Scicli's dining scene since September of 2016. Local owner Giuseppe Fiorilla's focus has always been on

good-quality food that pairs well with the selection of wines. Ùmmara is an ideal choice for a fun and casual wine bar. The simple house-made dishes will nourish visitors into the night while taste-testing their way through a selection of over 300 unique bottles.

Ristorante Baqqalà
Piazza Angelo Ficili, 3; tel. 0932/931028; www. facebook.com/baqqala.scicli; 12:30pm-2:30pm and 7:30pm-11pm Sun., 12:30pm-3pm and 7:30pm-11pm Mon., 12:30pm-3pm and 7pm-11pm Tues. and Thurs.- Sat.; dishes from €15-22
In the city center of Scicli, Ristorante Baqqalà is the top destination for a seafood-focused meal. The friendly staff and locally sourced products ensure a pleasant dining experience at a reasonable price. From raw seafood starters to pastas and fresh fish entrées featuring red mullet, snapper, amberjack, or red Sicilian shrimp, Baqqalá offers a wide selection of traditional dishes and daily specials.

Nivera
Via Francesco Mormino Penna, 14; tel. 393/8383833; www.facebook.com/nivera.gelateria; €2-5
Located on the edge of the Piazza Municipio town square, Nivera offers some of the best gelato, fruit sorbets, and granita in Scicli. The fine craftmanship results in a high-end artisanal product made from fresh, local ingredients. Try its unique seasonal flavors like Sicilian prickly pear, Bronte pistachio, fig, ricotta, and carob.

Getting There
By Car
From **Modica,** take the SP54 state road heading southwest on SP54 for 20 minutes (6.5 mi/10.5 km) to Scicli. From **Ragusa,** the drive south to Scicli will take approximately 40 minutes (16 mi/26 km), following directions for the SS115 to SP94. Modica is on the way and can be used as a place to stop off on the drive to or from Scicli. From **Noto,** the drive will take just under an hour (27 mi/43 km), following the SS115 to SP45, SP43, SP96, SP75, and SP41into Scicli.

By Train

Traveling to Scicli by train is also an option. The historic town center has a **central station** on Corso Mazzini that is serviced by **TrenItalia** (www.trenitalia.com). When arriving in Scicli, the town's main churches and restaurants will be an additional 15-minute walk from the station. Direct trains from local towns such as **Modica** (11 minutes; €2.10), **Ragusa** (35 minutes; €3.70), **Noto** (1 hour; €5.20), and **Siracusa** (1 hour 40 minutes; €8.40) are available multiple times during the day.

Coastal Ragusa

The beach destinations south of Ragusa and Scicli are popular in summertime but remain much less crowded than the surrounding areas on the eastern coast in the province of Siracusa. The 11-mile-long (18-km) coastline has stretches of soft sand beaches, many of which are free to the public, that can be a great option for a beach day, especially during the shoulder seasons of May and September/October when they are more isolated. From Marina di Ragusa to Donnalucata, Sampieri, Marina di Modica, and Pozzallo, guests can explore this part of the south best by car on short trips from the more popular destinations like Noto, Modica, Ragusa, and even Siracusa.

Food plays a large role in the celebrations of the region, with specific festivals including a local cherry tomato festival at the seaside in Sampieri at the end of April, and the Sagra della Seppia, a celebration of cuttlefish dishes in mid-May in Donnalucata.

MARINA DI RAGUSA

The small seaside hamlet of Marina di Ragusa, set directly in front of the island of Malta on Sicily's southeastern coast, can be a quiet getaway for those staying in Ragusa or Noto. Guests heading into the province's winemaking region near Vittoria can combine a day trip to Marina di Ragusa for a swim or a seafront meal. Locals flock to this area in summertime, where they might even have a second home, while tourists tend to visit for the afternoon and stay overnight in a bigger town like Modica or Scicli.

Beaches
Spiaggia di Marina di Ragusa

Lungomare Andrea Doria, Marina di Ragusa; open 24 hours; free

The coastline in the province of Ragusa spans 37 miles (60 km) running from Pozzallo to Scoglitti. The central Marina di Ragusa beach is a great place to enjoy a seaside break. The golden-sand beaches are not overcrowded on weekdays and offer options at lido beach clubs like **Lido Azzurro 1953 Da Serafino** (tel. 0932/239522; www.locandadonserafino.it), where guests can enjoy a delicious seafood meal and rent daily beach beds and umbrellas (May-Sept., €30 for 2 beds and 1 umbrella). The Marina di Ragusa beach was awarded the Bandiera Blu recognition for its clean and clear waters, and features amenities like stationed lifeguards, a volleyball court, bars, gelaterias, restaurants, showers, and bathroom facilities.

Food
Vossia il Mare

Via Benedetto Brin, 2, Marina di Ragusa; tel. 0932/734101; www.vossiailmare.it; 12:30pm-3pm and 7:30pm-11pm Thurs.-Tues., 7:30pm-11pm Wed.; mains €12-20

This restaurant, just 650 feet (200 m) from the sea, features plates of fresh pesce crudo and bottles of natural wine. Dishes like ruby red shrimp, oysters on the half-shell, golden saffron pasta, and perfectly pink langoustines bring a burst of color to the white and blue dining room. This casual, Sicilian nautical-themed restaurant is a perfect choice for a light seaside lunch in the Marina di Ragusa.

Trattoria da Carmelo
Lungomare Andrea Doria, Marina di Ragusa; tel. 0932/239913; www.facebook.com/trattoriadacarmelo; 12:45pm-2:45pm and 7:30pm-11pm Tues., 12:30pm-3pm and 7:30pm-11pm Wed., 12:30pm-3pm and 7:45pm-10:30pm Thurs., 12:45pm-3pm and 7:30pm-11pm Fri.-Sat., 12:45pm-3pm and 7:30pm-10pm Sun.; mains €12-22

Here you'll find simple coastal cuisine featuring Sicilian ingredients like sea urchin, swordfish, Mediterranean red tuna, and sea bass. Stop by for the freshest seafood in a local trattoria with an elegant dining area overlooking the sea.

Accommodations
Mangiabove Guesthouse
Contrada Mangiabove; tel. 334/9300441; www.mangiabove.com; rooms from €159

This heavenly four-star hotel overlooking the sea near Marina di Ragusa can be an ideal stop for a few nights while exploring Sicily's Baroque southeastern corner. It is a fully renovated family farmhouse built at the end of the 1800s. Mangiabove has a contemporary look and includes all the comforts of an upscale resort with the attention and care of a small farm guesthouse.

With eight units to choose from and plenty of shared spaces, guests can select the one that fits their needs, which might include additional perks such as a terrace, patio, or courtyard. Each apartment has sea and countryside views, a kitchen, a private bathroom, heating and air-conditioning, television, and Wi-Fi. All guests have access to the library, communal outdoor kitchen with barbecue, and private outdoor infinity pool equipped with lounge chairs and umbrellas. A common room is meant to be shared and has been decked out with a fireplace, sofas, a coffee bar, a breakfast area and communal kitchen, an honesty bar, and a mini food shop where local products and basic staples can be

purchased. Cooking classes, airport transfers, bike rentals, boating or fishing excursions, and spa treatments can be organized upon request.

Getting There
When exploring the southern coast of eastern Sicily, the seafront town of Marina di Ragusa is conveniently located just a short drive from a few of the main towns that might be on your itinerary. A 30-minute (16.5 mi/27 km) drive from Ragusa Ibla is practically a straight shot south on SP25. From the rural winemaking area of Vittoria, the 14.5-mile (23.3-km) drive via SP18 along SP20 to SP124 and SP36 will take approximately 30 minutes. The route from Modica on the state road SP54 runs through Scicli and continues on SP95 to Marina di Ragusa for a total of about 40 minutes (16 mi/26 km). There is no train station on the coast in Marina di Ragusa, and most travelers will head to the beach town by car.

DONNALUCATA
Donnalucata is an ancient fishing village of about 5,000 inhabitants, founded in 1091 after Count Ruggero d'Altavilla defeated the Saracens. Its seafront, Marinella, is featured in the Commissario Montalbano television series. The area thrives on tourism, fishing, and greenhouse agriculture. Similar to the other parts of the southeastern Sicilian coast in the provinces of Ragusa and Siracusa, these destinations are most popular in summertime, when they fill with beachgoers.

Beaches
Spiaggia di Ponente
SP89/Viale della Repubblica, Donnalucata; open 24 hours; free

On the western edge of Donnalucata, the Ponente Beach offers a stretch of clean water and sandy shores, perfect for families with small children. There are shower facilities and free street parking, as well as places to eat and even wood-planked walkways for easy access down to the water.

Spiaggia Micenci

Via Marina, Donnalucata; open 24 hours; free

In summertime, guests flock to the Spiaggia Micenci in the seaside town of Donnalucata. Located on the eastern side of the village, this stretch of golden-sand beach is much larger than the Spiaggia di Ponente on the opposite side. Spiaggia Micenci has stones lined along the shore to break waves, but it can still be a bit more challenging for small children swimming here. Cool freshwater streams into the sea at the Fonte delle Ore springs. This part of the shore will be more crowded but also offers calm water that can provide a refreshing temperature shock in summertime when the seawater warms up. The shore is equipped with a basketball court, bocce pitch, volleyball court, sun chairs and umbrellas for rent, a bar, changing rooms, showers, and bathrooms; in high season, a lifeguard is on duty here.

Food

Save time to stop by **Blue Moon** (Via Casmene, 1; tel. 0932/938158; www.donna lucatabluemoon.com) for a gelato or granita after a day at the seaside.

Il Consiglio di Sicilia

Via Casmene, 79, Donnalucata; tel. 340/9448923; www.ilconsigliodisicilia.com; 12:30pm-3pm and 7:30pm-11pm daily; tasting menus from €35-60; dishes from €15-32

Open since 2008, in chef Antonio Cicero's grandmother's house, Il Consiglio di Sicilia has a welcoming atmosphere that is fueled by owner Roberta Corradin's warm Sicilian hospitality. The menu's creative, minimalistic dishes elevate the natural flavors of the region's locally sourced seafood. For a more casual experience, check out their new wine bar/shop around the corner, **La Grande Sete** (Piazza Francesco Crispi, 1; 11:30am-2:30pm and 6:30pm-11pm daily).

Getting There

Take the SP39 road from Scicli to Donnalucata to arrive in just 15 minutes (6 mi/9.7 km) by car. It will take only 15 minutes (6.6 mi/10.6 km) from Marina di Ragusa, following SP63 and SP127. From Ragusa, drive south toward Scicli on SS25 to SP81 and SP89, following signs for SP127 and Via Regina Margherita/SP119 to Donnalucata for a total of about 35 minutes (19.4 mi/31 km).

SPIAGGIA DI CAVA D'ALIGA

Via Frine, Scicli; open 24 hours; free

The sandy shores of Cava d'Aliga, a seaside resort town, are protected from the wind by two cliffs on either side of the beach. Bars and restaurants are available for refreshments, and the clear, shallow waters are ideal for snorkeling. There are numerous beach club establishments nearby, equipped with sunbeds, umbrellas, and showers. It is also possible to rent pedal boats or canoes for the day.

Getting There

From Donnalucata, drive for approximately 15 minutes (5.6 mi/9 km) by taking SP119 to SP127, and SSP39 and SP84 to Via Madame Curiè, where you will see signs for Cava d'Aliga. From Ragusa, you can drive through Modica and Scicli, stopping off for some sightseeing then heading south to the coast, or take a faster route passing through Donnalucata, which will take about 45 minutes total.

SPIAGGIA DI SAMPIERI

Str. Demanio Forestale, Sampieri; open 24 hours; free

This is one of the most popular beaches in the Val di Noto area and one of the most beautiful landscapes on the southern coast of Ragusa. Sampieri shows up as the backdrop in several episodes of the Inspector Montalbano TV series.

The 1.9-mile-long (3.1-km) stretch of fine-grained shoreline is surrounded by sand dunes and a pine forest, which provides some shaded areas during the height of summer. Additional services include lifeguards on duty in summertime, paid parking lots nearby, and free showers that can be used by daily beach-goers. Try visiting on weekdays for a smaller crowd, especially in July and August.

1: Donnalucata 2: Spiaggia di Sampieri

Beach Club
Pata Pata
Via Miramare; tel. 0932/1846510; www.

patapatasampieri.com; 8am-midnight daily

Rent umbrellas and beach lounge chairs at the Pata Pata beach club and stop by for live music, DJ sets, an aperitivo, or a lunch break.

Getting There

Continue your beach day with a 5-minute drive (2.6 mi/4.2 km) on SP65 and Viale delle Pace from Cava d'Aliga to the Spiaggia di Sampieri. The 50-minute drive (23.7 mi/38 km) south from Ragusa passes through Scicli following SS115, SP94, and SP38 to Scicli, then SP40 to Via Sant'Elena and Via Miramare to the beach. From Noto, the 40-minute drive (26.5 mi/43 km) takes you along SS115 to the A18/E45 highway to SP66 in Modica. Follow the exit toward Marina di Modica/Sampieri until Via Miramare.

Background

The Landscape

GEOGRAPHY

The roughly triangular-shaped island off the toe of the Italian peninsula, Sicily is separated from the mainland by the thin Strait of Messina (only about 2 mi/3 km wide at its narrowest point) on its northeastern-most point. The island of Sicily is 9,927 square miles (25,711 sq km) in size, not including the area of its offshore islands, like the Aegadian and Aeolian archipelagoes and the minor islands of Pantelleria, Lampedusa, Linosa, and Ustica. The varied landscapes include mountainous areas dominated by the behemoth that is Mount

Etna, standing guard over the eastern side of the island, rolling hills in the entroterra countryside, and rough coasts along the shores mostly made up of rocky beaches and a handful of sandy coastlines. Sicily is the largest island in the Mediterranean Sea, which made it an extremely strategic position for cultures to conquer for centuries.

Coast

Covering 10,000 square miles (26,000 sq km), the island's 930-mile (1,500-km) coastline (longer if you include the sub-archipelagoes) is bordered by the Tyrrhenian Sea to the north, the Ionian Sea to the east, and the Mediterranean Sea to the south. Sicily's year-round warm weather and beautiful coastline make it a popular destination for travelers within Italy as well as abroad—not to mention its budget-friendly travel offerings.

Volcanoes and Volcanic Islands

Mount Etna (10,922 ft/3,329 m) is the largest active volcano in Europe and is part of a long volcanic chain, stretching north along Sicily's east coast to the Aeolian Islands, which include the famous volcanoes of Stromboli and Vulcano. This volcanic region of Italy comprises active, dormant, and extinct volcanoes.

CLIMATE

Sicily has a subtropical Mediterranean climate: In general, winters are mild (64°F/18°C on average with lows of 50-59°F/10-15°C), and summers are hot and dry (75-85°F/24-29°C). Limited annual rainfall reaches a maximum of 23 inches per year, with the wettest months

being October-December. Destinations at higher elevations, such as Mount Etna and the Madonie Mountains, can have cooler temperatures year-round. On Mount Etna, temperatures can even drop down to 10°F (-12°C). The Madonie Mountains, with average winter temperatures of 31°F (-1C°) and average summer temperatures of 63°F (17°C), get enough snow to boast a ski resort, Piano Battaglia. Snow is also possible on Mount Etna.

Coastal areas, which figure prominently in most trips to Sicily, start to get "beach weather" around April/May through September/October, which coincides with the period when most businesses are open in the coastal towns and on smaller islands. July and August are the hottest months, although in recent years, temperatures have been rising significantly and the warm summer season has stretched from June through September.

ENVIRONMENTAL ISSUES

Many of the potential threats and environmental issues Sicily is facing are related to climate change. Temperature changes and the reduction of four unique growing seasons affect the agricultural business on the island. Wildfires and specifically arson have become an issue in recent years. Sicily's dry climate, especially in summer months, makes the island susceptible to destructive damage during these periods. Extreme weather patterns like drought, torrential rains, and strong dry winds coming up from Africa are all a threat to keeping a harmonious environment on an island with continuously changing weather patterns.

Previous: Aegadian island landscape.

Plants and Animals

VEGETATION

Sicily is dotted with forests of beech, chestnut, and pine. Some of the oldest chestnut trees in Europe exist in the mountainous, inland, forested areas of Sicily. Around the island, visitors may also see carob trees, with their bean-like fruit pods; dwarf palms, a hallmark of beachy destinations; wild fennel on the sides of the roads; and various edible bitter greens and wild cardoons in the countryside. Olive trees, almond trees, and grapevines are also seen throughout Sicily and serve an important agricultural purpose. Capers thrive on the Aeoliean Islands and in Pantelleria.

The general term for the traditional plants growing especially on the minor islands and along Sicily's coastline is "macchia mediterranea." This Mediterranean scrub includes plants and trees such as myrtle, heather, strawberry tree, broom, rockrose, and hearty dry aromatic herbs like rosemary, oregano, and thyme.

Rare plants to watch out for include *Silene hicesiae,* a rare purple flowering plant in the carnation family that is native to the highest point on the Aeolian island of Panarea.

BIRDS AND WILDLIFE

Sicily is not a destination known for wildlife-watching, but visitors might be interested in some of the bird species that make their home here. It's possible to see greater flamingos in some coastal areas of Sicily. In spring and fall, migrating flamingos stop in Pantelleria, the Vendicari Nature Reserve, and the salt pans south of Trapani. The Trapani salt pans are a good spot for birders year-round, hosting other migrating birds like gray parrots, wild ducks, and herons. There is a population of peregrine falcons on the Aegadian island of Marettimo.

MARINE LIFE

With the array of seafood available at Sicilian restaurants and markets, it's no surprise that the waters around Sicily are home to an abundance of sea creatures. Fish like red mullet, mackerel, grouper, seabream, amberjack, and scorpion fish, as well as sea anemones, seafans, and endangered colorful corals, can be seen around Lo Zingaro Nature Reserve and the Aeolian island of Filicudi, among other spots. Fin whales migrate off the coast of Sicily, and it's also possible to spot *Stenella* spotted dolphins, sea turtles, starfish, and sea urchins.

History

EARLY HISTORY

Sicily's earliest inhabitants—the Elymians in western Sicily, the Sicani in central Sicily, and the Sicels (where the name Sicily comes from) in eastern Sicily—were groups who came to the island from neighboring lands. Later, Phoenicians settled parts of western Sicily, including Palermo, in 734 BCE. Phoenician ruins on the island of Mozia near Marsala can still be seen today.

MAGNA GRAECIA

The 8th century BCE saw the establishment of powerful Greek colonies around Sicily—this period of colonization, which also included other parts of southern Italy, is known as Magna Graecia. Greek settlements on the island included Akragas, later known as Agrigento, where the magnificent remains now known as Valle dei Templi can still be found. Syracuse was Magna Graecia's most important and beautiful city, with the historic center concentrated on the island of Ortigia, powerful enough to even defeat the Athenians in the Peloponnesian War in the 5th century BCE.

ROMANS

Roman expansion brought about the end of Magna Graecia in the 4th century BCE. After taking over the area around Neapolis in the 4th century, Roman expansion continued slowly southward. The main obstacle to Roman domination at the time was the Carthaginians, led by the renowned general Hannibal, who stacked up many important victories. Only Syracuse, leveraging its power, prosperity, and alliances with the Carthaginians, retained some sort of Greek independence a bit longer, but it too was eventually sacked and conquered in 212 BCE.

In many cases, the Romans built upon or repurposed Greek constructions, seen especially in the amphitheater in Taormina, which went from hosting plays by famous Greek writers to being filled with water to stage fake naval battles. Sicily was also considered an important breadbasket for the Roman empire, producing enormous quantities of wheat, olive oil, and wine during this time.

The Roman Empire declined in the early centuries of the Common Era, and its territories were won by various tribal powers, such as the Franks and Vandals. The Byzantines took hold in the 6th century CE, and the influence of the Byzantine Empire can be seen in many buildings in Sicily, especially in Palermo's main cathedral and its rival in nearby Monreale.

ARAB RULE

From the 9th-11th centuries, Sicily was dominated by the Arabs, who established an Islamic caliphate on the island. The Islamic influence is deeply felt on Sicily, from buildings like the Palazzo Normanni's peculiar mix of Byzantine, Arab, and Norman architecture, to regional dishes (like couscous) not seen elsewhere in Italy. The Arabs also introduced

new irrigation techniques and brought crops like citrus, chickpeas, sesame seeds, eggplants, and artichokes. This influence is still reflected in the cuisine of Sicily with the presence of sweet-and-sour dishes and couscous on the west coast, particularly in the province of Trapani.

NORMANS AND SWABIANS

The Normans eventually expelled all the Muslims from Sicily, in the course of conquering the rest of southern Italy between the 10th and 11th centuries. Sicily was conquered in 1071. What came to be called the **Kingdom of Sicily,** which then included modern-day Campania, Puglia, and Sicily, went on to become one of the most powerful and wealthy states in Europe at the time. The Normans were relatively tolerant rulers for the time, for the most part allowing southern Italy's mix of Arabs, Jews, and Christians to coexist, and most of the fortified castles seen throughout the region owe their construction to the Norman period.

Many of these castles were later expanded upon by the Swabians, who took over in 1194. The Swabian king of Sicily, Frederick II of the Hohenstaufen dynasty from Germany, has a mixed legacy: He founded the University of Naples in 1224, promoted a literary movement known as the Sicilian School from his court in Palermo, and constructed lasting buildings. But he also expelled all Muslims who remained from the kingdom, and got into a conflict with the Roman Catholic papacy, which eventually led to the Hohenstaufens' ouster.

FRENCH AND SPANISH RULE

Upon Frederick II's death in 1250, there was something of a power vacuum in Sicily and southern Italy, eventually filled by the Angevins of France, who were hand-selected by Pope Urban IV (who had long opposed Swabian rule) to take over. The Kingdom of Sicily was divided in two when Charles I of Anjou arrived in the region in 1266 and was crowned king. This was the beginning of a centuries-long period in which Sicily passed hands between different ruling dynasties of France and Spain. After decades of squabbling, the island of Sicily went to Frederick II of Aragon (Spain). In 1504, Spanish King Ferdinand III took power, beginning about 200 years of Spanish rule in Sicily, largely under the Hapsburg dynasty. This Spanish period is still evident in Sicily's unique styles of architecture—especially the Spanish-influenced Sicilian Baroque style of Noto, Ragusa, and other towns around the Catania area—as well as the low-temperature chocolate-making traditions in Modica, which leave the chocolate with a crisp bite due to sugar crystals that were not melted.

Devastating earthquakes and eruptions of Mount Etna rocked eastern Sicily in the late 17th century and destroyed much of Catania and other nearby towns. It was during this period, when corruption took hold of much of the region, that criminal groups formed and grew in power, forming the roots of the modern-day Sicilian mafia. Control of Sicily continued to change hands over the course of the 17th-early 19th centuries, at times going to Austria and Britain.

ITALIAN UNIFICATION AND THE 20TH CENTURY

Sicily resisted efforts to bring the island into a unified Italian state. Garibaldi set off from Genoa with a ragtag team of volunteers who were able to capture Palermo and the rest of Sicily with little violence. Sicily did not play a large role in World War I, but in the postwar period, during the rise of Mussolini and fascism in Italy, Sicily returned to its roots as a breadbasket for the nation, with Mussolini pushing the various regions to ramp up their agricultural production. Worried about the potential challenge the mafia might present to his regime, the dictator also made some progress cracking down on organized crime in the Italian south.

In World War II, Italy was initially part of the Axis powers, and Allied forces successfully invaded Sicily in July 1943. By this time, Mussolini and the Axis powers' decline was evident. Later that year, Italy switched sides in the war, joining the Allied powers.

After the war, in 1946, Italians voted in the Italian Republic and adopted a new constitution. Sicily retained its status as an autonomous region.

Government and Economy

GOVERNMENT

Italy is a parliamentary republic, governed by a head of state (president), legislative branch (Parliament), executive branch (prime minister), and judicial branch. Sicily is one of the country's 20 regions, which have a great deal of control over their own legislation; and as one of five regions in Italy with special autonomy, Sicily has a greater degree of individual legislative, administrative, and financial power.

Sicily (whose capital is Palermo) tends to be more center-right. Renato Schifani has been the Sicilian president since 2022.

ECONOMY

There are significant economic disparities between various Italian regions. The gap between the northern and southern Italian economy, evident since Italian unification in the late 19th century, has deep roots, from a feudalistic social system that retained its hold of southern Italy to the dominance of the mafia in the region. It is estimated that 70 percent of unemployed Italians reside in the southern part of the country. That said, this economic disparity is beginning to change, with a GDP growing at almost double the rate of northern Italy's, and increased investment in infrastructure and tourism.

Historical Timeline

8th century BCE	Greek founding of Syracuse, which went on to become Magna Graecia's most important city.
413 BCE	Syracuse, allied with Sparta, defeats Athens in the Peloponnesian War.
4th century BCE	Seven temples are built in Akragas, modern-day Agrigento, on the site now known as Valle dei Templi.
212 BCE	Syracuse, Sicily's last Greek stronghold, falls to the Romans, putting all of Sicily under Roman control.
9th-11th centuries	Sicily is under Arab rule.
1071	Normans conquer Sicily, expelling the Islamic caliphate from the island.
1302	Charles I of Anjou splits the Kingdom of Sicily from the Kingdom of Naples.
1669	Mount Etna's largest recorded eruption.
1693	Devastating earthquakes rock Catania and much of eastern Sicily.
1787	Goethe visits Sicily, making it a mandatory stop on the European Grand Tour.
1799	King Ferdinand IV flees to Palermo.
1860	Garibaldi's Expedition of the Thousand Lands in Sicily, hoping to unite Sicily and Naples with the Kingdom of Italy.
1861	Italian city-states and regions unify into a single nation governed by a constitutional monarchy.
1946	Italians choose to become a democratic republic in a national referendum.

Sicily is known for its agricultural production of wine, including unique volcanic wines grown on the slopes of Mount Etna, sweet wines like malvasia from the Aeolian Islands and passito from Pantelleria, and fortified marsala from western Sicily. Sicily's economic centers include Palermo, one of the major ports for cargo transport and one of the Mediterranean's busiest port cities; and Trapani, located on Sicily's western coast, which is the sixth-largest port in Italy, important for salt production and tuna fishing and known for its sea salt flats, fresh seafood, and excellent white wines.

Tourism plays an increasingly greater role in Sicily's economy. Sicily is in the top 10 most popular destinations in Italy.

People and Culture

DEMOGRAPHY

Just under 5 million people live in Sicily. The largest population center is the capital city of Palermo (680,000 inhabitants). As of 2006, foreign-born citizens in Palermo made up only 2.21 percent, coming from 127 different countries including Bangladesh, Sri Lanka, Romania, Ghana, Philippines, Morocco, and Tunisia. Since 2000, the foreign population has tripled to approximately 23,300. Palermo prides itself on its increasing diversity. Roman Catholicism is the main religion in Sicily. For the last 500 years, there have been no synagogues in Sicily; while one in three migrants to Italy is Muslim, there are several mosques, one of which is the oldest in Italy.

LANGUAGE

Italian is the main language spoken in Sicily. In many Italian cities, people in the hospitality industry may speak English, but Italians appreciate when you at least try to speak their language. Simple phrases like buongiorno ("good morning"), buonasera ("good evening"), and grazie mille ("thank you very much") will make your travels more enjoyable and sometimes improve customer service as well. They are always happy that you gave it a try.

In addition to Italian, Sicily is rich with local dialects such as Siciliano, which will be very difficult to understand, even to foreigners familiar with Italian. That said, most Sicilians will switch to speaking in Italian when addressing tourists. English skills are still fairly limited on the island, especially in small villages, but you'll find that within the hospitality and tourism industries, there will be English speakers to assist with your travel needs.

Sicilian

Sicilian is distinct enough from standard Italian to be considered its own separate language, not only a dialect. The story of the Sicilian dialect is the story of the island itself, influenced by Ancient Greek, Arabic, Norman, Germanic, and Spanish languages. Some Sicilian words sound so different from standard Italian that even native speakers may find themselves scratching their heads: For example, standard Italian O's turn to U's, B's are often turned into V's in Sicilian (broccoli to vrocculu), G's fall silent, and double L's become D's (bella to bedda). Today, there are estimated to be over five million Sicilian speakers worldwide. At times words in Sicilian will be more closely related to Spanish than Italian. When Sicilians emigrated to other countries, they often kept speaking in their local dialect. Sicilian Americans, for example, even at the third or fourth generation, will often know Sicilian words or phrases used in their families instead of formal Italian.

LITERATURE AND PHILOSOPHY

Sicily's associations with literature date back to classical times. Some of the adventures in Homer's *Odyssey* are associated with locations in Sicily, including the Faraglioni dei Ciclopi, off Sicily's eastern coast. The great Greek mathematician, Archimedes, was born in the Italian town of Syracuse.

A literary community known as the Sicilian School, founded in the 13th century, had a marked influence on writers like Dante Alighieri (1265-1321); their poetry is credited with the coining of the term Doce Stil Novo, or "sweet new style," and helping in the creation of the modern Italian language.

Sicily's most famous writer is probably Giuseppe Tomasi di Lampedusa, whose novel published in 1958, *The Leopard,* takes place during the Risorgimento movement to unite the Italian peninsula. On the lighter side, Sicilian author Andrea Camilleri's Inspector Salvo Montalbano series, written between 1994 and 2020, is tremendously popular across Italy and has been adapted into an extremely popular TV series.

ARCHITECTURE
Greek and Roman Ruins

In Sicily, the sites of Selinunte, Segesta, and Valle dei Templi offer Greek ruins as spectacular as any you might find in Athens. The Villa Romana del Casale, covered with around 16,145 square feet (3,500 sq m) of mosaics, is a sprawling example of an elite ancient Roman's country home. Speckled across the island, remnants of the past have become the highlights of present-day travel planning. No trip to Sicily is complete without at least one stop at the Valley of the Temples in Agrigento, the ancient Greek theater of Taormina, the limestone Orecchio di Dionisio in Siracusa, or a quick look at the Tempio di Apollo on the island of Ortigia.

Baroque Architecture

The Classic Sicilian Baroque decorated architectural style developed in the 1600-1700s under Spanish rule. Destructive 17th-century earthquakes in Sicily gave builders of the time an opportunity to rebuild towns like Noto and Modica in the lavish Baroque style, highlighting techniques like inlaid colored marble and concave or convex facades.

In 2002, the Late Baroque Towns of the Val di Noto were recognized as a UNESCO World Heritage Site. These towns include Scicli, Caltagirone, Militello Val di Catania, Catania, Modica, Noto, Palazzolo Acreide, and Ragusa. **Noto** is particularly notable and is considered the capital of Baroque. While the aforementioned towns have a larger concentration of monuments made in this style, Baroque architecture can be found in other parts of the island, including Palermo's octagonal Quattro

Canti piazza and the Chiesa del Purgatorio in Marsala.

Luxurious Palaces

In Palermo, the Palazzo dei Normanni is a stunning example of a royal residence, first constructed in the 9th century but renovated and expanded through the centuries. Noble palaces including Palazzo Biscari in Catania and Palazzo Borgia del Casale in Ortigia add to the hidden charm of digging a bit deeper with your travels in Sicily. Noble homes have been renovated into hotels or bed-and-breakfasts, or are open as historical building sites for guided visits. Many off-the-beaten-path private palaces will only be open for the annual Le Vie dei Tesori festival each autumn, although private licensed guides can be your connection to get into these hard-to-visit places.

DECORATIVE ARTS AND CRAFTS

The creative talents of generations of artisans have always brought an artistic touch to daily life in Sicily, from basket weaving to woodworking, silversmithing to pottery. **Ceramic production** is traditional in the entire area, especially terra-cotta, ceramics, and hand-painted maioliche tiles. The towns that are most famous for their ceramics in Sicily are Caltagirone in the province of Catania, Sciacca near Agrigento, and Santo Stefano di Camastra outside Messina.

MUSIC AND THEATER

Nineteenth-century opera composer Vincenzo Bellini, best known for his opera *Norma,* was born in Catania, in Sicily.

A Sicilian tradition, it's still possible to take in the unique experience of **puppet opera** (opera dei pupi) in Palermo, an art form that emerged in the region in the early 19th century. Though there are only a few performers keeping this theatrical tradition alive, a visit to the Museo Internazionale delle Marionette Antonio Pasqualino is a great way to get some background on opera dei pupi and find out where you can see one in action.

While there's no shame in enjoying being serenaded by the *Godfather* theme song played on an accordion during your Sicilian holiday, contemporary musicians such as Levante, Carmen Consoli, Colapesce Dimartino, Tinturia, Roy Paci, Alessio Bondì, and La Rappresentante di Lista have also been making their names known outside the island.

Essentials

Transportation

GETTING THERE

Sicily can be reached by train, bus, ferry, and rental car from mainland Italy, but flying is the fastest and most convenient way to arrive on the island.

By Air

Sicily has two main airports: **Aeroporto di Palermo Falcone e Borsellino** (PMO; Cinisi; tel. 800/541-880; www.aeroportodipalermo.it), also known as Punta Raisi, in Palermo and **Aeroporto di Catania**

Fontanarossa (CTA; Via Fontanarossa; tel. 095/723-9111; www.aeroporto.catania.it) in Catania. Of the two, the Catania airport is larger, but there are no direct flights from North America to either airport. Both are well connected to airports across Europe and Italy.

From North America

Getting to Sicily from North America involves at least one stop at a European hub, such as Rome, Amsterdam, Munich, or Frankfurt, before heading to Palermo or Catania. **ITA Airways** (www.ita-airways.com); **KLM Royal Dutch Airlines** (www.klm.com), which code shares with Delta; and **Lufthansa** (www.lufthansa.com) are among the airlines that fly between North America and Sicily. Trips between New York City and Catania take about 14 hours, including the layover.

From Europe and the UK

It is easy to reach Sicily from various cities in Italy, with multiple flights per day from Rome, Milan, and Venice; most flights take less than 2 hours. Among the airlines serving Palermo and Catania from within Italy are **ITA Airways** (www.ita-airways.com) and budget carrier **Ryanair** (www.ryanair.com).

Ryanair and fellow budget airline **easyJet** (www.easyjet.com) make daily nonstop flights to Palermo and Catania from London and other major European cities. Major European carriers, such as **British Airways** (www.britishairways.com), **KLM** (www.klm.com), **Lufthansa** (www.lufthansa.com), and **Air France** (www.airfrance.fr) also fly to Sicily from their respective hubs. Flights between Europe and Sicily take about 3-3.5 hours.

From Australia and New Zealand

Flying from Australia and New Zealand to Sicily is a lengthy proposition, usually involving at least two stops and being in transit for 24-36 or more hours. **Qantas** (www.qantas.com), **Air New Zealand** (www.airnewzealand.com), **Lufthansa** (www.lufthansa.com), **Aegean Air** (https://en.aegeanair.com), **Singapore Airlines** (www.singaporeair.com), and **Emirates** (www.emirates.com) offer routes with 2-3 stops between Sydney or Auckland and Sicily, usually with a leg on ITA Airways.

From South Africa

It's possible to fly to Palermo from Johannesburg with just one layover on **Swiss International Airlines** (www.swiss.com) or **Air France** (www.airfrance.fr), with flights taking about 14-15 hours, while returning to South Africa takes about 5-7 hours longer. Flights to Catania involve two layovers for around 20 hours of travel—**Ethiopian Air** (www.ethiopianairlines.com) and **Lufthansa** (www.lufthansa.com) operate along that route.

By Train

Traveling by train, run by **Trenitalia** (www.trenitalia.com), from Naples to Sicily usually takes about 6 hours. From Napoli Centrale, transfer at Salerno (sometimes farther south at Paola) to make it the rest of the way to Villa San Giovanni at the tip of mainland Italy. There, the train gets loaded onto a ferry to reach Messina on Sicily. From Messina, you can continue on by train to Palermo (3 hours), Taormina (1 hour), Catania (2 hours), or Syracuse (3 hours).

By Bus

FlixBus (www.flixbus.com) and **Itabus** (www.itabus.it) operate bus routes from mainland Italy to Sicily. The trip from Naples to Messina takes about 8 hours.

By Ferry

GNV (www.gnv.it) and **Tirrenia** (https://en.tirrenia.it) run ferries from Naples to the **port** of Palermo (www.adsppalermo.it), located on the western side of the city. Trips take

10.5-12.5 hours and cost €47.50-62.50 for passengers without vehicles.

The year-round, overnight ferry from Napoli to Palermo is organized by **Traghetti Lines** (www.traghettilines.it; seats €31, cabins €67, car transport €14-30). Tickets for the 11-hour trip can be reserved in advance online or in the Massa port of Naples ticket counter.

By Car

It's probably easier to fly to Sicily, then rent a car once you're on the island, rather than taking a car ferry over the Strait of Messina with a vehicle. Keep in mind that some rental companies do not allow rental cars to go on ferries.

GETTING AROUND

Though trains and buses reach larger cities in Sicily, driving may be a better option for travelers with limited time who want to see much of the island.

By Plane

Within the island of Sicily, it is not necessary to travel by air. If visiting the island of Pantelleria, part of the autonomous region of Sicily, the most efficient way to get there is to fly.

By Train

Most cities and some towns have a train station serving **Trenitalia** (www.trenitalia.it) trains. Trenitalia routes on the island of Sicily include:

- Palermo to Agrigento (through the center of the island, not traveling down the west coast)
- Trapani to Marsala
- Palermo to Messina
- Messina to Syracuse
- Syracuse to Ragusa

Here are some common train journeys, with station names, travel times, and prices:

- Between Palermo and Cefalù—Palermo Centrale to Cefalù (50 minutes, €6.80)
- Between Palermo and Agrigento through the center of the island—Palermo Centrale to Agrigento Centrale (2 hours 55 minutes, with one change in Roccapalumba-Alia, €10.90)
- Between Palermo and Messina—Palermo Centrale to Messina Centrale (2 hours 45 minutes, €15.50)
- Between Palermo and Milazzo—Palermo Centrale to Milazzo (2 hours 30 minutes, €13.60)
- Between Messina and Catania—Messina Centrale to Catania Centrale (1 hour 48 minutes, €9.20)
- Between Messina and Syracuse—Messina Centrale to Siracusa (2 hours 45 minutes, €12.80)
- Between Syracuse and Noto—Siracusa to Noto (38 minutes, €4.60)

Note that getting from Palermo to west coast towns like Trapani and Marsala is not practical by train; taking a bus is faster for travel to those cities.

Not run by Trenitalia, an additional regional train is the **Circumetnea** (www.circumetnea.it), which runs from Catania to Mount Etna, stopping at small villages around the volcano. Note that taxi services from these stations will not be readily available, it's best to use when traveling with a bicycle (when permitted) for cycling adventures or when a local guide or friend is going to meet you there.

By Car and Scooter

Renting a car for your time in Sicily can be a great option, offering maximum flexibility and the chance to discover tiny villages and beautiful countryside off the beaten path.

Car rental agencies are available at most airports and in larger cities, and off-season prices for rental cars are extremely affordable. Major international rental companies like

Hertz, Avis, and Budget are present in Sicily, as are smaller local companies.

Outside of large cities like Palermo or Catania, where driving is not generally recommended, it is easy to drive in Sicily, since the terrain is generally flat. That said, give yourself extra time on road trips, as many small regional roads will not be smoothly paved. Inland Sicily is famous for seemingly perpetual construction and detours.

If driving yourself, bring an international GPS of your own. Renting them through the agency will be expensive. In off-the-grid locations, cell service might be limited, so don't depend solely on your cell phone for directions, though the Google Maps app has a great option to download regional maps offline.

Renting a scooter while traveling in Sicily is only advised if you have previous experience driving a scooter. The traffic in larger cities will be hectic, and very close attention should be taken while following the local laws and being aware of your surroundings. Driving a scooter on the smaller islands or in rural parts of the island can also be a bit dangerous for an amateur driver, as the roads will not be lit or paved as well as you might expect in other parts of Italy or abroad.

Rules and Documentation

Rental car agencies will have requirements listed on their websites; take a look before reserving your car in advance. The requiremnts include a valid driver's license from your home country, an international driver's permit for non-EU citizens, an identification card such as a passport, and a credit card for the payment and incidental charges. Additional fees will be incurred when the driver is under 25 years old and when you request an automatic transmission vehicle. Follow the regional laws and signage for speed limits and never drive under the influence of drugs or alcohol.

Driving Tips

The best advice for driving in Italy and specifically Sicily is to give yourself additional time to make it from point A to point B. Take into consideration the scenic sights worth stopping off for, making time for refreshment breaks and refueling, and factor in extra time on rural roads and even a smidge extra in case you get off track.

By Bus

There are myriad bus companies operating in various regions of Sicily, but some of the most common are **Interbus** (www.interbus.it) and Azienda Siciliana Trasporti, or **AST** (www.aziendasicilianatrasporti.it). Although many trips between cities are more comfortable and efficient on trains, it is better to take the bus if traveling from Palermo to Trapani or Marsala.

Public transportation on islands and other smaller destinations, where it exists, is served by buses.

By Boat

Palermo's **port** (www.adsppalermo.it) is the point of arrival and departure for hydrofoils to the Aeolian Islands in the summer. Ferries to the Aeolian Islands operated by **Liberty Lines** (www.libertylines.it) and **Siremar** (https://carontetourist.it) also depart from Milazzo and Messina. To get to the Aegadian Islands, you'll need to depart from Trapani or Marsala (ferries also operated by Liberty Lines). It is best to buy tickets directly from the ferry line's website ahead of time. There are often information and ticketing booths at the ferry terminals, but they will be crowded in the high season and your preferred route might be sold out by the time you get there.

By Taxi

Taxis can be found throughout Sicily, including on most offshore islands, and can be convenient for people traveling without a car. Clearly marked taxi stands or a few cars on standby will most likely be available right at the main harbor where the ferry arrives on the small islands. Smaller towns in rural Sicily will not have taxis waiting when you arrive, but they will come when scheduled ahead or upon arrival, with a slight delay.

Visas and Officialdom

PASSPORTS AND VISAS

U.S., UK, Canadian, Australian, and **New Zealand** travelers do not need a visa to enter Italy, but in 2024, the ETIAS registration system (https://travel-europe.europa.eu/etias_en) is to go into effect, and visitors from visa-exempt countries will need to apply for authorization to enter Italy (and other European Union countries). Passports should be valid for six months after your departure date from the EU.

EU citizens have no visa or registration requirements to enter Italy. For travelers from **South Africa,** a Schengen Visa (€80 for adults) is required to enter Italy.

For more information, visit Italy's **Ministry of Foreign Affairs website** (http://vistoperitalia.esteri.it).

CONSULATES

For emergencies while abroad or to report lost or stolen passports, call the **U.S. Department of State** (tel. 888/407-4747 from the United States, 202/501-4444 from other countries; 8am-8pm EST Mon.-Fri.). The majority of foreign embassies and consulates in Italy are located in Rome. There is a **U.S. Consulate in Palermo** (Via Giovan Battista Vaccarini, 1). For emergencies, call 081/583-8111, which is a 24-hour hotline based in Naples.

CUSTOMS
Declarations

When entering Italy/EU, visitors must declare and pay duties on:

- Over €10,000 cash
- More than 1 liter alcohol
- More than 2 liters wine
- More than 200 cigarettes
- More than 250 grams tobacco

Meat and other animal products cannot be brought into Italy/EU.

Visit the following for customs regulations for reentering these countries:

- **U.S. Department of State:** www.state.gov
- **Canadian Border Services Agency:** www.cbsa-asfc.gc.ca
- **Australian Department of Immigration and Border Protection:** www.border.gov.au

Festivals and Events

From moving religious processions to gastronomic events, festivals offer a unique chance for visitors to experience local life and traditions in Sicily. There are many festivals throughout the year in this region. Here are a few highlights to mark on your calendar.

PALERMO
Zagara Festival
Mar. and Oct.

This three-day, semi-annual festival celebrating the zagara citrus flower takes place in the University of Palermo's Botanical Garden (Orto Botanico dell'Università di Palermo).

Ballarò Buskers
end of Oct.

Artists, bands, clowns, acrobats, jugglers, and dancers take to the streets of Palermo's Ballarò neighborhood, creating a lively atmosphere with music, parades, and other performances.

Le Vie dei Tesori

weekends late Sept.-Nov. and around Christmas

Palermo is the locus of this cultural heritage festival, where private buildings are opened to the public, but other cities around the island also participate.

CATANIA AND VICINITY

Festa di Sant'Agata

Feb. 5

One of the largest and most popular religious festivals in the world, the grand procession of Sant'Agata's silver reliquary through the sites of Catania is a sight to see.

SYRACUSE

Infiorata Flower Festival

third Sun. of May

The Infiorata Flower Festival and the Baroque historical parade in Noto is an annual celebration of spring. Since 1980, natural mosaics have been laid out on the town's main avenue every May to create a handmade tapestry of tiny, colorful flower petals.

Ortigia Sound System Music Festival

end of July

An international electronic music festival in the timeless city of Syracuse.

Recreation

BEACHES

No trip to Sicily is complete without a stop at the beach, especially in summertime. Most beaches found around the island will be rocky or pebbled, not smooth and sandy. Free public beaches are open 24/7 and tend to be more crowded. Private beach clubs can often be recognized by lines of umbrellas and beach chairs. These will incur a cost for the day that ranges from €10-20 per person on average. Sand beaches are ideal for traveling with small children, those with limited mobility, and elderly travelers. For the adventurous traveler in search of the rocky, hard-to-reach spots for a dip, make sure to plan accordingly, bringing your necessities for the day including water and protective footwear. Here, you will also swim at your own risk since there are no lifeguards on duty.

Food

Sicily is a melting pot of flavors. Each dish tells a story of the history of the island, with ingredients brought to Europe by way of Sicily from the Greeks, Arabs, Normans, and Spaniards. Try to make it a point to sample the local foods while you are here; they are called specialties for a reason. Ordering international dishes that you might be accustomed to at home or regional dishes that come from other parts of Italy might result in subpar flavors. Opt for what Sicilians do best, and get a taste for the island while you are here.

SICILIAN SPECIALTIES

The traditional eggplant **caponata** originated with the Arab influence in Sicily, and **couscous,** not seen in any other part of Italy, is made in the province of Trapani. Sicilians also have a sweet tooth, as evidenced by treasured ricotta-filled desserts and almond-based marzipan fruit sculptures, ice-cold creamy **granita,** and **torrone** nougat brittle.

All across Sicily, locals make the most of their pristine coasts and landscape: The coastal cuisine features **fresh seafood** like sardines, swordfish, red Mediterranean tuna, and anchovies. Most of the cheese here comes from local sheep's milk, like **pecorino, primo sale,** and **ricotta.** The diversity of Sicilian wines, from the historic fortified **marsala** to volcanic, organic, and natural wines makes them interesting to wine lovers from around the world. The easy-to-pair Sicilian native varieties of **nero d'avola** or **grillo** are among the most popular for their versatility, general low cost, and drinkability.

Vegetables and legumes are important parts of the traditional southern Italian diet, especially when it comes to home cooking. Cheap, healthy, and ubiquitous vegetables like zucchini, chickpeas, beans, and eggplant are essential parts of la cucina povera, or "poor cooking," the culinary ethos inextricable from the identity of most of Sicily. Vegetables appear on menus very seasonally, from artichokes and asparagus in the spring to zucchini, eggplant, and peppers in the summer to pumpkin and broccoli in the autumn. Other notable seasonal specialties include almonds.

COFFEE CULTURE

Coffee also plays an important role in everyday life across the region, from a morning **cappuccino** to an afternoon **espresso,** all enjoyed while sitting or standing at the café bar (not taken away in a to-go cup). There are funny signs hung in some small Sicilian coffee bars that translate to something along these lines:

- Make me a coffee—€1.50
- A coffee, please—€1.00
- Good morning, one coffee, please—€0.80

Note that it's frowned upon to order any coffee drink with milk after breakfast time. If you really want one, try ordering with a cheeky smile and a per favore, so they know that you are aware it is an unusual request. Although these are not strict rules, abiding by these small Italian quirks will help avoid embarrassment or poor customer service. One other tip on the coffee bar front: If you order while standing at the counter, your coffee will cost less than if a server brings it to you while seated at a table.

HOURS

Restaurants will tend to be open only at mealtimes from about noon to 3pm and from 7pm or 8pm to 10pm. Bars as well as more touristy restaurants will remain open throughout the day, catching guests who want to stop for a drink or have something to eat outside of standard Italian mealtimes. Pizzerias are often only open for dinner service. As tourism in Sicily continues to grow, making reservations ahead for restaurant meals is strongly advised.

TIPPING

Tipping in Sicily still remains a bit different from other international destinations, especially the United States. Add on an extra few euros to your bill when someone in the service industry directly helps you, gives excellent customer care, or goes above and beyond to make your trip more enjoyable. For example, leaving an extra €0.20 at a coffee bar will suffice, while €5-10 on a meal is greatly appreciated. Employees in Sicily do not depend on tips to make a fair wage; this is considered extra. Leaving a tip for housekeepers at a hotel, taxi drivers, a friendly bartender, street performer, tour guide, or someone who helps carry your luggage is a way to show your appreciation. Here in Sicily, it is not expected but can really make their day.

GROCERIES

Travelers can pick up staples like dry pasta, olive oil, salt, bottled water, and snacks from an alimentari deli or corner store. Supermarkets will have a larger selection of pantry items, fresh dairy products, bottled beverages, fruit and vegetables, bread, meat, and a limited range of seafood products. A better place to source your local and seasonal produce is in the outdoor markets or from fruit stands on the street. Supermarkets will have their hours posted online and usually on the front entrance door; they're typically open in the mornings about 8am-1pm with a break in the afternoon and open again 5pm-8pm or even later.

Accommodations

MAKING RESERVATIONS

Reserving accommodations in advance, especially in the height of the summer season (June-Aug.), is a must. Sicilians typically are not as adept at planning ahead; it is best to reconfirm your reservations before your arrival just to be sure everything is set.

HOTELS

Booking your accommodations at a proper hotel usually gives travelers the opportunity to reserve a room in advance, ask for an early check-in or late check-out, store their luggage, pay with a credit card, choose a room with an en suite bathroom, select the configuration of beds (singles or doubles), and request breakfast service.

RESORTS

The perk of staying in a resort on Sicily, especially on the smaller islands, is the possibility to have everything you need at your fingertips. Convenient amenities can include on-site restaurants, bars, and lounges, a pool, spa services, daily housekeeping, air-conditioning, laundry service, and more. Resorts can be found mainly in beach destinations along Sicily's coast, including Taormina, Palermo, Cefalù, and on the Aeolian island of Salina.

HOSTELS

Aside from a very short list, hostels are not traditionally an option in Sicily for travel accommodations. Bed-and-breakfasts are more commonly used and can be on the affordable end.

BED-AND-BREAKFASTS AND APARTMENTS

In recent years, the number of bed-and-breakfasts as well as apartment rentals has increased exponentially. Take care to read through customer reviews before booking these options. Make sure the necessities you need will be available, including laundry machines, coffeemakers, kitchen appliances, and so on. Websites like Airbnb and Booking.com will have additional options outside of the usual hotel or resorts available. Sometimes you can get a deal on booking a longer stay, such as a weeklong or monthly rental.

Health and Safety

Traveling within Sicily is fairly safe, and no out of the ordinary health precautions are necessary. Bring along any medications you are currently taking and have a copy of your doctor's prescription in case of an emergency. Sometimes it's as simple as showing the person working in the pharmacy the medicine that you have been taken in order to get a refill. Eyecare specialists can also sell you a pack of contact lenses without a prescription—just bring along a sample.

EMERGENCY NUMBERS

- **Medical emergency:** 118
- **Carabinieri (police):** 112
- **Police:** 113
- **Fire department:** 115

MEDICAL SERVICES AND VACCINATION REQUIREMENTS

Italian medical and emergency services are ranked fourth by the World Health

Organization. The emergency medical service number is **118.** If you can't wait, go directly to the pronto soccorso (emergency room), located in most hospitals.

No vaccinations, including for Covid-19, are required to enter Italy.

Resources

- **U.S. Centers for Disease Control and Prevention:** wwwnc.cdc.gov/travel/destinations/traveler/none/Italy

- **UK Government Foreign Travel Advice:** https://www.gov.uk/foreign-travel-advice/italy/health

- **Smart Traveler** (Australian Government Department of Foreign Affairs and Trade): www.smartraveller.gov.au/destinations/europe/italy

- **Italy Ministry of Health** (in Italian): www.salute.gov.it/portale/home.html

CRIME

As always when traveling, keep your eyes open, especially in larger cities like Palermo. Be aware of pickpockets. Don't leave your items unattended at any time, and carry only what you need with you for the day. When making purchases in outdoor markets or artisan shops, use small bills whenever possible. Keep your passport and valuables locked in a hotel safe whenever possible and carry only the amount of cash you need with you. Pulling out a wad of €50 or €100 bills that you just withdrew from an ATM in the middle of a piazza to pay for a souvenir or a snack is not a wise move. It is recommended to always pay close attention to your personal items, carry a crossbody bag, and not wear flashy jewelry.

Conduct and Customs

Appropriate attire is required to visit many churches (i.e., no shorts, miniskirts, or tank tops). It's also customary to remove hats when visiting churches. Italians are known for dressing on the formal side, and it's important to note that it is inappropriate to walk around in only swimwear or flip-flops outside of the beaches.

When entering shops, restaurants, and bars, a simple buongiorno or salve (the proper formal greeting for people you do not know) is polite and appreciated.

Traditionally, alcoholic beverages are served after the workday, in the evenings starting at aperitivo time around 6pm. Having a few cold beers at the beach during the day is also quite normal. Cocktails and mixed drinks are usually served as an aperitivo before dinner, while wine is more common with meals. After-dinner drinks include cordials and local spirits like amaro, grappa, or limoncello.

Unfortunately for health concerns, smoking cigarettes is still common in the south of Italy, including Sicily. Outdoor restaurants also allow guests to smoke at the tables. Cigarettes can be purchased from a tabacchi smoke shop by people over the age of 18. Once the shops are closed, automatic vending machines are only accessible to those who carry an Italian tessera sanitaria health service card. Please use ashtrays while smoking and properly dispose of your cigarette butts in a trash bin while you're out on the town or at the beach. Most hotels and resorts will not allow you to smoke inside their rooms. Just because you're on holiday in Europe doesn't mean you should pick up bad habits.

Practical Details

WHAT TO PACK

Sicily is very casual, with mild winters and hot summers. Beaches figure prominently in a trip to the island, so be sure to bring swimsuits and sun protection. Water shoes can help navigate rocky Sicilian beaches. If you're planning to hike, such as up Mount Etna, well-fitting hiking footwear is essential.

For travelers from outside the EU, pack a couple plug adapters—EU outlets take plugs with two round pins—to charge your devices.

To reduce waste, bring a refillable water bottle, reusable shopping bag, and your own toiletries.

MONEY
Currency

Italy uses the euro, which commonly comes in €5, €10, €20, €50, €100, and €200 bills and €0.01, €0.02, €0.05, €0.10, €0.20, €0.50, €1, and €2 coins. The exchange rates as of July 2023 for €1 are:

- US dollar: $1.08
- Canadian dollar: $1.44
- British pound: £0.86
- Australian dollar: $1.63

PUBLIC HOLIDAYS

- **January 1:** Capodanno (New Year's Day)
- **January 6:** Epifania (Epiphany)
- **Pasqua** (Easter Sunday)
- **Pasquetta** (Easter Monday)
- **April 25:** Festa della Liberazione (Liberation Day)
- **May 1:** Festa del Lavoro (International Worker's Day)
- **June 2:** Festa della Repubblica (Republic Day)
- **August 15:** Ferragosto (Assumption Day)
- **November 1:** Tutti i Santi (All Saints' Day)
- **December 8:** Immacolata (Immaculate Conception)
- **December 25:** Natale (Christmas)
- **December 26:** Santo Stefano (St. Stephen's Day)

WEIGHTS AND MEASURES

Italy uses the **metric system,** with the following units of measure:

- Distance: kilometers
- Weight: grams and kilograms
- Volumes: liters
- Temperature: Celsius

Italy is on **Central European Time,** six hours ahead of the U.S. East Coast and nine hours ahead of the West Coast. Military/24-hour time is frequently used (i.e., 13:00 is 1pm and 20:15 is 8:15pm). Italians order dates by day, month, and year.

Traveler Advice

ACCESS FOR TRAVELERS WITH DISABILITIES

Newer trains and city buses in Sicily will be wheelchair accessible. Travelers with mobility restrictions can request additional assistance in the airports and plan ahead to make sure their accommodations and touring destinations are going to be accessible depending on their specific needs. A list of accessible tours around the island, including city tours of Palermo, Catania, Noto, Syracuse, Cefalù, and Taormina and wine tours on Mount Etna, can be found online (www.romeanditaly.com/accessible/accessible-sicily-tours) and booked in advance.

Palermo has a fairly flat city center with large avenues for maneuvering through the town with more ease than the hillside towns of Modica and Taormina. Restaurants should have bathrooms with wheelchair access, and the main tourist attractions, such as the Cattedrale di Monreale and Duomo di Cefalù, have ramps available. This information should be posted somewhere such as Google Maps. For example, the Valle dei Templi in Agrigento provides a free rental service of electric wheelchairs for people with motor disabilities in order to make the park "accessible for all."

Sicily has a range of sand beaches in Mondello, Cefalù, Marsala, Trapani, San Vito lo Capo, Giardini Naxos, and the southeastern coast of Syracuse, which will be easier to access than the rocky shores. Cobblestone streets in the city centers can be particularly difficult to navigate. Small alleyways in Taormina, Caltagirone, Modica, and parts of Catania have staircases built into the street paths. Make sure to check with your accommodations ahead of time to avoid walk-up apartments or hotels that do not have elevators available to guests.

TRAVELING WITH CHILDREN

Sicily is a welcoming place for families traveling with small children. Southern Italian culture is quite hospitable toward including children in daily plans, including dining out. Advising a restaurant ahead of time is recommended, especially if you will need a high chair or will be bringing a baby stroller that might take up an additional seat at your table. Ordering a child's meal as soon as you sit down at the table can be a smart way to ensure that their dish comes out with as little of a wait as possible. Simple dishes like pasta bianca (with only olive oil and grated cheese) or pasta al pomodoro (with tomato sauce) are quick plates that Italian restaurants often prepare for little ones.

The island is known for its beautiful beaches. Sandy shores with shallow waters will be more family-friendly than those made up of stones, rocks, or shells. Bringing along a pair of water shoes is helpful—even—for adults when traveling to the beaches in Sicily.

Some high-end resorts or small boutique properties, especially those with pools, may have restrictions on access for small children. Spa services are often restricted to people of a certain age for safety concerns. The best thing to do is notify these places ahead of time if you will be traveling with children. The organizers of guided walking tours, vineyard visits, hikes, boat trips, and cooking classes may need to know if there are children in your group before booking.

Supermarkets and larger pharmacies usually have a small section for babies where you can purchase diapers, wipes, and toiletries. Packing everything you will need for the day will avoid any last-minute panic, including packing enough water, sunscreen, snacks, a change of clothes, proper footwear, and travel necessities. Check with your airline and car rental company when booking to allocate space for strollers, baby carriers, and car seats. **Mama Loves Italy** (www.mamalovesitaly. com) is a helpful resource for traveling with babies and toddlers in Italy and includes a few articles on Sicily.

WOMEN TRAVELERS

Solo women travelers should feel completely comfortable in busy areas, on central streets, and in well-lit areas after dark. Keep an eye on your possessions, keeping your bags closed and near your body, leaving valuable jewelry and large amounts of cash in a locked safe in your accommodations. Be sure to select your accommodations in a safe area and take taxi services home at night if you are far from your destination, heading home late in the night, or in any need of additional help arriving safely. Harassment on the street and catcalling is unacceptable yet still bothersome and common in Italy. In these cases, they are mostly seeking attention. Often the best response is to completely ignore it and keep walking to quickly dissuade the attention. Calling the **Police** (112) or the **Anti-Violence and Stalking hotline** (1522) is advised if you are in need of immediate assistance.

For those who prefer not to travel alone, there are options for group programs such as **Stellavision Travel** (www.stellavision-travel.com), which organizes boutique trips and private planning for feminist travelers, or **Cummari** (www.cummari.com), a luxury co-living and co-working space in Catania designed for female digital nomads, artists, and solo travelers.

SENIOR TRAVELERS

Senior travelers should give themselves additional time to get from point A to point B, especially during the hottest months of the year, when walking around under the Sicilian sun can be exhausting. Take a taxi ride when needed. Research your accommodations before booking. Check to see what floor your room is located on, if there is an elevator in the building, or how close a taxi or driver can

drop you to the entrance. Cobblestone roads, small alleyways, and narrow staircases can present issues for mobility. When taking a train, consider booking first class to ensure that there will be a seat, especially on longer journeys. There may be senior discounts available on train/ferry travel tickets, or on museum, monument, or archaeological park entrance fees. You may also want to consider a guided tour or private driver for additional help navigating the island.

LGBTQ+ TRAVELERS

LGBTQ+ couples are able to express themselves in a respectful way when in public. In more rural, conservative, and less accepting areas, this can still attract negative attention. Each year, Italy is becoming more accepting and welcoming of those who identify as LGBTQ+. Currently, same-sex couples cannot get married in Italy, but they have been able to access civil unions since 2016, which provide some rights, legal protections, and benefits.

Palermo and Catania host the island's annual gay pride celebrations each June. Both of Sicily's large city centers also offer a range of gay and gay-friendly bars and restaurants (sometimes also noted on Google Maps listings). Catania has a reputation for being much more open and welcoming to gay visitors.

ARCIGAY (www.arcigay.it) is Italy's first and largest worldwide LGBTI not-for-profit organization. Founded in Palermo in 1980, the organization became known throughout Italy for its campaign for civil unions. They have branches in Palermo, Catania, Ragusa, Syracuse, and Messina. This can be a resource for events as well as information about equality and marriage, fighting discrimination, health services, identity, and pride. The **International LGBTQ+ Travel Association** (www.iglta.org) also provides information and resources for LGBTQ+ travelers.

TRAVELERS OF COLOR

Although multiculturalism has been engrained in the Sicilian demographic for centuries, inclusion and representation for people of color in Sicily is a continuous work in progress. A city like Palermo tends to have a much higher number of foreign immigrants compared to small villages around the island, which are significantly less diverse. This region, populated with around five million people, remains a homogenous culture, populated with mainly white Italians. A boom in international tourism has opened the doors to people of diverse backgrounds being more represented and welcome here. In day-to-day interactions, locals' curiosity is most often just that, rather than criticism or hostility, although harmful stereotypes focusing on "exoticness" are still an issue.

Resources

Glossary

aliscafo: hydrofoil boat

aperitivo: pre-dinner drink; also used for the time of day/hour these drinks are typically consumed when restaurants and bars offer snacks with a drink order

belvedere: scenic lookout point

biglietto: ticket

borgo: village

bottega: shop

centro storico: historic center

ferrovia: railroad

funivia: aerial cable car

lido (singular)/lidi (plural): beach clubs with amenities for paying guests like lounge chairs, umbrellas, restrooms, and restaurants

lungomare: sea front promenade

parcheggio: parking

saline: salt flats

spiaggia: beach

tabacchi: literally "tobacco shop," but more like a corner store; bus tickets can often be purchased at tabacchi

tonnara: tuna fishery

Italian Phrasebook

Italians appreciate when you at least try to speak their language. Simple phrases like buongiorno (good morning), buonasera (good evening) and grazie mille (thank you very much) will make your travels more enjoyable and sometimes improve customer service as well. They are always happy that you gave it a try.

PRONUNCIATION

Vowels

a like *a* in *father*

e short like *e* in *set*

é long like *a* in *way*

i like *ee* in *feet*

o short like *o* in *often*, or long like *o* in *rope*

u like *oo* in *foot*, or *w* in *well*

Consonants

b like *b* in *boy*, but softer

c before e or i like *ch* in *chin*

ch like *c* in *cat*

d like *d* in *dog*

f like *f* in *fish*

g before e or i like *g* in *gymnastics* or like *g* in *go*

gh like *g* in *go*

gl like *ll* in *million*

gn like *ni* in *onion*

gu like *gu* in *anguish*

h always silent

l like *l* in *lime*

m like *m* in *me*

n like *n* in *nice*

p like *p* in *pit*

qu like *qu* in *quick*

r rolled/trilled similar to *r* in Spanish or Scottish

s between vowels like *s* in *nose* or *s* in *sit*

sc before e or i like *sh* in *shut* or *sk* in *skip*
t like *t* in *tape*
v like *v* in *vase*
z either like *ts* in *spits* or *ds* in *pads*

Accents
Accents are used to indicate which vowel should be stressed and to differentiate between words with different meanings that are spelled the same.

ESSENTIAL PHRASES
Hi Ciao
Hello Salve
Good morning Buongiorno
Good evening Buonasera
Good night Buonanotte
Good-bye Arrivederci
See you later A dopo
Nice to meet you Piacere
No problem Nessun problema
I'm sorry Mi dispiace
Thank you Grazie
Thank you very much Grazie mille
You're welcome Prego
Please Per favore
Do you speak English? Parla inglese?
How sweet! Che carino!
How kind! Che gentile!
I don't understand Non capisco
I don't know Non lo so
I would like... Vorrei...
I am running late Sono in ritardo
Have a nice day Buona giornata
Where is the restroom? Dov'è il bagno?
Yes Sì
Of course Certo
No No

TRANSPORTATION
Ticket(s) biglietto/biglietti
Where is...? Dov'è...?
How far is...? Quanto è distante...?
Is there a bus to...? C'è un autobus per...?
Does this bus go to...? Quest'autobus va a...?
Where do I get off? Dove devo scendere?
What time does the bus/train leave/arrive? A che ora parte/arriva l'autobus/treno?
Where is the nearest station? Dov'è la stazione più vicina?
Where can I buy a ticket? Dove posso comprare un biglietto?
A round-trip ticket/a single ticket to... Un biglietto di solo andata e ritorno/andata per...

FOOD
A table for two/three/four... Un tavolo per due/tre/quattro...
Do you have a menu in English? Avete un menu in inglese?
What is the dish of the day? Qual è il piatto del giorno?
We're ready to order. Siamo pronti per ordinare.
I'm a vegetarian. Sono vegetariano (male) / Sono vegetariana (female)
I am allergic to gluten. Sono celiaco.
I have a severe nut allergy. Ho una allergia grave alla frutta secca/noci.
May I have... Posso avere...
The check please Il conto per favore
beer birra
draft beer birra alla spina
bread pane
gluten-free bread pane senza glutine
glass of wine (white/red/rosè/sparkling) calice di vino bianco/rosso/rosato/spumante
breakfast colazione
cash contante
credit card carta di credito
croissant cornetto
check conto
coffee caffè
dinner cena
fresh juice spremuta
glass bicchiere
wine glass calice
hors d'oeuvre antipasto
side dishes contorni
ice ghiaccio
ice cream gelato
italian ice granita

lunch pranzo
restaurant ristorante
sandwich(es) panino/panini
snack spuntino
waiter/waitress cameriere/cameriera
water acqua
still water acqua naturale
sparkling water acqua frizzante/gassata
wine vino

SHOPPING

money soldi
shop negozio or putia (Sicilian dialect)
cheap/inexpensive economico
expensive caro/costoso
What time do the shops close? A che ora chiudono i negozi?
How much is it? Quanto costa?
I'm just looking. Sto guardando solamente.
What are the local specialties? Quali sono le specialità locali?

HEALTH

drugstore farmacia
pain dolore
fever febbre
headache mal di testa
stomachache mal di stomaco/pancia
seasickness mal di mare
toothache mal di denti
burn bruciatura
cramp crampo
nausea nausea
vomiting vomitare
medicine medicina
antibiotic antibiotico
pill/tablet pillola/pasticca
aspirin aspirina
mask maschera
thermometer termometro
I need to see a doctor. Ho bisogno di un medico.
I need to go to the hospital. Devo andare in ospedale.
I have a pain here... Ho un dolore qui...
Can I have a facemask? Posso avere una maschera?

She/he has been stung/bitten. È stata punta/morsa.
Jellyfish sting puntura di medusa
I am diabetic. Sono diabetico.
I am pregnant. Sono incinta.
I am allergic to penicillin/ cortisone. Sono allergico alla penicillina/ cortisone.
My blood group is...positive/ negative. Il mio gruppo sanguigno è... positivo/negative.

NUMBERS

0 zero
1 uno
2 due
3 tre
4 quattro
5 cinque
6 sei
7 sette
8 otto
9 nove
10 dieci
11 undici
12 dodici
13 tredici
14 quattordici
15 quindici
16 sedici
17 diciassette
18 diciotto
19 diciannove
20 venti
21 ventuno
30 trenta
40 quaranta
50 cinquanta
60 sessanta
70 settanta
80 ottanta
90 novanta
100 cento
101 centouno
200 duecento
500 cinquecento
1,000 mille
10,000 diecimila

100,000 centomila
1,000,000 un milione

TIME
What time is it? Che ora è?
It's one/three o'clock. E l'una/Sono le tre.
noon/midday mezzogiorno
midnight mezzanotte
morning mattino
afternoon pomeriggio
evening sera
night notte
yesterday ieri
today oggi
tonight stasera
tomorrow domani
tomorrow morning domani mattina
tomorrow night domani sera
sunrise alba
sunset tramonto

DAYS AND MONTHS
week settimana
month mese
Monday lunedì
Tuesday martedì
Wednesday mercoledì
Thursday giovedì
Friday venerdì
Saturday sabato
Sunday domenica
January gennaio
February febbraio
March marzo
April aprile

May maggio
June giugno
July luglio
August agosto
September settembre
October ottobre
November novembre
December dicembre
New Year's Day Capodanno
Easter Pasqua
August 15 Ferragosto
Christmas Natale

VERBS
to have avere
to be essere
to go andare
to come venire
to want volere
to eat mangiare
to drink bere
to buy comprare
to need necessitare
to read leggere
to write scrivere
to stop fermare
to get off scendere
to arrive arrivare
to return ritornare
to stay restare
to leave partire
to look at guardare
to look for cercare
to give dare
to take prendere

Suggested Reading

Inspector Montalbano series by Andrea Camilleri (1994-2020): This popular mystery series uses southern Sicily as its backdrop.

Palmento: A Sicilian Wine Odyssey by Robert V. Camuto (2010): This travel narrative through Sicily's wines delves into the island's history and culture.

The Heart of Sicily by Anna Tasca Lanza (1993): The utmost authority on Sicilian cuisine shares the recipes of her family's homeland along with family stories.

Coming Home to Sicily by Fabrizia Lanza (2012): This seasonal cookbook is written by Anna Tasca Lanza's only daughter, who carries on her mother's tradition at the cooking school on the family wine estate in Regaleali.

The Leopard by Giuseppe Tomasi di Lampedusa (1958): Written by arguably Sicily's most famous writer, *The Leopard* takes place during the Risorgimento movement to unite the Italian peninsula.

From Scratch: A Memoir of Love, Sicily, and Finding Home by Tembi Locke (2019):

Summers in Sicily are the backdrop for this memoir of a Black American woman healing from the loss of her Sicilian husband at her in-laws' home.

Bitter Almonds: Recollections & Recipes from a Sicilian Girlhood by Maria Grammatico and Mary Taylor Simeti (1994): The incredible life story of Maria Grammatico, founder of the pasticceria in Erice that bears her name, includes growing up in a Sicilian convent, where she "stole" secret recipes by watching the nuns through a crack in the floor above the kitchen.

On Persephone's Island by Mary Taylor Simeti (1986): This memoir is by a culinary anthropologist, ex-New Yorker who spent her entire adult life in Sicily and also co-wrote *Bitter Almonds*.

The New Wines of Mount Etna: An Insider's Guide to the History and Rebirth of a Wine Region by Benjamin North Spencer (2020): Written by the founder of Etna Wine School, this book is a great resource for wine lovers visiting the Mount Etna Area.

Suggested Films

Nuovo Cinema Paradiso directed by Giuseppe Tornatore (1988): The best-known of Sicily-born director Giuseppe Tornatore's many films (known in the U.S. as just Cinema Paradiso) tells the story of a child's friendship with the proprietor of a movie house in a small Sicilian town.

The Star Maker (1995), *Malèna* (2000), and *Baarìa* (2009) directed by Giuseppe Tornatore: These three films by Giuseppe Tornatore, who was born near Palermo, are set in small Sicilian towns.

Il Gattopardo directed by Luchino Visconti (1963): Known as *The Leopard* in English, this is the film adaptation of Giuseppe Tomasi di Lampedusa's famous novel.

La Terra Trema directed by Luchino Visconti (1948): A mix of fiction and documentary, this film illustrates the life of a fishing family in Sicily.

A Bigger Splash directed by Luca Guadagnino (2015): The island of Pantelleria serves as the backdrop of this drama starring Tilda Swinton and Ralph Fiennes.

Il Postino directed by Massimo Troisi (1994): This gorgeous film depicts the fictional friendship between a postman and the famous poet Pablo Neruda. The story is set in Procida, but Pollara, on the Aeolian island of Salina, served as a location in the film.

Stromboli directed by Roberto Rossellini (1950): This movie put the Aeolian island of Stromboli on the world scene. Its star, Ingrid Bergman, and its director, Roberto Rossellini, are said to have begun their infamous affair while filming on the island.

L'avventura directed by Michelangelo Antonioni (1960): The historic center of Noto and other locales in Sicily are the backdrop of this film about a mysterious disappearance starring Monica Vitti.

Internet and Digital Resources

www.visitsicily.info
Sicily's official tourism website is full of useful information, with an especially helpful, up-to-date list of events happening across the island.

www.trenitalia.com
Trenitalia is the main provider of train travel within Italy. Guests can book tickets online to save time waiting in line at the stations.

www.rome2rio.com
This website is handy for figuring out the best way to get from point A to point B. It easily explains the best transportation options, whether you'll need a train, bus, taxi, or ferry, while providing links to the affiliated companies where you can purchase tickets in advance.

www.viator.com
Viator is a subsidiary of TripAdvisor where travelers can book guided tours and experiences, reserve tickets to enter cultural sites and monuments, and explore the island on guided outdoor adventures, cooking classes, and more.

Index

List of Maps

Photo Credits

MOON
Tahiti
& FRENCH POLYNESIA

MOON
Japan

MOON

**BALI &
LOMBOK**

**NEW
ZEALAND**

MOON
Baja
TIJUANA TO LOS CABOS

BELIZE

MOON
CARTAGENA
& COLOMBIA'S
CARIBBEAN COAST

MOON
CHILE

MOON
Costa Rica

MOON
**Galápagos
Islands**

ECUADOR
& THE GALÁPAGOS ISLANDS

TRIP OF A LIFETIME
**MACHU
PICCHU**

OAXACA

TRIP OF A LIFETIME
PATAGONIA

MOON
**Puerto
Vallarta**
WITH SAYULITA, THE RIVIERA
NAYARIT & COSTALAGRE

MOON
YUCATÁN
PENINSULA

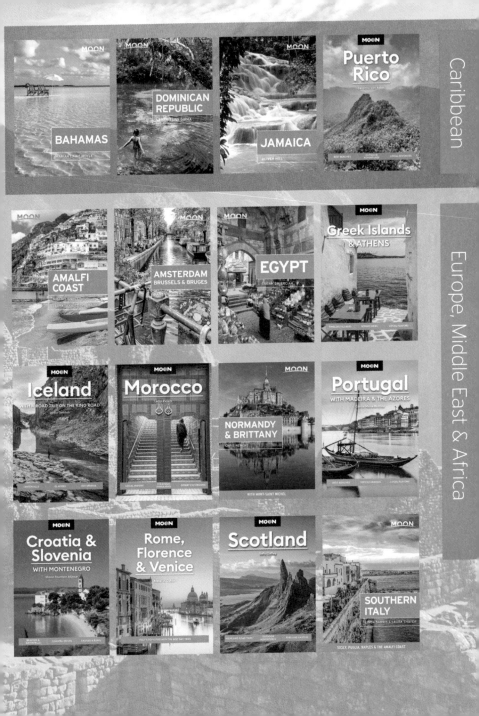

MOON

BAHAMAS

MOON

DOMINICAN
REPUBLIC

MOON

JAMAICA

MOON

Puerto
Rico

MOON

AMALFI
COAST

MOON

AMSTERDAM
BRUSSELS & BRUGES

MOON

EGYPT

MOON

Greek Islands
& ATHENS

MOON

Iceland
WITH A ROAD TRIP ON THE RING ROAD

MOON

Morocco

MOON

NORMANDY
& BRITTANY

WITH MONT-SAINT MICHEL

MOON

Portugal
WITH MADEIRA & THE AZORES

MOON

Croatia &
Slovenia
WITH MONTENEGRO

MOON

Rome,
Florence
& Venice

MOON

Scotland

MOON

SOUTHERN
ITALY

SICILY, PUGLIA, NAPLES & THE AMALFI COAST

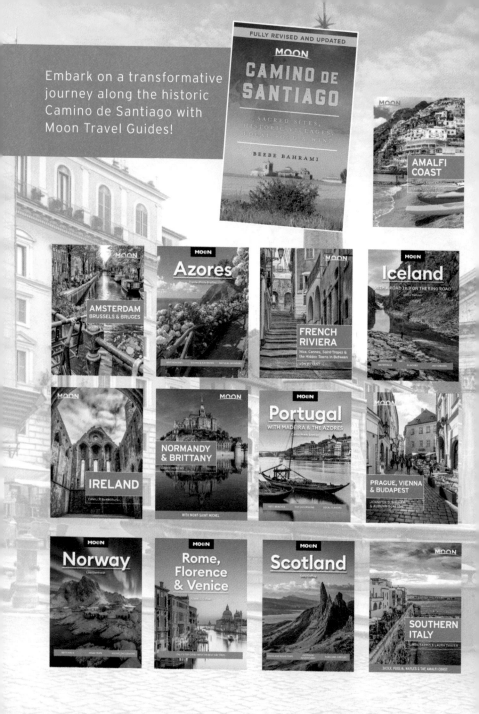

Embark on a transformative journey along the historic Camino de Santiago with Moon Travel Guides!

CREATE AN EPIC TRAVEL BUCKET LIST

MOON

WANDERLUST
Road Trips

40 BEAUTIFUL DRIVES
AROUND THE WORLD

MOON

WANDERLUST
a traveler's guide to the globe

EXPLORE CITY NEIGHBORHOOD WALKS

LONDON WALKS
See the City Like a Local

NEW YORK CITY WALKS
See the City Like a Local

PARIS WALKS
See the City Like a Local

ROME WALKS
See the City Like a Local

More Beachy Escapes from Moon

MAP SYMBOLS

Expressway	○ City/Town	ⓘ Information Center	♣ Park
Primary Road	◉ State Capital	🅿 Parking Area	⚲ Golf Course
Secondary Road	⊛ National Capital	⛪ Church	✦ Unique Feature
Unpaved Road	✪ Highlight	🍷 Winery/Vineyard	🌿 Waterfall
Trail	★ Point of Interest	🚩 Trailhead	Ⓐ Camping
Ferry	• Accommodation	🚆 Train Station	▲ Mountain
Railroad	▾ Restaurant/Bar	✈ Airport	⛷ Ski Area
Pedestrian Walkway	■ Other Location	✕ Airfield	◠◡ Glacier
Stairs			

CONVERSION TABLES

$$°C = (°F – 32) / 1.8$$
$$°F = (°C × 1.8) + 32$$

1 inch = 2.54 centimeters (cm)
1 foot = 0.304 meters (m)
1 yard = 0.914 meters
1 mile = 1.6093 kilometers (km)
1 km = 0.6214 miles
1 fathom = 1.8288 m
1 chain = 20.1168 m
1 furlong = 201.168 m
1 acre = 0.4047 hectares
1 sq km = 100 hectares
1 sq mile = 2.59 square km
1 ounce = 28.35 grams
1 pound = 0.4536 kilograms
1 short ton = 0.90718 metric ton
1 short ton = 2,000 pounds
1 long ton = 1.016 metric tons
1 long ton = 2,240 pounds
1 metric ton = 1,000 kilograms
1 quart = 0.94635 liters
1 US gallon = 3.7854 liters
1 Imperial gallon = 4.5459 liters
1 nautical mile = 1.852 km

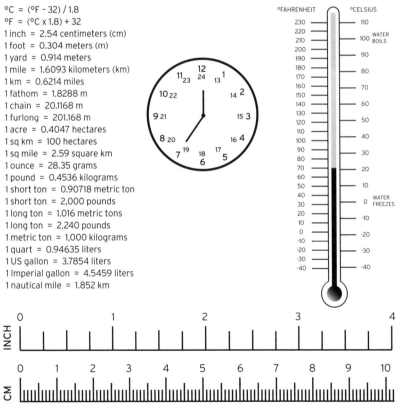

MOON SICILY

Avalon Travel
Hachette Book Group
1700 Fourth Street
Berkeley, CA 94710, USA
www.moon.com

Editor: Grace Fujimoto
Managing Editor: Hannah Brezack
Copy Editor: Ann Seifert
Graphics Coordinator: Darren Alessi
Production Coordinator: Darren Alessi
Cover Design: Toni Tajima
Interior Design: Avalon Travel
Map Editor: Kat Bennett
Cartographers: Erin Greb Cartography, John Culp,
  Mark Stroud (Moon Street Cartography), Abby
  Whelan, Kat Bennett
Proofreader: Deana Shields
Indexer: Rachel Lyon

ISBN-13: 979-8-88647-000-0

Printing History
1st Edition — March 2024
5 4 3 2 1

Front cover photo: Valle dei Templi
  © robertharding / Alamy Stock Photo
Back cover photo: Cefalù
  © Luca647 | Dreamstime.com

Printed in China by RR Donnelley APS

Avalon Travel is a division of Hachette Book Group,
Inc. Moon and the Moon logo are trademarks of
Hachette Book Group, Inc. All other marks and logos
depicted are the property of the original owners.